This study explores the nature of the conflict between science and religion. It shows through a detailed examination of this conflict as it was manifested in nineteenth-century Britain that religion and science, properly understood, cannot co-exist in mutual harmony. The legacy of their conflict in the last century has been passed on to the twentieth, greatly to the detriment of religious belief. It is the author's contention that a return to the essentials of Kant's critical philosophy would lay bare the profound differences between religious and scientific approaches to the world, and the nature of the choice to be made between them. In its effort to demarcate the outlines of a genuine biblical theology (and to articulate the proper procedures for producing one) the book casts light on important questions of biblical interpretation, and demands a radical reassessment of the meaning of science for society.

PHILOSOPHY AND BIBLICAL INTERPRETATION

PHILOSOPHY AND BIBLICAL INTERPRETATION

A study in nineteenth-century conflict

PETER ADDINALL

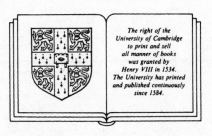

The right of the
University of Cambridge
to print and sell
all manner of books
was granted by
Henry VIII in 1534.
The University has printed
and published continuously
since 1584.

Cambridge University Press
Cambridge   New York   Port Chester
Melbourne   Sydney

Published by the Press Syndicate of the University of Cambridge
The Pitt Building, Trumpington Street, Cambridge CB2 IRP
40 West 20th Street, New York, NY 10011-4211, USA
10 Stamford Road, Oakleigh, Melbourne 3166, Australia

First published 1991

Printed in Great Britain at the University Press, Cambridge

British Library cataloguing in publication data
Addinall, Peter, *1932–*
Philosophy and biblical interpretation: a study in
nineteenth-century conflict.
1. Science – Christian viewpoints
1. Title
261.55

Library of Congress cataloguing in publication data
Addinall, Peter.
Philosophy and biblical interpretation: a study in nineteenth-
century conflict / by Peter Addinall.
p.   cm.
Based on the author's thesis (doctoral), University of Sheffield.
Includes bibliographical references and index.
ISBN 0 521 40423 1
1. Religion and science – Great Britain – History – 19th century.
2. Bible and science – History – 19th century. 3. Religious thought –
Great Britain – History – 19th century. 1. Title.
BL240.2.A33 1991
215.'0941'09034–DC 20   90–2544 CIP

ISBN 0 521 40423 1 hardback

To my parents, Stanley and Sarah Irene

Contents

Preface

This book had its origin in a doctoral thesis prepared under the supervision of the Revd Professor John Rogerson, Head of the Biblical Studies Department in the University of Sheffield. It is a pleasure to record my gratitude to Professor Rogerson for generous guidance and continual encouragement freely given over many years.

The book is, of course, entirely my own responsibility. It gives expression to certain convictions which became clearer and firmer as work proceeded, and to other convictions which only emerged as I studied the evidence relevant to the thesis. Among the latter are a sense of the reality and inevitability of the conflict between natural science and religion, the permanent insight enshrined in what is otherwise an outmoded conservative approach to biblical study, and the serious deficiency of liberal scholarship, despite the basic correctness of the critical approach to biblical texts and a multitude of fruitful results produced by it.

The historical aspect of the argument is no accident. The child is father of the man, and the true nature of man-come-of-age in the twentieth century can only be grasped when recognised as the more developed form of a troubled childhood and tempestuous adolescence going back to conception in the later eighteenth century.

The careful study of long-forgotten or generally neglected texts is no mere esoteric pastime to satisfy those who enjoy reliving distant controversies while remaining safe from painful exposure to current conflict. The Preacher's terse comment on novelty will be found to have remarkably frequent application, and the echoes of past controversy a disturbingly contemporary ring.

The book is a single argument, designed to be read straight through from start to finish, as the introduction will show; but

xi

chapters can be treated as individual studies by those who have a special interest in the topic concerned. Endnotes contain only references to sources, and may be ignored by those who wish to read through the main text without interruption.

Translations of German texts are my own when not otherwise indicated.

Introduction

Religious belief has always had its critics, and outstanding among them was the eighteenth-century Scottish philosopher David Hume, whose critique of religion is perhaps unsurpassed for its lucidity and persuasive force.

Hume's attack evoked two very different replies: one from the Englishman William Paley, and the other from the Prussian philosopher Immanuel Kant. In Britain Paley's reply was very popular and influential, but it was fatally flawed. Kant's response, on the other hand, was thoroughgoing and fundamentally correct, but not popular in Britain, and often not properly understood even by the few who were prepared to give it serious consideration.

During the nineteenth century the natural sciences underwent rapid development and provided religion's critics with massive evidence supporting Hume's suggestion that the world might turn out to be entirely explicable in terms of its own inherent forces, thereby making reference to God not merely redundant, but a positive hindrance to the proper understanding of human existence.

At the same time, scientific discoveries contradicted certain statements in the Bible, thus threatening the authority of sacred literature which was generally regarded as essential to the life of both Church and State. The mounting pressure of scientific evidence during the nineteenth century led to a split in the ranks of biblical scholars, into conservatives and liberals. The former endeavoured to maintain traditional views of biblical authority and what were supposed to be traditional or plain interpretations of disputed texts, while the latter admitted the validity of German critical scholarship and turned biblical studies into a humanistic

I

enterprise with what might be called a scientific validity of its own.

Neither the conservative nor the liberal responses to scientifically based scepticism was satisfactory from the point of view of religious belief, and what was valuable in both needed to be taken up into a wider philosophy which would provide the justification for both.

This wider philosophy was provided by Kant, but his insights and what was of permanent value and validity in his arguments were not, and still are not generally recognised, either by those who assert or by those who deny religious belief. It must be admitted that he by no means did full justice to the content of Christian faith, but he did lay a firm foundation for religious belief in general human experience, and his critical philosophy is directly relevant to the construction of a theology which is meaningful and persuasive to men and women belonging to a science-dominated culture.

Chapter 1 is concerned to establish the fact, against some who have maintained otherwise, that there was a real conflict between science and religion in the nineteenth century, and that this conflict was passed on into the twentieth century and still exists today.

Chapter 2 describes and evaluates Hume's criticisms of religious belief in his *Dialogues Concerning Natural Religion*, and chapter 3 the response of William Paley in his *Natural Theology*.

Chapters 4–7 provide illustrations at some length of the different kinds of response made by religious thinkers in Britain to the threat of science, covering the first half of the nineteenth century up to roughly 1860. These thinkers are divided into three categories, and are taken to reflect much more widespread currents of opinion, doubt and argument, as people in general increasingly felt the impact of scientific research and its challenge to a traditional outlook. A careful consideration of these ideals reveals much highly intelligent reflection, a genuine concern to preserve what is valuable in human life and frequent insights, but overall confusion and mere progress up an intellectual blind alley. Similar ideas and arguments are not infrequently repeated today, and with similar consequences.

Chapter 4 first briefly explains the fundamental weakness of religious thought in Britain in the nineteenth century, and then goes on to consider examples of very conservative thinkers in the first half of the century who tried to make an infallible Bible the sole basis of their reply to scepticism.

Chapters 5 and 6 consider conservative thinkers in the first half of the century who not only appealed to the authority of the Bible, but who also depended on the kind of natural theology put forward by Paley. Chapter 5 is entirely devoted to the Bridgewater Treatises, a massive attempt to illustrate and justify Paley's natural theology.

Chapter 7 considers the ideas of certain more liberal religious thinkers in the first half of the century; their recognition that the successes of scientific method could not go on being simply denied; their consequent surrender of an infallible Bible; and their unsuccessful attempt to make natural theology the proper reply of religious believers to sceptical criticism.

Chapter 8 illustrates the variety and inadequacy of religious thought in Britain after about 1860. It also describes the triumph of liberal scholarship in serious biblical study as justified in itself, but deceptive as an attempt to escape the strictures of scientific scepticism on religious belief.

The disarray of British religious belief confronted by a scientific world outlook and the continuing domination of twentieth-century thought concerning religion by nineteenth-century ideas suggest that there might be profit for all concerned in a return to the critical philosophy of Kant. There is good reason to believe that where thought dependent upon a flawed natural theology and a false view of biblical authority failed, thought based upon a correct estimate of the powers of human reason will succeed. This is a lesson in the history of ideas which it is not – yet – too late to learn.

Chapter 9 therefore considers the critical philosophy of Kant, and chapter 10 offers suggestions concerning the lines on which biblical interpretation and other thought about religion might develop in the light of Kant's achievement.

CHAPTER I

The general picture

There was a real conflict between science and religion throughout the nineteenth century in Britain, and it was passed on by the nineteenth as a legacy to the twentieth century. Religious belief was defended by appeals to natural theology and the authority of the Bible, but the defence failed in both respects, while at the same time massive developments took place in the natural sciences. While scientific methods registered one success after another, it became increasingly evident that the popular natural theology was invalid and the Bible fallible. Scientific statements about the natural world were sometimes at variance with biblical assertions, and this shattered the simple and straightforward view of the Bible, that God had spoken to the inspired writers much as a father addresses his children, conveying truths to them which otherwise they could never discover but which are essential to their health and welfare. If God had conveyed untruths to his children then he lost face, just as a deceitful or careless earthly father does; but with the significant difference that a fallible God is no longer God, and the Scriptures no longer possess their unique character and authority.

Sometimes children play games which involve setting aside a given spot as 'safe', a kind of sanctuary where you cannot be caught or 'tigged'. Without wishing to overstress the analogy one could say that British biblical scholars and theologians adopted a similar tactic in the later nineteenth century, deliberately limiting their work to the religious-cum-moral area of life and conceding the right of scientists to explore the natural world and come to their own legitimate conclusions. The Bible was then defended as a storehouse of religious and moral truth, and its mistakes concerning the natural world ignored or dismissed; and the same became true for all theology, which could not be caught out provided it was confined to the non-natural aspects of existence.

The last assertion, however, immediately suggests the fundamental problem which neither religious belief nor scientific commitment can ignore: What happens when the game stops? If the rough boys suddenly decide to engage in activities which rule out safe places and forbidden areas, there is nothing to prevent them; and the question then is whether or not the analogy still holds. Are religious beliefs and moral feelings 'safe', that is, non-natural? They are held and felt by human beings, and it is arguable, to say the least, that human beings are part of the natural world; and this includes the human beings who wrote the Bible, and whose deeds and words are recorded in it.

To shift the analogy somewhat: to play a game at all means constructing rules and artificially isolating some area for legitimate and limited conflict; but football and cricket pitches, the boxing ring and tennis court, along with the players, do not cease to be governed by nature's rules, and the artificiality of game situations is often revealed by injury or the intervention of the weather. Throughout the nineteenth century in Britain science inflicted wounds on religious belief and interrupted the smooth flow of religious worship, and the sharpness of these challenges lay in the implicit or explicit assertion that religious attitudes and activities, however happily and consistently they might operate within their own rules, remained ultimately under the overarching government of nature's laws.

While therefore biblical scholars and theologians were claiming that their studies concerned an area beyond the reach of natural science so that they could get on with their work undistracted by scientific discovery and controversy, there was an uneasy feeling among both believers and sceptics that the setting apart of religion and morality was a purely artificial procedure, useful for certain purposes but untrue to the real nature of religious and moral claims; and also untrue to the character of the biblical literature itself.

It was perfectly clear that much scientific work did not directly impinge on religious and moral beliefs, and that much biblical study and theological assertion bore no direct relation to technical questions in science; yet science overall presented a picture of the world, including human beings, which seemed to contra-

dict the religious outlook. Already in the eighteenth century David
Hume had suggested a view of the world in which its origin and
continuance were wholly explicable in terms of its own life and
energy, a necessity inherent in matter itself. This was the basic
principle of the natural sciences, and therefore every scientific
success was a piece of evidence strengthening the suggestion.
Such evidence was produced on a vast and ever-increasing scale in
the nineteenth century, and therefore the felt need for belief in
God as the author and preserver of this world correspondingly
decreased.

Biblical scholarship in later nineteenth-century Britain came to
be dominated by the criticial approach already long established in
Germany.[1] This critical study of the Bible could itself be described
as 'scientific', and the description was sometimes offered as a commendation of a methodical approach to the text which confined
itself to matters susceptible of reasonable demonstration in the
eyes of any honest and unprejudiced inquirer. A biblical scholarship thus freed from ecclesiastical control and the tyranny of fore-
ordained dogmatic conclusion, free to explore vast areas of study
opened up by the interpretation of a thousand years of ancient
literature, was rightly called 'liberal'. It was a truly liberating influence on many minds and offered tremendous scope to a great
variety of talents in the attempt to establish the meaning of the
sacred books: but at the expense of discounting their sacredness.
Of course, any given scholar or student could have the utmost
veneration for the texts, but it was essential to the critical method
to treat the literature like any other. Whatever the attitude in worship and the conduct of daily life, study was expected to be critical
and objective.

By no means all biblical scholars and students were prepared to
accept the liberal critical approach. One thinker who did welcome
it nevertheless gave forceful expression to what he perceived to be
its fundamental weakness:

Inspiration, deprived of its old intelligible sense, is watered down into a
mystification. The Scriptures are, indeed, inspired; but they contain a
wholly undefined and indefinable 'human element'; and this unfortunate intruder is converted into a sort of biblical whipping boy. Whatsoever scientific investigation, historical or physical, proves to be
erroneous, the 'human element' bears the blame; while the divine
inspiration of such statements, as by their nature are out of reach of

proof or disproof, is still asserted with all the vigour inspired by conscious safety from attack.[2]

Thus Thomas Henry Huxley, no friend to conservative religious thought, but expressing as clearly as any conservative could wish the mortal danger of setting off along the broad road of liberal biblical criticism.

Such critical study might create the impression of bringing biblical scholarship into closer touch with other intellectual disciplines through the adoption of methods generally recognised as valid, but such an impression would be false. As long as the biblical literature was studied like any other body of literature, it could safely be confined to its own department, and frequently has been. The restoration of genuine contact with other intellectual disciplines, including the natural sciences, would depend on full recognition of the Bible's claim to be asserting truth of fundamental significance for the whole human race, but the restored contact would inevitably involve conflict; and it was from conflict that the later nineteenth-century biblical critic wanted to escape. It was, however, one thing to end futile attempts to make Genesis and geology say the same thing by recognising that the Bible is a guide to religion and not a textbook of science, but a very different matter to ignore the wider implications of the recognition. The liberal critical stance treated biblical texts much as would a Shakespearean scholar who has no interest in dramatic performance, or a musicologist who never plays an instrument or attends a concert. Their criticism can achieve much that is useful and even necessary, but the original intentions of creative genius are ignored. However the original intentions of particular biblical authors might be viewed, both authors and texts had, and still do have, an essential relationship with Judaeo-Christian traditions and institutions, that is, the Church; and the self-conscious stance of the Church in the world is integral to the character of the biblical literature.

Conservative religious thinkers knew or sensed this and instinctively reacted against liberalism for denying or ignoring something which they felt to be essential. With conservatives it had been a much-reiterated principle that 'the truth is one', that God's revelation of himself in nature and the Book of Books must be a unity: a principle which could form the major premise in any

argument concerning religion and science. It might lead, however, to a reductio ad absurdum rather than the hoped-for theistic
conclusion, and a confession of what ought to have been the case
if religion were true rather than what was the case because religion
was true. Conservatives in the early nineteenth century had also
approached their task of interpretation in the conviction that
astronomical, geological and developmental theories of the
world's origin could be dismissed as the offspring of overheated
human imagination impregnated by overweening human pride;
and that a correct, even if novel reading of the biblical text would
prove it to be consistent with any properly established scientific
fact. The double risk involved in this twofold conviction turned
out to be fatal, even though a dead conservatism still refuses to lie
down. The scientific picture of the physical universe became quite
irreconcilable with any picture which could be derived from the
Bible, and conservative interpreters found themselves at logger-
heads with one another over the 'correct' interpretation of crucial
texts. Liberalism was repulsed with horror as a betrayal, and
philosophy regarded as the natural ally of the enemy.

This left conservatives with no choice but the simple reiteration
rather than justification of what they sincerely believed to be true.
The dogmatic attitude was modified in varying degrees through
limited concessions to liberal critical findings, but it was also
encouraged by emphasis on the reality of the miraculous and the
inflexible refusal to face real difficulties posed for conservatism by
the text. The suspicion of reason which had always characterised
conservatism became in effect an article of the Creed.

It has been maintained that there was no real conflict between
science and religion in the nineteenth century. Owen Chadwick
states:

Churches are institutions concerned with truth . . . When a theory could
be shown to be well founded, they hesitated and cast regretful glances
backward, but they accepted it because it was true and soon were again
serene. Let us not confuse secularization with the perpetual task of
adjusting religious understanding of the world to any new knowledge
about the world.[3]

Some moralists . . . seized upon Vogt, who by denying free will, and asserting that thoughts are only a response to a physical condition, removed all
moral responsibility. Of course, many moralists were aware of the real
state of affairs; and most scientists were aware of the real state of affairs –

that the advances of science could hardly touch God. Huxley knew it –
no enquiry in the realm of the physical could produce results in the
realm of the spiritual.[4]

Does the entity Science say, down with Religion? Nowhere. The entity
Science did not say, down with Religion. But a few scientists said that
Science said, down with Religion.[5]

This gives the impression of whistling in the dark to keep up
courage. Chadwick himself tells us that Vogt, Professor of Geology
in Geneva, translated the notorious *Vestiges of the Natural History of
Creation* into German, and was 'a hater of clergymen and fierce
advocate of a materialist philosophy'.[6] Bernard M. G. Reardon
much more truly says in speaking of the growth of the scientific
outlook that

for multitudes today [it] renders traditional Christian belief not merely
unacceptable – for the great majority have never seriously examined it –
but irrelevant. This is the hard fact which the teacher of religion must
now face and it should not be obscured by a complacent assumption that
the 'Victorian' conflict between religion and science is happily at an end.
The psychological impact of science continues to make itself felt, with
results no more favourable to religious valuations than formerly.[7]

It is a pity that elsewhere Reardon adopts a much more dismissive attitude to those involved in the science/religion conflicts
of the early and mid nineteenth century. With reference to
Genesis and geology: 'The details of these disputes are both amus-
ing and lamentable, but it would be pointless to dwell on them.'
'British Protestantism was inveterately biblicist and took it as a
matter of course that statements of holy writ could not be false.'[8]
It is important to note that the impact of science was not merely
psychological. If a completely scientific explanation of the universe is possible, at least in principle, then morality and religion
are illusions; and this was clearly perceived by many in nineteenth-
century Britain.

James R. Moore, in a volume which contains much material of
permanent value for a study of the subject, argues against the use
of the war analogy in describing the relationship between religion
and science, or religious believers and scientists, in the period of
the post-Darwinian controversies.[9] According to Moore, Protestant responses to Darwin showed their affinities with metaphysical and theological traditions from which Darwinism and post-

Darwinian evolutionary thought derived. By offering a non-violent interpretation of the post-Darwinian controversies Moore aims to support the revisionist thesis that Christian theology has been congenial, or, one may add, even essential to the development of modern science. He argues that

Darwin's theory of evolution by natural selection could be accepted in substance only by those whose theology was distinctly orthodox; that this was so because the theory itself presupposed a cosmology and a causality, which, owing much to orthodox doctrines of creation and providence, could be made consonant a priori with orthodox theistic beliefs.[10]

The war analogy obscures the metaphysical origins of the theory of evolution, and the reconciliation between science and religion which can be effected by a return to these metaphysical origins in the shape of traditional Christian theology. The actual arguments which have taken place are simply the result of mis-understanding. The real conflict which took place concerned matters which are no part of specifically Christian belief: first, that a scientific theory, to be established, must achieve full certainty through inductive inference: a demand impossible for Darwin's theory to fulfil. Second, that all forms of life have been fixed by divine will.[11]

Suspicions regarding this thesis are aroused by the amount of evidence produced by Moore himself that really fierce controversy did take place. In so far as the well-known use of the war analogy by writers like J. W. Draper and A. D. White suggests a clear-cut division between two sides, each with clearly defined and clearly incompatible views, Moore has made an overwhelming case against it; but this is more in the nature of a refinement of the picture than the substitution of one picture for another. Moore's own description of the fate of St George Mivart fits the war analogy remarkably well despite Moore's opinion to the contrary. Mivart apparently suffered precisely the treatment to be expected from both sides in a war of one who tried, no matter how sincerely, to compromise both. The impression created by Moore's description is that Mivart was regarded by both the Church and Darwinists as a traitor. 'Mivart was haunted by the hostility . . . of the small circle which had surrounded Darwin';[12] while Cardinal Vaughan demanded 'his unconditional surrender'.[13]

Moore's attempt to depict Darwin as a kind of neo-Paleyan

despite himself is not convincing, to put it mildly. The fact that Darwin was much impressed by Paley's *Natural Theology* in his student days does not mean that this was an effective basis for his work as a naturalist, which would have taken place even if he had never heard of Paley. Nor does it alter the fact that this early influence had to be decisively rejected as observations grew and theoretical interpretation developed.

Moore refers to T. H. Huxley's 'An Apologetic Irenicon' as containing a 'frank admission of the theological affinities of his scientific faith'.[14] The doctrines quoted from page 569 of the article are in fact referred to by Huxley as 'faulty', and are merely used in order to emphasise his rejection of ' "liberal" popular illusions that babies are all born good'. The whole article reaffirms Huxley's agnosticism and is a clearly rhetorical rejection of the views and criticisms of a Mr Harrison, and it would be very unwise to read anything more positive into it. The doctrine of Providence means for Huxley 'the total exclusion of chance from a place even in the most insignificant corner of Nature . . . the strong conviction that the cosmic process is rational; and the faith that, throughout all duration, unbroken order has reigned in the universe'.[15] For Huxley there can be no such thing as the 'ethics of evolution', although morals can have a very limited meaning as applied to certain rules of conduct 'essential to the maintenance of social existence'.[16] Otherwise Huxley can discover only 'a stream of tendency towards the consummation of the cosmic process, chiefly by means of the struggle for existence, which is no more righteous or unrighteous than the operation of any other mechanism'.[17]

Huxley gave expression to precisely those beliefs, based on scientific research, which horrified religious believers, and with very good reason.

The more fundamental criticism of Moore must be that the revisionist thesis is far from proved, and is perhaps unprovable; and that even if it is true as an account of historical change, it does not remove the real conflict between science and religion. The child does not necessarily inherit the parent's philosophy of life. Or, to put the matter another way, the Church could have generated its own Trojan Horse.

The appeal to Calvinistic theology raises considerable problems of its own and can scarcely be accepted as simply a return to traditional orthodox theology. Furthermore, we may in principle see divine sovereignty and predestination as including the evolutionary process, so that this process becomes for us the inevitable and irresistible unfolding of God's will; but we are not obliged to see evolution in this light, and scientific explanations like Darwin's confine attention to the natural process itself and deliberately exclude the supernatural. A recent example is Richard Dawkins' *The Blind Watchmaker*. Moore leans on a selection of theologians to support his thesis, but states their views rather than examining them.[18] His closing remarks are significant:

the Christian Darwinians were never more than a tiny minority, their writing never more than marginally effective against the rising tide of evolutionary naturalism and evolutionary liberalism and the strong undercurrent of popular anti-evolutionary beliefs. They failed to persuade the greatest minds of their generation; they failed to impress the least . . . The struggle to come to terms with Darwin has not yet ceased.[19]

This is only too true.

Dr Tess Cosslett has produced a useful collection of selections from literature illustrating the conflict of science and religion in the nineteenth century, and some helpful comment;[20] but her overall view of their relationship is seriously misleading. In commenting on Paley's *Natural Theology* she states:

Thus neither empiricism nor mechanism were seen as threats to religion – instead, both were used to strengthen religious belief . . . The nineteenth century begins with science and religion not just in harmony, but mutually interdependent. Not only did theologians use scientific evidence, but scientists investigated Nature with a religious reverence for the wonders of Divine design. Science was thus seen as a religious pursuit, providing ever more evidence for God's existence.[21]

According to Cosslett, it was natural selection which inflicted a devastating blow against 'the widely accepted relationship between science and religion'. 'What had been a prop of religion was now turned against it.'[22] With reference to John Tyndall's presidential address before the British Association in Belfast in 1874, Cosslett accuses Tyndall of completely ignoring 'the huge debt that nineteenth century science owed to natural theology'.[23] Tyndall is quoted as saying of science, 'Single-handed . . . by inward force, it has built at least one great wing of the many-mansioned house which man in his totality demands.'[24] On which

Cosslett comments: 'This is a serious misrepresentation of the contribution of theology to scientific advance. It is a myth created by scientific naturalists like Tyndall, who want to detach science from its traditional association with religion.'[25] Huxley is represented as playing a similar villainous part:

Huxley's image of a necessary conflict between two deadly enemies became the received account of the relations between science and religion in the nineteenth century.

Yet:

Up to about 1860, most scientists and clergymen in England assumed that natural theology guaranteed a productive harmony between science and religion. The discoveries of the scientists provided religion with ever-more complex demonstrations of the design and order of God's universe; in this light, science was a religious pursuit.[26]

Darwin's natural selection destroyed all this. The triumph of a 'value-free' science in the modern world 'explains why we have been so ready to accept the science-versus-religion myth of its partisans, such as Huxley'. 'It has been pointed out that if there was a "conflict" between science and religion after the publication of the *Origin of Species*, it was scientists like Huxley and Tyndall, rather than theologians, who were the aggressors.'[27]

In reply to Dr Cosslett we must first recognise that early nineteenth-century writers on natural theology attempted to put a religious interpretation on scientific discovery, and endeavoured to use the facts it had uncovered to support the design argument, precisely because they knew the evidence was capable of very different interpretation. Lengthy argument was made out by men like Paley and the Bridgewater authors because they saw in natural science a serious potential threat to religion.

The same fear of science lies behind the bitter controversies over geology and frequent references to the nebular hypothesis. It lies behind the uproar over *Vestiges* and the frantic denunciations of it made by Sedgwick (see pp. 155–61 below). Nor is it good enough to explain the attitude of Huxley and Tyndall as the result of their being educated outside the usual English system, with a consequent natural opposition to an establishment dominated by the clergy.[28] If science had been seen as a prop to religion, if it was in fact a religious pursuit, young scientists like Huxley and Tyndall would have developed in an atmosphere where their endeavours were welcomed and the clergy would have been their warmest allies. In fact, they entered upon a scene of already prolonged and bitter conflict, and, like Draper and White, wanted scientific research freed from the dead hand of ecclesiastical control, however indirect.

The real position is made perfectly clear in Tyndall's Belfast address:

Cardinal Cullen, I am told, is also actively engaged in erecting spiritual barriers against the intrusion of 'Infidelity' into Ireland. His Eminence, I believe, has reason to suspect that the Catholic youth around him are not proof to seductions of science. The youth of Ireland will imbibe science . . . And to its inward modifying power . . . I look for the abatement of various incongruities.[29]

The Cardinal's view should be compared with that of another Cardinal-to-be a little earlier in the century with reference to the mechanics' institutes, and 'those classes which, external to Ireland, are the problem and perplexity of patriotic statesmen, and the natural opponents of the teachers of every kind of religion'.[30]

Cosslett's interpretation of the evidence implies that without religious belief and natural theology, science would have been seriously impeded in its development, or not developed at all: scientists would not have pursued their investigations without religious motivation, or would have suppressed personal observation, theorising and classification unless they felt that this was fulfilling some religious purpose. In fact, men followed naturalistic and scientific pursuits because they had a strong desire to do so, whether this was the dominant influence in their lives or more of a sideline. To claim that such motivation was combined with religious ideas and beliefs is one thing, and was in many cases true; but to claim that the latter were the moving force in scientific investigation is a very different matter and is not true.

Natural theology was also a comfort to those who were not scientifically inclined but who were alarmed at the implications of scientific discovery. We must also bear in mind the fact that natural theology dependent on the design argument was invalid; that there were widely varying estimates of the precise religious conclusions to be drawn from it; and that it was opposed by a substantial number of religious believers who regarded revealed truth as the sole hope of salvation. Natural theology was far more of a prop to religious faith than to scientific endeavour, and a very poor one at that, wholly inadequate to its purpose. It is little wonder that theologians in the latter part of the century were defensive rather than aggressive. Scientific knowledge had become much too specialised for plausible and persuasive criticism of its contents from lay sources, while at the same time no generally agreed philosophy was available for the inspection of its wider implications.

It is, then, true that men like Draper and White, Huxley and Tyndall were perfectly happy to leave the Church to its own religious sphere on the understanding that scientists were left free from interference on religious grounds. It is also true that many individuals combined in their own persons sincere religious belief and scientific interest and accomplishment. Yet the case for scientific freedom was argued aggressively by men who felt with unshakeable confidence that history, up to the very moment of presenting their case, was wholly on their side. They were men on the offensive, certain of victory over what they regarded as obscurantism; and concessions to religion were not based upon a clearly grasped appreciation of any real contribution theology could make to our understanding of the world, but were the impatient gestures of those who want to get on with the real work unimpeded by the irrelevant. Peace bought for religion on the terms offered meant intellectual suicide and the reduction of faith to a forlorn hope. Tyndall, for example, makes room for religion in his overall view of the world by assigning it to the realm of feeling and sentiment, with science firmly ruling over the realm of knowledge: precisely the view which so horrified John Henry Newman, and which he rightly saw as utterly incompatible with the proper claims of religion and theology.

Religious belief put into propositions about nature, man and God was somehow incompatible with propositions about nature and man, along with the deliberate exclusion of propositions about God, made by science. The incompatibility was a fact and remained so regardless of any given individual's reaction to it. It might be recognised and it could be stressed; or it might be ignored, or the illusion might be maintained that it had been explained away; but particular attitudes could only be related to the fact; they could not remove it. Science was not merely a collection of experiments, hypotheses and generalisations about natural phenomena, but the exhibition on a large scale of rational inquiry which set no limits to the areas of life which it might investigate, and which refused to compromise its demand for evidence, reasonable demonstration and proof. Any department of life which closed its gates firmly in the face of reason was suspected of having something to hide. Claims which resisted investigation must be fraudulent, and this reflected badly on the institutions which made them.

Hence the historical approach of Draper and White, who believed that they could demonstrate by reference to actual examples the utter foolishness of using religion as a barricade to stop scientific entry into some new area of investigation and inquiry. Scientific progress and the benefits it could bring were impeded and religion was discredited because the barricade was invariably smashed. The clear implication was that religion should keep to its own sphere and give up the pretence of setting bounds to rational, scientific inquiry; but the question was not properly addressed as to how religion could establish its own legitimate sphere of influence without setting purely artificial bounds to rationalism. According to what criteria could such frontiers be drawn? Who or what would be the impartial boundary-maker independent of both religion and science but with authority recognised by both? Was not this judge reason itself, the only faculty we have for making judgments? Any claimant to the position of arbiter would have to submit credentials for examination at the bar of reason, which implied that reason was itself the inescapable final authority.

If religious believers proposed God as the rival candidate, then either his revelations would themselves have to be received and grasped by reason, as Locke had pointed out long before,[31] or else reason would have to be overruled by the miraculous. In the latter case Church leaders ran the grave risk of attempting the impossible, since they would have to show that the occurrence of miracles which defied all rational explanation was self-evident, while at the same time they would have to explain why the Bible itself bore ample witness to the failure of miracle as an instrument of persuasion. On the other hand, the surrender of religion to the supreme rule of reason was what the arbitration procedure had been supposed to avoid.

The mention of scepticism suggests that it would be more

accurate to speak of the war between religion and scepticism than religion and science. T. H. Huxley, on one of those occasions when he was in the mood to play down the atheistic implications of scientific study, rightly asserted that Kant's three problems of God, free will and immortality existed long before physical science and would remain if it ceased to exist; but he made a considerable understatement when he went on to say, 'All that physical science has done has been to make, as it were, visible and tangible some difficulties that formerly were more hard of apprehension.'[32] The quoted statement cannot be accepted as it stands. Natural science was a body of knowledge which grew by feeding on itself, which developed under the powerful influence of an internal drive, limitless energy within nature and the universe, within humanity, rendering the supernatural superfluous and demonstrating in concrete achievements what reason could accomplish when freed from the bonds of superstition.

If all the particular items of knowledge which comprised science were added up, the encyclopaedic result did not in itself deny God, but it did ignore God and prove itself an altogether more useful volume than the Bible. It was only too easy for the sceptic to point to the natural sciences as the gods which were already delivering a captive people from the land of oppressive ignorance. Any given scientist might object to this use of his or her technical studies, just as certain scientists objected to the use of their research work to produce the atom bomb; but just as the bomb was a perfectly valid conclusion in the realm of applied military technology, insisted on by those who had the will, the aim and the power to make that particular use of experiment and discovery, so also the sceptic could legitimately make his own particular use of the picture of the universe ruled by secondary causes. And those who think that this picture is now outdated should ask themselves to what extent this is really the case, and if the replacement of necessity by the rule of uncertainty and statistical probability really offers greater comfort to religion.

At the same time, the correctness of Huxley's assertion about Kant's three problems and their existence independently of the sciences must be given full recognition. There is no evading the crucial role of scientific witness in any discussion of religion's claims to truth, but the problems calling for an answer are philosophical. The conflict of science was and is a real one because it is part of a larger battle between religion and scepticism in which science appears all too readily as scepticism's natural ally. It was Hume's devastating critique of religious belief which required an answer, and that answer could only be provided by a reconstructed theology, that is, metaphysics, which fully recognised and accepted what was true in the sceptic's case, including the ever-developing picture of the universe presented by the natural sciences. If theology could not accomplish this task then the believer could give no account of his faith to the challenge of inquiry, or to the questions and doubts which must inevitably arise in his own mind and feelings. Religion and morality might well remain as the disposition of individuals, but claims to truth would be inadmissible. Assertions of religious belief could not reasonably be supposed to have any objective reference.

It would be an absurd mistake to suppose that the conflict of science and religion was the only one to occupy the minds of thoughtful people in nineteenth-century Britain. It is an easier mistake, but more profound, not to see in that conflict a particularly striking example of a far more widespread awareness of the tension between religious faith and unfettered reason, liberalism. For example, the science/religion conflict and the Oxford Movement would occupy different chapters in a textbook of Church history, and for practical teaching purposes this is necessary. Yet the Movement's hostility to liberalism sprang from a deep-seated realisation that reason let loose was a threat to faith, the destructive tendencies of which were limitless. When members of the Oxford Movement attacked liberalism, they had in mind rational reflection set free from dogmatic control in theology and biblical criticism; but when the same kind of rational inquiry took the whole of nature for its subject, with first the hint and later the more explicit assertion of mankind's inclusion, it threatened the ecclesiastical issues with total loss of significance.

Ironically, it would be those who sought truth by objective scientific methods who would emerge into the light of day, while those whose minds were still ruled by inherited dogmatic tradition would remain in cave-like obscurity, absorbed in fierce or fascinating argument concerning shadows bearing no relation to reality. There was no more rational movement in history than the Tractarian, but it was reason within the limits of religion alone. When church thinkers were eventually compelled to take note of the scepticism inherent in natural science, they were at a loss how to cope with it, since the framework of religion was itself being smashed.

Newman had to argue for the place of theology in a university education, and he felt obliged to relate such theological study to the world as seen by the natural scientist. His attempt was a failure, despite some penetrating insights of permanent value. In his *Apologia* Newman tells us that as a man in his thirties he viewed the angels 'as the real causes of motion, light, and life, and of those elementary principles of the physical universe, which, when offered in their developments to our senses, suggest to us the notion of cause and effect, and of what are called the laws of nature'.[33] John Keble in a well-known hymn could speak with clear conviction of heaven revealed in nature to those who gazed upon it with eyes purified by Christian virtue. In these two cases the temper displayed and the mode of approach to the natural world are poles apart from the ideal purity of science, which is freedom from any kind of prejudice, above all the religious, and dedication to the objectively demonstrable.[34] Seen in the light of the latter, the former could only appear as some kind of fairy tale.

The Tractarians were also very much alive to what they perceived as threats posed by Whigs, radicals and all those imbued with the spirit of the French Revolution. At the same time, many of those who felt the need for change found a natural ally in the sciences. This is not to say that reformers made frequent explicit appeals to science or that scientists naturally gravitated to the political left: but it would be equally mistaken to ignore the attempt to educate working men in the principles and achievements of science, the obvious benefits in terms of health and wealth brought by science in its train, the link between self-help, useful knowledge and political and economic freedom, and the demand that authority should give account of itself to the reason and sense possessed by all men. If there were appalling conditions and injustices to be remedied, the will might be provided by the politically motivated, but the techniques necessary to improvement were provided by scientific method. Humanitarian aims might or might not be allied to religious commitment, but religion too often appeared as the protector of privilege and preserver of the status quo. When men had within their own grasp the means to positive achievement there was no point in deferring to a transcendent deity who was, perhaps, merely the grandiose reflection of man himself. The story that Marx sought to dedicate the second volume of *Capital* to Charles Darwin may be a legend, but if so it is an even more telling symbol of nineteenth-century ideological connections than an isolated historical detail could be.[35]

The presence of the burgeoning natural sciences in nineteenth-century Britain affected the whole ethos and conduct of society, much as the arrival of the first baby transforms a hitherto childless household. Scepticism was in the air, and the sciences fed it. The multitude of volumes and articles on the conflict of science and religion produced in the nineteenth century are not likely to have been merely the fruit of some simple misunderstanding.

However, if the conflict was, and is, real, this implies that religion must be something more than superstition and comforting illusion. The Church has not simply disappeared before the advance of science, and the large majority in Britain outside regular church membership have not thereby placed themselves beyond religious thought and sentiment. The persistent, widespread and varied expression of religious belief, however we evaluate particular instances of it, suggests some deep-seated need or assurance in human nature which only faith in the supernatural can satisfy. The universality of spontaneous moral judgment and genuineness of moral feeling, however chaotic and inconsistent the overall picture may be, can only have real significance in the context of wider metaphysical truth. The naive belief in progress to be found in nineteenth-century thought has found ample and even astonishing fulfilment in twentieth-century scientific and technological achievement; but that very achievement, far from bringing solutions to the serious problems which have their roots in defects of personality and character, has seriously aggravated them.

Nevertheless the question remains, Is religion true? The affirmative answers often given to that question in the nineteenth century and passed on into the twentieth generally lacked proper or full justification. No coherent system was agreed among the churches; there was no commonly recognised foothold whereon the Church could stand and move the world. David Hume had done his work thoroughly, and an equally thoroughgoing reply was needed. Although that reply was provided, religious thought in Britain was dominated by a wholly inadequate response, while the true answer was ignored and has yet to make its proper impact on British thought.

First, however, we must appreciate the considerable strength, and also the weakness, of Humean scepticism.

CHAPTER 2

David Hume

David Hume, the eighteenth-century Scottish philosopher, published in 1739–40 his *Treatise of Human Nature*. Hume's main interest was in morals, politics and the passions and inclinations which move human beings; but as a preliminary to the study of human nature in its moral and political aspects he carried out a critique of reason. His aim was to show that self-conscious human reasoning does not have the significance in human thinking and experience which it is generally assumed to have, and that its contribution to knowledge is and must be much more limited than has often been supposed. The most famous illustration of this contention given by Hume concerns the causal connection, axiomatic alike for common sense and natural science.

It is important to recognise that Hume did not deny the necessity whereby one event or set of circumstances gives rise to another, or that an event or thing is the effect of some antecedent cause. What he denied was that reason can give any explanation or justification for our acceptance of necessary causal connection. We accept it, indeed assume it because we are so constituted as to have no choice in the matter. Belief in necessary causal connection is alike unavoidable and inexplicable.[1]

Hume by temperament had a strong antipathy to the dogmatic religious outlook and the intolerance and zeal or enthusiasm that went with it. He was subjected to frequent criticism by both Presbyterians and Anglicans, and was branded as an infidel before the General Assembly of the Church of Scotland. His application in 1744 for the Chair of Ethics and Pneumatic Philosophy at Edinburgh University was rejected because of suspicion about his moral and religious views. It is therefore not surprising that when he turned to the congenial task of subjecting reasoned religious belief to sceptical analysis the result of his endeavours was not

22

published during his lifetime. This work, *Dialogues Concerning Natural Religion*, appeared in 1779, three years after his death and tacitly excludes revealed, biblical religion as a subject for investigation. In this imaginary discussion between three men, Demea represents dogmatic belief founded on what is claimed to be infallible a priori argument; Cleanthes represents religious belief founded on rational reflection on human experience of the world; and Philo is a sceptic whose aim throughout is to demonstrate the incapacity of reason to bear the weight put on it by Demea and Cleanthes.

Hume explains that he uses the dialogue form, first to avoid tediousness in emphasising important points which at the same time are obvious; and second, because it is best suited to dealing with a matter in which human reason can reach no certain conclusion. The second point is of fundamental importance in understanding the *Dialogues*. Hume is asserting from the very beginning that being reasonable means acknowledging that neither the assertion of Christian theism nor its denial can be proved on the basis of our observation and knowledge of the natural world, although any given individual will feel that the evidence supports one view rather than the other. Such belief is a matter of opinion, however well informed and carefully worked out that opinion may be. Recognition of this fact leads to tolerance, a cardinal virtue in the eyes of Hume.

It also leads to a certain tension in his philosophy. He obviously resented what he regarded as lack of tolerance on the part of religious dogmatists and he therefore emphasised the strength of sceptical criticism in opposition to them. This strictly rational criticism receives no convincing answer and suggests that complete agnosticism is the only reasonable attitude we can adopt. On the other hand, all three participants in the discussion assert the importance of religion, and the conclusion of the *Dialogues* is that Cleanthes has put forward the most convincing argument of all. In Part XII Philo makes a sharp distinction between popular religion or superstition on the one hand, and a thoughtful religious belief on the other, and he makes what is in the context of the whole argument a surprising return to the argument from design. Philo now qualifies his earlier severe criticism of this argument, excusing himself on the ground of his strong opposition to bigotry and the 'vulgar superstition' on which it is based. He is now prepared

to allow that there is a vast number of pieces of evidence to support the view that an intelligence something like our own has
brought the world into existence. 'In many views of the universe
and of its parts . . . the beauty and fitness of final causes strike us
with such irresistible force that all objections appear (what I
believe they really are) mere cavils and sophisms; nor can we then
imagine how it was ever possible for us to repose any weight on
them.' Natural theology can really be summed up in the proposition 'That the cause or causes of order in the universe probably
bear some remote analogy to human intelligence'.[2] Theists
emphasise the analogy, the possibility of comparison between the
human creature and the divine creator. Sceptics emphasise the
remoteness of the one from the other: but reasonable theists and
sceptics will recognise how much they have in common and will
see their differences as really only differences of emphasis.
Indeed, any genuine religious believer will welcome scepticism as
a confession of the weakness of human reason, and this will compel those who really want to know the truth to turn to revelation
for it.[3]

We may compare with all this a statement in the *Treatise*: 'The
order of the universe proves an omnipotent mind . . . Nothing
more is requisite to give a foundation to all the articles of religion;
nor is it necessary we should form a distinct idea of the force and
energy of the Supreme Being.'[4] Similar assertions are made
throughout *The Natural History of Religion*, although no attempt is
made to defend this view.[5]

If Hume himself really believed this, we must suppose that he
genuinely respected a thoughtful and tolerant religious philosophy, and hoped that his own would provide common ground
upon which believers and sceptics could meet to their mutual
advantage. This interpretation of the *Dialogues* fits well into the
general context of Hume's philosophy and his rejection of
extreme scepticism. In that case we must see the forceful presentation of Philo's sceptical outlook as the consequence of his dislike
of religious dogmatism.

The difficulty with this interpretation lies in the simple fact that
Philo's arguments not only challenge Demea's dogmatic a priori
defence of theistic belief, but destroy Cleanthes' argument from
design; and this is also in keeping with Hume's overall philosophical outlook. Reason can no more demonstrate the truth of

God's existence by reflection upon the natural world than it can prove the existence of necessary causal connection. We accept necessary causal connection nevertheless because it is natural for us to do so, and in any case we really do not have any choice in the matter. If Hume's arguments are meant to effect a reconciliation between religious belief and scepticism, then the same must be true for the existence of God. We should all be by nature believers in God and only capable of regarding the world as the manifestation of divine benevolence and purpose. Unfortunately for the cause of tolerance, this proposition is untrue. As Philo himself says, 'A man's natural inclination works incessantly upon him; it is for ever present to the mind, and mingles itself with every view and consideration; whereas religious motives, where they act at all, operate only by starts and bounds, and it is scarcely possible for them to become altogether habitual.'[6]

Furthermore, such a mere inclination would be wholly inadequate as a justification of theistic belief. We might as well believe in fairies or the Olympic pantheon. For Christian and Jewish belief, naturalistic explanation is merely explaining away.

One is left wondering how much irony there is in Philo's ultimate concessions to religious belief, or possibly the desire to soften the animosity of religious leaders when the *Dialogues* were finally published. It is interesting and perhaps instructive to compare a closing remark of the *Dialogues* with a more notorious one at the end of the essay on miracles:

A person, seasoned with a just sense of the imperfections of natural reason, will fly to revealed truth with the greatest avidity . . . To be a philosophical sceptic is, in a man of letters, the first and most essential step towards being a sound, believing Christian.

So that upon the whole we may conclude, that the *Christian Religion* not only was at first attended with miracles, but even at this day cannot be believed by any reasonable person without one. Mere reason is insufficient to convince us of its veracity. And whoever is moved by *faith* to assent to it, is conscious of a continued miracle in his own person, which subverts all the principles of his understanding, and gives him a determination to believe what is most contrary to custom and experience.[7]

The savage sarcasm of the latter statement could scarcely have been applied to the necessity linking cause and effect. Hume's scepticism with respect to the causal connection demonstrates the weakness of reason. The tendency of his scepticism regarding religious belief is to destroy the notion that it has any rational basis.

Whatever may have been Hume's own beliefs, it is Philo in the *Dialogues* whose arguments are the most impressive. After some brief pleasantries Demea opens the discussion with remarks on the limits of human reason, especially in religious matters, and Philo picks up the point and emphasises it. Cleanthes objects that sceptics are not really as sceptical as they make out. In his reply Philo agrees that in ordinary daily affairs sceptics act, and must act, like other men.

> But when we look beyond human affairs and the properties of the surrounding bodies; when we carry our speculations into the two eternities, before and after the present state of things: into the creation and formation of the universe, the existence and properties of spirits, the powers and operations of one universal Spirit existing without beginning and without end, omnipotent, omniscient, immutable, infinite, and incomprehensible – we must be far removed from the smallest tendency to scepticism not to be apprehensive that we have here got quite beyond the reach of our faculties.[8]

A little later Demea once more gives Philo an opening by insisting that the nature of God is 'altogether incomprehensible and unknown to us', a point which Philo is very happy to stress. 'Our ideas reach no farther than our experience. We have no experience of divine attributes and operations': and the reader is left to draw the obvious conclusion.[9]

Cleanthes replies with the argument from design, likening the world to a great machine, divided up into a vast number of smaller machines, all with parts beautifully adjusted to one another to accomplish given ends. This adaptation of means to ends can only be the result of deliberate intention and intelligence, similar in the case of the world and all its parts to human artefacts, but so much the greater as the world and all it contains is so much greater and more refined than any man-made machine.

Philo demolishes this argument by making four points: first, an argument from analogy depends on the closeness of the analogy for its persuasiveness. The comparison between human artefacts and the universe is too remote to be persuasive. Second, matter may have an inherent tendency towards order. This is not true for things made by man, but we cannot apply to the whole universe what is true of some of its parts. Third, thought is a little agitation of the human brain, and we have no right to select this one small part of the universe and make it the ruling principle of the whole. Fourth, even if human intelligence were now vastly more influential in the universe, it would not follow that it was so in the beginning.

Philo concludes by pointing out that men like Copernicus and Galileo, to whom Cleanthes has appealed to show the power of reason, differed from Cleanthes precisely in this, that they reasoned on the basis of analogies between things which fall within our experience and really are similar. Cleanthes, on the other hand, speaks as if he had witnessed the origin of worlds and the first arrangement of the elements, which is utterly impossible.

What Philo's case implies, not only here but taken as a whole throughout the *Dialogues*, is that the argument from analogy can never demonstrate the truth of a proposition because the assertion that there is an analogy assumes what it is meant to demonstrate. As Philo states later in Part vii,

> To say that all this order in animals and vegetables proceeds ultimately from design is begging the question; nor can that great point be ascertained otherwise than by providing, a priori, both that order is, from its nature, inseparably attached to thought and that it can never of itself or from original unknown principles belong to matter.[10]

We may add that the natural sciences strengthened Hume's supposition concerning matter on a grand scale, not least the science of chemistry, which began to come into its own not long after his death. This also means with reference to the second point above, that things made by man not only lack an inherent tendency towards order, but actually require such order in matter. If raw materials lacked stability, artefacts as we know them would be an impossibility.

Philo's reply to Cleanthes' design argument is what we might call the hard core of Hume's scepticism, and no theistic philosophy can be established which fails to take into account its correctness. Philo, however, has by no means finished his work of demolition.

He goes on to point out that positing a divine intelligence and ideal world as the origin of this one only lands us in an infinite regress, since the origin of this ideal world also demands explanation. What makes matters worse is that the ideal world is also purely imaginary:

It were better, therefore, never to look beyond the present material World. By supposing it to contain the principle of its order within itself, we really assert it to be God, and the sooner we arrive at that divine being, the better. When you go one step beyond the mundane system, you only excite an imaginative humour which it is impossible ever to satisfy.[11]

Philo then considers what conclusions we may draw from Cleanthes' analogical argument if we waive the insuperable objections to it and pretend that it is true. He asserts that a collection of imperfect deities is at least as likely a conclusion as a single perfect deity. If we look at a beautiful ship we are struck with admiration for the carpenter who designed and made it: but it might turn out to be nothing more than a copy made by 'a stupid mechanic', and the excellent ship itself the ultimate product of long years of trial and error involving innumerable workmen. Similarly,

Many worlds might have been botched and bungled, throughout an eternity, ere this system was struck out; much labour lost, many fruitless trials made, and a slow but continued improvement carried on during infinite ages in the art of world-making. In such subjects, who can determine where the truth, nay, who can conjecture where the probability lies, amidst a great number of hypotheses which may be proposed, and a still greater which may be imagined?[12]

Furthermore, the world much more resembles an organism than a machine, and may have come into being by some process of natural growth. 'Judging by our limited and imperfect experience, generation has some privileges above reason; for we see every day the latter arise from the former, never the former from the latter.'[13]

If we combine Hume's two ideas of the organic, and development over long periods of time, we have an evolutionary hypothesis, and once again the natural sciences went on to produce the evidence which turned Hume's speculative possibilities into what looks very much like the truth. In the words of Richard Dawkins, Reader in Zoology in the University of Oxford, 'But what Hume did was criticize the logic of using apparent design in nature as *positive* evidence for the existence of a God. He did not offer any *alternative* explanation for apparent design, but left the question open.' Dawkins goes on to say, 'Darwin made it possible to be an intellectually fulfilled atheist.' It must be admitted that one does not get the impression from Darwin himself that there was anything intellectually fulfilling about atheism, but Dawkins is right to make the connection between the philosopher and the scientist.[14]

Demea has all along found Cleanthes' approach unsatisfactory. He now repeats his opinion that the only dependable kind of argument for the existence of God is a priori, and he offers what he regards as the common one: everything must have a cause outside itself, and this cause in turn must have a cause, and so on. Either the succession of causes and effects goes back to infinity; or else it had its beginning in a necessarily existent cause, a being who must necessarily exist. If we accept the first alternative then we have an infinite chain of causes and effects, the existence of which itself demands some explanation. Simply to accept an infinite regress is an absurdity, and we must therefore accept the second alternative; and the necessarily existent being who constitutes the First Cause is God.

Cleanthes rejects Demea's argument on the ground that it is impossible to demonstrate a matter of fact a priori. For such a demonstration to be possible, the opposite of what is asserted must be a contradiction. No denial of an assertion of fact can involve a contradiction, and this is the essential difference between the a priori propositions of mathematics and statements of fact; therefore the phrase 'necessarily existent being' is nonsense. This is because, according to Cleanthes' line of argument, it involves a contradiction: an existent being is a fact; but we can conceive that there is no such fact without contradicting ourselves; and therefore its existence is not necessary.

However, Cleanthes and Philo then go on to consider 'this pretended explication of necessity' in relation to matter. Hume here simply returns to a point he has already made and proceeds to emphasise it. They suggest that if we understood the nature of matter fully, we might be compelled to recognise that the denial of facts as they are does involve a contradiction: it might be that things are as they are by a kind of mathematical necessity. Matter 'may contain some qualities which . . . would make its nonexistence appear as great a contradiction as that twice two is five'. Philo speaks of the possibility that the whole economy of the universe is conducted by algebraic necessity.[15] Cleanthes also asserts that it is meaningless to ask about the first cause of an infinite chain of causes and effects. If we can speak of a First

Cause, the chain is not infinite. If we ask about the cause of the chain as a whole, we are playing with words. The idea of the chain as a whole is one which we can form in our minds for our own convenience in thought and discussion, and it does not correspond to some sort of extra thing, over and above the constituent parts of the chain, which requires explanation.

It is in this Part IX of the *Dialogues* that the weakness of Hume's scepticism begins to show. Cleanthes' assertion that it is meaningless to speak of the First Cause of an infinite chain of causes and effects is scarcely a criticism of Demea, who has posited a First Cause precisely because he regards an infinite regress of causes and effects as an absurdity. Although the ontological argument is not referred to by name, its validity would be assumed by the kind of thinker whom Demea represents, and it is implicit in his reference to God as necessarily existent. It receives no refutation from Cleanthes or Philo, since the claim that no assertion of a matter of fact can involve a contradiction is precisely what is in question when considering the ontological argument. The denial of the assertion that God exists is the one case, according to the argument, which does involve a contradiction. God is that than which no greater can be conceived; but to exist is greater than not to exist: therefore if we think of God as not existing, we are not thinking of that than which no greater can be conceived: that is, we are not thinking of God.

This may seem to be a logic-chopping exercise and not worth Hume's attention considering the overall strength of his sceptical arguments against the powers of human reason; but a proper attempt to understand and refute the ontological argument might have compelled Hume to face the question what we believe to be the ultimate reality, than which no greater can be conceived. Anselm, who gave classic expression to this argument, based it on an appeal to experience, the unique nature of God and the adequacy of a very limited knowledge of God for its valid application to human reasoning. If we mean by mentally conceiving not merely conjuring up any image or idea which an extravagant imagination can produce, but sensible thinking about what can be proved to exist or reasonably be believed to exist, we shall find ourselves concerned with the nature of that ultimate power which alone is adequate to account for the world as we know it. Anselm quite clearly insisted that the ontological argument was based upon experience, that it was the expression of a deeply held faith, and could only be intelligible in that context.

When Hume can first dismiss the phrase 'necessarily existent being' as nonsense, and then argue for its possible application to matter, he is enjoying the luxury of playing the purely negative critic. As Hume himself fully appreciated, we have inescapable beliefs and assumptions related to everyday events and behaviour. If we try to see their implications and offer some positive justification for them, we must make up our minds whether necessity operates in the universe or not. Regardless of the limitations of human reasoning, we must acknowledge that the complete rejection of necessity involves acceptance of the totally random. If the latter is rejected in theory as it is in practice, we must then try to determine with whatever degree of probability we can just what the nature of this necessity is. The difference between Hume on the one hand, and Anselm and the thinkers represented by Demea on the other, is not that the latter thought in some confused and invalid way about God as a necessarily existent being whereas Hume did not because he had spotted the logical flaw in the expression; but that Hume wanted to apply the phrase to matter, the physical world, whereas the latter believed that it could be applied legitimately only to the transcendent being known to theists as God.

Hume emphasises the possibility of a necessity inherent in matter, and this idea received considerable support from the wide-ranging successes of the natural sciences. The assumed necessity of causal connections may or may not be demonstrable, but the evidence of common sense has been supplemented on a vast scale by scientific investigation. This makes such an assertion as 'Halley's comet appeared in 1984' a contradiction. If a comet appeared in 1984, it not only *was not* Halley's comet; it *could not* have been Halley's comet, and no doubt Patrick Moore would insist on this way of putting it. It is part of the definition of Halley's comet that it should appear in 1985 and not 1984. Synthetic propositions are thus ultimately reducible to analytic, and Philo's contemplation of an algebraic universe is shown to be a fact by the significance of mathematics in the accepted system of laws of nature. Our preferred distinction between analytic and synthetic, a priori and a posteriori, merely reflects our ignorance of the real nature of events.

This line of reasoning, allied with rigorous rejection of an anthropomorphic-type theism, leads directly into Spinozistic monism. The world is here because it is here and it could not be otherwise, and we may call it 'God' or 'nature'. Hume was dismissive of Spinoza, whom he used a stick wherewith to beat the theologians;[16] but this belonged to his role as the negative sceptic. Once we step outside the charmed circle of scepticism and try to give a positive account of experience along the lines laid down by Hume in the *Dialogues*, our ultimate destination is Spinozistic monism, and this is as good as admitted in the words of Philo in which he refers to the world as an organism containing the principle of its order within itself and thereby really asserts it to be God.

Hume might reply that necessary existence in God and in matter are equally unknowable and that we are not entitled to go beyond an ad hominem argument the sole intention of which was to shake theological complacency and dogmatism. The fact remains, however, that devastating arguments against theism are produced by Hume and never answered, whereas for Hume the acknowledgement of necessary causal connection remains an unavoidable element in everyday experience as well as being the foundation principle of all scientific investigation. There can be no doubt that if we try to draw a positive view out of the discussion in the *Dialogues*, it must either be plain atheism, or atheism in the thin disguise of pantheism.

In Parts x and xi we come to a lengthy consideration of the problem of evil. The evil of the world is its widespread misery and wickedness, and Philo suggests that if someone who did not yet know the world were told beforehand that it had been created by a very wise, powerful and benevolent deity, even if this deity were not the infinitely powerful, wise and good God of orthodox theology, he would expect to find something very different from the world as it is. If we were shown a building which caused its inhabitants as much proportionate suffering and inconvenience, we should form no high opinion of the architect, and if we follow the method of reasoning found in natural theology, we shall be driven to a similar low opinion of the deity. Even those aspects of nature which seem to reveal purpose and design, some systematic and coherent plan, nevertheless also reveal what can only be called slipshod divine workmanship. Winds, rain and heat, for example, are often excessive, causing immense damage and suffering which a little alteration on the part of divine power could easily avoid. A survey of the world in no way enables us to infer morality in the deity in any sense that we can give to the term.

Look round this universe. What an immense profusion of beings, animated and organized, sensible and active! You admire this prodigious variety and fecundity. But inspect a little more narrowly these living existences, the only beings worth regarding. How hostile and destructive to each other! How insufficient all of them for their own happiness! How contemptible or odious to the spectator! The whole presents nothing but the idea of a blind nature, impregnated by a great vivifying principle, and pouring forth from her lap, without discernment or parental care, her maimed and abortive children![17]

Hume immediately goes on to mention, only in order to dismiss it, the idea that the mixture of good and evil in the world implies the existence of a malevolent as well as a benevolent deity, both at war with each other. 'The true conclusion is that the original Source of all things is entirely indifferent to all these principles, and has no more regard to good above ill than to heat above cold, or to drought above moisture, or to light above heavy.'[18]

The main points in Hume's scepticism are therefore as follows:

(1) We cannot by reasoning alone demonstrate the truth of any assertion of fact.
(2) The subject-matter for all reasoning concerning matters of fact is drawn from experience.
(3) When reasoning shakes itself loose from the bond of experience it may display validity in the connection of ideas, but the demonstration of truth regarding matters of fact is in this case an absolute impossibility.
(4) Dogmatic assertions about God can therefore find no foundation in mere reasoning.
(5) If we then try to use experience as the foundation for metaphysical claims, we find that no analogy is adequate to the task; that a variety of religious views of the origin of the universe is possible, but none demonstrable; that matter may itself contain innate tendencies to change, such as could have produced the world we know; that metaphysical as well as physical explanation of the world's origin leads us into infinite regress; that mind could well have its origin in matter.
(6) The problem of evil lays bare the fatal weaknesses in both a priori and empirical attempts to demonstrate the existence of God.

It is impossible to assess precisely Hume's direct influence on British thought in general, but he gave very clear and forceful expression to those doubts which most, if not all, individuals feel concerning the claims of religion. It is likely that his influence on thinking people gradually became strong, directly or indirectly, with the passage of time.[19] Norman Kemp Smith states, 'If the problems of Divine Existence are now seldom approached in the manner favoured in the eighteenth century and so conservatively held to also in the nineteenth century, this is traceable in no small degree to the influence of Hume, as conveyed through many channels, most notably through Kant.'[20] Gerald R. Cragg asserts of Hume's scepticism that it reduced natural religion 'to a tenuous shadow of its former self'; although he also correctly remarks of Hume that his position as a neutral observer was also his greatest weakness.[21]

Nevertheless, despite the neutral stance or pose, there is no denying the powerful sceptical thrust of Hume's thought, and it is only too easy to derive from it a positively atheistic or pantheistic outlook. As we must now see, William Paley felt it necessary to give a full and systematic reply to Hume.

CHAPTER 3

William Paley

William Paley exercised a strong influence on religious thought in nineteenth-century Britain, to which even his detractors bear witness. Shelley's comment is well known: 'For my part, I had rather be damned with Plato and Lord Bacon, than go to heaven with Paley and Malthus.'[1] To which we may add Mary Shelley's remark, 'Shelley loved to idealize the real – to gift the mechanism of the material universe with a soul and a voice', which readily explains his antipathy to arguments based on the machine analogy.[2] Hazlitt made scathing comment on Paley's moral philosophy and refers to his 'loose casuistry, which is his strong-hold and chief attraction', but even that derived from Abraham Tucker.[3] In describing a conversation with Coleridge, Hazlitt tells us that 'He mentioned Paley, praised the naturalness and clearness of his style, but condemned his sentiments, thought him a time-serving casuist, and said that "the fact of his work on Moral and Political Philosophy being made a text-book in our Universities was a disgrace to the national character".'[4] Coleridge described the *Natural Theology* as 'the utter rejection of all present and living communion with the universal Spirit';[5] and among several references to Paley in his *Aids to Reflection* there occur the following:

Hence, I more than fear, the prevailing taste for books of Natural Theology, Physico-Theology, Demonstrations of God from Nature, Evidences of Christianity, and the like. *Evidences* of Christianity! I am weary of the word. Make a man feel the *want* of it; rouse him, if you can, to the self-knowledge of his *need* of it; and you may safely trust it to its own Evidence . . .

I have, I am aware, in this present work furnished occasion for a charge of having expressed myself with slight and irreverence of celebrated Names, especially of the late Dr Paley. O, if I were fond and ambitious of literary honour, of public applause, how well content should I be to excite but one third of the admiration which, in my inmost being, I feel for the head and heart of Paley! And how gladly would I surrender all hope of contemporary praise, could I even approach to the incomparable grace, propriety, and persuasive facility of his writings! But on this very account I believe myself bound in conscience to throw the whole force of my intellect in the way of this triumphal car, on which the tutelary genius of modern Idolatry is borne, even at the risk of being crushed under the wheels![6]

F. D. Maurice makes reference to Paley's influence in Cambridge, a demoralising one according to Maurice, who says in a letter to Charles Kingsley, 'I have been fighting against him all my days.'[7] In the University of Durham, Paley's *Evidences of Christianity* was a set text for first-year Arts students from at least 1837 to 1841 and then for the final year of the pass degree and for honours in classics from 1842. The *Natural Theology*, with the exception of a few chapters, became a set text in 1871.[8] Paley's prominence as a lecturer at Cambridge was attested by William Frend. 'Paley "shone as a lecturer at a place where the art of lecturing is better understood than in any other part of the world".'[9] The continuing influence of Paley through his writings was clearly attested by Charles Darwin:

In order to pass the B.A. examination, it was also necessary to get up Paley's *Evidences of Christianity*, and his *Moral Philosophy*. This was done in a thorough manner, and I am convinced that I could have written out the whole of the *Evidences* with perfect correctness . . . The logic of the book and, as I may add, of his *Natural Theology*, gave me as much delight as did Euclid. The careful study of these works . . . was the only part of the academical course which, as I then felt, and as I still believe, was of the least use to me in the education of my mind. I did not at that time trouble myself about Paley's premises; and taking these on trust, I was charmed and convinced by the long line of argumentation.[10]

F. le Gros Clarke, FRS, published a revised edition of Paley's *Natural Theology* in 1875, referring in the Preface to 'this standard work', and stating that while scientific references had been brought up to date, 'Yet care has been exercised not in any way to interfere with the general plan and argument of Paley'; and reference is made to 'the high and just estimation in which it continues to be held'.[11] The hymn-writer W. H. Turton, in a volume first published in 1895, and which I consulted in the seventh edition of 1908, makes explicit appeal to Paley's watch argument and, like Clarke, regards evolution as illustrating, not contradicting it.[12]

Lord Kelvin confessed in 1903 that he was still persuaded by the argument of the *Natural Theology*, 'that excellent old book';[13] and even in 1986, Richard Dawkins can entitle his advocacy of natural selection as the sufficient explanation for the appearance of life as we know it *The Blind Watchmaker*, in conscious acknowledgement of Paley's significance, if not his correctness in attributing the appearance of design in nature to the supernatural deity.[14] The readings of Dawkins' book which were given on BBC Radio 3 in October 1986 included his explicit references to and refutation of Paley. Long before, in the nineteenth century, J. S. Mill, George Romanes and Benjamin Jowett had correctly rejected Paley's argument, but they could not ignore him. Jowett demolished the argument from final causes and denounced Paley and Butler as false props to Christianity in an 'Essay on Natural Theology', the second edition of which was published in 1859, and which reappeared in a collection of Jowett's essays in 1906.[15]

D. H. LeMahieu refers to the 'numerous editions of Paley published in the nineteenth century'; and M. L. Clarke states, 'Apart from the collected editions of Paley's works, *Natural Theology* was reprinted many times.'[16] It is therefore certain that Paley was a figure in British thought to be reckoned with, whether for good or ill; but it is also clear that we must take account of him not merely for historical reasons, but because he gave particularly forceful and persuasive expression to a mode of thought which persists and spontaneously governs much human thinking, not least that of biologists consciously committed to an evolutionary theory utterly destructive of Paley's point of view. We shall be specifically concerned with his *Natural Theology*.

It is necessary to emphasise that this work, published in 1802, was a deliberate reply to Hume's *Dialogues*. It has been supposed that Paley wrote in ignorance of Hume's book, not realising that his arguments had already been destroyed. John Hick regarded it as 'a lamentable instance of the lack of communication between the philosophical and theological worlds that Paley was apparently unaware that his arguments had been devastatingly criticised by Hume twenty-three years earlier'; and A. N. Whitehead expressed a similar view.[17] Anthony Quinton accuses Paley of not taking Hume into account and clearly implies that Paley was not one of those philosophers who answered Hume or had any dominating influence in the first half of the nineteenth century. In a later

volume of the same work, Elmer Sprague comments on the
Natural Theology, 'It is to be regretted that Paley does not meet
Hume's argument head-on.'[18] B. M. G. Reardon in his *Religious
Thought in the Nineteenth Century* makes no mention of Paley, and in
his later volume, *From Coleridge to Gore: A Century of Religious
Thought in Britain*, dismisses Paley's natural theology as not the
work of a philosopher and asserts that as far as the archdeacon was
concerned, Hume's writings might never have seen the light of
day.[19] Leslie Stephen expressed admiration for the *Natural
Theology* as 'a marvel of skilful statement', but also accused Paley of
'a complete unconsciousness of the metaphysical difficulties
which might be suggested', and wrongly asserted, 'To Hume's
arguments on the same topic he makes no allusion.'[20] As a matter
of fact, towards the end of his *Natural Theology* Paley explicitly
refers to an assertion concerning idleness by 'Mr Hume, in his
posthumous dialogues', an assertion which occurs in a lengthy
statement by Philo in Part XI.[21]

Furthermore, the famous watch analogy which opens Paley's
argument reads like a blow-by-blow refutation of Hume; and we
must remember that the *Evidences of Christianity* was an explicit
reply to Hume's essay on miracles. If in the *Natural Theology* Paley
does not make explicit reference to criticisms of theism as coming
from Hume, we have to remember Hume's use of the dialogue
form to express such criticism, the guarded admission of respect
for the argument from design given in the *Dialogues*, and his own
confession of belief in it elsewhere in his writings. In his essay 'Of
a Particular Providence and a Future State', Hume puts in a nut-
shell the scepticism of the *Dialogues*, and clearly implies the
invalidity of the design argument; but even this essay is a conversation, and it opens with reference to sceptical paradoxes and
curious principles of which the author 'can by no means
approve'.[22]

In view of the safeguards with which Hume had surrounded
himself, Paley could not openly accuse him of actually accepting
the devastating critique of natural theology which he had
expressed through the mouths of fictitious characters; and in any
case Paley was concerned with the critique itself and not the precise state of Hume's mind, much as is the case with the modern
reader. Nevertheless Paley does meet Hume head-on with what
must be recognised as a classic restatement of the argument from

design, astute and lucid and with a powerful appeal to the imagination. To move immediately from Hume to Paley is to become
aware of a perennial conflict between two standpoints which, far
from being settled once and for all by the unquestionable victory
of Hume, is continually being refought in every generation; and
while Paley loses battle after battle, he somehow never loses the
war.

A second point which requires emphasis is that Paley presented
his argument in the *Natural Theology* as a demonstrative proof of
God's existence which would persuade any unprejudiced person.
It is necessary to insist on this, because it can be maintained that
the argument from design is presented by any given thinker as
simply a clearly articulated expression of his antecedent belief in
God. In this case the aim is to confirm the belief of the faithful
rather than to persuade the sceptical, and criticisms which treat
the 'argument' as claiming the force of demonstration or proof
will therefore be wide of the mark.

D. L. LeMahieu has asserted that the arguments of natural
religion were an expression of deeply held Christian faith, and
that some preferred to express their faith in this rational form
because they disliked the emotionalism of religious enthusiasm.
According to LeMahieu natural theologians, including William
Paley, never supposed that their arguments would persuade non-
believers or atheists. The arguments of natural religion were the
rational form in which Christians expressed their beliefs among
themselves; and therefore Hume's merely rational objections were
doomed to failure from the start since he was setting out from a
different standpoint and not touching the foundation upon which
such arguments as that from design were based.[23] LeMahieu states
concerning the *Natural Theology, Evidences* and *Horae Paulinae* that
'the purpose of these works . . . was not to persuade the unbeliever,
but to subject God and the Bible to the same kind of dispassionate
analysis employed by a scientist when studying, say, the flight of
birds or the movement of tides'.[24]

However, LeMahieu presents a confused and misleading
picture in this respect. He acknowledges that the arguments of
natural religion were put forward as proofs and were either
accepted or rejected as such.[25] Along with his assertion that Paley
intended to strengthen faith rather than answer unbelief, there
is also the claim that 'the teleological argument assured the

Enlightenment Christian that his religious faith was not founded
solely on the treacherous sands of the human emotions. Religion
was based on fact as well as feeling. As an arbiter of conduct and
of belief, it could be justified before the stern tribunal of logic and
science.'[26] And after rightly pointing out that Paley looked on
natural theology as leading to revelation, LeMahieu says 'Yet,
revelation itself could not be inviolate from the scrutiny of reason;
it also should submit to the rigorous examination of objective
analysis.'[27] Also, 'The object of natural theology was, of course, to
demonstrate rationally the existence of God and to establish by
inductive reasoning his attributes.'[28]

It must surely be conceded that a natural theology which could
meet such demands ought to persuade any honest thinker regardless of his original standpoint; and if, as LeMahieu indicates,
Hume and Kant proved that the argument from design had no
logical foundation, then it would equally persuade no one, again
regardless of belief or unbelief. It would neither convert the
sceptic nor strengthen the faithful.

This double aspect to LeMahieu's interpretation of Paley's work
leads him into a certain ambiguity when he is considering Paley's
relationship to Hume. If Paley was deliberately replying to Hume,
then he must have believed that his arguments had the validity
and force of rational demonstration, and such validity and force
would inhere in the argument regardless of a thinker's already-
held beliefs. On the other hand, if Paley deployed his argument
simply as the clear expression of a faith held on grounds other
than the mere contemplation of nature, then he was not making
a direct reply to Hume. Caught on the horns of this dilemma,
LeMahieu refers to Paley's 'rebuttal of Hume's *Dialogues*'; and he
refers to Philo's argument that the acceptance of universal causation within the universe does not mean that the universe itself
had a cause, and claims that Paley countered this argument 'without mentioning Hume by name'. Yet he also claims that the
Natural Theology 'repeated virtually every one of Cleanthes' arguments . . . In essence, Paley utterly ignored Hume's objections.'[29]

There can be no doubt that Paley and many of the thinkers who
agreed with him believed that they were putting forward a conclusive argument which if not sufficient of itself to make someone
a Christian would lead any honest thinker to revelation and ultimate commitment to the Christian faith. From beginning to end

the *Natural Theology* is dominated by the feeling that those who fail to draw the proper conclusion are being wilfully blind. The closing words of chapter II equate 'absurdity' and 'atheism', while the concluding chapter XXVII is clearly the work of an author who feels that he has offered his readers unassailable proof which now leaves them free to open their minds to revealed truths beyond the reach of reason. Paley's explanation and apology, indeed, is to those who already believe in case they should feel that they are being offered unwanted and pointless proofs, and his sentiments are echoed in full by an early editor of his complete works.[30] For this editor, those who can believe in God without demonstration are fortunate:

Others are constitutionally doubters . . . and the far greater portion of mankind are troubled by difficulties that appear in this most important of inquiries. Moreover everyone . . . meets with those who impugn the grounds of his belief; to such persons it is important to have an unrefutable reply; important, for the sake of the objector, important for the mental quietude of the believer.[31]

This is not to deny that there were some who saw such argument in a different light, but there can be no doubt that the quoted opinion represents the view of Paley and many who were influenced by him. It also well expresses the supposedly self-evident nature of the argument as presented by Paley, which is nothing if not a cast-iron demonstration guaranteed to win the approval of unprejudiced reflection.

THE ARGUMENT OF PALEY'S NATURAL THEOLOGY

If, says Paley, we come across a stone when walking across a heath, we think nothing of it. For all we know it could always have been there. If, on the other hand, we come across a watch, we wonder how it got there, and we do so for one sufficient reason: the watch is made up of parts which function together to produce an effect. Unlike a stone, the watch gives evidence of contrivance, design, and we therefore deduce the existence of a contriver, a designer who made the watch.

Paley goes on to point out that our conclusion is not weakened if we have never seen a watch made; or if the watch sometimes goes wrong; or if there are some parts whose function we cannot understand; and if the watch had the capacity to produce other watches, this would only increase our admiration for the original maker. To suppose that watch-producing watches could in themselves account for the whole process is merely absurd, and applied to the world at large, atheism. 'It is the same with any and every succession of these machines; a succession of ten, of a hundred, of a thousand; with one series as with another; a series which is finite, as with a series which is infinite. In what other respects they may differ, in this they do not. In all equally, contrivance and design are unaccounted for.'[32]

Dr Cosslett speaks of Paley's analogies between the natural and the man-made as strange and grotesquely charming, as, for example, in the case of the watch which is imagined capable of reproducing itself;[33] but this is to treat the analogies as merely subtle imagery developed for its own sake. They appear in an altogether different light when it is recognised that they are integral to Paley's direct reply to Hume, taking up the sceptic's points one by one and judging them by the canons of common sense.

Paley continues that we should not be impressed if someone asserted that an object must have a particular structure and the watch just happened to have this one; or if it were claimed that the watch was the product of innate tendencies in matter or the laws of nature. Finally, ignorance about the making of watches in no way shakes confidence in the conclusion: 'He knows enough for his argument: he knows the utility of the end: he knows the subserviency and adaptation of the means to the end . . . The consciousness of knowing little need not beget a distrust of that which he does know.'[34]

The watch symbolises the natural world whose contriver and designer must be God, and the remainder of the book is very largely taken up with concrete illustrations of mechanisms in nature which demonstrate the existence of the divine maker.

In chapter III, after some illustrations of contrivance in nature by reference to the eye, Paley raises the question why God should not have made it possible for the creature to be immediately aware of what is presented to the sight without the elaborate means referred to. Contrivance implies limitation of divine power. Paley's answer is that God deliberately limited himself, creating according to what we call the laws of nature in order to provide mankind with evidences of his existence, power and wisdom:

It is only by the display of contrivance, that the existence, the agency, the wisdom of the Deity, *could* be testified to his rational creatures. This is the scale by which we ascend to all the knowledge of our Creator which we possess, so far as it depends upon the phenomena, or the works of nature.35

The imperfections of nature do not destroy the argument from design, nor does the existence of apparently useless organs. The overwhelming evidence supports the existence of a creator, and it is with God's existence we are concerned. If such imperfections be taken to reflect imperfection in God, the vast evidence of 'skill, power, and benevolence' should lead us to see in them rather a reflection of our own ignorance.36

For Paley, just one example, such as the eye, is sufficient to prove the existence of a creator, just as only one watch or other machine in the world would indicate a maker; and no amount of confusion in the world can disprove this conclusion. With reference to a ligament in the thigh bone Paley states,

It is an instance upon which I lay my hand. One single fact, weighed by a mind in earnest, leaves oftentimes the deepest impression. For the purpose of addressing different understandings and different apprehensions, – for the purpose of sentiment, for the purpose of exciting admiration of the Creator's works, we diversify our views, we multiply our examples; but for the purpose of strict argument, one clear instance is sufficient; and not only sufficient, but capable perhaps of generating a firmer assurance than what can arise from a divided attention.37

Paley goes into some detail concerning muscles, joints, the action of the heart, veins and arteries, the digestive system, etc., to give concrete illustrations of evidence for design, and this detail is impressive. With reference to bones, muscles and vessels Paley states, 'The wisdom of the Creator is seen, not in their separate but their collective action . . . in their contributing *together* to one effect and one use. It has been said, that a man cannot lift his hand to his head, without finding enough to convince him of the existence of a God.'38

Paley is quite explicit that the only possible explanation of natural facts is in terms of final causes. The claws of the chicken automatically close when its legs are bent, giving it security in perching even when asleep; human teeth are not covered with the same substance as other bones, but with an enamel of ivory which exactly suits the purpose for which they are used; the brain had a

thick bony protection just suited to its nature, although other
similar organs have a soft protective covering. Various animals
have precisely the kinds of coat or clothing, the kinds of eye,
mouth or beak which enable them to get food or evade capture.
Paley is insistent that such adaptations could not have simply
appeared through habit and usage, the 'blind conatus of nature':[39]

Suppose we had never seen an animal move upon the ground without
feet, and that the problem was; Muscular action, i.e. reciprocal contrac-
tion and relaxation being given, to describe how such an animal might
be constructed, capable of voluntarily changing place. Something, perhaps, like the organisation of reptiles, might have been hit upon by the
ingenuity of an artist: or might have been exhibited in an automaton, by
the combination of springs, spiral wires, and ringlets: but to the solution
of the problem would not be denied, surely, the praise of invention and
of successful thought: least of all could it ever be questioned, whether
intelligence had been employed about it, or not.[40]

With respect to the structure of our organs and the properties
of our atmosphere, it is evident that they were made for each
other; and 'the mandate of the Deity' is alone sufficient to account
for such facts.[41] God cannot be perceived, but we know of his
existence because that which is contrived cannot have contrived
itself; it must have a contriver independent of and prior to itself.
The universe therefore cannot have existed externally but must
have come into existence after God who designed it. It is the essential distinction of the deity that he alone is self-sufficient; he does
not require the prior existence of some other being. ' "Self-
existence" is another negative idea, viz. the negation of a preceding cause, as of a progenitor, a maker, an author, a creator.
"Necessary existence" means demonstrable existence.' And the
uniformity of nature demonstrates that there is but one God.[42]

According to Paley the natural attributes of the deity are
omnipotence, omniscience (infinite power, infinite knowledge),
omnipresence, eternity, self-existence, necessary existence and
spirituality. For Paley they not only have a positive aspect in so far
as they attribute intelligible properties to the deity, but also a
negative aspect in so far as they implicitly acknowledge our
ignorance of God's true nature. If God is 'infinite' this is simply an
acknowledgement by ourselves that we are in no position to assign
any limits to him. And we may deduce these attributes as part of
natural religion without recourse to revelation. 'Upon the whole;

after all the schemes and struggles of a reluctant philosophy, the necessary resort is to a Deity. The marks of *design* are too strong to be gotten over. Design must have had a designer. That designer must have been a person. That person is God.'[43]

Thus Paley, to his own satisfaction, established his large and significant conclusion by irrefutable argument; an argument not only presented in words but revealed in myriad concrete examples surrounding and a very part of every human being. Only the most wilful scepticism could reject the manifold clear illustrations of such unanswerable argument.

THE FATAL FLAW

As a proof of the existence of God the argument from design is invalid; but it is essential for religious belief that the invalidity and the reason for it should be quite clearly understood. It is possible to dismiss the argument as invalid and yet still be influenced by it. This is because there are countless items in the natural world which may very readily be seen as exhibiting design, and the whole realm of nature may be so viewed. No one knew better than Paley how to deploy the argument, and when his watch analogy has been rejected, the concrete zoological illustrations he offers nevertheless retain their force. Furthermore, many religious believers would find it incredible that the hand of God should not be seen in the obvious and numerous examples of order and harmony in the life of nature, and the feeling remains that while the argument may be formally invalid, it nevertheless gives legitimate expression to a fundamental truth.

Whether or not we may truly see divine purpose exhibited in nature is, however, a very different question from whether or not design and purpose are exhibited in nature in such a way as both to be undeniable and to entail acknowledgement of a supremely powerful being of whom we may think in personal terms, a designer or contriver fulfilling deliberate intentions. The distinction is the essential one between truth and falsity on the one hand, and validity and invalidity on the other. Even if it is true that the world is created, this truth cannot stand as the valid conclusion of the design argument.

The reason for this is that the conclusion is already contained in the minor premise: All watches are made by someone; the world is like a watch; therefore the world was made by someone. The second premise unfortunately asserts precisely that which is in question. Is the world like a watch? The fatal flaw in Paley's classic statement of a classic argument is that he assumes just that which he is attempting to demonstrate; and this is the hinge upon which all turns. It is perfectly true that if we approach the natural world, including our own bodies, and ask if the various parts can be described as if they were machines, the answer is yes. We can bring the machine analogy to our observation of the natural world, and often do, and it is very useful to think of parts functioning together to accomplish some end. What we observe then becomes intelligible to us. Nevertheless we have no right to assume or deduce that what is convenient or even almost unavoidable in human ways of thinking about the natural world is a characteristic of that world in itself. It must also be added that some parts do not answer to the ideas of design, and the contemplation of the ultimate observable end of all plants and creatures, and the highly probable end of our planet itself, suggest rather that denial of purpose to which Macbeth gave such eloquent expression, and which is by no means unknown in the biblical literature.

The contrast between a stone and a watch was a useful one for Paley, but the presence of the stone in the argument harbours a question of crucial importance. The watch obviously has parts functioning together for a purpose, while the stone equally obviously does not display parts or purpose. The stone is therefore a nice contrast to a watch. By the same token, however, the stone and countless millions of others like it could not figure among Paley's illustrations of mechanism in nature. For Paley this was no problem: plenty of natural objects do seem to display mechanical design, and if others do not, this is presumably because God did not wish or need to mould them in this fashion. They are, as it were, part of the debris left over from the work of creation.

Nevertheless, if the same natural forces which produce stones also produce plants and animals, why should not the natural forces which are a sufficient explanation for the appearance of stones be a sufficient explanation for the appearance of plants and animals? If the reply is that the latter display design while the former do not, we are once more begging the question. Interestingly, both William Buckland in his Bridgewater Treatise and Lord Brougham in his edition of the *Natural Theology* recognised the artificiality of distinguishing the stone from other natural objects, but without grasping the full significance of the point.

If we go walking on the moors and choose a flower instead of a stone to compare with our watch we shall have a natural object in which parts function together, but not for any purpose. It may so happen that the flower gives pleasure to someone or occupation to a passing bee, but we are not entitled to deduce that this is its purpose. All we observe is an organism which has parts functioning together in such a way as to develop and sustain it. The mere fact of possessing parts which function together does not indicate purpose. Paley's question about the stone is therefore deceptive. The stone just happens to be there, the result in both its existence and its position in time and space of the play of natural forces. Exactly the same is true of the flower. It is not so obvious that the stone has parts, nor can we so easily trace the forces which have placed it at just that spot at that moment, but flower and stone are essentially the same.

We may even reverse Paley's argument. If there really is an analogy between artefacts and natural objects, we may interpret the former in terms of the latter. Suppose we were out walking with Paley and we came across a watch lying beside the path across the moor. We should immediately conclude that someone had dropped it there by accident. Let us suppose, however, that another companion pointed out that there were also flowers growing beside the path and that therefore the watch might have appeared like them in quite natural fashion. He could argue that the flowers have parts which function together in an intricate way, that they play their part in the whole economy of nature and that they serve a useful purpose among human beings in that they create happiness. That is, there is an essential similarity between the flowers and the watch, and we must therefore conclude that the watch has an origin similar to that of the flowers.

The absurdity of the conclusion reflects the flaw in Paley's premises. We simply know from experience that watches are made and that flowers grow and that there is an essential difference between them. This prevents us arguing from the origin of flowers to the origin of watches, but if the essential difference prevents argument from the natural to the artificial, it also prevents argument from the artificial to the natural. When we look at the watch and the flower we are confronted not by an answer but by a question: Are the flower and all else in nature ultimately the products of a divine maker? Or is the human constitution, symbolised in its workmanship, simply an integral part of nature, itself the flowering of physical forces not susceptible of further explanation? Admiring surveys of the natural world cannot of themselves provide the answer, but merely reiterate the question.

When G. J. Romanes considered Paley's illustration, he imagined a man finding a watch on a heath and then going on to observe the adaptation of means to ends illustrated on the sea shore. In both he would see design: 'But there is this great difference between the two cases. Whereas by subsequent inquiry he could ascertain as a matter of fact that the watch was due to intelligent contrivance, he could make no such discovery with reference to the marine bay.'[44]

It would, of course, be a grave mistake to suppose that Paley made this error because he was naive or unintelligent, and the mistake would be grave, not merely because of the wholly unjustified slander on Paley, but because it would divert attention from a conspicuous feature of the natural world and the instinctive manner in which the human mind apprehends it. Paley would reply to the allegation of a fatal flaw in his argument by returning to his illustrations of the fact that in organic nature parts function together and achieve effects; and Paley's mind, like the human mind in general, was irresistibly drawn to replace 'function together *and*' by 'function together *to*'. The manufacture of machines and the observation of design in nature both illustrate the essential constitution of the human mind as something which tends to envisage ends, to devise means and to seek explanations in terms of purpose; but this raises rather than answers Hume's question whether or not we are entitled to explain the origin of the universe according to the tendency of our peculiar mental constitution.

Paley was insistent that adaptation to environment could not simply have appeared through habit and usage, and without the vast and systematised knowledge of a Darwin or a Wallace and the crucial capacity they possessed for giving positive credence to a radically different approach to the biological facts, Paley's argument was not merely highly plausible but appeared as no more than a clear objective description of what any honest observer could see for himself. As Cleanthes puts the matter to Philo, 'Are you not aware . . . that it is by no means necessary that theists should prove the similarity of the works of *nature* to those of *art* because this similarity is self-evident and undeniable?'[45] We may compare with this the difficulty Copernicus and his disciples had in persuading the world that it is the earth which moves. 'Copernicus was a dedicated specialist . . . To anyone who did not share his specialty Copernicus' view of the universe was narrow and his sense of values distorted.'[46]

Nevertheless the flaw in the Paleyan argument remains, and it means that the existence of God can never be the valid inference from mere observation of the natural order.

'OF THE GOODNESS OF THE DEITY'

This is the title of the penultimate chapter of the *Natural Theology*. In it Paley argues from the general condition of creatures in the natural world to the benevolence of God, and then seeks to demonstrate the consistency of belief in divine benevolence with the general human condition, and with the existence of chance amidst the multifarious evidences of design.

Paley believed by this stage in the argument that he had established beyond doubt the existence of a creator of the world. The character of this creator is for Paley established beyond reasonable doubt by the beneficial nature 'of the vast plurality of instances in which contrivance is perceived',[47] and by the vast extent of pleasure and happiness among the creatures, which are by no means necessary for their ongoing life. To a mind already thus persuaded it was obvious not only that such a world could not be the product of malicious intent but also that it could not be the accidental product of indifference. Finally, viewed from this standpoint much that is advantageous but taken for granted could be brought to self-conscious recognition, and much that appears as needless suffering shown to be unwarranted distortion or exaggeration of situations revealed as beneficial to a more careful observation.[48]

Leaving aside for the moment reference to mankind, it is clear that Paley's assertions, no matter how true with respect to his selected facts of natural history, are incapable of bearing the weight put upon them. One weakness is that the claims of an indifferent deity to recognition are more powerful than Paley realised, or perhaps could have realised. The beneficial contrivance is the necessary means to existence. Under the dominion of an indifferent evolutionary process 'nature' is the collective name at any given moment for the sum total of successful candidates for existence, and in the never-ceasing competition, today's beneficial contrivance may become tomorrow's fatal handicap. Nor is the beneficial contrivance even a guarantee of survival.

Furthermore this is not merely a fact but an essential characteristic of nature, with vast numbers in many populations doomed to early extinction before ever they are born. In the words of Charles Darwin:

Natural selection will never produce in a being anything injurious to itself . . . No organ will be formed, as Paley has remarked, for the purpose of causing pain or for doing an injury to its possessor . . . After the lapse of time, under changing conditions of life, if any part comes to be injurious, it will be modified; or if it be not so, the being will become extinct, as myriads have become extinct.[49]

Nor may we gloss over the actual suffering of the natural world. If insects, birds, fishes and animals are capable of the enjoyment of life which Paley attributes to them, they are capable of corresponding suffering when deprived, preyed upon and killed.

This brings us to the second and more fundamental weakness in Paley's argument. Assuming the beneficence and power attributed to the creator by Paley, why should there be any suffering among creatures at all? Even one instance of needless pain frustrates this creator's will, but such frustration contradicts the very conception of the creator whom we now find either will not or cannot prevent it. In this part of his argument Paley had been drawn on to Hume's ground, where a decision concerning the character of this world's origin was to be made by reference to happiness. Hume chose his ground well, and Paley's rearguard action merely postponed inevitable defeat.

Quite early in his book Paley discusses the concept of 'chance', and also returns to it later.[50] It is a word and concept which appears frequently in the literature concerning religion and science, and Paley himself well illustrates the problems which could arise from failure to appreciate its proper meaning in any given context. He defines chance as 'the operation of causes without design', and in that sense is prepared to see the appearance of 'a wen, a mole, a pimple . . . a clod, a pebble, a liquid drop' as products of chance: 'but never an eye'. Likewise, 'never was a watch, a telescope, an organised body of any kind, answering a valuable purpose by a complicated mechanism, the effect of chance'. According to this definition, however, the assertion is either a tautology or a begging of the question, since the word 'design' is ambiguous. It may mean either 'plan, scheme, pattern'; or 'purpose, intent'; or both these ideas together. The statement that the eye is the product of design therefore means either 'This purposefully constructed mechanism was purposefully constructed'; or 'The pattern displayed in this organism was purposefully produced.' The first is a tautology, the second simply an example of the question-begging central to the argument from design. The ambiguity of 'design' gives Paley's assertions all the logical, undeniable force of the tautology, while at the same time presenting us with a substantial but unjustified assertion about natural phenomena.

Paley himself was not happy with the bare assertion that 'the stone' is what it is just by chance, but this is not followed up. Stones do not obviously display design and therefore for Paley do not enter into the argument; but what would he have said about the designs made by frost on a window, or displayed in countless crystalline structures which appear spontaneously in nature? Or the fossil in a stone suggested by Buckland? As Buckland himself commented, such a fossil would as much exhibit contrivance and design, on Paley's principles, as 'a watch or steam engine'.

Paley even considers the theory of evolution, the idea that this present world presents 'only so many out of the possible varieties and combinations of being which the lapse of infinite ages has brought into existence . . . millions of other bodily forms and other species having perished, being, by the defect of their constitution, incapable of preservation, or of continuance by generation'. He rejects this idea as groundless since there is no evidence that such a process is actually going on, and because a similar hypothesis applied to a collection of machines would be absurd and immediately recognised as such, since no one in their right mind could attribute the appearance of machines to 'chance'. As we have seen, Paley could hardly have been expected to come to any other conclusion than he did; nor is his analogy with machines simply to be dismissed as fantastic. Richard Dawkins in a television programme referred to and illustrated what is known in Germany as *Evolutionstechnik*, the application of the principles of natural selection to computer programming in attempts to solve engineering design problems. By a strange irony the hypothesis which Paley dismissed itself illustrates the dangerous ease with which analogies can operate between the natural and the artificial and the care which has to be exercised in distinguishing those which are legitimate from those which are not. The structures to be found in nature may teach us much to our advantage in matters of design, but it does not follow that they were themselves designed, and there is much in nature which occurs in a manner far removed from that energy-conserving efficiency which is the aim of the human technician.

Paley's later explanation of chance is that it indicates human ignorance, and that this can be seen in the most ordinary affairs of life; as, for example, when two people set out on separate journeys but meet 'by chance'.[51] Both journeys exhibit purpose, and granted such purposes and their fulfilment the meeting is inevitable; but because this cannot be realised beforehand, 'chance' enters into our description of the situation. The fall of a die is a matter of chance, not in the sense that physical laws are not at work but in the sense that we cannot possibly be properly acquainted with their working in such a case. If this is so in such commonplace affairs of daily life, how much more when we are viewing all the works of God!

What Paley says here is true as far as it goes, but the inadequacy of his remarks is revealed in the illustration of throwing dice. Chance is revealed as compatible not with ends purposefully achieved, but with the play of forces which exclude such achievement. I may intend to throw a double six, but even if this end is accomplished it is 'by chance', indicating not merely ignorance of the forces producing such a result, but inability to control them. The acknowledgement of chance is therefore compatible with both the purposeful and the purposeless, either the mighty designs of God which stretch far beyond our comprehension, or the mindless interplay of physical forces which does likewise. Paley rightly argued for the first possibility but gave no attention to the second. 'The question in its whole compass lies beyond our reach.' For Paley the existence of a benevolent deity was already firmly established and he was solely interested in demonstrating the compatibility of chance as a concept legitimately applied to certain circumstances with his theistic conclusion.

Brougham in his notes on Paley correctly speaks of 'chance' being used when ignorance of causes is meant, and correctly recognises that this is compatible with the existence of purpose; but he incorrectly refuses to recognise that it is equally compatible with complete absence of purpose and that it can sensibly be maintained that all present animal species have appeared as the result of chance.

The concept of chance leads Paley on to consider that of uncertainty and the large place it has in human affairs. He sees this as necessarily involved in our present life, which is one of preparation for a future existence. The uncertainty of life in this world is essential for the exercise of human choice and initiative and the consequent opportunity to develop virtue. This is why God cannot be perpetually intervening in the world's affairs to put things right. The facts which present themselves for human consideration give sufficient ground for believing in beneficent design, even though at the same time it is true that we are surrounded by much uncertainty and unhappiness.

The state in which we are placed is most probably

a state of moral probation . . . It is not a state of unmixed happiness, or of happiness simply; it is not a state of designed misery, or of misery simply: it is not a state of retribution; it is not a state of punishment . . . It accords much better with the idea of its being a condition calculated for the production, exercise, and improvement of moral qualities, with a view to a future state, in which these qualities, after being so produced, exercised, and improved, may, by a new and more favouring constitution of things, receive their reward, or become their own.

The acceptance of Providence and belief in a future state must stand or fall together, and Paley continues:

In the wide scale of human condition, there is not perhaps one of its manifold diversities, which does not bear upon the design here suggested. Virtue is infinitely various. There is no situation in which a rational being is placed, from that of the best instructed Christian, down to the condition of the rudest barbarian, which affords not room for moral agency; for the acquisition, exercise, and display, of voluntary qualities, good and bad. Health and sickness, enjoyment and suffering, riches and poverty, knowledge and ignorance, power and subjection, liberty and bondage, have all their offices and duties, all serve for the *formation* of character . . . characters are not only tried, or proved, or detected, but . . . are generated also, and *formed*, by circumstances.[52]

There was nothing new in this argument, nor as it stands is it an adequate reply to the wide-ranging scepticism of Hume. Its considerable value lies in the refusal to look at the problem of evil in Humean terms at all. For Hume it was sufficient to characterise the theistic view as thinking of the world like a ship or a building, an object which may be well or badly made by its creator. On this view the well-made world is harmonious and happy, and the degree to which misery and pain appear is the degree to which the world is badly made. For Paley, as for Joseph Butler and many others, the world does not simply lie like plastic in the maker's hands. Human beings in limited but crucial ways can shape their own lives, and they are aware of moral principles, which lay a peculiar kind of claim upon them, even if recognition of the claim brings unhappiness. Indeed, happiness itself is not all of a piece and must be subjected to moral scrutiny. Human character and personality may in fact develop or deteriorate, and we have reason to hope that development will continue beyond the grave into a life where virtue is its own very true reward.

Paley's thinking and that of many others in the nineteenth century was dominated by the machine analogy and what was believed to be the conclusive argument from design. This inevitably excludes the far more profitable approach to a solution of Hume's doubts to be found in a realm at once dynamic and morally demanding, the realm of human life. In Paley's thought this realm was separate from the realm of 'nature'; nature in this case being that vast area of the world which is active indeed but incapable of originality and the initiative which breaks established moulds, a realm of fixed species behaving as they always have done, always will do, and always must, just like the machine which displays vast energy, but necessarily channelled within the limits established by its maker and designer. The only hope in this realm is indeed for happiness and the exclusion of fear and misery, and it is a legitimate question why the creator has not made a much better job of it; and this remains the case even if we exchange the idea of the world as a machine for that of the world as a self-originating, self-perpetuating and self-developing organism, as Hume did.

When natural theology attempts to deal with the problems

arising from this outlook its only hope of success is in bringing the two realms together, so that 'nature' includes reference to human life in every aspect and recognises it as an integral and crucial part of the whole. The machine analogy, and even the organic, create two closely related but essentially distinct realms, that of the observer and that of the so-called natural world, whereas in reality there exists but one.

CHAPTER 4

Biblical conservatism

The false response to Humean scepticism in Britain received tremendous impetus from Paley's *Natural Theology*. Religious thinkers seeking a firm ground for their faith were therefore left with the choice between biblical authority or an invalid natural theology or a combination of the two. If the Bible was infallible, then its authority was obvious. If it contained errors, then its authority might still be justified by concentrating on its religious and moral message, but natural theology would then have to be called in to justify the idea that there could be a true religious message at all. If we have no good reason to believe in God, we have no good reason to believe that he has spoken. Conversely, if natural theology cannot provide us with convincing evidence that God has spoken, has expressed himself in some way accessible to human beings, then belief in God itself has no ground. We need, as it were, our 'burning bush' to get us away from the pressures and promises of a purely secular existence on to that holy ground where the voice of God can be heard. The natural theology on offer in nineteenth-century Britain, however, failed to provide that demonstration which could be the starting point or foundation of a thoroughly worked out justification of religious commitment; and the situation has not essentially changed.

People do not, of course, accept or reject religious belief simply as a response to rational argument. Often enough thinkers have set out on the basis of belief and proceeded to rationalise it as best they could; nor is rationalisation unknown to scepticism. Furthermore, religious thinking has often displayed highly significant insights, and it would be astounding if this were not the case. Nevertheless, intellect is an essential part of human life, and we do not normally choose to behave in ways which contradict the demands of reason. Isolated insights may give rise to questions as well as being accepted as answers. The insights need to be welded into a system generally recognised and accepted, and no such system has been produced in Britain. In the absence of well-worked out positive reasons for religious commitment, it is not surprising that an all too plausible scepticism should come to rule most people's minds, even if many would find it hard to express in words; and that doubts in the hearts of believers should all too often be smothered under some brand of so-called evangelical zeal, or even fanaticism.

Shelley is remembered for his poetry rather than his prose works, and there is no reason to suppose that the latter had much influence on nineteenth-century thought; yet copies of his pamphlet 'The Necessity of Atheism' were removed from an Oxford bookshop and burnt on the advice of the Revd John Walker, Fellow of New College, and Shelley himself was expelled from the university in March 1811. Such writing was dangerous because it gave clear and incisive expression to the feelings of the less articulate and the less bold. In another essay, 'On a Future State', part of which was published in the *Athenaeum* (29 September 1832), the link with science is also explicit. 'Some philosophers – and those to whom we are indebted for the most stupendous discoveries in physical science, suppose . . . that intelligence is the mere result of certain combinations among the particles of its objects.' In all material combinations there is the tendency 'to dissipate and be absorbed into other forms', and in death the organs of sense are thus destroyed 'and the intellectual operations dependent on them have perished with their sources'. 'It is probable that what we call thought is not an actual being, but no more than the relation of certain parts of that infinitely varied mass, of which the rest of the universe is composed, and which ceases to exist so soon as those parts change their position with regard to each other.'[1] Thus was Hume's speculation being turned into something like certainty by the growing sciences, and his insistence that the supernatural deity worshipped by the Church could never be deduced from observations of nature increasingly borne out by vast numbers of such observations.

A reply to Hume very different from that of Paley was given in Germany by Immanuel Kant. Kant's insights provided the proper answer to Hume, and his critical philosophy provided the right preparation for a genuine theology: that is to say, a theology, a metaphysics, which absorbs the worst blows that scepticism can inflict and goes on to deal with human experience in its wholeness, including the human experience reflected in the Bible and that large expanse of human experience known as scientific knowledge. Kant has, however, exercised little influence on British religious thought.

If, instead of Paley's natural theology, the Kantian critical philosophy had been accepted into the mainstream of British religious thought by the beginning of the nineteenth century, the Bible could have been studied and theology developed to the present day as part of philosophical thinking in general, instead of in separation from it; and the term 'philosophy' would have retained its wider nineteenth-century meaning, taking into account all the results and methods of scientific research as a matter of course. Naturally, there would always have been technical historical, literary and linguistic studies on the biblical side, just as there would have been chemistry, physics, botany, etc., on the scientific side; but the attempt to assess the value and relevance of such studies for human life in general would have been the meeting point and ought to be the meeting point for all such specialist disciplines.

The terms 'theology' and 'metaphysics' ought to be and would have been but two names for the same intellectual enterprise; and there would not only have been no need for an increasingly apologetic tone in presenting the claims of religion alongside the triumphs of science and technology, but the legitimate claims of religious belief could have led society to a more cautious and critical estimate of the scientific approach to nature and the world itself. The treatment of science and religion as if they belonged to two distinct contexts of thought has had disastrous consequences, which, if they could scarcely have been foreseen in the nineteenth century, we have no excuse for ignoring in the twentieth.

It was to the credit of conservative religious thinkers in the earlier half of the nineteenth century that they insisted upon the principle 'the truth is one', that the revelation of God in Bible and nature must be a unity; and it was a principle acknowledged alike by those for whom unaided human reason could see God in nature, and those for whom corrupted human reason needed the enlightenment of biblical revelation first before the divine character could be seen reflected in the natural world. It was also a principle readily appreciated by common sense, which then wanted to know why there appeared to be contradictions between revelation proper, that is, the Bible, and certain facts concerning God's handiwork in nature, including the fundamental fact that nature seemed to contain the principles of its own explanations within itself. The correct answer to the question depended on having a philosophy which could legitimise claims that the Bible taught essential truths about God and man, while at the same time not only recognising the validity of scientific methods within their own sphere, but showing how these could be related together in one system with religious assertions. This philosophy was lacking in Britain.

As a result, various solutions were proposed by religious thinkers to the problems raised by science, and it is convenient for the period up to about 1860 to place them in three groups, provided it is realised that the lines between the first two are not hard and fast, and that none of them corresponded to actual self-conscious groupings in nineteenth-century Britain. First there were those who were suspicious of natural theology and emphasised biblical authority. Second, there were those who whole-heartedly accepted the value of natural theology, but regarded it as subordinate to the Bible. Third, there were those who emphasised natural theology and tended to make it a determining factor in biblical interpretation.

The difference between the first two groups was not necessarily very marked as far as biblical authority was concerned, but the first was very suspicious of the supposed contribution an unaided and sinfully corrupt reason could make to the defence of the faith, and thinkers of this type were afraid that its use would undermine confidence in the authority of the biblical revelation. We shall consider examples of the arguments used by all three groups, and then illustrate some of the diverse views which appeared in the latter part of the century. We shall then be in a position to examine the Kantian critical philosophy and its relevance to the construction of a soundly based theology.

The remainder of this chapter is taken up with examples of the first group of thinkers, and no one illustrates the strength and weakness of this approach more clearly than Samuel Horsley, one time Lord Bishop of St Asaph. His papers were collected together and edited by H. Horsley to make a four-volume work on biblical criticism.[2] The bishop tells us that Genesis 1 was produced as if the events it describes had been witnessed by an imaginary spectator, probably because there was no other way in which such facts could be expressed. The strength of Horsley's brief exegesis lies in its absolute refusal to compromise the meaning of the text in the interests of real or supposed accommodation to modern knowledge or speculation. For example, light was produced on the first day of creation, and the luminaries on the fourth. The familiar 'difficulty' of reconciling these two statements did not exist for Horsley: 'The luminaries therefore are not the cause, nor the makers of light, as the principles of Materialism require; but merely the receptacles or magazines of light previously made.' Nor was the earliest vegetable and animal life dependent on the sun, for the simple reason that the sun did not exist. The notion that mankind originally existed in a savage state 'is a falsehood, and an idle fiction' since the text plainly tells us that man was created in the image of God. It also tells us that man immediately conversed with God, and 'The notion, therefore, of a religion of nature, prior to revelation, is a falsehood, and a wicked fiction.'[3]

Whenever these remarks were committed to paper, they were published in 1820, and they were certainly not produced in ignorance of the difficulties created for the biblical expositor by astronomy and geology. The weakness of such an approach is obvious to us today, but we must also recognise the strength of an insistence on the integrity of the text which refuses to be budged by modern discovery. Simply to dismiss a commentator like Horsley is merely to confess how far we have travelled without an adequate religious philosophy.

A later writer who adopted a similar robust stand was C. M. Burnett, a member of the Royal College of Surgeons. At first sight Burnett's volume is not unlike those of the Bridgewater Treatises in its general aim, but references to the Treatises are by no means uncritical, and the only reference to Paley is in a footnote correcting a zoological detail.[4] The book is made up of a series of imaginary letters, and at the head of the first two is a quotation from Bird Sumner's *Records of the Creation*: 'The real use of natural theology is to shew the strong probability of that being true which revelation declares.' These first two letters are severely critical of geology because of the doubt it has cast upon the plain truth of the Bible. The idea that 'day' in Genesis 1 means anything other than the normal twenty-four-hour day is firmly rejected, as is the view that light existed before the Adamic creation and that the darkness of chaos was merely temporary.

Furthermore, geological evidence of catastrophes in the early history of the earth is quite unnecessary since that evidence is contained in the biblical record of the Flood. Burnett clearly envisages the breaking open of the fountains of the deep as meaning colossal volcanic activity, and the whole narrative as indicating an upheaval approaching the dimensions of the original creation itself. It was quite literally an act of God as described in the text, and to think of it in terms of secondary causes is already to have cast unwarranted doubt on the divinely inspired text. Burnett implies that if the text is approached in this latter way, misunderstanding will inevitably follow, but if taken in its plain meaning, there is no problem about the vast tonnage of rock being shifted; and the fossils in the ancient strata, indicating different species from those which now exist, were simply adapted to the very different conditions of the earth before the Flood. Also, if we push the origin of the world back so far in time that we cannot grasp it, and do so on the basis of an appeal to secondary causes, we in effect deny the first cause altogether and teach the eternity of matter.[5]

An article on Buckland's Bridgewater Treatise appeared in the *Edinburgh Review* for April 1837, in which the reviewer maintained that 'the geologist . . . has nothing to do with revealed religion in his scientific inquiries'; upon which Burnett comments, 'any geological deductions which stand opposed to the revealed word of God must be false', and later remarks that safe geological conclusions can only be arrived at when 'the compass of God's sacred word' is taken on board.[6] It is obvious to us today, as it was to many in 1838, that science cannot be conducted on this basis, but we then have to answer the question why a man of Burnett's intelligence and education should make such an assertion; and the answer must be that he was clinging to this quite untenable support because he could see no other way to continue in religious belief which had some semblance of rational justification. The alternative was to fall into some unfathomable abyss of unbelief.

John Bird Sumner, quoted by Burnett, published in 1816 a prize-winning treatise. This was made possible by a bequest which

provided money for the regular production of two treatises on
'The Evidence that there is a Being all-powerful, wise, and good,
by whom everything exists; and particularly to obviate Difficulties
regarding the Wisdom and the Goodness of the Deity . . . and this
. . . from Considerations independent of . . . Revelation'.[7] What is
particularly interesting about Sumner's approach is his manipulation of the explicit demand for an essay in natural theology so as
to produce a strong emphasis on the need for revelation, that is,
the Bible. With Malthus in mind he tries to show how the suffering inevitably associated with population growth nevertheless
bears testimony to God's wisdom and goodness. There is much
argument to the effect that the inequalities of society are necessary
in mankind's present circumstances if virtue is to be practised,
since the pressure of population upon subsistence compels those
virtues, including civilisation and intercourse between nations,
which only inequalities can produce. Suffering is part of the trial
mankind needs in the present state of moral probation, as preparation for a future life which reason and revelation alike
demonstrate.

The usual argument from design appears and there is reference
to the mechanism of the natural world, but we are also left in no
doubt about the severe limitations of natural theology. In the
words already quoted by C. M. Burnett: 'The real use of Natural
Theology, is to show the strong probability of that being true
which Revelation declares.' Although 'Reason and Revelation
mutually support and assist each other', reason is inadequate to
satisfy questioning and gain obedience. 'Natural reason conducts
us to the door of the temple', but we must then be led by revelation. There is much in the world to suggest that the creator does
not communicate with it; and the ancients who made use of
natural theology

knew more than enough of the harmony and design of the universe to
draw out an unanswerable argument from final causes: and, in point of
fact, they did draw out both that and other arguments so far as to leave
us indisputable proof that the God of NATURAL THEOLOGY will never be
anything more than the dumb idol of philosophy; neglected by the
philosopher himself, and unknowable to the multitude.

As it stands Sumner's argument is inconsistent: natural theology
is a dumb idol, but it can tell us enough to silence doubts based on
Malthus and lead us to revelation's temple. Yet despite the

inconsistency, it has the ring of truth. According to Sumner, it is foolish to pretend that we are in the same position as Socrates and Cicero:

The experiment of vindicating the moral administration of the universe without the help of a future state, has been sufficiently tried. The necessity of general laws, or the imperfection of matter, or the inevitable consequences of human liberty, or the degrees of perfection of possible worlds, may serve by turns to exercise, or amuse, or perplex the reasoning powers of a few philosophers. But something more satisfactory must confute the sceptic; something more consolatory must soothe the afflicted; something more irresistible must arm the moralist.[8]

Half recognised in Sumner's work, but not brought to full consciousness, is the fact that we bring to nature the divine purposes which we see there. Sumner was struggling to escape from the dominating influence of Paley and other proponents of the design argument, and he obviously felt that some larger view of the universe was required than could be inferred by mere unaided reason from the observation of phenomena, whether natural or human. At the same time he could not simply deny that God is revealed in his world and leave it as the happy hunting ground of an atheistic materialism. According to Sumner, men do not spontaneously infer the creator from the observation of nature. They take this for granted, and it is only through the development of reason that a genuine inference can be made. He then has to recognise, however, that trained reason can envisage three possibilities: that the world existed from eternity, that it was formed by chance, that it was created by an omnipotent and intelligent being. The first idea is dismissed as scarcely worthy of attention, but the second demands more comment.

Sumner appeals to the contingent nature of geographical features and astronomical facts:

Can we conceive it otherwise than arbitrary, whether our earth should be attended by a single moon, or be surrounded by as many satellites as Jupiter or Saturn? But if the world be *necessarily* existent, these things are not arbitrary, but governed by the same immutable necessity by which the world itself exists: unless it can be denied, that to suppose the possibility of alteration in that which exists necessarily, involves contradiction, and is absurd.[9]

What was unthinkable to Sumner was precisely what Hume had proposed as a real possibility and what natural philosophy was

beginning to establish on a large scale as actual fact; but although
Sumner was very much aware of Hume, who finds mention at the
very opening of Volume I, he makes no attempt to meet the
arguments of the *Dialogues*. In an Appendix devoted to geology
Sumner refers to

an apparent tendency to attribute various catastrophes or revolutions
. . . to a sort of mechanical agency of its own . . . to natural causes arising
out of its constitution. The effect of such philosophy is, of course, to keep
out of sight the interference of the Creator: it would be more consistent
in the advocates of the eternity of the world, than in those who admit the
fact of its creation by an Intelligent Power.

Similarly, some have been misled by the infinite variety of
nature's productions into the false conclusion that there is a
'chain of existence' which destroys the essential distinction
between man and the animals.[10]

Since Sumner knew of no valid philosophy to substitute for the
invalid natural theology he had inherited, he turned to the only
other authority there was and rested his principal evidence of the
existence of the creator 'upon the credibility of the Mosaic
records'.[11] Volume I is largely taken up with a rationalising
approach to the Old Testament.

Reason may lead us to a belief which was made certain for the
Hebrews by the miracles which they witnessed. Sumner argues at
length that Moses knew the creator by revelation, and that this was
not merely so that he should be aware of the divine origin of
Israel's laws. The knowledge of the world's creator was the truth
for which the organised nation was brought into existence, so that
it could teach it to the rest of the world. That is to say, 'the Hebrew
polity . . . was divinely instituted, for the purpose of preserving the
records of creation'.[12] The literal truth of Genesis chapters I–II
must therefore be accepted even though certain of the Fathers saw
them as allegorical. 'Either the first eleven chapters of Genesis . . .
are true, or the whole fabric of our national religion is false.'[13] The
supposed inconsistency between the Hebrew cosmogony and
geology is merely apparent, and Cuvier's *Theory of the Earth* is
appealed to in support of this view. Sumner also wishes to dis-
sociate himself from 'some friends of Revelation' who attack
geology, since Genesis had a more elevated purpose than the
description of details which can be supplied by science.[14] And thus
did Sumner use a treatise on natural theology to withdraw from

the arena of futile argument which it engendered, so that he could rest the case for religion on an infallible Bible. This, regrettably, depended upon the fiction that scientific discovery not only did not, but could not and never would contradict the literal meaning of Genesis I-II.

A later writer, John H. Pratt, was much more clearly aware of the serious threat to faith posed by scientific discovery, and his book gives evidence of strong feeling on the subject.[15] According to Pratt, many were at a loss how to repel charges that scientific discovery was opposed to scriptural statements:

The names of geologist and sceptic were regarded by the mass of sensible but uninformed and astonished minds as all but synonymous.

The existence of Animals and Plants previous to the six days' work, when first announced, was regarded with the same indignant scorn, as the fabrication of ungodly men, enemies of the sacred volume, and fearless in their profane inventions. The Press teemed with attacks upon such reckless theorists.

With religious belief in mind, Lyell is quoted at length lamenting the gulf between 'the opinions of scientific men and the great mass of the community', a statement which occurred during his 'Address to the British Association' in 1846.[16] Pratt's solution was to reiterate the commonplace principle that nature and Bible both have the same author and therefore cannot be at variance, but at the same time he insisted on the basic truth that 'the Scriptures, as being inspired by God, must be free from all error. Where terms are used and facts are affirmed, which belong to the natural world alone, they can in no instance be wrong, nor involve any error.'

Scripture is inspired and therefore 'infallible in every respect'. The chief cause of conflict between the Bible and science has been the fallibility of man as an interpreter both of the Bible and nature.[17] This meant that while Pratt regarded the Bible as primarily concerned with spiritual and moral matters, this fact could in no way be used as an excuse for mistakes regarding the natural world. In the Preface to the second edition of his book he refers to a section which has been added 'to show the high value we should put upon the opening portion of the Book of Genesis, on account of the important information it conveys'. When we look to Pratt for the correct interpretation of Genesis we find him appealing to Chalmers, Pye Smith and Hugh Miller (see pp. 107–18, 126–33 below). Lyell's address is quoted as confirming the

view that scientific research will increasingly 'elevate our conceptions of the Divine Artificer'. Some room for error is left in the
Bible as we have it by asserting that it was infallible only as originally given; nor could the biblical writers use the language of
science, because this is forever changing as discovery proceeds.

Yet throughout Pratt's book there is an inarticulate sense of the
very real threat posed by science to religion, and a desperate
attempt to cling to unerring Scripture in the face of an enemy
whose demands, by the 1850s, were not to be denied. The result
was the usual rationalising of the Old Testament text, the authority of which is at the same time proved by the way Jesus and the
apostles used it; although one feels that the interpretations
espoused by Pratt would have made strange listening in the syna-
gogues of first-century Palestine, despite the elasticity permitted to
rabbinic comment. He illustrates the closeness of the first two
groups of thinkers to each other, although his own emphasis on
scriptural authority and apparent alienation from real sympathy
with scientific method place him in the first rather than the second; but at the same time it brings out the gulf which separated
conservatives from those who were really prepared to face the
facts. Professor Baden Powell, in his *Essay on the Philosophy of
Creation,* spoke explicitly of the irreconcilable contradiction
between geology and Genesis and asserted that the Judaical
cosmogony had died a natural death. Pratt quoted from the
volume with horror.

Donald MacDonald was another writer of the 1850s in roughly
the same sort of position as Pratt. He undertook to defend and
expound the first three chapters of Genesis, and while he believed
that nature and the Bible both came from God, there is no
suggestion that anything of religious significance can be learnt
from the former, and he implies hostility to a natural religion
'which may be proved by demonstration'.[18]

In his Introduction MacDonald makes it clear that rejection of
Genesis 1–3 as a record of fact had become commonplace, and in
his Preface he quotes a letter to *The Times* in which the correspondent refers to a sermon in a London church in which it was
admitted that the discoveries of geology irreconcilably contradicted the Mosaic narrative of creation. The correspondent had
heard with obvious relief that the truth of the New Testament was
quite independent of such questions concerning the Old. For

MacDonald this was a view to be countered. He apparently regarded Genesis as the oldest book in the world, and Genesis 1–3 contains 'literal historical statements' as against 'poetry, allegory or mythology'. The Scriptures are a unity, and to impugn part is to destroy the whole.[19]

Nevertheless, MacDonald appears to have been well acquainted with German scholarship, and he appeals to Hugh Miller, Lyell, Pye Smith and Sedgwick in support of his interpretations of the text. He is really too well aware of the issues surrounding biblical exegesis to make a clear and convincing conservative case. Room is left for some degree of figurative language, since otherwise we have a 'jejeune literalism' which converts statements into 'puerilities'. The literary unity of Genesis 1–3 is maintained against Document or Fragment hypotheses, but he admits that even as a compilation of earlier documents it could be a genuine and authentic historical work inspired by God. There is a lengthy reconciliation of science and Genesis 1, even though the Bible is concerned with moral and not scientific matters, and is expressed in a language all can understand. Purely naturalistic accounts of creation are dismissed, including the nebular hypothesis, the development hypothesis of Lamarck and that of the author of *Vestiges*; but geology and astronomy can be appealed to as proving that the world and mankind had a beginning.[20]

MacDonald is prepared to follow Chalmers in his view that the biblical text tells us nothing about the date of the original creation, but he is not happy with the assignment of the geological record to an indefinite period between Genesis 1:1 and 1:2, not least because of the continuity of the geological record. Pye Smith's idea of a localised chaos is also rejected as an artificial reading of the text; but MacDonald is prepared to argue that 'day' in Genesis 1 means a long period of time, and that God's sabbath is the period of God's work of salvation in the hearts of men.[21]

One closes his book in bewilderment and with a lively sympathy for *The Times*' correspondent who escaped with relief from the complexities of such controversy into the haven of the New Testament.

MacDonald appealed to an earlier writer, George Holden, as an ally, while Holden appealed to Horsley. A reading of these works makes clear the tension put on the older conservative position by the increase of scientific discovery, and the persistent threat of

German scholarship. Holden asserts that the Holy Scriptures must be accepted 'with full assurance of faith in their natural and obvious sense', and those who favour the mythical, allegorical approach are strongly attacked, including a good number of German scholars. 'Modern liberality can go no farther than to degrade the holy Scriptures into mere human, fallible, uninspired writings, and to reject almost every ancient and established article of faith. Surely, surely open enemies are preferable to such pretended friends, whose smiles conceal a lurking venom, and who have treachery even in their warmest professions.'[22]

The Book of Job is regarded as the oldest composition in the world, and next to it, the Pentateuch. Moses was an historian inspired to tell plain historical truth, and it is plainly anathema to Holden to argue against specific biblical assertions that they are absurd to us. The true analogy of nature shows that we must not be surprised if revelation contains many things different from what we should have expected and such as appear open to great objections.[23] Even Holden, however, found the position of faith alone a little difficult to maintain. A literary-critical analysis of Genesis 2–3 is naturally firmly rejected, but it is also argued against at some length and in some detail. 'Cavils' must be removed, such as the objection that it is an anachronism to suppose that Adam and Eve used needle and thread to make themselves aprons of fig leaves; and this is on the general principle that if Moses 'made the mistake of representing events impossible to be accomplished in the time specified, and of mentioning the use of certain instruments before their invention, it must detract from his authority as an historian, and weaken our belief of his inspiration'.[24]

It must, of course, actually destroy belief in his inspiration as Holden understood it.

At about the same time as Holden was publishing his book, William Buckland and Granville Penn were attempting to defend the Mosaic narrative against doubts based on geology, but their approaches were very different. In his *Comparative Estimate* Penn makes reference to a review of Buckland's *Reliquiae Diluvianae*, and to a review of the first edition of his own book.[25] Both reviewers had questioned the wisdom of connecting the discoveries of natural science with sacred writings. For Penn, it was a fundamental tenet that we must make the connection, since the Bible does in fact speak of such things, its authority is divine, the

God of Scripture and the God of nature are one, and therefore one truth must be witnessed to by both. Penn refers to the frequent fear that a connection will not be found, and to the bewilderment of the believer in revelation when confronted by a geology expounded without any reference to Scripture: 'there are many, very many, who, in this age of mineralogical scrutiny and geological theorisation, anxiously and reasonably seek for a *plain evidence of the coincidence,* to give a sound, unperplexed, and comfortable establishment to their belief. It is to these that the *Comparative Estimate* is especially addressed.'[26]

At this point, however, Penn parts company with the likes of Buckland. According to Penn we are not entitled to say beforehand what it would please God to reveal or not to reveal, and in truth he has revealed geological fact; and all the geological conclusions of the *Comparative Estimate* are ultimately deduced from 'the revealed record of Moses', a record sharply contrasted with 'the inventive speculations of a *Mineral Geology*', 'the versatility of geological invention', 'attempts to raise an edifice on vacuity', mere theory which 'originates in the *human brain*'.[27] Later we come to an even more fundamental objection to the speculations of unaided reason:

It is revolting to *reason,* and therefore to *true philosophy* to observe how strenuously *physical science,* though expatiating on the wonders of *creation,* has laboured to exclude the *Creator* from the details of His own work, straining every nerve of ingenuity to ascribe them *all to secondary causes,* and, with what undisguised *relief of thought,* it exchanges the idea of *God,* for the idea of *Nature.*

This leads inevitably to materialism. It is not enough to presuppose a first intellectual cause. 'It is indisputably necessary to propound it . . . to proclaim it . . . to recur to it *repeatedly* and *constantly*', the alternative being to stray into error and 'become ultimately lost, in all the horrors of *moral darkness*'.[28]

Of the three thinkers who remain to be considered, Thomas Hartwell Horne and Adam Clarke were famous as biblical commentators. In *Essays and Reviews* C. W. Goodwin referred to 'Horne's *Introduction to the Holy Scriptures* (1856 tenth Edition)' as 'a text book of theological instruction widely used'.[29] Horne, however, was interested not only in the details of biblical exegesis, but also in the defence of biblical authority, a defence which he obviously felt to be necessary. In his *Deism Refuted*[30] he clearly asserts the need for revelation and that this was to be found in the divinely inspired Bible. 'I am convinced that we are incapable of discovering for ourselves a religion that is worthy of God, suited to our wants, and conducive to our true interest.' This is shown by the appalling state of mankind where this revelation has not been received. Nevertheless, the Bible will be found to pass 'the test of a fair and rational examination', and 'there is . . . evidence for the genuineness and authenticity of the Bible', which is proved to be the inspired Word of God. A survey of the evidence shows that the Bible can be depended on as the product of honest and well-informed men, and this includes Moses' account of the creation, which 'is perfectly *philosophical*, as well as sublime'.[31]

However, even well-informed and honest men may be mistaken in drawing conclusions or repeating the opinions of others, and it must therefore be shown that they 'were under the immediate guidance and direction of God'. Evidences of inspiration should be provided 'with which every rational creature ought to be perfectly satisfied'.[32]

Thus does Horne become an excellent example of what happens to a conservative who allows reason to get its foot in the door by being asked to adjudicate in the question of biblical credibility. His case rests on the evidence of miracles and prophecy, but this is essentially an appeal to the miraculous, since prophecy is for Horne a kind of miracle, the predictions of biblical prophets going well beyond what an intelligent and informed person could foresee without inspiration. He defines a miracle as 'a sensible suspension or controlment of, or deviation from, the known laws of nature'. There is a certain order or course of nature which has been established by God, and this is seen in the invariable laws of nature. When an event occurs in keeping with these laws it is 'natural'; when an event deviates from them it is a 'miracle' which God alone can perform through the suspension of nature's laws. The fact that miracles are incomprehensible does not make them contrary to reason. Many natural occurrences are incomprehensible to us, but this is a fact we overlook because they are commonplace; and therefore incomprehensibility is not an objection to the occurrence of miracles.

Reason, however, is rightly concerned about the reliability of the evidence that a miracle has actually occurred. 'I have no more reason to disbelieve them, when well attested and not repugnant to the goodness and justice of God, only because they were performed several ages ago, than I have to disbelieve the more ordinary occurrences of Providence which passed before my own time, because the same occurrences *may* never happen again during my life.'

The purpose of miracles must warrant the suspension by God of his own laws, and can therefore never be trivial. They occur in order to authenticate an individual's divine mission, as is illustrated in the lives of Moses, the prophets, Jesus Christ and the apostles. 'These extraordinary acts of power prove the divine commission of that person who performs them.' They 'mark *clearly* the divine interposition; and the Scriptures intimate this to be their design'. Horne goes on to consider the historical criteria which must be satisfied in order that a miraculous event shall be accepted as having actually occurred, and this includes a fairly lengthy discussion of the evidence for Jesus' resurrection.[33]

Prophecies in the Scriptures 'respect contingencies too wonderful for the powers of man to conjecture or to effect'; to which may be added what Horne calls 'internal evidences' of the divine authority of the Bible: 'the sublime doctrine and moral precepts revealed in the Scriptures – the harmony subsisting between every part, – their miraculous preservation, – and the tendency of the whole to promote the present and eternal happiness of mankind, as evinced by the blessed effects which are invariably produced by a cordial reception and belief of the Bible'. Furthermore, 'Nothing false or immoral can be taught by a God of truth and purity.'[34]

Horne presented his case with lucidity and force, and there are many statements with which no one can quarrel; but this kind of approach becomes a weakness if such statements are not carried through to their proper conclusion. There is an attractive simplicity about asserting the utter inadequacy or even impossibility of belief in God on the basis of so-called natural theology, and the clearness and sureness of such belief based on a handy collection of inspired literature; but once the call to rational inquiry is taken seriously, structural defects are revealed which make it wholly unsuitable as a temple for those who wish to worship God with the mind. Much of what Horne says in his *Deism Refuted* creates the impression that any honest reader of the Bible is engaged in a straightforward task whereby he immediately becomes aware of its revelatory character and divine authority. This is confirmed by other statements in Horne's works. Quoting Bishop Horsley, he says: 'every sentence of the Bible is from God, and every man is interested in the meaning of it'; and that it is 'a discovery by God to man of himself or his will, over and above what he has made known by the light of nature, or reason'.[35] The Mosaic narratives of creation and Fall are to be taken in their plain, literal sense: they are 'strictly historical' and betray 'no vestige whatever of allegorical or figurative description'.[36]

As we have seen in connection with Horsley, this did at least have the by no means negligible advantage of drawing attention to the natural meaning of the text, and taken seriously was a warning not to bend biblical statements into artificial conformity with the statements of modern knowledge when there was real inconsistency between them; but Horne was no more equipped to face this fact than any other conservative. The fiction of a plain scriptural revelation could not be sustained, and Horne knew it.[37] The invitation to examine the Bible critically or to interpret it is an implicit admission that the Scriptures by no means present a complete set of plain meanings to every honest mind or confine their challenge to the spiritual and moral state of the reader. The very titles of two of Horne's famous works link critical study with knowledge of the Bible, and criticism with interpretation. In the revised edition of the latter we are advised that

It will be well . . . to bear in mind the progressive character of revelation. There is, indeed, a substantial unity in the Bible . . . the various parts contributing to make up that *whole* which the master mind of God intended from the beginning. Yet the full understanding of his great plan was not at once communicated. Fresh lessons, as time flowed on, were taught the church of God. The new things never contradict the old; but they were further developments of them.[38]

An approach which can be accepted for just so long as we do not put it to the test of investigation. Once biblical credibility had ceased to be an article of faith and had become an object of rational inquiry, conclusions devastating to conservative belief were inevitable, and one can easily sense this in Horne's works themselves. The dogmatism and assertiveness are those of a defence becoming desperate for arguments and allies. Although Genesis 1–3 is said to relate 'real facts' in literal fashion, Granville Penn is quoted to the effect that 'Moses speaks according to optical, not physical truth: that is, he describes the effects of creation *optically*, or as they would have appeared to the eye.' The effects have been described accurately 'according to their sensible appearance'. This has two supposed advantages: (1) the narrative was adapted 'to the apprehension of mankind in an infant state of society'; and (2) having an accurate record of the effects, we can ourselves proceed to a more accurate determination of the causes.[39]

The insistent repetitious emphasis on optical effect is noteworthy. It is the lever by means of which biblical assertions are going to be bent into an acceptable significance, and it is an instrument which must be firmly grasped.

For Horne, objections against the chronology of Genesis 'because it makes the world less ancient than is necessary to support the theories of some modern self-styled philosophers' are futile. Admittedly, those who wish to see the Genesis narratives as mythical do not therefore regard it as merely baseless fiction. The allegorical statement is a veil for 'real events'. 'But . . . any such theory must be taken as irreconcilable with the facts of the case. For otherwise the tendency of Genesis would be to mislead the world. There is no indication on the part of the writer that he is describing allegorically.'[40]

For Horne and his later editor Ayre the Mosaic history is either wholly allegorical or wholly literal, and to take it in any other than its obvious sense it to put the whole Pentateuch in doubt and shake Christianity to its foundations. The mythical or 'poetic fiction' approach is said to be a 'notion . . . current among the divines of Germany', Bauer and Gramberg being named. Dr Geddes is said to have adopted it, and it is said to be current among 'the modern Socinians in this country'. In his Preface Ayre states:

I have made considerable use of recent German writers. From the principles of some of these I must plainly say I entirely dissent. Such men as De Wette, Gesenius, Ewald, are profound scholars; but I consider their views in many respects most erroneous . . . The works of Hengstenberg, Hävernick, Kurtz, and Keill, are far more in accordance with my principles.[41]

The persecution of Samuel Davidson consequent upon his modest attempt to introduce the principles of genuine criticism into his revision of the Old Testament volume of Horne's *Intro-duction* is well known.[42]

Nevertheless, it was only a rationalising rather than a rational approach which could impose the restraint of 'caution' on honest inquiry, and the distinctions of literary and historical criticism arise naturally out of a proper study of the biblical text, regardless of ill-advised meandering among the minefields of German scholarship; and once critical examination is conceded, it raises far more fundamental issues, and it is these which prompted the evasions and desperate expedients essential to the defence of the literal meaning of the text. As we have seen, it was the very foundations of Christian belief which were regarded as threatened by the application to the text of what is only a literary category, not only harmless but necessary and useful. The real enemy was the threat to belief in revelation and inspiration on the assumption that an inspired revelation must be expressed in plain, literally meant sentences and phrases, unless there is clear indication in the text itself to the contrary. Minor accidents to the record in its human transmission could be safely conceded, but no more.

This, however, creates a dilemma: if we query the assumption about the literal expression of revelation, we are in effect suggesting a revision of accepted ideas about inspiration and revelation and are moving into the dangerous realm of natural theology, since we must then face more general questions about the nature and existence of God and his relationship with the world. If we avoid this danger by refusing to be misled by corrupt reason and its dependence on nature and human experience, we are forced back to a defence of the Bible which can be conducted only by suppressing legitimate questions and denying obvious conclusions.

Horne must have been aware of this dilemma to some extent, even if it were only a vague uneasiness in his mind. On the one hand, natural religion and theology are characterised by him as spiritually and morally useless, or even worse. He outlines the dreadful consequences of being left to operate with the light of nature alone, and one wonders if any truth about God at all could be deduced from mere observation of the natural world. The pagan thinkers of antiquity are used to illustrate the blindness of fallen mankind left to its own intellectual devices.[43] On the other hand, Horne asserts that we know God has the power to reveal himself and that being good, he would reveal himself for the benefit of mankind; so that 'the works of creation prove that He is a being of infinite power and goodness', and 'the works of nature sufficiently evidence a deity'. If the pagan nations failed to recognise God, this was because they 'made so little use of their reason' even where 'he was easy to be found'.[44] In the middle of a passage expressing severe criticism of natural theology we read, 'To a reflecting and observant mind, the harmony, beauty, and wisdom of all the varied works of creation are demonstrative evidence of a First Great Cause; and the continued preservation of all things in their order attests a divine and superintending Providence.'

Likewise 'divine goodness, as displayed in the works of creation' could give hope of reconciliation with God, but not at all how this might be brought about.[45]

When Horne is telling us how hopelessly inadequate or even corrupt natural religion is, consistency demands that this should simply be the prelude to the appearance of the Bible as the sole, unique revelation; and his passages emphasising the evils of natural religion do serve as a contrast to the saving truth known only through the Bible. If the Bible was inspired, as Horne believed it to be, and if divine grace operated as he believed it to operate, natural theology was an irrelevance, and one should turn immediately to the Bible as the only necessary and sufficient source of the truth about God and man, and learn there that God has the power and the benevolent will to reveal himself to mankind. Why, then, introduce quite inconsistent assertions about God revealed in nature? and maintain that in certain aspects of nature he was 'easy to be found'?

The answer is that when human beings did investigate nature rationally they really did find out facts which were not immediately obvious to common sense, some of them very remarkable facts, and some of them completely at variance with scriptural assertions. Furthermore, these facts were related by secondary causes which excluded any need for reference to God. Philosophy therefore was not wholly corrupt, since it did reveal some truths, and as we have seen, Horne was happy to commend Moses' account of creation as '*perfectly philosophical*', and to appeal to 'modern discoveries in philosophy' as confirming it.[46] On the other hand, it seemed to destroy the plain scriptural revelation fundamental to Horne's thinking, and seemed to bow God out of his own

creation. The dilemma existed for Horne, even if not clearly
recognised, because he had no philosophy which would enable
him to acknowledge all the facts while at the same time retaining
his faith. The result was a very half-hearted and spasmodic acceptance of a natural theology at variance with his main outlook, and
a determined effort to retain the Bible as the unique, indisputable
revelation of God expressed in terms which any honest person
could understand.

Horne's need of philosophy is obvious once we examine the
supports of biblical authority to which he appeals, namely, miracle
and prophecy; the latter being, as already mentioned, really a
species of miracle in Horne's argument. Let us leave aside the
internal inconsistencies and ethical problems in the text and the
use or influence of the Bible in some of the wars, massacres,
violent dissensions and power struggles which have disfigured
history; and let us acknowledge that Horne makes shrewd and
valid points in his discussion of the miraculous. Nevertheless, no
hostility to religion or Church would be needed to compel further
questions from an open-minded inquirer, even sympathiser. Is
there not a difference between establishing through the examination of testimony that an extraordinary event has occurred, and
that it is in Horne's sense a miracle? Why should we believe that
God has intervened rather than that further inquiry would bring
to light a naturalistic explanation of the event? Is there not a
crucial difference between the incomprehensibility of commonly
perceived events, and the incomprehensibility of events we never
perceive and which are by definition impossible? If all biblical
miracles occurred as described, why are such miracles never perceived now, even in similar circumstances? Why was Jesus rejected
by people who witnessed his public performances of the impossible, bearing in mind that they were, according to the argument,
for the specific purpose of authenticating his person and message?
And why did Jesus offer such signs, and then denounce as 'evil and
adulterous' the generation which demanded them?

Horne's stress upon the relevance of historical criteria is
welcome, but he himself accepts the Nile turned to blood and
'millions . . . fed with manna', which reveals considerable naivety
in the handling of historical evidence.[47]

Similarly, even those who believe in prophetic inspiration will
acknowledge the serious problems involved in turning this into

unanswerable proof of irresistible divine intervention in human thinking. Why, for example, could Isaiah but not Ahaz or Hezekiah foresee and judge the political situation correctly? If God simply wished Ahaz or Hezekiah to know the truth, he could have intervened in their thinking just as easily as he could in the case of Isaiah's. To reject this assertion because we prefer to think of God responding to Isaiah's faith and commitment is to adopt a view of God's relationship with mankind which is not that accepted by Horne. Once faith and commitment are admitted, it is always open to the sceptic to argue that people who held the views they did, and who felt the way they did, and lived in the situation they did, would foresee certain things which others could not; and could not simply because they were not willing to do so.

No doubt Horne believed that he had replied in advance to such an objection by showing that biblical prophecies were made about verifiable historical events which it was *absolutely* impossible for a human being to make without being directly informed by God; but not only does this raise serious literary and historical problems; much more to the point is it that Horne's implied view of God and man leaves us with the unanswerable question why in that case God did not and does not simply make all men see and believe what is true.

Adam Clarke, like Horne, believed that the Bible was the infallible Word of God, spoken to the contemporary reader as directly as God spoke to his original hearers, but also requiring rational reflection for its proper understanding. He was also very willing to use the latest scientific views in order to elucidate the text. As was so often the case, the Bible is treated basically as an history book, and we are invited to put confidence in it as such by a mixture of appeal to common-sense considerations and encouragement to trust in the Holy Spirit. According to Clarke the Pentateuch is unquestionably the oldest record in the universe and the Decalogue probably the first regular production in alphabetical character.[48] 'True knowledge is from Heaven, and is never contradictory to itself; therefore *reason* and *learning* not only coincide with Divine Revelation, but serve to illustrate and establish it'; and Clarke's own aim in his studies is to attain to 'a proper understanding of the literal sense of Scripture'.[49] In the antediluvian period there were very few people, closely related to one another and living to great ages, which means that they could

easily pass on information until it reached Moses, who wrote everything down. 'Yet, to preclude all possibility of mistake, the
unerring Spirit of God directed Moses in the selection of his *facts*,
and the ascertaining of his *dates*.'⁵⁰

Nevertheless, Clarke is well aware of problems. The essential
truths of divine revelation may be agreed upon, but there is much
difference of opinion among competent and sincere thinkers on
points of great importance. The Authorised Version contains
gross corruptions in the English words added to what is found in
the original Hebrew and Greek texts, and thereby attributes words
to God which he never spoke. Religious people engage in controversies, and it is implied that this is scarcely what one would expect
granted a perfectly clear revelation. Clarke hopes to state the
meaning and truth of each passage in a way acceptable to all those
who really want to know it.⁵¹ It does not, however, occur to him to
ask why the Holy Spirit should act as guide in the period when conditions almost guaranteed accurate transmission of the records,
but fail so to guide in the increasingly complex circumstances of
later ages.

The relationship of New and Old Testaments in Clarke's
exegesis also raises serious questions about inspiration and literal
truth. In commenting on Genesis 3:1 he rejects the Septuagint's
ophis as a translation of the Hebrew *nachash*, and asserts that New
Testament writers have simply followed the Septuagint in this
mistake, and that they seem to lose sight of the animal and refer
only to Satan himself.⁵² Nevertheless, he was prepared to appeal to
the New Testament in settling the meaning of an Old Testament
text. The *ruach Elohim* of Genesis 1:2 has received various translations: 'a very strong wind', 'elementary fire', 'Sun', 'angels',
'*anima mundi*', 'magnetic attraction'. Clarke favours 'Spirit' since
the Spirit is referred to as wind in John 3 and Acts 2.The remarks
of Jesus and the apostles prove Mosaic authorship of the Pentateuch; but Jesus' reference to the Flood, according to Matthew
24:36–44 and Luke 17:24–30, seems to be ignored in Clarke's
opinion that God gave 120 years' warning that the Flood was to
take place and that many thousands must have availed themselves
of this offer of divine grace.⁵³

Clarke's own transparent honesty and sincerity destroy the idea
of infallibly guided authors producing a literally true text, and
equally his willingness to take account of current science raises

questions about a religious interpretation of the universe which
only a wide-ranging philosophy could hope to answer. 'The origin,
constitution, and nature, of the universe, could never have been
known, had not God given us a revelation of his *works*.' 'Moses
alone, under the inspiration of the Spirit of God, gave a consistent
and rational account of the Creation: an account which has been
confirmed by the investigation of the most accurate philosophers.'[54] When we turn to the detailed commentary on Genesis 1
we are told that verse 2 seems to indicate that God first created the
elementary principles of all things, and that this formed the grand
mass of matter, the chaos; which was then arranged during six days
into the solar system. The 'light' of verse 3 is interpreted to mean
caloric or latent heat, spread through all nature, both light and
heat becoming actual through friction. Verse 4 refers to the
rotation of the earth 'by anticipation'. Verse 6 cannot refer to a
solid sky, which would deprive the passage of all sense and meaning. The Vulgate's *firmamentum* is a misleading translation based
on the Septuagint's *stereoma*. What is actually referred to is 'space'.
On verse 10, the earth's rotation and the relative proportions of
land and water have made it into an oblate spheroid. On verse 12,
the immense power of generation within the vegetable creation is
revealed in the fact that if all the seeds produced from one
original elm tree matured, within a few generations there would
be enough to cover every planet in the solar system. On verse 24,
it is acknowledged that animal life is revealed in 'infinitely varied
gradations' and that the polype 'seems equally to share the
vegetable and animal life'. Verse 25 means that everything in the
animal and vegetable worlds was created in its own genus and
species, with all future generations seminally included in those
first made.

We begin to wonder if those who have suggested a developmental, an evolutionary view of life may not be right; and if
secondary causes are so much in evidence why we should see God
in these purely natural events. Clarke would apparently have
fallen back on the traditional natural theology in answer to such
questions: 'The contrivance, arrangement, action, and reaction,
of the different parts of the body, shew the admirable skill of the
wondrous Creator.'[55] He certainly expected to see the divine
purposes at work in creation, and perhaps this was for him more a
self-evident truth than an argument. It is more than a mere

curiosity that he regarded the sun and moon as habitable, and
thought that all planets and their satellites are inhabited and that
all stars or suns have a similar system of inhabited planets
attached: 'for matter seems only to exist for the sake of intelligent
beings'. There are 'innumerable worlds, all dependent on the
power, protection, and providence of God', who 'supports' these
worlds.[56] When further astronomical research shows that the
extent of matter or energy is indescribably greater than Clarke
could ever have supposed and that there is precious little indication of life like our own anywhere in it, we begin to see the
danger of applying the results of rational inquiry to the eluci-
dation of ancient texts, without the benefit of some overarching
philosophy which can embrace both. And we wonder what the
purpose can be in creating elm trees which left to themselves
would in no time at all annihilate all life, real or supposed,
throughout the whole solar system. In commenting on Genesis
3:18 Clarke tells us that the enormous fertility of thorns and
thistles demonstrates the fulfilment of God's curse; but this is only
because thorns and thistles are often inconvenient to mankind,
whereas elm trees are not, and we are still left with the question
why members of all species produce vastly more offspring than can
possibly survive to mature life, especially when such survival would
in any case be disastrous for all other forms of life. It is scarcely
surprising that many should have later preferred natural selection
to explanations in terms of divine purpose.[57]

It was the aim of W. J. Irons, in his book *On the Whole Doctrine of
Final Causes*,[58] to establish the unique authority of revelation by
general argument rather than by biblical exegesis, and it is an
argument which for the time contained remarkable insights. In
order to fulfil his main purpose Irons wished to show that a strictly
natural theology is unattainable, and that attempted proofs of
God's existence which start out from the fact of causation in
nature fail in their object. This applies to what we should call both
the teleological and cosmological arguments.

The great enemies for Irons are Romanism and a powerful
infidelity which takes the forms of deism, natural theology and
'liberality'. Romanism and infidelity 'have united their forces, for
open war, beneath banners inscribed with the outraged name of
"Liberal"'.[59] Liberalism is particularly dangerous because it often
appears to favour religion; but for Irons this is merely obscuring

the fact that human reason left to itself cannot give certain proof of any single theological truth. Lord Brougham, whose view of the significance of reason in religious belief was certainly very different from Irons', is repeatedly attacked, and this includes strong criticism of his edition of Paley's *Natural Theology*.

Irons pays incidental tribute to the great influence of Paley and refers to his *Natural Theology* as 'confessedly a popular treatise', while elsewhere he speaks of 'the unjustifiable idolatry of Paley, which has been prevalent in this country'.[60] As a prelude to his criticism of Paley he makes use of the argument of Epicurus

That before the existence of the eye . . . it could not be known what *sight* was; – therefore it could not be said that the eye was made *for* seeing. All sight and consequently all knowledge of sight, must be subsequent to the eye. Which argument can only be overthrown by showing, on other, and quite independent grounds, that there existed previously a Being of infinite knowledge and skill. It is clearly a very different thing to say – certain things are well adapted *to* certain uses; and to say – certain things were 'created *for*' certain uses. This latter sentence implies a Creator and a Designer, who must *first* be acknowledged . . .[61]

Irons is perfectly willing to assert that there is divine design in nature, but he rightly insists that this is a belief which we bring with us to the observation of the world. Therefore, as he clearly and correctly points out, Paley's argument is, as such, a *petitio principii*:

This constant appeal to facts of fitness, can, of itself, prove nothing *certainly*. To one who believes in God, on *other grounds*, these facts are invaluable. The Christian rejoices in believing, that these facts of fitness, or adaptation, all result from the design of his Gracious God; the Natural Theologian has first to *prove* his God. He may then admit design in Nature; but not till then.[62]

He goes on to give a clear and fully justified critique of Paley's watch analogy.[63]

Irons not only recognises but lays great stress on the fact that the evils of the world, including appalling human suffering, contradict design and the idea of an all-powerful wisdom and benevolence. He makes a fierce attack on the underestimating or playing down of the evil and pain in the world, and Paley receives scathing comment in this respect.[64] It is an interesting question, in that case, whether or not Irons was entitled to retain teleology as an article of faith, having destroyed it as an argument for faith, but it is not one which he raises or attempts to answer.

He then engages in a lengthy discussion of various meanings of 'cause' and comes to the conclusion that the word can only legitimately be applied to that which of itself makes anything begin to be. On the analogy of human experience of what it means to be an originator or cause of events he asserts that every cause must be an agent, and that this implies intelligence in every cause; and this in turn means that so-called physical causes are not causes at all, but only the instruments or occasions of causation. We are then left with the choice of attributing intelligent agency to nature itself, pantheism, or recognising in such causation the power of God. 'Wherever there is Originating Efficiency there must be Life – Power — Spontaneous Motion – in a word, Intelligence. Therefore, to say that any "Laws" or Nominal "Powers of Nature" are Efficient, Self-originating, or Self-operating, is to deify Nature.'[65]

We might feel at this point that Irons is inconsistently offering us his own natural theology: pantheism is the reductio ad absurdum which leaves us with no option but to acknowledge the transcendent deity's presence in nature, provided, of course, we are also prepared to go along with the dubious analogy between human agency and physical causation; but this would be a mistake. Irons consistently maintains that no knowledge of God can be derived from nature:

It appears that, by the unassisted efforts of Nature, we could no more arrive at a knowledge of the Character, than of the Personality or Unity of God. The union of goodness, wisdom, and power, in the Creator and Governor of the Universe, seems incredible, on natural grounds . . . I conclude, therefore, that though, without a revelation, we might arrive at a certain knowledge that there was a Cause (or Causes) for all things in Nature; yet we could never tell, whether there was only one Cause? or, whether there were many? – We could not know even the Personality of any such Cause, nor the moral character of it; we *must* disbelieve either its wisdom, its goodness, or its power. So that not one single truth of Theology could, by any possibility, be arrived at, on Natural principles.[66]

Why, then, does he offer us the argument about causation? The answer is that Irons clearly appreciated that a natural world operating simply by means of necessary physical causes not only could not be made the basis for a demonstration of God's existence, but is 'utterly destructive of every such argument'. A self-sufficient natural world is a self-sufficient natural world, and while the increase of knowledge may continually widen the physical context of which it is a part, and although this context may appear to have no limits, we are not entitled to establish a limit by the arbitrary introduction of a transcendent deity.

Furthermore, Irons well knew that the chain of physical causation which was supposed to require God as its origin also created problems for human freedom, thereby threatening to destroy both morality and religion. He hoped to overcome this threat to freedom, morality and religion by making God the only true cause or agent in the physical universe. 'We thus make the Law of Causation not merely consistent with, but the very basis of, all possible Morality – the sole foundation of Human Responsibility.'[67] The personally conceived deity thus becomes the guarantee of all that is most profoundly significant in human life; but since the sole justification for interpreting the law of causation in this way is the false analogy with human initiative, the argument cannot stand. Irons displays a fine awareness of the aspects of human experience which demand the revelation of God if they are to have in reality the substance which they seem to have in practice,[68] but regrettably this is not worked out as a proper reply to scepticism, and we are left simply with the basic facts of religious and moral experience plus an unacceptable explanation of causation.

Although there can be no doubt about Irons' independence of thought, the similarity between his demolition of the generally accepted natural theology and that of Hume is striking, and Irons has no hesitation in appealing to Hume for support. His assessment of Hume's overall argument is correct: 'It appears to me that while Mr Hume confines himself to demonstrating the *insufficiency* of the proof of Natural Religion, he is unanswerable.'[69] He also correctly sums up Hume's scepticism in his own words:

Mr Hume had denied that Man could obtain any knowledge of the Moral Governor of the Universe from the works of Nature – even if the theory of Causation were admitted; *because* we have no right to *argue* that any Cause is *more* than the alleged Effect shows him to be . . . Now this Argument cannot be answered by those who derive all our knowledge from

Sense. Therefore, if there be no Truths except empirical Truths . . .
'Truths of Understanding' – there can be no Religion.[70]

Irons means by 'Truths of Understanding' those which lie
'within the province of sense and experience' and which therefore
cannot give us theological truth, which lies beyond experience.
On the other hand, 'Truths of Reason', which include the fundamental doctrines of religion, are unattainable by mere finite
intelligence. Such concepts as the unity, or the combined infinity
and personality, of God cannot possibly be reached by argument
or reflection.[71]

In his own way Irons anticipated H. L. Mansel's line of argument
in his Bampton Lectures of 1858. Human reason cannot grasp the
knowledge of God and we must therefore turn to revelation, that
is, the Bible, for it. We also detect in Irons' argument what is
present in Mansel's, the influence of Kant, and Irons does refer to
Kant a number of times, but there is no suggestion that he had
even begun to appreciate the critical philosophy in its full scope.
This was no doubt the consequence in Irons' case of other
demands upon his time and energy, but the further inevitable consequence is that we are then left with a question of fundamental
importance concerning the authority of the Bible: Were the persons who wrote the Bible and whose deeds and words are recorded
in it like human beings today, or not? If they were, how could they
understand what we are, according to the argument, incapable of
understanding? If they were different, how can the Word of God
which came to them come to us? The words in which they express
themselves can never really mean anything to us, since we are
incapable of sharing their religious experience.

The conservative reply must be to choose the first alternative,
that there is no essential difference between men and women of
biblical times and men and women now, but that external circumstances were different in that God performed miracles, intervened
in human history, in ways which do not occur now. The Bible is the
miraculous record of miracles, and that is why we call it revelation
in a special sense which cannot be given to any other recorded
experience; but this is no real answer to the problem, since we are
left again with a biblical world significantly different from our
own, not to speak of other problems such as those referred to in
connection with Horne, questions which cry out all the more for

an answer if we believe that miracles do still happen. If the biblical world is essentially the same as our own, it may be that human experience within it has something to teach us, but in that case biblical exegesis and contemporary philosophy must go hand in hand.

CHAPTER 5

Conservative natural theology: Paley's design argument

Those thinkers who illustrate the second line of approach to the religious problems with which we are concerned are not distinguished from those who illustrate the first by their view of the Bible, but by their view of natural science and philosophy.

All those in the second group felt compelled for one reason or another to acknowledge the legitimacy of philosophical reflection and research, which at the time included what we should call scientific study, and they were more or less sensitive to possible charges of dishonesty in the refusal to accept established facts and valid conclusions and in the attempt to bend the meaning of biblical texts to make them consistent with such facts and conclusions. This did not alter the fact that interpretations and reinterpretations of the Bible had to be made, and that there were frequent disagreements between the interpreters, and some changes of mind. The assertions of rational inquiry were and are irreconcilable with the plain meaning of certain biblical texts, not least those concerning the creation of the world and its dissolution and re-creation through the Deluge; and therefore attempts to preserve the plain meaning of the text in the light of new knowledge were doomed to failure from the start, and what was plain to one interpreter was far from plain to another.

At the same time, the only natural theology available to such thinkers was invalid. The rational inquiry and reflection they rightly recognised as legitimate did not offer firm ground for belief in God, any more than it could be reconciled, in the way they wanted, with the assertions of biblical revelation. They therefore resembled a man standing with a foot in each of two boats, the two vessels being gradually pushed apart by the steady current of thought, despite Quixotic endeavours to hold them together; and the alternatives were either a leap back into conservatism, a leap forward into a fresh but inadequate religious philosophy, or disappearance beneath the advancing waves.

These thinkers will be considered in two chapters: this one is concerned with an attempt to illustrate Paley's design argument on a truly vast scale, taking into account all the major fields of scientific inquiry known to the early nineteenth century. The first of the eight authors involved in the enterprise, Thomas Chalmers, will be dealt with in the next chapter.

THE BRIDGEWATER TREATISES

The Rt Hon. and Revd Francis Henry, Earl of Bridgewater, died in February 1829. By his last will and testament a bequest of £8,000 was put at the disposal of the President of the Royal Society of London so that he could nominate a person or persons to write, print and publish a thousand copies of a work 'On The Power Wisdom And Goodness of God As Manifested In The Creation'. President Gilbert Davies, in consultation with the Archbishop of Canterbury, the Bishop of London and a noble relative of the deceased, appointed eight gentlemen to write on different aspects of the subject. The result was the publication in the 1830s of eight treatises in twelve substantial volumes.

The influence of Paley is not to be seen merely in the occasional references to him, but much more profoundly in the domination of the argument by the analogy between nature and a machine, an analogy which could be illustrated from the treatises at length. The words of Sir Leslie Stephen are apt: 'God has been civilised like man; he has become scientific and ingenious; he is superior to Watt and Priestley in devising mechanical and chemical con- trivances, and is, therefore, made in the image of that generation of which Watt and Priestley were conspicuous lights.'[1] William Prout in his brief Introduction offers his own illustration of the argument from design: human beings provide themselves with clothing against the cold, and animals are similarly so provided. Animals, however, do not clothe themselves, and therefore this end must have been accomplished by their creator. Prout thus assumes that the product of human workmanship and design is equivalent to the product of natural growth, although no one has ever witnessed God clothing an animal, and such 'clothing' is an integral part of the animal without which it would not exist at all.[2]

It is not surprising that Prout, in common with his colleagues, could not help giving expression to doubts and difficulties in the presentation of the overall argument:

the instances . . . in which man is thus able to trace the designs of his Creator, are really few. Man not only sees means directed to certain ends; but ends accomplished by means, which he is totally unable to understand. He also sees, everywhere, things, the nature and the end of which are utterly beyond his comprehension; and respecting which, he is obliged to content himself with simply inferring the existence of design.

We are here close to an admission that design is read into rather than read off the works of nature. Prout, the pioneer chemist, was more impressed by the incomprehensibility of nature's processes than their clarity, and he admits that design in nature cannot be *proved* 'by any argument founded on *reason* or *necessity*'. Instead, we have to depend on common sense, which recognises design in nature just as readily as it does in human artefacts.[3] A similar position is taken up by Whewell, who denies that we infer design in the natural world: it presents itself to us just as it does in the case of artificial products, and it is just as unavoidable in the one case as in the other. 'It is not therefore at the end, but at the beginning of our syllogisms, not among the remote conclusions, but among original principles, that we must place the truth, that such arrangements, manifestations, and proceedings as we behold about us imply a Being endowed with consciousness, design, and will, from whom they proceed.'[4]

This direct, immediate intuition is likened by Whewell to our recognition of a person, our spontaneous knowledge of mind and will inhabiting the physical frame confronting us; and once again we come close to the admission of seeing in nature the reflection of our own belief, the premises of the argument being supplied with the truth which we wish to find in the conclusion. In fact, we do not meet God in nature as we meet our friends and acquaintances, and if we did, there would scarcely be that threat to religious belief from the developing sciences to which Whewell refers early in his treatise.[5]

Roget momentarily teeters on the edge of giving the game away. He explains that he refers to 'nature' rather than 'God' producing life in its multifarious forms in order to avoid the too frequent and therefore irreverent use of the divine name: 'the term Nature' is used 'as a synonym, expressive of the same power, but veiling from our feeble sight the too dazzling splendour of the glory'.[6] Roget did not, of course, think of 'God' and 'nature' as synonymous, and if he had made the experiment of writing 'God' throughout, he would have been compelled to think again. We do not observe God; we observe natural processes.

The recognition of *mind and instinct* in human beings and animals, and a certain vitality in both them and plants, fitted ill with the machine analogy. John Kidd candidly acknowledges the intimate connection between intelligence and instinct on the one hand and physical nature on the other:

Should it be said, for instance, that the bee or the ant shews greater indications of intelligence than many species much higher in the scale of animal creation, it may be answered that those indications are manifested in actions which are referable to instinct, rather than intelligence; actions namely, which being essential to the existence of the individuals, and the preservation of the species, are apparently determined by some internal impulse which animals unconsciously obey.

Kidd finds instinct impossible to define since we are ignorant of its real nature, and when he interprets the way in which insects and animals cope with unusual circumstances he can refer to it as both 'modification of instinct' and evidence of 'intellectual prudence'. In speaking of the brain he states, 'no one can doubt that the organ itself is the mysterious instrument by means of which, principally, if not exclusively, a communication is maintained between the external world and the soul . . . it must on every consideration be admitted to be the instrument by which the various degrees of intelligence are manifested'.

Although soul and body are distinct parts of our nature, Kidd knows that they exercise a 'reciprocal influence' on each other, which shows that the immaterial soul 'may be manifested by means of a material instrument'. He also knows that the body can determine or modify the moral and intellectual tendencies of the soul, although determination is 'in a qualified sense'. He also knows that changes in the physical state of the brain can effect marked changes in mental activity. His fear of what a more detailed analysis of the brain and its physiology might reveal may be felt in his strictures on a certain Dr Gall, who, despite excellent work in this sphere, carried his investigations too far, his work being marred by 'indiscreet zeal'.[7]

It would be possible to develop out of the facts which Kidd

recognised an approach to organic life which sees it developing by reciprocal interaction with its environment, the two being utterly inseparable and producing the 'intelligence' of ants and bees and higher intelligences alike. He was, indeed, impressed by the unity of nature which could nevertheless embrace immense variety even within species, and by the fine gradations between ever-changing phenomena which at times made biological definition and precise classification difficult, if not impossible. He was aware of the claim that rock strata demonstrate an evolutionary change from simpler to more complicated forms, although it was a claim which he thought had been disproved.[8] It is not surprising that he disclaims any attempt to put forward a formal argument such as would persuade a sceptic, and aims rather to provide for believers concrete illustrations of how the physical world contributes to the advancement of mankind.[9]

The dilemma confronting those who accepted the Paleyan approach to nature was that it was impossible to square the facts of observation with the machine analogy. Everything we mean by 'life' can only be related to nature's 'mechanisms' in some crude and artificial manner. On the other hand, if we recognise nature's organic character, she takes on a life of her own independent of some contriving and supervising divine mechanic. She bears the seeds of development within herself, and natural change neither demands nor reveals purposeful design.

This dilemma is most clearly seen in Roget's treatise. In the opening chapter on final causes, as part of the considerable emphasis Roget lays on the machine analogy, he states that the animal is made up of 'lifeless and inert materials'; it is an 'elaborate machine' in which life and energy mysteriously appear, these qualities being 'apparently so foreign' to the 'inherent properties' of the material particles composing its body. Later he says that 'mere machinery is incapable of generating force'. 'The living body differs from inorganic machinery in containing within itself a principle of motion.' When we take this with Roget's acknowledgement of the 'dormant vitality' found in nature, we wonder why it did not lead him to question the wisdom of making an analogy between things so unalike.[10]

Later in Volume II we do find an admission of the limitations of the machine analogy. According to Roget, an analysis of chemical changes in creatures reveals processes which are subtle and complex and which cannot be repeated by men. A process of growth and decay takes place in animals and plants which is different from the building up, maintenance and wearing out of a machine. There is a vitality not to be found in machines, and the formation of each creature or plant is closely related to that of many others: it is part of 'the great scheme of nature'. Much later in the same volume we read, 'No conceivable combinations of mechanical, or of chemical powers, bear the slightest resemblance, or the most remote analogy, to organic reproduction, or can afford the least clue to the solution of this dark and hopeless enigma.'[11]

Roget speaks of vital force being conferred 'on the organized fabric', but offers no defence of the view that higher energies have been conferred rather than that they have appeared naturally in the course of unified organic development.[12] He himself refers to the essential and complete interdependence of parts in any given organism and the striking similarities in the overall structure of widely varying species of animal revealed by comparative anatomy. He mentions the hypothesis that all organic beings form a continuous chain of life from the simplest to the most sophisticated; and also the hypothesis 'that the original creation of species has been successive and took place in the order of their relative complexity of structure . . . Many apparent anomalies which are inexplicable upon any other supposition, are easily reconcilable with this theory.'[13] The first hypothesis is dismissed on the ground that the suggested system is incomplete, although Roget well knew that gaps in knowledge were being rapidly filled and that four-fifths of the insects then known had been discovered within the previous ninety years. The second hypothesis is rejected in favour of the idea of development according to divine plan, but this is a tacit admission that much of the evidence produced to support the rubric could be very differently interpreted.

The concept of *adaptation* was both crucial to the Paleyan argument and fatal to it. With the benefit of post-Darwinian hindsight we can see that it is an essential, integral part of the whole organic process and not, in itself, evidence of some external guiding hand. And yet post-Darwinian hindsight was not really necessary for the appreciation of this truth. A selective and rationalising attitude to the evidence would have been clearly recognised for what it was by any thinker adopting a genuinely objective approach rather than setting out to defend a cause, and both Paley's *Natural Theology* and the Bridgewater Treatises offer ample proof of the fact.

Whewell, for example, argues that 'The length of the solar year is so determined as to be adapted to the constitution of most vegetables; or the construction of vegetables is so adjusted as to be suited to the length which the year really has.' As he truly remarks, if the earth were placed where Mars and Venus now are, all vegetable life would be destroyed. He is dimly aware of the fact that it is the conditions of this planet which have produced vegetation as we know it, but this possible line of explanation is simply dismissed.[14] He refers to Laplace's objection to explanations in terms of final causes, an objection based on the fact, for example, that the moon's light is often hidden, whereas it could have been arranged to shine all the time. Whewell's answer is partly that we simply do not and cannot know why this is so; and partly that any rearrangement we can think of would disturb the stability of the whole system.[15] This is, of course, tantamount to an admission that the only sensible explanation we can offer based on observation of natural phenomena is in terms of efficient, not final causation. Later in the treatise he states,

Laplace himself, in describing the arrangements by which the stability of the solar system is secured, uses language which shows that these arrangements irresistibly suggest an adaptation to its preservation as an *end*. If in his expressions he were to substitute the Deity for the abstraction 'nature' which he employs, his reflexion would coincide with that which the most religious philosopher would entertain.

It is, however, precisely our entitlement to make the substitution which is in question, and Whewell's idea that the whole mass of the earth is 'employed in keeping a snowdrop in the position most suited to the promotion of its vegetable health' does not encourage confidence in the suggestion.[16]

As an illustration of divine purpose, Kidd tells us that 'almost all the tropical islands . . . are guarded from the sea . . . by a reef of coral rocks . . . and thus nature has effectually secured these islands from the encroachments of the sea'. This is despite the fact that shortly afterwards he gives a careful description of how coral reefs are formed purely in terms of efficient causation.[17]

Buckland, in a striking and lucid opening to his treatise, shows how the distribution of population and predominant occupations are the consequence of geological conditions, ending with the remark, 'Their physical condition also . . . depending on the more or less salubrious nature of their employments, are directly affected by the geological causes in which their various occupations originate.' He notes the dependence of geology for its development as a science upon other sciences: physics, mineralogy, chemistry, botany, zoology, comparative anatomy; and this leads to the acknowledgement that the large effects studied by geologists have their ultimate cause in atomic reactions which 'are, and ever have been, governed by laws . . . regular and uniform'.[18] He even declares at one point that the production of soil and the way in which metals are disposed 'were almost essential conditions of the earth's habitability', and that the advantages man derives from 'great geological phenomena' should be regarded as 'incidental and residuary consequences'. Yet he can also express the view that the deposits of coal were placed where they are for the use and benefit of the human race; and the phenomena of geology are 'decidedly opposed' to all evolutionary theories, and along with all the other sciences produce conclusive evidence of design, 'the operations of the Almighty Author of the Universe'.[19]

Further illustrations of this kind of confusion and rationalisation with respect to adaptation could be multiplied at length from the Treatises, and it is closely related to the concept of *chance*, and what Chalmers called *collocation*, that is, the putting together of the various parts which go to make up each item of nature and nature as a whole; the latter idea is based on the machine analogy as an assumption.

Once nature is approached in this way it becomes absurd to suppose that the various parts which make up a plant or animal have simply come together in some haphazard fashion, by chance, and unthinkable that this should be true for the whole of nature. Purpose must have been at work, and thus does chance become the reductio ad absurdum to which natural theology can appeal as the final, indisputable demonstration of divine design manifested in nature, in whole and in part.

In speaking of the mutual adaptation of the vegetable cycle and the solar year, Whewell asserts, 'No chance could produce such a result'; and in his description of the solar system as an exhibition of design he asserts that planetary orbits cannot be nearly circular 'by chance' but have been chosen 'with some design'. The

stability of the solar system cannot be 'the work of chance', and
the fact that the sun is at the centre of the solar system 'could
hardly have occurred by anything which we can call chance'. A
candle does not appear upon a candlestick and a fire does not
appear in the hearth 'by the casual operation of gravity'.[20]

For Sir Charles Bell, the idea that the relationship of animals
and man to the changing conditions of the earth is to be
explained as a matter of chance is an 'idle' supposition; and for
Roget the myriad organisms in the vegetable and animal worlds
cannot be the consequence of chance, which is as good as to say
they had no cause at all: 'such a conclusion is contrary to the
constitution of human thought'.[21] Kirby dismisses as absurd the
idea that the complex and numberless adaptations of the natural
world could have come about by chance, or 'nature, as some love
to speak'. For Kirby, the alternative to purpose is the random, the
only effect of which would be chaos. Similarly, for Prout the idea
that matter came into existence by chance is monstrous, and
we must therefore accept the only alternative of intentional
creation.[22]

The concept of chance will require further investigation when
we consider Chalmers, but that of 'collocation' was in itself disastrous as a clue to understanding adaptation. When Roget notes
the correspondence between the horizontal spread of a tree's
branches and the spread of its roots, so that rain off the leaves
provides nutrition for the roots, he sees 'a striking instance of that
beautiful correspondence, which has been established between
processes belonging to different departments of nature, and
which are made to concur in the production of remote effects,
that could never have been accomplished without these pre-
concerted and harmonious adjustments'.[23]

Nature, however, is not a gigantic department store, and the
harmonious adjustments spring from within and are not compelled from without. In reply to Whewell we must point out that
the sun is not an item independent of the solar system as the fire
is of the grate, nor is our planetary system merely adapted to
receive the sun as the wick is to receive the flame. When Sir
Charles Bell promises to refute the opinion that outward circumstances are the cause of variety in and among animals, the fulfilment of the promise is both inevitable and insignificant since the
refutation is based upon the supposed fundamental distinctness

of creature and environment.[24] If Prout felt obliged to confess to some difficulty in supplying examples of design from the subject-matter of his own discipline, this is not surprising: the force at work in nature manifests itself in multifarious reactions and combinations, the mere observation of which gives no clue as to why it is just these reactions and combinations which occur and not others. Out of these reactions and combinations multifarious organisms appear, and the natural world we now perceive is the present consequence of processes spanning vast eras, to which artificial production cannot provide the remotest analogy. Nothing could be more different from such processes of growth than the assembling of a watch or a steam engine.

As we have seen, there is from time to time in the Treatises the recognition or hint of a very different way of reading the evidence from that laid down in the noble bequest. The immense age of the earth, the lessons of comparative anatomy, the fossil evidence, fine gradations between species and wide variations within species, interrelationships in nature and the harmony and unity of the whole, adaptation of creatures to environment, the existence of rudimentary and useless organs, the balance in populations maintained through the struggle for existence, nature's own vitality, the evidence of development from simpler to more complex: all these are recognised and make readily intelligible the emergence of Darwin and Wallace with their theory of evolution, but the Bridgewater authors preferred to force a preconceived interpretation on the evidence, which they could only do by filling the universe with innumerable gaps between innumerable parts, gaps which only God could fill and parts which only God could join according to a preordained plan. If we ask why men of intelligence, integrity and learning should have adopted such a method of argument, we must remember that what seemed to them the alternative, chance, was not merely a handy stick wherewith to beat opponents, but also the symbol of a barren universe in which human life becomes meaningless. Deep-seated resistance to this view of things was and is by no means confined to the authors of the Bridgewater Treatises.

When the question is raised in the Treatises as to exactly how we should envisage *God's relationship with the natural world*, no clear and consistent answer is forthcoming. The operative picture is that of a craftsman, a Platonic-type demiurge, assembling parts like a watchmaker, but on a breathtakingly larger scale. The crucial question is, When does the assembling take place? If it took place at the original creation, if the world sprang into being an already functioning whole, we may preserve the doctrine of creatio ex nihilo; but the problem in this case is that the self-perpetuating world of harmoniously functioning forces may, to all appearances, contain the seeds of origin within itself. We are not obliged from mere observation of the natural world to suppose that it was made by a being external to it.

If, on the other hand, the assembling is going on all the time, we are presented with a staggeringly impressive piece of divine juggling, and we must redefine our concept of creation to include the idea of ongoing processes, creatio continua. The fundamental problem in this case is that this continuous creation is not open to observation. The performance is indeed remarkable, and perhaps all the more so because the performer is imperceptible. We may be experiencing God at work in the processes of nature, but this is not apparent. The world does not have the maker's name stamped on it.

The words of Leslie Stephen are once again appropriate as we confront the alternatives:

Place your creative impulse at any distance you please, at six thousand or sixty million years, and Paley's God stands for the aggregate of the preceding forces. Since that date, the field is open as widely as possible to the researches of science; before it everything is hid in mystery, which we call God.

On the other hand, if the creative God is ever-present:

God, indeed, has all but become an object of scientific investigation; had we but a sixth sense, we might expect actually to detect him in the act of creating; and yet science may investigate the working of the machinery, instead of its original construction, without risk of meeting the supernatural. The man of science may examine the functions, when he cannot inquire into the origin of the organs.[25]

We shall be more concerned with Thomas Chalmers later, but it is worth noting here that he endeavoured to preserve the doctrine of creatio ex nihilo while at the same time wishing to see the divine power and wisdom displayed in the production of order out of the complexities of chaos. According to Chalmers, we may think of God as being like a human artificer, but with the significant difference that while a human workman manipulates matter with its inherent properties, God created both matter and its inherent properties. This, however, only gives rise to the question why God made things so difficult for himself. We admire the human skill and strength which can overcome material obstacles or turn the recalcitrance of matter to its own advantage, but it is difficult to see why God should create obstacles merely in order to overcome them. After briefly wrestling unsuccessfully with this problem Chalmers escapes with relief from what he calls 'this digression'; but it is no digression. The analogy of human work-manship, basic to the whole argument of the Treatises and supposedly providing a firm ground for belief in God through the contemplation of his workmanship, is quite inconsistent with the doctrine of creatio ex nihilo, which is a confession that divine cre-ation is a complete and impenetrable mystery to which there is not and could not be the remotest human parallel. Men do not create ex nihilo. We must allow Hume to remind us that the creating of worlds is something of which we have no experience, and there-fore no idea.[26]

William Whewell asserts that we cannot know how God has made and continues to sustain the universe, and that events occur according to general laws and not by the exertion of divine power in each particular case. Nevertheless, 'The properties of matter, even the most fundamental and universal ones, do not obtain by any absolute necessity, resembling that which belongs to the prop-erties of geometry' – or, we may add, remembering Hume again, algebra. It is only the universal presence of God's power and agency which enables conditions to endure or changes to occur, and Whewell quotes with approval a statement of the Bishop of London that 'all the events, which are continually taking place in the different parts of the material universe, are the *immediate* effects of the divine agency'.[27] Whewell concludes from this that there is a vast difference between the way human beings create things and the way God has created and sustained them; men can only make use of matter as it already exists.

Whewell is obviously torn between his scientific knowledge and his desire not to hand over the world to the operation of imper-sonal forces. The result is the assertion of creatio continua, although this is not clear, and we are left with a point of view which denies the possibility of comparison between divine creation and human manufacture, despite the fact that this is the basic assumption of the Treatises. The denial of necessity in natural processes is more than we know, and it is contrary to the assumptions of common sense and natural science. The analogy with geometry as presented by Whewell is misleading, since geometry is a product of the human mind, a set of definitions and logical connections whose consistencies or inconsistencies we are directly aware of. The connections we discover in nature are presented to us and *for all we can tell* might have been different; but it does not follow from this that in reality they could have been different, and the general assumption is that they could not.

Both Kirby and Prout wrestled unsuccessfully with this problem, Kirby insisting on using the Bible as a guide to finding the deity in the works of creation. Kirby wishes 'to counteract that tendency . . . to ascribe too much to the action of second causes . . . as if they were sufficient of themselves, and without the intervention of the First Cause, to do all in all, and keep the whole machine and all its parts together and at work'.

Therefore, when Kirby's thinking is dominated by the Bible, we learn that God is always in active control of the whole world through instrumental powers symbolised by cherubim, clouds and wings of the wind; but when Kirby turns his attention to the actual subject of his treatise we learn that there are physical forces in nature not controlled immediately by God, and we find ourselves back in the familiar world of secondary causes and experimental methods.[28]

Prout is likewise caught between acknowledgement of the forces at work in nature and the desire to present evidence of divine activity. Following Paley, he asserts that God operates in nature through subordinate agents, acting according to rules which he has prescribed to himself. There is no necessity in the natural elements to make them act as they do, and the laws of nature as we understand them are descriptive generalisations based on experience of what actually happens. Chemical elements have within themselves no power to act or react, and the qualitative distinction between compounds is somehow determined by God. On his concluding page he refers to laws of nature as 'mere delegated agencies', and to 'the GREAT FIRST CAUSE; who exists and acts throughout the universe'.[29]

Nevertheless, we also learn that the most common and the

simplest natural operations, in the minutest fragments of matter, take place of necessity; and even at the original creation God may have operated through 'delegated agencies and laws'. Certainly, once the new forms of life had come into existence they were given the capacity to reproduce themselves, and God himself ceased to operate.[30] Prout also thinks of primary arrangements which create problems and secondary arrangements which overcome the problems and thereby provide evidence of divine design.[31] The world has gone through different states in which different laws of nature have prevailed; God strictly adheres to the laws of nature, which are therefore unalterably stable; there is a distinction between laws of nature rigidly adhered to and others, which God breaks; but since laws of nature are only descriptive, they cannot really be 'broken'; in any case, what appears to us to be anomalous or defective may in reality be part of some vast cycle or series beyond human comprehension; yet such infringements are indispensably necessary to organic existence and disprove the supposed omnipotence of the laws of nature; but the events which chemists observe are necessarily connected and we are led irresistibly to inevitable conclusions which are increasingly being expressed in mathematical terms.

That is to say, inconsistency and confusion are scattered throughout Prout's treatise, and on the subject of God's relationship to the world this is characteristic of the Treatises as a whole. It reflects the inadequacy of the basic analogy upon which Paley and the Bridgewater authors relied and their failure to recognise this and the need for a fresh philosophical approach to the age-old problems of religious belief: problems which had received powerful expression in the scepticism of Hume, and which were being increasingly underlined by the developing picture of nature provided by the burgeoning sciences.

Although the aim of the Bridgewater Treatises is to tell us what man can learn about God by reflection on the natural order, some attention is given to *revelation, the Bible*. God had revealed in the Scriptures truths not to be found in nature, yet there is much mention of nature in the Bible, and it was assumed that God would not mislead readers in references to nature which are incidental to his main purpose. From ancient times, of course, biblical interpretation had provided students with problems which admitted of no certain or generally agreed solution. Centuries of comment and controversy provide ample evidence of well-meant and well-informed variety in expositions and explanations of what the Bible means. Serious controversy, however, was based not merely upon the acceptance of the Bible as true, but upon the belief that this truth was of such vital significance that one had to get it right; and the meaning did not by any means always lie plainly on the surface of the text.

By the time the Bridgewater authors wrote, it was obvious that natural scientists had produced and were producing a picture of the world quite at variance with that given in the Scriptures, and this created a new and uncomfortable situation for the interpreter, who now not only had to answer the question, What is the truth here revealed? but also the question, Is it, can it be, true?

Roget quotes Job 12:7-9 opposite the title-page of Volume I, apparently in the belief that this gives scriptural support to the idea of the deity whòse beneficent designs are revealed in nature. A reading of chapters 11-13 shows that nothing could be further from the truth. Job invites Zophar to look at the facts: 'The tents of robbers prosper, And they that provoke God are secure; Into whose hand God bringeth abundantly.' God does as he pleases, and there is striking arbitrariness in the fates of men. It is the absoluteness of God's power coupled with the arbitrariness of his will which we are taught by beasts, fowls, earth and fishes.[32]

William Kirby stretched the meaning of the rubric beyond its intended limit, but the only effect of his effort is to suggest a biblical view of nature very different from that of natural science. Kirby believed that he could show by careful attention to the text that the cherubim symbolise all powers in the universe, physical and other, and since God directly controls the cherubim, this means that he directly controls all events in the natural world. 'God acts upon the earth by what we call symbolically his feet', producing whirlwinds and storms in the atmosphere and the evaporation which produces clouds.

The Deity superintends his whole creation, not only supporting the system he has established, and seeing that the powers to which he has given it in charge to govern under him, execute his physical laws; but himself, where he sees fit, in particular instances dispensing with these laws; restraining the clouds, in one instance from shedding their treasures; and in another permitting them to descend in blessings. Acting everywhere upon the atmosphere, and those secondary powers that produce atmospheric phenomena, as circumstances connected with his moral government require.[33]

The vagaries of weather forecasting may incline us to sympathise with this view, but the scientific explanation of failures in prediction is necessarily in terms of human error and ignorance, and not the nature of reality. Like his colleagues in the Bridgewater enterprise, Kirby wanted to acknowledge the laws of nature but not give any credence to the view that they represented physical forces operating of their own necessity. As we have seen, when he turned in Volume II to give primary consideration to natural facts, it was these forces which were recognised.

We turn from Kirby's bizarre exegesis to William Buckland for a more sober attempt to reconcile Bible and science. Buckland's task was more specific: to reconcile the geological record with the account of creation in Genesis I. This biblical text is not an incidental reference to the natural world, nor is it poetic or merely rhetorical. It is a short collection of plain assertions placed significantly at the very opening of the Scriptures. The geological evidence that the earth, along with animals and plants, had existed a very long time before the appearance of man is in conflict with the biblical assertions that the whole process of creation took place in six days, and that the animals and mankind were created on the same day. Buckland was one of those conservative interpreters who refused to attempt a solution of the problem by taking 'day' to mean a very long period of time.

Instead, he adopted the view which had been put forward by Thomas Chalmers that the long geological eras are by implication referred to in verse I. 'In the beginning' refers to the immeasurably distant past, whereas the chaos of verse 2 refers to the state of the universe immediately preceding the creation of the world inhabited by man. The Bible is primarily concerned with the life and salvation of mankind and therefore omits details of the vast period between the 'beginning', when matter was created, and the formation of the present world. Geologists are thus provided with a happy hunting ground in which they can pursue their interests without the slightest danger of trespassing on theological property. No less an authority than Professor E. B. Pusey is quoted in support of this reading of Genesis I:I.[34]

It is, nevertheless, a reading of which no one would have

thought without the threat of science to stimulate it, and does no justice either to the continuity of the geological record or to that of the biblical text. 'That is not to say that conservatives consciously sought to impose their interpretations upon Scripture; far from it. But the fact that for them it was inconceivable that Scripture should speak contrary to the fundamental direction of scientific thinking inevitably determined their interpretation of crucial passages.'[35] Quite so, and well said: but false and forced interpretations remain just that, whatever the motives of the interpreter. Buckland's honesty makes further reflection on the subject well worth while since it shows that such unconvincing reconciliations of Bible and science were and still are but the symptoms of a more profound disease, that is, lack of philosophy.

Buckland admits that light must have existed during the long geological period, since there were animals and vegetation which could not have existed without it. This means that the command of verse 3, 'Let there be light', is the restoration of light after a merely temporary darkness referred to in verse 2. It also means that the actual making of sun, moon and stars is included in the original creation of verse 1, since they are part of 'the heavens' referred to, and that verses 14–19 describe not the making but the appearance of these luminaries as the vapours surrounding the earth gradually cleared.

This last statement, however, is a plain contradiction of the text, as anyone can see who cares to read it; and including sun, moon and stars in 'the heavens' is simply to ignore a distinction which is also quite clear in the text. There is nothing in the text to suggest that the dark chaos of verse 2 was purely temporary, and verse 3 most naturally reads as the first creation of light. It is therefore not surprising that Buckland should require 'some little concession' from 'the literal interpreter of scripture', but when we recollect Bishop Horsley's uncompromising insistence on the plain meaning of Genesis 1, we realise that what is being asked for is no 'little concession'. Furthermore, Buckland has to assume that no human being existed in the long geological period supposedly covered by Genesis 1:1, and this put his biblical interpretation at the direct mercy of further geological and palaeontological research.

Buckland, however, did more than bend the Bible in a vain endeavour to make it and science speak with one voice. He

enunciated two principles which should guide biblical interpretation: first, that the Bible is solely 'a guide of religious belief and
moral conduct' and therefore never intended to give information
about divine operations 'with which the human race has no concern'; and second, that the record of the creation of our world is
relative to the needs and perceptions of mankind, and the details
of the text must be understood accordingly.[36] He himself pushes
the second principle too far, but it is more important to note that
it is capable of application far beyond the boundaries of Genesis 1.
The notion of revelation adapted to human capacity opens wide
the gates to acknowledgement of marks of human frailty in the
sacred text as a whole, and the need to disengage this from the
genuine divine message; which then demands production and
justification of the principles according to which we make the
distinction.

The first principle leads to the same conclusion. As it appears in
Buckland's argument, it suggests that any reconciliation between
Genesis and geology is unnecessary. He claims that it is 'proper
. . . to consider how far the brief account of creation . . . can be
shown to accord with those natural phenomena'; but this is not
proper at all if the Bible is a religious and moral guide and not a
manual of science. He claims that 'the results of geological
enquiry throw important light on parts of this history, which are
otherwise involved in much obscurity', forgetting that the
obscurity was divinely inspired and concerned 'matters with which
the human race has no concern'. The inconsistency is that of an
honest man caught between the idea on the one hand that God
cannot inspire error, and the fact, on the other hand, that human
error is all too manifest in the sacred writings, while at the same
time he wants to remain loyal to the profound truths which the
Bible contains. This could only be done by undertaking a
thoroughgoing revision of theology which would include restate-
ments of what we can mean or ought to mean by 'inspiration' and
'revelation', but the dominant natural theology not only did not
encourage such restatement but was a positive hindrance to it.

Within the Treatises themselves there are occasional hints of a
wholly different approach to the problems of rethinking and
restating religious belief in the light of a rapidly changing outlook
on the world. Bell asserts that there are other things in life which
make religious hope and belief profoundly significant for us, and

that these lie within the realm of personal relationships; that it is possible for human beings to know too much, to gather facts too great for the imagination to grasp. Such remarks reflect a certain uneasiness with the whole of the preceding argument of the treatise and betray an awareness that a much more fruitful line of thought lay in a quite different direction.[37]

William Whewell, in Book III of his treatise, 'Religious Views', argues that there is but one God. Man's moral and spiritual nature is intimately and necessarily related to the physical world, in which we see evidences of design and therefore the 'designer', God; but close interrelationship of the moral and spiritual with the physical argues for one God, himself of a moral nature. This is suggested by moral awareness, since there must surely be something corresponding to it in the universe at large.

This leads Whewell on to distinguish between the great discoverers in science, and those who engage in mathematical and mechanical deductions from great discoveries. The former are very few in number and often of a definite religious disposition. The latter are much greater in number, not always favourable to religion, and supporting wholly naturalistic explanations of the universe. Having reached this last point, the fundamental issue behind all other argument in the conflict between science and religion, Whewell argues that religious believers should not be alarmed, since a wholly naturalistic explanation of the universe is what might be expected from the kind of reasoning used by such mathematicians and technologists. According to Whewell, they take for granted the premises they are given and become too much impressed by chains of deductive reasoning and their application to given problems, forgetting the need for a power which designed the whole and which alone can give it life.

All of this might seem to be little better than a repetition with some variation of the invalid natural theology already so much in evidence, but Whewell was led on to the assertion that mathematical reasoning and that of 'mechanical philosophers' is wholly unsuited to demonstrating the existence and nature of God. For this we must turn to the moral experience of mankind, the awareness of moral commands which are sufficient of themselves to merit obedience, and to the personal hopes and values known to everyone. 'There can be no wider interval in philosophy than the separation which must exist between the laws of mechanical force and motion, and the laws of free moral action.'[38] This recognition of the limitations of scientific reasoning and strict deduction, combined with emphasis upon the moral and personal elements in experience, offered the possibility of far more fruitful argument than the main theme of the Bridgewater Treatises. It is a pity that Whewell's mind was too much dominated by the design argument and the vague concept of creatio continua to break away from the traditional approach altogether and follow his own insights into the nature of the evidence required for proper judgment in this case. His inconsistency had a potential for development regrettably not realised.

We may conclude this chapter with brief reference to *the problem of suffering*. It receives scant and superficial attention in a natural theology which is supposed to be demonstrating above all the extensive evidence of benevolent design in nature: a demonstration which is particularly urgent for those who wish to see the hand of God immediately evident in the processes of nature. Chalmers is the notable exception to this criticism, but the rest are lured, as Paley was when simply viewing nature as an external human observer, on to ground where God can only be defended on the Utilitarian principle; which merely raises the question why the omnipotent God should be a Utilitarian.

Roget, for example, declares that the intention of the deity is the enjoyment of life, and the immense and inevitable suffering of the animal world is dismissed as a minor evil which is permitted for the sake of vastly superior good. The laws of nature secure, on the whole, the greatest and most permanent good. Making one creature the food of another extends the benefits of existence to an infinitely greater number of beings than could otherwise have enjoyed them:

Thus does the animated creation present a busy scene of activity and employment: thus are a variety of powers called forth, and an infinite diversity of pleasures derived from their exercise; existence is on the whole rendered the source of incomparably higher degrees, as well as of a larger amount of enjoyment, than appears to have been compatible with any other imaginable system.[39]

Goethe gave expression to a rather different view and an interesting twist to the anthropological analogy:

> Denn unfühlend
> Ist die Natur:
> Es leuchtet die Sonne
> Über Bös und Gute,
> Und dem Verbrecher
> Glänzen wie dem Besten
> Der Mond und die Sterne.
> Wind und Ströme,
> Donner und Hagel
> Rauschen ihren Weg
> Und ergreifen
> Vorüber eilend
> Einen um den andern.

The echo of the Sermon on the Mount is unmistakable. Goethe's conclusion is that we have no choice but to imagine the gods, the 'unbekannten Höheren Wesen, Die wir ahnen', on the analogy of mankind. The divinely appointed laws of nature operate indifferently for all alike, and if rain falls on the just and the unjust, if the sun shines on both good and bad, then we cannot deduce the God of the Bridgewater authors simply by inspecting the rain and the sunshine.[40]

CHAPTER 6

Conservative natural theology:
Thomas Chalmers

Thomas Chalmers was the one theologian to contribute to the Bridgewater Treatises, with a work entitled *The Adaptation of External Nature to the Moral and Intellectual Constitution of Man.* To some extent he shared in the failings of the rest of the enterprise. He started out on the basis of the machine analogy and Paley's teleology, and he regarded it as self-evident that intelligence must spring from intelligence and that mind cannot spring from the workings of 'unconscious matter'.[1] Thus, from the very beginning there is built into the subject of Chalmers' treatise a profound division between the observing and reflecting human mind, and the natural environment.

What Chalmers claims to be self-evident is, of course, by no means so, and it certainly wasn't to Hume. Even if the point is granted, we are still left with the question how mind and person-ality are related to the material world, including our own bodies. This line of reasoning leaves us with the crude 'Ghost in the Machine' made famous by Gilbert Ryle, and all the problems of Cartesian dualism.[2] It emphasises the distinctness of observer and observed nature, an emphasis of crucial significance only too easily assumed rather than explicitly recognised, and leaves us with the question how an object of one kind is, or can be adapted to an object of a quite different kind. It may be that no answer to the question is possible, but in that case some explanation is required concerning the subject-matter of Chalmers' treatise as it appears in the title.

The dividing up of what is essentially a unity also vitiates Chalmers' attempt to demonstrate the absurdity of proposing chance as the governing force in the production of the present world rather than divine design. He argues that when two or more parts of a given whole function together for some purpose, the more parts there are, the less likely it is that they came together by accident and the more likely it is that design is exhibited. On this basis it is obvious that structures such as the human eye or the solar system comprise so many parts functioning together that the probability of accidental combination is remote indeed, and in the case of nature as a whole the probability against is well nigh infinite.

It is perhaps worth commenting, before going on, that discussion of such argument is no mere shadow-boxing with the ghosts of history. James Ward felt it necessary to deal with Chalmers' 'collocations' in his Gifford Lectures for 1896–8, and nearly a century further on Fred Hoyle makes precisely the same mistake as Chalmers in trying to destroy Darwin's theory of natural selection and demonstrate the need for a guiding intelligence in evolution. Hoyle presents us with the idea that evolution is arranging things and that they cannot possibly have been arranged as they are by means of random variations; and granted the initial assumption, the conclusion is irresistible.[3] If countless parts have to be combined in nature, it is unbelievable that they should have come together by accident.

As a matter of fact, however, parts of natural objects are only found existing in nature as parts of a whole and never separately. We do not find retinas or the ligaments and muscles of the human body or the fruit, leaves and branches of a tree coming into existence separately and then somehow coming together. Such separate parts are the product of human analysis. We are actually confronted by organic wholes which are themselves parts of larger communities of interdependent organic wholes, and all together form the great organic whole we call 'nature'. Artificial products, on the other hand, are made up of parts, and this makes them radically different from what appears by natural growth.

Furthermore, Chalmers is thinking of relatively large-scale parts: in the case of the eye, for example, parts which could be laid out on a plate or represented in an elementary diagram, each with its own properties and function; but these parts also have parts, and analysis can continue until we come to atoms and molecules, and then the forms of energy studied in physics. It is out of physical processes that the interrelated creatures of nature appear, and observation can provide no justification for the distinction between properties of matter on the one hand, and 'collocations' on the other. On Chalmers' view, if we start with fifty parts of a watch and fifty parts of an organism it is equally unlikely that either watch or organism will appear spontaneously, by chance. As a matter of fact, it is quite impossible for either of them to appear spontaneously, and no amount of juggling with the parts or leaving them alone will ever produce a watch or an organism. The one is irrevocably dead, and the parts of the other have to be fitted; and dressing up in terms of probability a comparison between things which are essentially different is merely misleading.

Nor is probability itself a matter of purely statistical calculation. Mere figures never tell us anything about the chances or probability of something being the case, and when they are held to do so, this is always because they are combined with knowledge of or assumptions about things and forces involved. If, for example, we throw dice a million times and get double six every time, the chances of the million and first throw being a double six are very high: but only because we have explicitly or implicitly drawn conclusions about the state of the dice or the will and skill of the thrower or some other such determining condition. Statistics may reveal patterns which suggest how forces are operating and therefore enable us to work out probabilities with greater accuracy.

This fact is obscured because in some situations we express *total* ignorance of the relevant conditions in terms of figures. If a full pack of cards including two Jokers has been assembled at random in our absence and left on the table, we might say that the chances of the Queen of Spades lying on top are one in fifty-four, thereby creating the impression of an accurate calculation, when all the figure represents is the confession that we have no basis for making any calculation at all. Some card must be at the top and it is just as likely or unlikely to be the Queen of Spades as any other. That is to say, mathematics by itself is useless as an instrument of discovery. In the words of A. N. Whitehead, 'There is no valid inference from mere possibility to matter of fact, or, in other words, from mere mathematics to concrete nature.'[4]

The concept of chance is never defined or explained by Chalmers, and yet the word may convey different meanings. We may use it to refer to the absolutely random or purely arbitrary, that which has no antecedent cause whatever. Or we may be acknowledging the existence of natural forces at work but confessing our ignorance of or inability to measure or control them, as in games of chance. Or we may be drawing attention to lack of intention, the purposeless, also to be seen in games of chance where the wishes of the participants cannot influence the course of events. Both the wholly random and the absolutely determined are purposeless, and 'chance' may refer to either case. Certain processes may be determined by antecedent conditions and also partially determined by will or choice, intention, aim, purpose. An 'accident' ceases to be such upon the discovery that the course of events was crucially influenced by deliberate action directed to the accomplishment of the actual end. In the absence of such influence, even if choices or aims affect circumstances in other ways, we still speak of chance and the 'accident' remains just that.

Chalmers, like his colleagues, rejected chance in the sense of the wholly random, and by using a false analogy in which the application of 'chance' in this sense is absurd, asserted what was obvious or even tautological at the expense of dodging the main issue. A sceptic who chooses to maintain that the world has come into existence by chance, in the sense that it is the consequence of physical processes working in a wholly determined way, uninfluenced by any conscious aim or purpose, is only referring to it as an 'accident' in a commonly accepted sense of the term. We may think the choice of analogy wrong, but we cannot brand it as absurd. If it is argued that the world has appeared by chance in the same sense that a double six may appear by chance when dice are thrown, this merely means that the forces at work operated without the control or understanding of some personality external to them: once again, a view we may reject, but which is no reductio ad absurdum. A century and a half after the publication of Chalmers' treatise Richard Dawkins has argued for precisely this alternative on the basis of considerable scientific research, although he prefers to speak of tamed chance rather than pure chance, a linguistic tribute to the ambiguities of the concept.[5]

Nevertheless, Chalmers began to develop a different and altogether more helpful approach to the problems of religion and science, as we can see from the second volume of his treatise and certain other of his works, especially his *On Natural Theology*, which contains passages closely parallel to some in the treatise.[6] In the *Natural Theology* Chalmers makes his own independent attempt to meet Hume's challenge. He had read the *Dialogues* and the *Essay on Providence and a Future State* and had taken the point. Paley's authority is still explicitly acknowledged, but there are clear signs of an attempt to break away from that devastating intellectual influence. He says of Paley, 'He . . . brings it forward as a general position, that wherever we meet with an organic structure where there is the adaptation of complicated means to an end, the cause for its being must be found out of itself and apart from itself.'[7]

Chalmers rightly finds this far from self-evident, and elsewhere in the same work, in a long passage expressing warm appreciation of Paley, nevertheless speculates, 'it were curious to have ascertained how he would have stood affected by the perusal of a volume of Kant'.[8] Curious indeed! Chalmers has for a moment forgotten about 'collocations' and glimpsed a view which would have revolutionised British thought if it had been fully appreciated.

Adam Clarke's a priori argument for the existence of God is firmly rejected: 'we fear that when he attempts to demonstrate the non-eternity of matter, and that to spirit alone belong the attributes of primeval necessity and self-existence, he leaves behind him that world of sense and observation within which alone the human mind is yet able to expatiate'.

Chalmers rejects the argument that an existence must be contingent if we can assert its non-existence without contradiction, and rightly insists that we cannot impose on reality a certain character merely because we can conceive things in a certain way without contradiction:

Because we do not see the reason why matter should have been placed here and not there in immensity – because we cannot tell the specific cause of its various forms, and modifications, and movements – because of our inability to explore the hidden recesses of the past – and so to find out the necessary ground . . . for the being and the properties of every planet and of every particle – are we therefore to infer, that there is no such ground, and for no better reason than that just by us it is undiscoverable.

According to Chalmers, the mere existence of matter does not prove the existence of God, and as far as mere observation goes, it could have been eternal. Furthermore, 'matter may . . . have the necessity within itself of its own existence – and yet that be neither a logical nor a mathematical necessity. It may be a physical

necessity – a ground of which I understand not.'⁹ The doubts
about Paley and the criticisms of Clarke amount to an admission
that the world revealed to the investigations of natural science
could have emerged through the working of purely natural processes which have continued to determine its manifold changes.

Early in his *Natural Theology* Chalmers confesses with respect
to Hume, 'The truth is that we do not conceive the infidelity of
this philosopher to have been adequately met, by any of his
opponents; whether as it respects the question of a God or the
question of the truth of Christianity.'¹⁰ Part of the strength of a
sound natural theology, according to Chalmers, is its initial recognition that we do not know God as we know other persons and
things:

> Our first remark on the science of Theology is, that the objects of it, by
> their remoteness, and by their elevation, seem to be inaccessible. The
> objects of the other sciences are either placed, as those of matter, within
> the ken of our senses; or, as in the science of the mind, they come under
> a nearer and more direct recognition still, by the faculty of conscious-
> ness. But no man hath seen God at any time. We 'have neither heard His
> voice nor seen His shape'. And neither do the felt operations of our own
> busy and ever thinking spirits immediately announce themselves to be
> the stirrings of the divinity within us. So that the knowledge of that Being,
> whose existence, and whose character, and whose ways, it is the business
> of Theology to ascertain, stands distinguished from all other knowledge
> by the peculiar avenues through which it is conveyed to us . . . certain it
> is, that we can take no direct cognizance of Him by our faculties whether
> of external or internal observation.¹¹

Chalmers answers this point by drawing attention to an element
in experience which can begin to lead us beyond those facts made
available to our consciousness through sense-perception and
mere introspection, and this element is our moral sense. He is
careful to distinguish between observation of the mind in a
Baconian sense, and the peculiar nature of the ideas of right and
wrong which form the subject-matter of ethics. Moral sense has a
special character which means that it cannot be satisfactorily
described or explained merely as one among all the other
phenomena of the mind. In his treatise Chalmers raises the question how the emotions which arise naturally within us can receive
moral praise or blame, and he finds the answer in determinations
of the will, through the selection of feelings to be encouraged and
those to be discouraged. This in turn means that judgment has to

be exercised, and it is here that morality enters in. Will is essential to the existence of moral worth or worthlessness. Moral sense, therefore, lies firmly embedded in human experience but cannot be explained simply in terms of it.[12]

Does this mean that morality points beyond itself to God? No clear and consistent answer to this question is given by Chalmers. He wishes to stress the categorical character of the moral demand: virtue has its own distinctive character apart from happiness or beauty or even the right of God to obedience. It is a fundamental truth that moral values remain even if there is no God. 'Though the world were to be transported beyond the limits of the divine economy . . . all sense of a ruling Divinity were expunged . . . still there would be a morality among men, a recognition of the difference between right and wrong, just as distinct and decided as a recognition of the difference between beauty and deformity.'[13]

It is easy to appreciate why Chalmers uses such emphasis, but if moral sense and aesthetic sense are to be thus equated, we also begin to wonder if moral feelings and judgments may not after all be susceptible of naturalistic explanation. If they exist as part of human experience regardless of God's existence, how can they lead us from the solitary confinement of that experience to God? The fact that moral feelings and ideas exist with their own identifiable character may turn out to be entirely explicable in the categories of social anthropology. We must sympathise with Chalmers to the extent of recognising that if that is the case, such moral feelings, and the judgments based on them, have been explained away; but perhaps this is the truth of the matter.

Chalmers' attempt to overcome the problem by comparing ethics with mathematics merely makes matters worse. According to him, ethical principles exist independently of actual facts, just as mathematical principles do. Mathematics may be applied to our observations of sun, moon, planets and stars, but the mathematics would remain with its own validity and truth even if these celestial objects did not exist. Similarly, ethical values remain even if there are no facts to which they may be applied, even if there is no God.[14]

Yet if this comparison is true, it follows that it is just as impossible to get from morals to God as it is to get from pure mathematics to the facts of astronomy. We may, of course, combine mathematics with some facts in order to infer other facts, and the inference can then be subject to confirmation or denial by experiment; and Chalmers produces an argument somewhat along these lines by asserting that we have an obligation to search for knowledge of God if there is no positive proof that God does not exist; and because there cannot in the nature of the case be such proof, since it would have to be based on omniscience, we must follow those inklings in experience that God does exist. All human beings have some idea of God, we are surrounded by evidences of design in nature, and there is the gospel of Jesus Christ. Thus does natural theology lead us to revelation.

By this time, though, Chalmers has forgotten his acknowledgement of what is correct in Hume's scepticism, the destruction of the design argument and the demonstration that human inklings can lead to conclusions about deity very different from those of Christian theism. Furthermore, mathematical demonstration and moral certainty are very different, a difference clearly revealed by reflection on the ways in which disagreements in the former are settled compared with attempts to resolve problems involving the latter. In his treatise we find a very different view of morality, containing precisely that rational potential for which Chalmers was seeking. There he tells us that the distinctive character of virtue derives from the fact that it is the nature of God himself. 'He acts virtuously, not because He is bidden, but because virtue hath its inherent and eternal residence in His own nature. Instead of deriving morality from law, we should derive law, even the law of God, from the primeval morality of His own character.' Morality 'is seated in the depths of His unchangeable essence, and is eternal as the nature of Godhead'.[15] If Chalmers had let his argument start out from this conviction, the real nature of religion's claim to commitment and its complete incompatibility with the use of reason in scientific investigation would have been laid bare.

This aspect of Chalmers' thought also enables him to offer the one attempt in the Bridgewater Treatises to give serious and extended consideration to the problem of evil. He firmly refuses either in his treatise or his *Natural Theology* to be drawn on to Hume's ground, and seeing virtue as the reflection of God's righteous nature, infers that we are not entitled to judge the divine exercise of creative power and providence merely in terms of beneficence. Nor is the attempt to establish a balance of good over evil sufficient, since we are still left with the question, 'why, under a Being of infinite power and infinite benevolence, there should

be suffering at all'.[16] The clue to the real answer lies within ourselves. The supremacy of conscience bears witness to the fact that
mere happiness is not the prime concern of God: 'however much
he may love the happiness of His creatures, He loves their virtue
more'. It is also the case that a great proportion of the evils which
trouble mankind have their origin in the human heart, and if we
try to imagine what life would be like 'were perfect virtue to revisit
the earth', we shall gain a much truer idea of why there is so much
misery in the world. This in turn means that we must avoid crude
misunderstanding of the divine omnipotence, since suffering, and
even sin, may be necessary to the accomplishment of greater good
in ways which we cannot understand.[17]

Such an argument was not, of course, a complete answer to the
problem of evil, and Chalmers freely admitted as much; but he did
claim that it was a sufficient answer to scepticism, granted that we
have other good reasons for belief in God, and his claim to have
'neutralized' scepticism in this way is reasonable enough.

Chalmers was moved by a genuine revulsion against the idea of
a universe ruled by physical necessity, indifferent to human joys
and sorrows and all that gives life significance. The *Natural
Theology* leaves us with a deep sense of human need, brought into
focus by death, the horror of which is emphasised by Chalmers,
who, like many others of his generation, knew from experience
the meaning of serious illness and the premature loss of family
and friends. 'Let the picture of all those joys which gladden the
family circle be rendered as touching as it may – it is death . . .
which turns it all to cruellest mockery.'[18] The design argument was
not inadequate merely on account of its invalidity: a watchmaker
God is too remote and impersonal. Human beings need a God
whose presence can be felt, and whatever confusions there may be
in Chalmers' overall argument, he clearly recognised that if
Christian belief is to be justified, a place must be found in our view
of the world for divine Providence and efficacious prayer. Inklings
of eternity are not demonstrations, and they may be regarded as
merely wishful thinking, but if they are dismissed we are left with
a universe which throws up and annihilates human life in a
manner wholly at variance with our own deepest feelings about its
significance.

At the same time Chalmers was too honest and well informed
not to gain a glimpse at least of what the developing sciences

implied for a general view of the world, and the way in which they were fleshing out what had been a genuine but abstract possibility in Hume's discursive philosophy. He was therefore placed in a quandary. It was all very well to use the limitations of natural theology as an introduction to the hope and consolation which only the revelation of the Scriptures could supply, but a more positive philosophy of nature was required, without which the Bible would stand isolated from the main currents of thought and the claim that it should be taken seriously would be increasingly ignored or contradicted. Like many contemporary religious thinkers Chalmers assumed that natural and revealed must be knit together in a unified philosophy. The uniformity of nature seen simply as the expression of regular physical causation was the great obstacle to the achievement of such a philosophy. He therefore grasped the nettle and attempted to reconcile science's basic principle with the essentials of Christian faith, divine Providence and prayer.

Chalmers believed that it was sufficient for him to provide a possible view of God's relationship to the world consistent with scientific method, and this leads him, regrettably, to depend on the analogy of human intervention in natural processes in order to justify the assertion of divine creatio continua: human influence in the natural world does not violate the laws of nature, and therefore the personal influence of divine Providence and response to human prayer do not violate such laws. When he then has to face the objection that such effects are not, as in the case of human action, actually witnessed, he replies at length that God's intervention takes place at points beyond the reach of observation and philosophy. For example, if we pray about a harvest or a voyage, what we actually observe are natural phenomena behaving according to their usual properties, but behind the scenes, as it were, God is determining these sequences in accordance with his own will.

This is clearly no argument at all. Chalmers cannot enjoy the luxury of the sceptic in this instance, for he is an advocate; and asserting that God is operating all the time in nature but that the divine operations are beyond the reach of observation and philosophy is mystification of the worst sort, not to speak of the dangers of a pantheism wholly at variance with his fundamental beliefs. It is perfectly true, as Chalmers insists, that there are conflicts between natural forces, and that we do not therefore surrender the established laws of nature. If magnetic power overcomes gravitational attraction in any given instance, there is not only no contradiction between the laws of nature, but we are simply provided with an example of that continual tension between forces which illustrates the laws and is their basis. In no way, though, does this justify the introduction of some force for which there is by definition no evidence. Even if belief in God is already satisfactorily established, this is no ground in itself for accepting the immediate divine presence and activity in natural processes.

Nevertheless, Chalmers did come close to a much more plausible answer to the problem, and this was at the point where prayer is likened to our attempts to influence other human beings, coupled with the fact that such influences do operate and that human beings do in turn influence the course of nature. If we take Chalmers' own examples of harvest and voyage, it is obvious that scientists can predict what will happen to a given acre of land left to itself or an abandoned vessel drifting in the open seas, even though such predictions will be limited, and even severely limited, by the number and complexity of the relevant facts. If, however, we incorporate the acre in a farm and man the ship, prediction becomes impossible when we are unaware of the human choices involved, but becomes much easier when we do know those choices. That is to say, the presence or absence of human life in any situation is crucial to the understanding of it, and if we can believe that the divine influence is exerted through that crucial factor, then the reconciliation between Providence and prediction has been accomplished. As we have seen, Chalmers elsewhere speculates about the transformation of a world ruled by perfect human virtue, and the speculation is not an idle one. In a Discourse concerning the connection between theology and science he refers to a sermon preached on the occasion of a cholera epidemic and in answer to the scorn which had been poured on the idea of a national fast, a spiritual discipline which it was hoped would persuade God to intervene and stop the epidemic. It is instructive to compare this view with his acknowledgement on a later page of the vigorous medical aid given to victims in Edinburgh and the consequent relative fewness of deaths in that city. Further reflection might have led him to see in this latter situation a true indication of how God can intervene in this world,

not merely to alter the course of nature, but to fulfil the moral
ends which are as much an integral part of the world's life as the
natural forces through which they may be expressed.[19]

Chalmers' thought contains a proper appreciation of Hume's
scepticism, along with positive insights and many passages of
sound argument; but loyalty to an invalid design theology and the
barren doctrine of creatio continua stifled the coherent development of a systematic philosophy. If Chalmers wondered how Paley
might have responded to the perusal of Kant, we may ourselves
wonder what the consequences for British thought might have
been if Chalmers himself had properly appreciated the Kantian
rather than the Paleyan reply to Hume.

Other authors who illustrate the second approach must be
considered more briefly, and in relation to certain major topics of
discussion.

Geology unquestionably constituted the major threat to
religious belief, but the fundamental reason for this implicated all
other natural sciences. This reason was the explanation of the
world's appearance purely in terms of *secondary, or efficient causation*, God being tacitly excluded from the process. In principle, of
course, this should have offered no difficulty to thinkers dominated by a design theology for which the machine analogy was a
basic assumption; but confronted by the detailed presentation of
nature as a system of spontaneously operating causes and effects,
believers were made more sharply aware of the need for clear,
positive demonstration of the divine contribution to events; and
the position was not improved, as Hume had shown, when nature
was viewed as a great organism. The inevitable evolution of one
state of things out of another had an alarmingly self-sufficient
character about it, and one which also threatened to overwhelm
human consciousness, and religious belief along with it. In this
desperate situation the desperate remedy was all too often an
appeal to the doctrine of creatio continua.

E. W. Grinfield rightly perceived that if the moral government
of the world is to have any significance man must be a free agent,
and that without this free agency the universe 'would be but a
mighty machine'.[20] However, this free agency is not merely human
but includes the activity of God: there is no demonstrable necessary connection between causes and effects, such connection being
established by 'the positive will of the Creator'. Laws of nature are

'the operations of an intelligent mind: not the blind results of necessity, not the capricious evolution of chance'.[21]

William Buckland's Inaugural Lecture at the University of Oxford, 15 May 1819, is an explicit justification of geology in the face of fears that it does harm to religion, as the title makes clear.[22] If geology lies under the imputation of being dangerous to religion, this is because of the attempt 'to explain every thing by the sole agency of second causes'. Fortunately 'the same proofs of subserviency to final causes' are found in geology 'which are so strikingly exhibited in the animal and vegetable creation'; but geology goes further in exhibiting the continuing divine superintendence of the world. The phrase 'laws impressed on matter' is a verbal fallacy and can only really denote 'the continued exertion of the Lawgiver, the first Mover'. The secondary causes investigated by geology give 'proofs of an overruling Intelligence continuing to superintend, direct, modify, and control the operations of agents, which he originally ordained', and 'the hypothesis of an eternal succession of causes is thus . . . removed'.[23] Whether or not such a view can be rendered consistent with Buckland's recognition of 'chemical and mechanical forces' regulated by 'the laws of matter and motion', effects which have their ultimate cause in atomic reactions which are and ever have been governed by regular and uniform laws, is another question.[24]

A writer who welcomed Buckland's *Vindiciae*, with its emphasis on design and the divine control of secondary causes, was James Kennedy, who gave the Donnellan Lectures for 1824 in the Chapel of Trinity College, Dublin.[25] In a Postscript to the Preface in the published lectures Kennedy refers to a review of Penn's *Comparative Estimate* in the *Westminster Review* for October 1825, in which the reviewer asserts that it had never been held derogatory to Almighty power that both creation and preservation took place through 'intermediate agents or secondary causes'. Kennedy rightly maintains against this that the difference between creation and preservation must be recognised and that secondary causes, being part of nature, cannot have existed until after the 'course of nature' had been created, and that creation itself is unique.[26] He gladly accepts the reviewer's opinion that geology supports the doctrine of final causes as well as giving evidence of upheavals in nature which cannot have resulted from secondary causation, but reveal divine 'interpositions'; yet Kennedy wishes to anticipate the possible discovery that such upheavals are actually explicable in natural terms. He therefore denies that secondary causes operate according to their own internal necessity, and sees them as selected and continually imposed by God on matter according to his will. He admits that it makes little difference in that case whether we regard God as acting through secondary causes or directly, but believes that concentration on secondary causes does introduce the danger of giving them undue importance and worshipping the creature rather than the creator. Accepting the independent efficiency of second causes is 'atheistic belief', since they 'are themselves creations'.[27]

Needless to say, no evidence is offered in support of these assertions. For Kennedy they are the necessary conclusions of religious belief, although they obliterate the distinction between creation and preservation upon which he first insisted, and contradict common experience and highly successful scientific method.

John Anderson, the minister at Newburgh, well illustrates the tension felt in the mid nineteenth century by the sincere religious believer also moved by a genuine interest in natural science, and the Preface in his book is an 'apology' for the publication of a work on geology. 'I have often, and with severity at times, questioned myself as to the propriety of my geological pursuits, my ardent love of them, and their compatibility with the strict discharge of professional duty.'[28] Design theology comes to his rescue, but he was nevertheless left uneasy with developmental hypotheses since he himself had to admit the existence of 'a gradual progression from the little to the great, from the insignificant . . . to the noble and the grand'. He tries to overcome this problem by asserting that each link in the chain is perfect in its kind and that all is controlled by God, although it is not theology's concern to decide whether that control is mediate or immediate.[29] Later, in an attempt to fit such ideas into an honest interpretation of Genesis 1, Anderson suggests that the ineffable acts of creation took place on literal days, but subsequent development took place over long periods: thereby preserving a distinction between the original unique creation beyond geological inquiry, and lengthy changes in the life of the planet which are open to such inquiry. However, no attempt is made to render this suggestion consistent with the idea of a gradual progression of life with its perfect links all under the direct or indirect control of God. It is precisely the idea of gradual progression over long periods which is utterly inconsistent with the Genesis account taken in its plain sense, whereas if the days of creation are slotted into the gradual progression from time to time, the consequent radical innovations should be striking features of the geological record – but such features do not appear. Not surprisingly, despite his own alternative suggestion Anderson felt reluctantly obliged to interpret the days of Genesis 1 as epochs, but his basic problem was how to avoid interpreting the geological record entirely in terms of efficient causation working gradually to produce the species we now observe.

In a popular work, the Revd Thomas Pearson of Eyemouth identified the fundamental enemy as a picture of the world dominated by secondary causes and thereby excluding providential care.[30] Pearson appeals to the usual design theology, Brougham's emphasis on the significance of the mental in human existence, and biblical miracles, but he admits that the machine analogy is defective. Men use already existing natural forces in making machines, and those forces themselves require explanation. Pearson finds this explanation in effect in the doctrine of creatio continua, supported by an appeal to geology as providing concrete evidence of repeated creations. He frequently attacks 'naturalism', the idea that physical processes can be entirely explained in terms of secondary causes, and he sees a link between 'The extreme scepticism of Hume, the old French atheistical philosophy', and 'exclusive attention to mere secondary causes', and the exclusion of 'a superintending providence'.[31] There are hints of an altogether more profitable approach in Pearson's book, but these hints are never developed.[32]

At about the same time as Pearson, Horace Bushnell in America was struggling to resolve the tension, not merely between science and religion, but between the view of Christianity and modern science as involved in a war of life and death, and the view of Christianity as 'the foster-mother of science' and science as 'the certain handmaid of Christianity'. Bushnell wanted harmony, but he was painfully aware of discord.[33] He sees the battle as one which religion is losing, and he also knows that there is no denying scientific method or the facts it uncovers. Nature 'is that created realm of being or substance which has an acting, a going on or process from within itself, under and by its own laws'. He correctly indicates the weakness of creatio continua: 'It is yet *as if* the laws, the powers, the actings, were inherent in the substances, and were by them determined . . . a chain of causes and effects, or a scheme of orderly succession, determined from within the scheme itself.'[34]

Bushnell's answer is to argue that the human power of choice and decision which manipulates and directs the system of causes and effects is the immediate obvious evidence of the supernatural, and that this provides us with the analogy of the way in which God operates on nature without destroying it. The miracles of Christ illustrate this, and it is essential to 'moral government'.[35] He also appeals to geology as witness to the intervention of God, who alone could have produced life on earth; which is tantamount to making geology as much a witness to the miraculous as the gospels. It would seem that Bushnell had not properly appreciated his own comment on the apparent self-sufficiency of causation: God's presence is not immediately evident in the workings of nature, not even in its upheavals and exceptional occurrences; but if we are treating the exceptional nature of the case as evidence of miracle, we are putting ourselves at the mercy of scientific advance, which may reveal exceptions to be evidence of ignorance rather than signs of the divine. If, on the other hand, Bushnell is really arguing that it is the moral and spiritual character of such events which makes them miracles, he must show in what sense such qualities, when revealed in otherwise apparently ordinary or natural events, transform these events also into samples of the miraculous. This is not a reductio ad absurdum of Bushnell's case, but a plain statement of what is required if, as with Pearson and Chalmers, more fruitful lines of thought are to receive their proper development.

Thomas A. G. Balfour, MD, published a volume which started out as an address to medical students, in which he wished to demonstrate nature's symbolic witness to Christian truth.[36] It was sufficient for Balfour that nature was readily susceptible of interpretation in the light of Christian revelation, provided only, we may add, that the pious imagination was restrained by some care in the selection of rationalised illustrations; but shortly afterwards he produced another volume intended as an introduction to *The Typical Character*, and to prove that nature symbolises the kingdom of grace.[37] Basic to his argument is the identification of divine power with forces at work in nature. He therefore has no qualms about the fact that 'we find no distinct boundaries in nature, no abrupt transitions; but in this grand picture we have a most beautiful example of perfect shading, so that we insensibly find ourselves contemplating the subject of another kingdom, while we were not aware of having crossed any boundary line'.[38] Nature's perfect shading had already been subjected to a much more rigorous analysis and a conclusion drawn utterly devastating to Balfour's kind of religious fantasising; and if nature could be appealed to in support of belief, she could also prove fickle and bestow her favours on undisguised scepticism. If nature really is the picture of God continually at work, Hume's question as to what we must infer about God becomes pressing indeed.

The conflict between the findings of geologists and the assertions of the Bible is notorious, and it is one which seems scarcely worth reviving. Today we sympathise spontaneously with the geologists. The dating of a fossil in a lump of rock, or the dating of the rock by means of the fossil, was a fascinating exercise for some people, and no one could blame them for disputing the relevance of ancient religious texts to its proper conduct. On the other hand, innumerable fossils in the multifarious strata of the earth's crust might be taken to imply an evolution of the earth and its creatures during an unimaginable span of time entirely explicable in terms of secondary causes; and while such causes are still with us, perceptible and more or less intelligible, God, however dressed up in such laudatory terms as the great First Cause, has become too remote to be significant. The attempt to restore God to his creation by means of teleology was invalid, and by means of a thinly disguised pantheism even worse. It is not surprising, therefore, that religious believers clung to the authority of the Bible with the tenacity of survivors at sea clinging to substantial, if gradually disintegrating, wreckage. Whatever might be true of current philosophy, the Bible offered the hope of genuine life, and the endeavours of believers to get the right understanding of a few sentences in an ancient religious text formed part of a whole metaphysical enterprise in which Genesis and geology do meet: and the basic issue is still with us.

Chalmers, writing early in the century, could be dismissive of geology.[39] The contrast is made between Moses the acknowledged historian who lived at a time near to the recorded facts, and the airy-fairy speculations of a distant posterity, 'the fanciful and ever-varying interpretations of philosophers'.[40] Geologists are infidels who have strayed into the domain of the historian, and the burden of proof lies on them, not the defenders of the faith. We cannot place confidence in scientific conjecture, even when used to support religious belief, over against the weighty testimony of Moses.

Yet despite this robust confidence, Chalmers is obliged to make concessions which ominously foreshadow the shape of things to come. Robert Jameson, in his notes on Cuvier's *Essay on the Theory of the Earth*, had suggested that the 'days' of Genesis 1 should not be taken literally but as representing the long epochs uncovered by geologists. For Chalmers, this attempt at reconciling Genesis and geology smacks too much of the merely defensive, and such laxity of comment, 'if suffered in one chapter of the Bible, may be carried to all of them, may unsettle the dearest articles of our faith, and throw a baleful uncertainty over the condition and the prospects of the species'.[41] Nevertheless, he accepts that all geologists are agreed on the vast antiquity of the earth: there is no division of scientific opinion here in which the religious believer may seek refuge. This in turn means that he has to provide his own interpretation of Genesis 1:1–2, according to which the vast expanse of geological time is implicitly located between the initial creatio ex nihilo of verse 1, and the chaos out of which our own world emerged in verse 2: a reading just as artificial as Jameson's, and just as fraught with danger for the believer in unquestionable biblical authority.

Buckland was able to dispose of geological eras after the manner of Chalmers, but the Deluge was another matter, since it took place within the lifetime of mankind on the planet and could not be conveniently ignored as part of the chronological void supposedly implicit in Genesis 1:1. Yet all argument would go for nothing and the worst fears of many churchmen be confirmed if it had to be admitted that geology contradicted the biblical narrative; and if the Deluge did occur, geologists must surely find some trace of it. A few years after his Inaugural Lecture, therefore, Buckland devoted a whole volume to the subject, the lengthy title making quite explicit the attestation of geological phenomena to 'An Universal Deluge'.[42]

The work is dedicated to Bishop Shute Barrington, who had

encouraged the investigation upon which it is based, and the dedication acknowledges the relevance of geological studies to the truth of the Mosaic narrative and therefore, by implication, to the authority of the Bible. Nevertheless, what is striking about the book's contents is the way in which they reflect Buckland's enthusiasm for geological research and the irrelevance of the biblical Deluge to the interpretation of the mass of findings he recorded. A cave at Kirkdale in Yorkshire was discovered in the summer of 1821 and examined by Buckland in the following December, and a comparison was then made with similar caves in England and Germany. The general picture to emerge was of mud, pebbles and animal remains so disposed as to demonstrate the action of flood water rushing in with great force and then gradually retiring, consistently with the biblical narrative. Ironically, however, Buckland had to admit that the remains at Kirkdale, along with those at Kühloch, gave no evidence of disturbance at all, and he concluded that they had been somehow protected from the flood's ravages. The proper conclusion, of course, was that they offered evidence against the identification of the contemporary flood waters with a universal deluge, above all a deluge of the dimensions described in the Bible.

It was inevitable that a man like Buckland, continually confronted by fact and reason, should eventually be compelled to recognise the futility of trying to square the facts of the geological record with the details of an ancient myth, and in his Bridgewater Treatise the argument for the Deluge is laid to rest.[43]

Along with geology, *astronomy* sometimes forced conservative commentators into the reconciling mode of interpretation. The Westminster reviewer with whom James Kennedy concerned himself in his Donnellan Lectures was so bold as to assert that 'No ingenuity, nor any perversion of Scriptural commentary, can reconcile the solar system, or that of astronomy at large, to the Mosaic history.'[44] Astronomical facts were too well established and too closely associated with the name of Newton for anyone to dream of challenging them; and Kennedy himself starts out with the acknowledgement of geology as a genuine science. His response therefore comprises a mixture of qualifications and forced renderings of the text which are obviously, if unintentionally, fatal to the idea of biblical inspiration generally accepted. According to Kennedy, the biblical writers used a popular style and were not concerned to present their readers with the full principles of science. He refers to Bird Sumner's view that pre-Adamite convulsions of the earth, like the galaxies, 'are matters of curious reflection and sublime interest', but of no concern to specifically religious belief. The sharp discrepancies supposed to exist between Genesis and the findings of science disappear when the language of Scripture is 'duly appreciated', and it is even strong evidence of inspiration that in certain instances there is deviation from the exactness of philosophical language, since such language would have baffled those for whom revelation was originally intended, and would interfere with the main aim of Scripture, which is to convey moral and religious instruction.

As one struggles through the intricacies of Kennedy's lengthy argument one wonders if it would not have been wiser simply to admit that the accounts of creation and the assertion of a universal deluge are wrong, but for Kennedy the pentateuchal records 'are incomparably the most ancient, the most precise, and the most authentic documents which have been transmitted, relative to the first formation of the physical and moral world', and the facts they record coincide with those revealed by science, such coincidence being itself strong evidence of inspiration. Kennedy's justification of this claim, which must ultimately stand or fall according to the meaning of the text, takes the form of a long and complicated exposition: the geological record is implicit in Genesis 1:1–2; the recorded order of events in Genesis 1 is dictated by reference to final causes; the 'firmament' is not solid but denotes the atmosphere; the 'heavens' of verse 1 include sun, moon and stars; the light of the first day is an independent agent of vision with which the sun is later invested; the moon is at the same time in inferior conjunction, but in just the right position to 'rule the night' when this is stated to have happened.[45]

Kennedy had taken the reviewer's challenge to heart, but his mentally exhausting display of ingenuity merely proves the reviewer's point.

John Pye Smith, Divinity Tutor in the Protestant Dissenting College at Homerton, read the text somewhat differently in his attempt to make science and an infallible Bible speak with one voice. He acknowledged that there was no clear geological evidence for a universal deluge, and he dwelt at length on the impossibility of the Ark containing all species and the equal impossibility of their dispersal from Ararat. Geology also bore witness to a continuity of animal and vegetable life which was incompatible with the existence of a universal chaos immediately preceding the creation of our present world at anything like the sort of date indicated in the text, and an honest recognition of these facts led Smith to surrender the idea that chaos and flood were universal and to see them as localised, confined to the area inhabited by mankind.

This suggestion is implausible enough, but Smith's honesty led him into further difficulties over the general picture of the world presented in Genesis chapters 1 and 2, which is one of perfect peace and harmony, with death entering the world as the penalty for human sin. Let it be immediately conceded that there is room for disagreement over exactly how to understand the text on the subject of death: nevertheless, the pain and carnage among animals to which science testifies has been continuous throughout the earth's history, and, as Smith himself agreed, an essential condition of organised existence. To deny it would therefore be to deny the laws of nature, which are also expressions of God's will, and for Smith this was an intolerable contradiction.

He argues therefore that death and the knowledge of it are implicit in the biblical narrative before the Fall. Adam and Eve must have known what death meant, since they understood the divine warning that they would die if they ate the forbidden fruit; and there must have been carnivores, since otherwise all animals would have had to be herbivorous. The divine command to be fruitful and multiply means the preservation of the species but the inevitable passing away of the individual; yet this cannot apply to individual human beings before the Fall, and so they must have been exempted from natural death in the original state of innocence, simply passing from one state to another without dying. The laws governing the dissolution of animal bodies did not apply to the human constitution.

Smith seems to have forgotten that in the original condition of the world according to Genesis, the animals and mankind feed on the earth's vegetation: an ideal state of affairs which the prophet Isaiah believed would return under the reign of the Messiah. Nor would Adam and Eve have to be acquainted with actual death in order to grasp the meaning of God's warning; and to deny the gradual dissolution and death of human bodies is not to reconcile nature's laws with the text but to imply their irrelevance to its proper understanding, which is the exact opposite of Smith's intention.

In dealing with certain other texts, Smith has to invoke further principles of interpretation to help out a struggling exegesis. We gather that since mankind does not have direct knowledge of God, God can be thought of only in terms of analogy drawn from experience and that therefore revelation must take place in the same terms. This principle is reasonable enough, but it is next applied to the Bible when it speaks of natural phenomena, and is interpreted to mean that expressions and ideas were used 'such as comported with the knowledge of the age in which they were delivered': in fact, a very different matter. Smith, however, goes even further and claims that the New Testament provides us with a

justness and purity of conception concerning 'the things of God', far superior to that which the ministration of Moses and the prophets could supply. The one was obscure, tinctured with the spirit of bondage, only a preparatory and temporary system.

We are therefore

fully warranted by divine authority, to *translate* the language of the Old Testament upon physical subjects, into such modern expressions as shall be *agreeable to the reality* of the things spoken of.

Thus armed Smith can, for example, reject the false translation of *raquia*, 'the firmament', as 'expanse' or 'atmosphere', and admit that it refers to a solid sky. In discussing the meaning of 'earth' he can insist that the biblical language is not meant to convey physical knowledge; that it is adapted to the ideas and capacities, the wants and conveniences of mankind, and this means that the creation of the heavenly bodies refers to their appearance through the atmosphere and their being instituted as lights and a calendar for human beings. All of which is tantamount to admitting that there is no reconciling the biblical picture of the universe and that being unfolded by the natural sciences, and that if the latter is right, the former is wrong. It was also difficult, to say the least, to reconcile such comments on the Old Testament with Smith's own definitions of inspiration and revelation, and it is not surprising that he was accused by some conservatives of being himself tainted with anti-evangelical German Neologism.[46]

Hugh Miller's attractive piety and reverence for the Bible are unquestionable. So also is the fact that he was a born naturalist, with a special interest in geology, but keenly observant of the men, women, and lesser creatures in his environment. As with Buckland and others in a similar position, honest recognition of the facts uncovered by scientific research was integral to his outlook, and was part of his active life. The facts, therefore, once established by observation and reasonable inference, could not be gainsaid. This leads him to recognise the cruelties and killing among the creatures which took place long before the appearance of mankind on the earth, and therefore long before the Fall. He rightly rejects Pye Smith's attempt to localise the pre-creation chaos as not in accord with the actual assertion and clear intention of the text, as well as lacking geological support; and he also rejects the long gap proposed by Chalmers and Buckland between the original creation and the production of the present world. At times he even seems to be on the point of breaking away from the conservative approach altogether:

The geologist, as certainly as the theologian, has a province exclusively his own; and were the theologian ever to remember that the Scriptures could not possibly have been given to us as revelation of scientific truth, seeing that a single scientific truth they never yet revealed, and the geologist that it must be in vain to seek in science those truths which lead to salvation, seeing that in science these truths were never yet found, there would be little danger even of difference among them, and none of collision.

'Plain men' have made false deductions from the Bible: that the earth is flat, the sun moves, the earth is about six thousand years old. They have been corrected by geographer, astronomer and geologist. The Bible is 'in reality intended to teach, – the way of salvation . . . in every instance in which they have sought to deduce from it what it was *not* intended to teach, – the truths of physical science, – they have fallen into extravagant error'.

Science is concerned with what is discoverable by investigation. The Scriptures are concerned with what passes beyond the investigable: the divine authorship of the universe, the progressive character of God's workings, the sabbath as 'a prophetic reference to the great dynasty to come'. Miller therefore rejects those who try to find natural philosophy revealed in Genesis: 'men such as the Granville Penns, Moses Stewarts, Eleazar Lords, Dean

Cockburns, and Peter Macfarlanes'. 'No true geologist ever professes to deduce his geology from Scripture.'

The conclusion we naturally expect is that the Gordian Knot shall be cut, the futile endeavour to find consistent accuracy in biblical assertions concerning the world and universe completely surrendered, and some more appropriate ground of biblical religious belief looked for than the facts discoverable to systematised human curiosity; but our expectations are disappointed. Instead we are plunged back into the fantasy world of make-believe interpretation and foregone conclusion. In the conflict between contemporary scientific fact and biblical scientific fiction, the former is recognised, but the natural recognition of the latter blocked by some kind of spiritual and intellectual apprehension. The Revd Dr M'Cosh is quoted to the effect that 'Science has a foundation . . . and so has religion. Let them unite their foundations, and the basis will be broader, and they will be two compartments of one great fabric reared to the glory of God.' Miller's true insights should have made him suspicious of the idea of uniting foundations so unalike, but in the absence of a concept of revelation which could include the notion of God communicating spiritual truth either by means of or despite biblical fiction, there was no alternative.

Miller therefore had to find room for geological time somewhere, and this was accomplished by making the six days of Genesis 1 into vastly extended periods, although he had initially taken them to be ordinary days of twenty-four hours each. He also argues at length for a localised deluge, biblical phrases which suggest universality being regarded as metonymic. The miracle whereby all species would survive a truly universal flood was more than the experienced naturalist could allow, and a restricted flood could still make the moral point.[47]

It was still necessary, of course, to show that the order of creation in Genesis 1 and in the geological record was the same, and Miller believed this to be so. He was defended against criticism by a certain James C. Fisher, who may be referred to as a final example of what can be done to the biblical text if we really put our mind to it.[48] Fisher refers to and rejects Chalmers' and Pye Smith's attempts to reconcile Genesis and geology, and supports the view of Miller and others that the Genesis day is actually a vast period of time, claiming that the great majority of geologists adopt the same interpretation. He then makes the geological record relevant only to the third, fifth and sixth days of creation. Days one and two concern the initial creation of matter and its dispersal throughout space; and day four the arrangement of the heavenly bodies in their proper working order. In verse 5, 'day' first means 'light' and expresses its principal character 'and is in this respect like our word *caloric*, with which it seems to be identical in meaning'. In the latter part of the verse it means a long period of time. The Hebrew grammatical particle *eth* in verse 1, which indicates that the following noun is in the accusative case, is translated by Fisher as a noun itself, meaning 'the substance of'; and translations of *raquia* as meaning something solid are rejected as merely childish. For Fisher it means the expansion throughout space of already existent matter.

Such gross misinterpretation is not to be dismissed as simply silly. It is ingenious and not uninformed: but it is a rationalisation of the text based upon the fatal principle, held to by both Miller and Fisher, that 'philology' can only be sound when it does not commit the Scriptures to assertions which science has shown to be untrue; and this despite Miller's acknowledgement that science cannot be derived from the Bible, which is concerned with truths beyond scientific investigation.

One of these truths was *the unique character of divine creation*, partly recognised by Miller and partly ignored. He took the seventh day 'rest' of God to mean the period of redemption, the saving and elevating of mankind, and he rightly saw in the divine sabbath a clear indication that God's creative work had ceased and could not in the nature of the case be repeated. He was also aware, however, of the sceptical conclusions Hume had drawn from the necessary ignorance of human beings concerning creation, but instead of holding to his genuine insight and facing the essentially philosophical issues which had been raised, turned to geology for the answer. With reference to Hume's essay on Providence and the future life he says,

Now, it has been well said of the author of this ingenious sophism – by far the most sagacious of the sceptics, – that if we admit his premises, we will find it difficult indeed to set aside his conclusions. And how, in this case, does geology deal with his premises? By opening to us the history of the remote past of our planet, and introducing us, through the present, to former creations, it breaks down that *singularity* of effect on which he built, and for one creation gives us many. It gives us exactly that which, as he truly argued, his contemporaries had not, – an *experience in creations.*[49]

Elsewhere Miller argues that geology supports natural theology by demonstrating that what exists now had a beginning and that this cannot be explained in terms of natural development: 'But when the Lamarckian affirms that all our recent species of plants and animals were developed out of previously existing plants and animals of species entirely different, he affirms what, if true, *would* be capable of proof; and so, if it cannot be proven, it is only because it is not true.' The point is emphasised, and it is stated with reference to certain shells, 'But no such genealogy can be formed. We cannot link on a single recent shell to a single extinct one.'[50]

This was a dangerous path to follow: once links were established where previously they had been unexpected and unknown, it was Hume who would appear as victor; while at the same time the real, philosophical issues, had not been addressed.

Pye Smith had a philosophy of sorts, and as we have seen, recognised that *analogy* was essential in human talk of God, and therefore, we must assume, in talk of divine creation. Smith depended on the generally accepted design theology and such writers as Clarke, Paley and the Bridgewater authors for detailed discussion; but he also himself argued that what is contingent and dependent presents itself to our senses, but that reason compels us to infer a First Cause which brought the world into existence and gave it motion. The original creation referred to in Genesis 1:1 was ex nihilo, and Pusey's note in Buckland's Bridgewater Treatise is criticised as 'very obscure and quite nugatory', presumably because Pusey refused to see in the verb *bara* itself any reference to creatio ex nihilo. According to Smith, the vast succession of changes taking place over vast periods of time has continued ever since the original creation, and according to processes still in operation. The temperature and constitution of the atmosphere is the same now as when God first created man and the animals associated with mankind, and the state of matter as first created 'falls within the province of General Physics to examine'; and there is therefore nothing wrong in principle with the nebular hypothesis, since God endowed these original simple bodies 'each with its own wondrous properties'; and these properties worked and are still working according to God's ways, that is, our 'laws'.[51]

On reading such assertions one feels that Hume might never have lived; but whether or not, the alternative reading of the evidence remains, and was and is a threat to religious conviction in the absence of a valid response. If figurative talk of God and his creative work is not based on direct acquaintance, it must have its basis elsewhere, but it will not be found simply by observing natural events.

The Revd Renn D. Hampden, later to achieve notoriety over his appointment as Regius Professor of Divinity in the University of Oxford, acknowledged that the use of language to convey truth about God necessarily involves analogy, and that scriptural revelation must use human ideas and language, these being the expression of minds adapted to the course of 'outward nature'.[52] Thomas Balfour made this the basis of his whole appeal to nature as a revelation of God, obviously unaware that his statements were capable of very different interpretation. Balfour criticised Paley for claiming to prove the existence of God independently of revelation, but actually bringing to his argument the assumption, which can only be learnt from the Bible, that man is made in the image of God. If the assumption were wrong, then we might be misreading the divine mind. Balfour aims to supply the deficiency by concentrating on nature alone, and his first proposition is that 'all language is originally a symbol borrowed from Nature: therefore, all our knowledge of spiritual things is derived, indirectly at least, from Nature'. God adapts his ways to our corporeal constitution, and therefore 'no *direct* knowledge of spiritual truth can be obtained, since it is only by material objects that the mind takes cognizance of the truth'. 'The *material* element in language appears if we attempt to describe the spiritual world.' 'That all language was originally figurative is very manifest also . . . '[53]

The sceptical empiricist could scarcely ask for more. If spiritual, divine truth is so bound up with nature, why look elsewhere for its origin? Balfour read his biblically based theology into the natural world, just as did Gisborne, who saw geological evidences of tremendous convulsions in the earth as signs of God's wrath against sin; and Grinfield, for whom the world presented the picture of a Paradise in ruins.

Dubious interpretations of the Bible, or nature, in the interest of forced reconciliations between the Bible and science could only in the end destroy biblical authority, and at the same time threaten to destroy religious faith itself and any hope of a meaningful life for humanity; although the religious thinkers who made the attempt did not see things that way. Pye Smith maintained that the truth of his biblical interpretation was quite independent of natural science and stood upon its own evidence: an assertion which was both absolutely sincere and absolutely false. He and others like him saw themselves as honest believers basing their faith and biblical exegesis on the obvious principle that the Word of God in creation and the Word of God in revelation must be in perfect harmony. Belief in the historical character of the Mosaic narratives, let alone faith in their accuracy, may seem to us to be no more than an interesting intellectual fossil, helping the curious to reconstruct what seems to be an infinitely remote climate of religious opinion, and throwing into sharp relief the truly threatening character of critical scholarship for the people of the time. Science has long since triumphed over the protestations of the ignorant or prejudiced, and disputes about the so-called Mosaic narratives carry us back to the age of alchemy. It would seem best to leave the curious to their harmless pursuit.

Nevertheless, if this is our decision, we are guilty of a serious misjudgment. Charles Gillispie in his *Genesis and Geology* states:

The most embarrassing obstacles faced by the new sciences were cast up by the curious providential materialism of the scientists themselves and of those who relied upon them to show that the materials of a material universe exhibit the sort of necessity which results from control instead of the sort which springs from self-sufficiency. The work of the scientists supported a providentialist view which managed to be at the same time mundane and supernatural – mundane as to appearances and supernatural as to inferences.

Later Gillispie returns to the theme: 'if the infinity of physical adaptations on which this popular theology rested turned out to stem from their own interactions and not from a managing Providence, what became of the Supreme Lawgiver?' The question shows that the providential materialism referred to was not merely 'curious'.[54] Humean scepticism presented the possibility of a world entirely governed by physical necessity, and 'natural philosophy' threatened to transform the possibility into reality. This same scepticism also apparently destroyed the claims of reason to draw conclusions about God and the future life because reason could only operate on the foundations of human experience within this world, and never get beyond it.

When, therefore, religious thinkers tried to produce a reading of the Bible consistent with the facts established by scientific research, they did so as part of an overall attempt to meet a scepticism utterly destructive of Christian religious belief. If they had merely been concerned to preserve the value of ancient writings despite their outmoded view of the physical world, they would have had no more difficulty in doing so than in a similar exercise with respect to the Dialogues of Plato or the works of Roman and Greek poets and dramatists. The case of the ancient literature sacred to Jews and Christians was different because it was regarded as revelation from God. Thus did metaphysics and natural philosophy compel a response from nineteenth-century religious believers never before experienced in the history of the Church.

A self-consciously strict conservative response was, at least in theory, possible. In the face of reason's confessed poverty the Bible would be accepted as a divine revelation, the miraculous record of self-evidencing miracles. We cannot rise to God and he therefore comes to us, and in this way human experience and the Bible might be supposed to combine and thus provide us with the basis of a sound incarnational theology. Miracles are by definition breaches of nature's uniformity, and that would be precisely why they should offer irrefutable helps to human weakness in the acceptance of the religious and moral truths of the Bible.

Anyone who could swallow this religious philosophy was and is in an impregnable position. He could swallow Hume's scepticism whole as well, provided his faith was large enough, as Hume himself indicated in the bitterly sarcastic conclusion to his essay on miracles. There were, and there are, those who are prepared to make the attempt, although this is not to be confused with the innocent conservatism which knows nothing of metaphysical scepticism, biblical scholarship or scientific methodology. Sophisticated and self-conscious conservatism requires determination, and involves concentration upon religious and moral lessons of the Bible selected according to the culture or sub-culture to which the believer belongs. It implies a clear-cut division between those who believe and those who do not, because the biblical message is

simply accepted as the bearer of salvation, or it is not. Reason may
be allowed to frisk happily among its natural companions, but into
the pastures ruled by faith it comes not at all; or only on a tight
leash and under strict prohibition of worrying the sheep. Therefore as knowledge grows in the community at large, and argument
proceeds, the tension between biblically based faith and a secular
outlook becomes more and more powerful. As increasing numbers of people find the abdication of reason an impossibility in
that area of life which is most important to any human being, so
the circle of the truly faithful, Bible in hand, shrinks, making a
virtue of its own paucity.

Those believers who were not prepared to abdicate reason were
also unable to swallow Humean scepticism, and this in turn meant
finding an answer to it. Whatever the reply might have been, the
actual response involved combining biblical revelation with a
mixed acknowledgement and denial of truths in Hume's arguments. The honest endeavour to produce a system of belief doing
justice to all the facts demanded an account of the concept of
revelation, as applied both to the Bible and to the world of the
present-day believer. The thinkers who made the attempt were
fighting a war on two fronts: one concerning the truth revealed in
the present to natural scientists about the world and human life;
and the other concerning the truth revealed in the Bible about the
world and human life. It was absurd to suppose that the two could
remain separate, because this would imply that there were two
mutually exclusive truths relating to the same subject. The principle to which Buckland and others made half-hearted appeal, of
making the Bible the authority on moral and religious matters,
and thereby relieving the inspired authors of the responsibility of
getting their science right, itself raised rather than solved problems. Religious beliefs and moral judgments cannot simply be
divorced from the rest of experience, and they have implications
for the world of which we are a part, and either fit in with the rest
of our knowledge of the world, or do not; and this includes the
concept of revelation, which itself requires some explanation if
significant parts of the 'revelation' are false.

If, for example, Moses' teaching that the world was created, a
religious belief, is bound up in the text with assertions about the
order of creation and the time it took wholly at variance with growing knowledge, the explanation that God's purpose in communi-

cating with Moses was purely religious and moral is inadequate. The conveying of religious truth does not explain or excuse the misleading of Moses as to matters of fact. If we then speak of divine adaptation to human ignorance, it is difficult to imagine what state of mind Moses must have been in not to be capable of comprehending that the world he knew had been brought into existence over a very long period rather than six days, or that the sun and stars had been made before rather than after the appearance of the earth.

An adequate metaphysical response to Hume would have made possible and encouraged a complete reappraisal of the concept of revelation, and in that case biblical critical scholarship would have been welcomed as a friend and incorporated into a larger intellectual outlook and discipline. Instead, British natural theology was flawed and inadequate, and weakness on this front involved the desperate attempt to preserve inherited notions of revelation on the other, and the implicit obligation to preserve the text, the whole text, and nothing but the text. From this point of view critical scholarship could be seen as nothing other than an enemy, the virtual surrender not only of this or that biblical assertion, but a whole religious philosophy. Nevertheless, the conservative thinkers who fought this battle are not simply to be dismissed. A repetition of their mistakes can be avoided and their genuine insights welcomed. Above all, it is possible to appreciate their instinctive awareness that a biblically based Christianity faced a challenge, the evasion of which would be as serious as defeat: and the challenge has remained and is stronger than ever.

CHAPTER 7

Liberal natural theology

It is obvious, but perhaps all the more worth stating on that
account, that much scientific research was carried out in the nineteenth century without any reference to actual or possible conflict
with religion. Many technical issues had no apparent connection
with religious belief, and in any case the truths revealed to careful
observation and intelligent experiment remained truths regardless of human taste, feeling and judgment. Furthermore, such
matters had their own fascination for certain minds, whereas
theology and biblical study did not; and if the essence of religion
was to walk humbly with one's God, such humility could only be
deepened by an increased appreciation of the works of God in
nature. Indeed, contemplating the wonders of creation might
seem to be a far more elevating occupation that participating in
endless, and at times acrimonious, theological and biblical debate;
and the pursuit of scientific research had nothing to gain by
attaching to itself the burden of ecclesiastical censure.

A glance at the early volumes of the *Edinburgh Review* reveals
much free discussion of scientific matters: chemistry, mineralogy,
geology and a new French Natural History in twenty-four volumes,
involving reference to such men as Black, Irvine, De Luc, Werner
and Lavoisier. The *Edinburgh New Philosophical Journal* was very
largely devoted to technical scientific matters, this being actually a
cause for complaint by the Very Revd Dean Ramsay in his Opening Address to the Royal Society of Edinburgh, 2 December 1861.
The Dean wanted, alongside such technical subjects, more time
and space devoted to topics of a more general cultural interest;
thus bearing indirect witness to the dominating influence
exercised over many reflective minds by the novel revelations of
practical empiricism.[1]

Problems arose for religious belief only when the believer saw in science as a whole, or more particularly in evolutionary ideas, an alternative explanation of things which excluded God; or when scientifically based assertions about the world contradicted biblical assertions. For example, Erasmus Darwin's poem 'The Temple of Nature; or, the Origin of Society' received severely critical comment in the second volume of the *Edinburgh Review* for 1803: Darwin was accused of leaving behind the proper role of observer because he had proposed spontaneous evolution of 'living, intelligent, and moral existence' through 'the spontaneous operation of chemical laws and affinities', 'from sluggish and unorganized matter'; all of which was 'in *substance* little else than some of the wildest theories of "Zoonomia" done into verse'.[2] Likewise, when his grandson published *The Origin of Species* later in the century, critical responses appeared in the *Edinburgh New Philosophical Journal*, motivated at least as much by religious as scientific considerations. We have already seen that the threat to the Bible could have similar consequences.

On the one hand, therefore, scientific research could produce a mass of results which no one dreamt of denying, thereby bestowing on scientific method almost unquestionable authority; while on the other hand that authority could be challenged where evolutionary hypotheses were concerned because such hypotheses went well beyond the immediately observable and the clearly demonstrable. Serious disagreements among eminent scientists could also lend specious plausibility to such challenges, especially if religious-minded scientists were prepared to go along with them. Nevertheless, there were those who saw the fundamental danger to religion in this kind of approach. This was the unlikelihood of scientific methodology being proved ultimately wrong, and the much greater likelihood of disagreements, uncertainties and mistakes being the fruit of ignorance; ignorance destined to be removed by the patient application of that same methodology to the solution of empirical problems. To accept science in most areas of its activity but to deny it in some other area where it was or appeared to be inconsistent with religious belief was to deny the uniformity of nature, the rationality of the universe.

The third approach to the conflict of religion and science was therefore characterised by insistence that properly established facts and the uniformity of nature which they exhibited must be accepted; that the truth or falsity of scientific hypotheses and theories must be decided by expert investigation and discussion, and could not be settled a priori by religious considerations; and that natural theology must show how to incorporate new knowledge into the overall view of the world held by the Church. Thinkers in this category were also not interested in defending the infallibility of the Bible and were not prepared to cling to biblical assertions if these were contradicted by scientific discovery. In this last respect Horace Bushnell was a borderline case between the second and third approaches, and illustrates the danger of taking historical generalisations too literally. Bushnell asserted that Christianity cannot be defended by an appeal to infallible Scriptures, since if only one error is found, then the authority of the whole corpus is destroyed; and he believed that both textual criticism and geology had already ruled out such verbal infallibility. Nevertheless, he appealed to the authority of the Bible to correct what he felt was wrong with scientific method, and made it the basis of his attempt to reunite the supernatural and the natural; the more specific basis being St Paul's teaching in Colossians that Christ is the one in whom all things con-sist. The overall balance of his thought was therefore nearer the second than the third approach.[3]

Representatives of this third approach will be found to vary somewhat, in their attitude both to the Bible and natural theology, although some kind of convincing natural theology would have to be produced if such an approach were to become generally acceptable; and this theology would have to include constructive statements about inspiration and revelation which would preserve or strengthen the authority of the Bible while at the same time surrendering the idea of biblical infallibility. Thinkers in this group generally failed to meet the challenge, Baden Powell being a notable exception, in that he did make the attempt. There was strong interest in freeing scientific research from interference on religious grounds, and a strong tendency to accept design theology without further examination, even if sometimes Paley was felt to be open to criticism; and the Bible received what could only be regarded by conservatives as cavalier treatment, and by those inclined to scepticism as a tacit confession that modern knowledge had utterly destroyed the idea of the Bible as 'revelation'.

Sir John Herschel's famous *Preliminary Discourse* for example, is based on the bland assumption that all will be well between science and religion provided scientists are allowed to get on with their work unimpeded by considerations extraneous to such research. Herschel refers to strong feelings which have been expressed on the supposed threat of science to religion and which are 'still occasionally brought forward'. The suggestion, in 1830, that conflict belongs largely to the past is noteworthy, although Herschel still feels the need to combat and comment on it. Herschel rejects the attempt to reconcile specific scientific assertions and apparently inconsistent biblical assertions: we may be confident in the basic principle that 'truth can never be opposed to truth', and that the answer to such problems lies in free inquiry which will uncover truth at present obscure to us. The deity is revealed in an harmonious nature: 'the testimony of natural reason, on whatever exercised, must of necessity stop short of those truths which it is the object of revelation to make known'; but in itself 'it places the existence and principal attributes of a Deity on such grounds as to render doubt absurd and atheism ridiculous'. However, 'to ascend to the origin of things, and speculate on the creation, is not the business of the natural philosopher'.[4]

The machine analogy was clearly a basic assumption for Herschel, but his chief wish was to engage in research without the distraction of engagement in wider controversy. The result was facile optimism and unintentional hints at an atheistic view of life. According to Herschel science is pursued primarily for its own sake, but it does have many practical advantages, and he believes that the success of scientific method will have a beneficial influence 'on the more complicated conduct of our social and moral relations'. Furthermore, 'In whatever state of knowledge we may conceive man to be placed, his progress towards a yet higher state need never fear a check, but must continue till the last existence of society.'[5] A closer acquaintance with history and human nature suggests otherwise.

Charles Babbage also assumed the truth of the design argument and believed that this enabled him to justify the progress of mathematics and the sciences in religious terms, while at the same time dismissing the relevance of awkward biblical texts to such matters. He produced what he chose to call *The Ninth Bridgewater Treatise*, although it formed no part of the original project.[6] It was intended as a rebuttal of Whewell's view that mathematical and mechanical reasoning are incapable of leading us to knowledge of the existence and nature of God. According to Babbage, the analogy between human manufacture and divine creation is inevitably imperfect but essentially true: and therefore, just as we admire most the machine which requires no interference for its proper working, so we admire in the creation the display of laws of nature which reflect an intelligence and foresight infinitely superior to our own. Consequently every increase in the knowledge of nature draws attention to objective facts which strengthen the design argument.

Likewise, what we call 'miracles' are events obeying laws of which we are at present ignorant. It would be possible to make a machine working with perfect regularity which nevertheless produced occasional results quite out of keeping with the usual pattern, and this is the way in which nature produces so-called miracles.[7]

For Babbage it followed from all this that natural religion had the advantage of being based on present knowledge and experience, while revelation depends on human testimony, the reliability of which weakens with the passage of time; and this was well illustrated for him by the impossibility of reconciling Genesis and geology. The plain evidence of the senses and reason presented by geological research could not be denied; on the other hand, Moses wrote long ago for a scientifically ignorant people, adapting his message to their intellectual capacity and expressing it in a language the precise meaning of which is now lost to us. If Genesis and geology cannot be reconciled, neither can they be said to contradict each other: we simply cannot know the original sense of the text.

Thus was Babbage able to skate over the awkward problems of biblical exegesis along with those raised by an invalid natural theology, and he thereby illustrated Whewell's point about the limitations of mathematics and the mechanical philosophy rather than replying to it. A clever model of the universe might be produced which simulates the complex unfolding of events according to laws expressible in relatively simple equations, and as a pioneer in the construction of the computer, Babbage was well able to appreciate the fact; but such a deterministic model throws no light on the problems of evil and the opportunities for good in human and animal existence. Babbage himself recognised the serious difficulty which exists for the religious believer in accepting the idea that all is determined beforehand by an all-wise and good creator, when the 'all' includes so much that is evil and painful, but he had no answer to it; nor, within the intellectual limits he had set himself could he have had.

Sir Charles Lyell well illustrates the need of an adequate religious philosophy and the strength this would have given to the Church. It is customary to associate the name of Huxley with strong opposition to the baleful influence of conservative clergy on science and education, and with crucial powerful support for Darwin's evolutionary hypothesis, but Lyell rivalled Huxley in the first respect and was of distinctly greater significance in the second. Unlike Huxley, however, Lyell remained a faithful member of the Church and paid something more than lip service to the value of religious belief.

Lyell regarded geology, biblical interpretation and religious philosophy as distinct disciplines, and was quite explicitly opposed to any kind of interference by the second and third with the first. He saw clearly the utter futility of trying to find geological evidence in support of the biblical Deluge, and delightedly reported in a letter to Dr Fleming, Professor of Natural Philosophy in King's College, Aberdeen, that Sedgwick 'Throws overboard all the diluvian hypothesis; is vexed he ever lost time about such a complete humbug . . . '[8] He was intrigued by Buckland's endeavours to reconcile Genesis and geology, but with the curiosity of one gazing at the spectacle of an attempt at the impossible. In November 1839 Pye Smith wrote to Lyell, 'My views of the restricted locality of the Adamic Creation and Deluge appear to me to be fully in accordance with the phraseology of Scripture; and they liberate Science and Theology from difficulties which seem to be otherwise insuperable';[9] but we may doubt that Lyell was impressed. Years earlier, in a letter to his sister Marianne, Lyell stated that he had written to Copleston, Bishop of Llandaff, 'to tell him among other pleasant news, that I meant to do my best to show in volume ii that no deluge has swamped Europe within 4,000 (I might have said 40,000) years. On his other points I was fully agreed with him, and on this I told him I had no objection to his drowning as many people as he pleased on such parts as can be shown to have been inhabited in the days of Noah.'[10] In other

words, biblical interpretation could be left to those who were
interested in it, provided geologists were likewise left to draw their
own conclusions by their own legitimate methods. Ironically,
Lyell's impatience with forced reconciliations is also revealed in
his admiration for Horsley's comments on Genesis. In his Journal
to Miss Horner, 2 December 1831, he says regarding a volume of
Horsley's sermons, 'one of which on the discrepancy of Genesis
with certain philosophical discoveries is very striking, and perhaps
the most straightforward, manly, and to-the-point declaration that
any eminent divine has made'.[11] As we have seen, there was no
inclination in Horsley to bend the meaning of Scripture to bring
it into accord with contemporary thought.

The virtues Lyell admired in Horsley were displayed by himself
in his epoch-making *Principles of Geology*, the first volume of which
was published in 1830. After the opening chapter Lyell gives an
outline of ancient religious and philosophical speculations, and
an outline history of geological investigation, illustrating in particular controversies bedevilled by extrinsic considerations. His
aim was very clearly to get geology separated from such religious
and philosophical speculations, to distinguish physical theory and
its appropriate evidence from religious views. The Bible is rejected
as a guide in geological matters, and Lyell makes clear the retard-
ing effect of conservative theological and religious views on the
progress of science as such. With respect to the Mosaic deluge he
asserts, 'Never did a theoretical fallacy, in any branch of science,
interfere more seriously with accurate observation and the systematic classification of facts.'

In short, a sketch of the progress of geology is the history of a constant
and violent struggle between new opinions, and doctrines sanctioned by
the implicit faith of many generations, and supposed to rest on scriptural
authority. The inquiry, therefore, although highly interesting to one who
studies the philosophy of the human mind, is too often barren of instruction to him who searches for truths in physical science.[12]

It was, however, one thing to speak of sinking the religious
diluvianists and all such theological sophists,[13] but a very different
matter to proceed from there to the construction of a correct
theology and a reasonable approach to biblical interpretation. It
was relatively easy to show that the Bible and geology made
irreconcilable assertions and to praise the manly honesty of
Horsley; but for the serious religious believer this was not so much

the conclusion of the argument as the beginning. In a letter to George Ticknor written in 1850 Lyell complained,

The vulgar hear the first chapter of Genesis read out without comment or the smallest explanation from ninety-nine out of a hundred pulpits, and they grow up in the belief of the modern origin of the globe, and the unity of the creation of man and the globe, and all the inhabitants which have ever lived upon it since the beginning. Hence they regard scientific men with suspicion and with prejudice . . . [14]

Precisely, one may add, the view of Horsley. The Bishop, in common with many other churchmen, would have wondered what kind of authority the Bible possessed if it stood to be corrected by men like Lyell.

Even worse were the broader implications of Lyell's strictly scientific views. These implications were drawn out by Charles Darwin from the premises supplied by Lyell in his *Principles*, and with typical modesty Darwin gladly acknowledged the fact. ' "I always feel", he wrote, "as if my books came half out of Lyell's brain, and that I never acknowledge this sufficiently; nor do I know how I can without saying so in so many words – for I have always thought that the great merit of the *Principles* was that it altered the whole tone of one's mind, and therefore that, when seeing a thing never seen by Lyell, one yet saw it partially through his eyes." '[15] It is well known that Darwin took with him the first volume of the *Principles* on his voyage with the *Beagle* and picked up the second volume during the journey. This reading had been recommended by Henslow, Professor of Botany at Cambridge, but with the additional warning not to accept Lyell's views. A warning, however, which was to no avail. In his *Autobiography* Darwin stated, 'I have always felt that I owe to the voyage the first real training or education of my mind'; geological study brought reasoning, as against mere observation, into play; and practical experience 'showed me clearly the wonderful superiority of Lyell's manner of treating geology'.[16]

Lyell's methods of investigation depended on explaining all physical changes in terms of secondary causes; causes which have operated throughout the earth's history, and which are observable today, operating according to immutable laws. He could see that such explanation could be applied to organic as well as inorganic change, including the origin of species; but he hesitated to accept the idea that secondary causation was a sufficient explanation,

however necessary its recognition might be in any complete picture of the world's origins and development. In a letter to Sir John
Herschel, dated 1 June 1836, he stated, 'In regard to the origination of new species, I am very glad to find that you think it
probable that it may be carried on through the intervention of
intermediate causes.' Lyell had been severely criticised by a
German audience for denying spontaneous generation but not
putting anything in its place, thus requiring the continual miraculous intervention of the First Cause, and contradicting his own
'doctrine of revolutions carried on by a regular system of secondary causes'. Lyell goes on to speak with admiration of the idea
that there has been a succession of species, coming and going in
relation to changing physical conditions; and he refers to the considerable effect which even very slight changes, such as those seen
in varieties, could have on survival.[17]

Darwin's development of such evolutionary ideas remains his
own unique achievement, but the difference between Lyell and
Darwin was not merely one of scientific emphasis in their chosen
areas of research. The complete explanation of the origin of
species, especially including the human, in terms of secondary
causation inevitably led to an agnosticism which Lyell was not
prepared to embrace. On the one hand, Lyell wanted to separate
geological research as completely from philosophy as from
biblical study. On the other hand, in neither case could he escape
the connection. In the *Principles* he distinguished geology from
cosmogony, just as the history of mankind should be distinguished
from speculations concerning man's creation, and while embracing and encouraging naturalistic explanation, he wanted to retain
an element of the unknowable or mysterious in causal sequences.
A few years after the publication of Darwin's *Origin* he wrote to
Hooker, 'I feel that Darwin and Huxley deify secondary causes too
much. They think they have got farther into the domain of the
"unknowable" than they have by the aid of variation and natural
selection.' Nevertheless, he could write to Haeckel in 1868 thank-
ing him for the recognition that he, Lyell, had advocated as early
as January 1832 a law of continuity applicable to the organic as well
as the inorganic world. 'I contended that this succession of species
was now going on, and always had been', although the cause of
new species was beyond comprehension, and 'it remained for
Darwin to accumulate proof that there is no break between the

incoming and the outgoing species, that they are the work of evolution, and not of special creation'. 'I had certainly prepared the way in this country, in six editions of my work before the "Vestiges of Creation" appeared in 1842, for the reception of Darwin's gradual and insensible evolution of species.'[18]

It is not surprising that Lyell's German hearers accused him of sidestepping the issue. The advancement of science itself, with its revelations of the infinitely complex and subtle outworkings of nature's very varied 'laws', enables us to sympathise readily with talk of unknowability and mystery; but confessions of scientific ignorance and helplessness are no basis for affirmations of positive religious belief. Today's scientific ignorance is also today's scientific opportunity. If the present state of our earth, galaxy and the universe is the inevitable, determined outcome of its whole previous dynamic state, then there is no room for the workings of or evidences for transcendent deity; and the situation is not improved for religious belief by the introduction of a significant element of the purely random. Despite disclaimers about the connection of geology and metaphysics, Lyell was driven to make the connection, but all he could do was to fall back on the current design theology. In his *Principles* he refers to past controversy in order to introduce his own view:

Hutton answered Kirwan's attacks with great warmth, and with the indignation justly excited by unmerited reproach. 'He had always displayed', says Playfair, 'the utmost disposition to admire the beneficent design manifested in the structure of the world; and he contemplated with delight those parts of his theory which made the greatest additions to our knowledge of final causes.' We may say with equal truth, that in no scientific works in our language can more eloquent passages be found, concerning the fitness, harmony, and grandeur of all the parts of creation, than in those of Playfair. They are evidently the unaffected expressions of a mind, which contemplated the study of nature, as best calculated to elevate our conceptions of the attributes of the First Cause.[19]

In part of his Journal to Miss Horner, dated May 1832, Lyell admitted that during a lecture, 'I worked hard upon the subject of the connection of geology and natural theology . . . concluding with a truly noble and eloquent passage from the Bishop of London's inaugural discourse at King's College, in which he says that the truth must always add to our admiration of the works of the Creator, that one need never fear the result of free inquiry.'[20]

This was unfortunately more an assertion of pious hope than well-grounded belief. Lyell's appointment to the post of Professor of Geology in the newly established King's College, London, was in the hands of the Archbishop of Canterbury, the Bishop of Llandaff and 'two strictly orthodox doctors'. The Bishop, Copleston, opposed the appointment, but doubts were for the moment overcome. 'The prelates declared "that they considered some of my doctrines startling enough, but could not find that they were come by otherwise than in a straightforward manner, and (as *I* appeared to think) logically deducible from the facts, so that . . . there was no reason to infer that I had made my theory from any hostile feeling towards revelation."'[21] Clearing Lyell of ill-motivation, however, could not settle the main issue, and in 1833 he resigned. He wrote to Fleming, 'I regret that the bishops cut short my career at King's College', and the regret was genuine because he saw in this institution the first formidable and much-needed opposition to or competition with the old universities. He accepted the opinion of Agassiz that the prospects for science in England were very poor 'because of the power of the English Church' and 'narrow views of our dissenters'. He believed the cause of science would suffer if ever the clergy got the mechanics' institutes into their power, and the Puseyites were bitterly accused of excluding science from Oxford. He feared that the sales of his *Principles* would be harmed because of its implications for 'the Mosaico-geological system', and his fears were strengthened by the unexpectedly sharp reaction to Milman's *History of the Jews*.[22]

Nevertheless, Lyell's conflict with the religious establishment cannot simply be explained as the confrontation of enlightenment and dark bigotry, any more than it can be explained away by pointing out that he combined in his own person genuine scientific interest of a high order and genuine religious belief. Lyell received a copy of Lamarck's *Philosophie zoologique* early in 1827 and was delighted and fascinated with it. Yet it raised disturbing questions with which he wrestled to the end of his life. If naturalistic explanation, the tracing out of unbroken chains of cause and effect, was sufficient to account for the appearance of plants and animals, it was surely sufficient to account for the appearance of man. If natural forces could produce new species, we would seem to be ascribing to them a creative power proper to God alone. On the other hand, if God intervened directly in the processes of nature to create new species, this contradicted the basic principle of explaining natural phenomena in naturalistic terms. Persistent divine intervention would blur the distinction between First Cause and secondary causes, and possibly make God directly responsible for monsters and a host of other evils in nature. In the end Lyell could only fall back on the design argument, but if genuine difficulties arose for the religious view of human life out of the kind of work he and Darwin were doing, then such difficulties existed for Puseyites, bishops and dissenters, too. This is not to deny that there was a natural jarring between Lyell's liberal, tolerant outlook and the real narrowness and bigotry of many conservative-minded clergy, but it is to deny that the nineteenth-century conflict of science and religion can be adequately described in such terms. Lyell and his ecclesiastical critics were all alike hamstrung by the lack of a valid philosophy.

Thomas Dick produced a relatively light and popular work which no doubt fulfilled its main purpose of bringing to a large section of the population up-to-date information concerning the wonders of scientific discovery and technical invention. However, it also raised issues which Dick was neither willing nor able to tackle.[23] Charles Gillispie refers to Dick's fears that religion and science were becoming separated because mechanics' institutes often forbade discussion of religious topics and because British scientists had begun to omit allusions to God and his physical providence from their publications and lectures. Gillispie thinks that Dick's fears were premature as far as the first half of the century was concerned; but Dick is not likely to have been mistaken in such a matter. Pye Smith complained that Lyell too often spoke of creation and nature when he should have spoken of God, and we have already noted Roget's recognition of the linguistic problem in his Bridgewater Treatise.[24] It is significant that Dick should not only want to keep the general reading public informed concerning the achievements of science and technology, but should feel obliged to do this in relation to possible offence against religious belief. Dick reveals obvious enthusiasm for the work of scientists and inventors: but references to the Bible and natural theology are introduced in order to demonstrate against hostile theological criticism that the study of nature ought to be a recognised part of

Christian thought and reflection. Regrettably he showed no conception of what was really needed for the establishment of
harmony between inspiration and rational investigation.

Dick has no doubt that reason left to itself is utterly depraved
and that only revelation can enable reason to abolish the reign of
ignorance and degrading superstition; but once so enlightened,
reason can greatly increase our appreciation of the revelation of
God in both nature and Scripture. Contrary to the fears of certain
theologians, the expansion of the human mind does not
endanger Christianity, and the message of the Church in its
proper fullness contains something more than what are known as
the doctrines of grace. The scripturally enlightened mind will find
God in nature, as indicated by Paley and the design philosophy.

So far, so good. The real trouble comes when Dick feels compelled to make more specific remarks about the declarations of
science over against those of Scripture:

If, in any one instance, a Record claiming to be a revelation from heaven,
were found to contradict a well-known fact in the material world . . . it
would be a fair conclusion, either that the revelation is not Divine – or
that the passages embodying such assertions are interpolations – or that
science, in reference to these points, has not yet arrived at the truth.[25]

Dick, however, has in mind scientifically established facts which
cannot reasonably be disputed, and where these are concerned 'It
may be laid down as a universal principle, that there can be no real
discrepancy between a just interpretation of Scripture and the
facts of physical science.' From which it follows

as an infallible rule for Scripture interpretation . . . *That no interpretation
of Scripture ought to be admitted which is inconsistent with any well authenticated
facts in the material world . . . Where a passage of Scripture is of doubtful meaning, or capable of different interpretations, that interpretation ought to be preferred
which will best agree with the established discoveries of science.*[26]

Dick goes on to illustrate what he means by reference to specific
passages, a hotch-potch of not unfamiliar forced reconciliations
between scientific and biblical assertion.

There were no doubt those in the Church who felt that with
friends like Dick, enemies were superfluous. Biblical interpretation and therefore Christian doctrine would be at the mercy of
ever-changing scientific opinion; and if the day should come, or,
who knows, had already come, when the 'facts of physical science'

really contradicted the sacred text, there could be no doubt, on Dick's principles, as to which must give way. Not one to spare the theologians, Dick plainly asserts:

Now, the scientific student of Scripture alone can judiciously apply the canon to which I have adverted; he alone can appreciate its utility in the interpretation of the sacred oracles; for he knows the facts which philosopher and astronomer have ascertained to exist in the system of nature; from want of which information many divines, whose comments on Scripture have in other respects been judicious, have displayed their ignorance, and fallen into egregious blunders, when attempting to explain the first chapters of Genesis, and several parts of the book of Job – which have tended to bring discredit on the oracles of heaven.[27]

At another time and in another place Dick would have been fortunate to escape with the fate of Galileo, but like that impetuous genius, he did have the future on his side. There is nothing subtle or profound about Dick's volume. Indeed, it gives the impression of a certain innocence, but of the variety which does know an unclothed emperor when it sees one: and his book must have found a large number of readers. What is sad about this well-meant venture is that, like the child in the tale, Dick could only sum up the essentials of the situation without being able to offer real clothing as a replacement for purely imaginary protection.

An altogether more sophisticated thinker than Dick was Henry, Lord Brougham, who nevertheless suffered just as much as Dick from the lack of a valid and coherent philosophy. The Society for the Diffusion of Useful Knowledge, founded by Brougham, had been strongly urged to publish an edition of 'Dr Paley's popular work' with far more scientific illustration; but some members felt that this enterprise 'might open the door to the introduction of religious controversy among us, against our fundamental principles', and the project was therefore abandoned. Brougham, however, was determined to proceed, and the result was a four-volume edition containing not only Paley's *Natural Theology* with Brougham's comments, but a great deal of supplementary argument from Brougham and 'A Treatise on Animal Mechanics' by Sir Charles Bell.[28]

In the dedication to John Charles Viscount Althorpe, Brougham justified the presentation of his own opening 'Discourse' by the need to re-establish the importance of natural theology in view of the scepticism with which it was regarded by many thinking people. Brougham did not share Dick's belief that revelation is needed to release reason from its depravity before it can become a help to religious belief. Indeed, he adopted the very different stance that natural theology is actually

necessary to the support of Revelation. It may be proved or allowed, that there is a God, though it be denied that he ever sent any message to man, through men or other intermediate agents . . . But Revelation cannot be true if Natural Religion is false, and cannot be demonstrated strictly by any argument, or established by any evidence, without proving or assuming the latter.[29]

Brougham appealed for support to Locke's well-known statement that removing reason to make way for revelation puts out the light of both, since reason is truth's mode of entry into the human mind, whatever its source. Natural theology in this case becomes not only a defence of religion against sceptics and atheists, but also a reply to 'friends of Revelation' who have contended 'that by the light of unassisted reason we can know absolutely nothing of God and a Future State', and who look upon natural theology as discrediting the gospel.[30]

Brougham's view implies that the men and women involved in the biblical 'revelation' had themselves to receive the truth through their human reason, and this is the way we must all receive the truth about God; and it is therefore better to receive such truth direct rather than on the basis of secondhand testimony. Indeed, we really have no alternative.

Brougham, however, was well aware that the friend of revelation would appeal to the evidence of miracles to show that God had acted in exceptional ways to convey otherwise inaccessible truth to the specially chosen individuals who produced the Bible; and this created a dilemma for him, although he seems not to have been conscious of the fact. To accept the miraculous would be to surrender his stance; but to reject the miraculous would be to embrace the scepticism of Hume while at the same time maintaining the dubious proposition that the whole of Christian doctrine could be established by natural theology.

According to Brougham, the claims of revelation rest upon miracles; but even if miracles have taken place, they do not establish the unity, benevolence or omnipotence of deity, or that man is destined for a future state, or even that deity created man in his present condition. Even worse, the belief that miracles took place might be false since this depends on testimony for all but the actual witnesses, and the strength of such testimony weakens the further removed it is from the actual occurrences. Nevertheless, he refutes Hume's essay on miracles and argues for the possible strength of testimonies to the miraculous, rather along the lines of Paley's *Evidences*, although without referring to Paley. The charge of inconsistency is avoided because he explicitly stops short in his note on Hume's essay of discussing the actual evidence for biblical miracles, but in his main text he does no justice to the varying character of miracles, and therefore does not face very pertinent questions about the nature of Jesus' miracles or the reliability of the apostles and evangelists. He says of Jesus' miracles that they were not denied by the ancients, presumably meaning Jesus' and the Church's Jewish enemies; 'but it was asserted that they came from evil beings, and that he was a magician. Such an explanation was consistent with the kind of belief to which the votaries of polytheism were accustomed. They were habitually credulous of miracles and of divine interpositions. But their argument was not at all unphilosophical.'[31]

Like all those impaled on the horns of an unrecognised dilemma Brougham wants to have it both ways: against Hume he insists that a kind of testimony to miracle is possible, and that this would have to be accepted even if it meant surrendering the absolute uniformity of nature. At the same time, unlike Paley, he dismisses the actual evidence that Jesus performed miracles, makes it virtually impossible that his criteria for reliable testimony should be fulfilled, and denies that any religiously or philosophically worthwhile conclusions can be drawn from the occurrence of miracles even if such testimony should be accepted. Hume would not have complained.

Brougham looked at the Bible with eyes dazzled by the achievements of natural science, and he clearly regarded any attempt to found religion on miracle as extremely hazardous, and instinctively leaned towards an appeal to the facts of nature which were, or could at least in principle be universally recognised. He appealed to Bacon's dictum that atheism is not to be refuted by miracles, but by the contemplation of nature, and he tried to make a distinction between the function of revelation to teach us proper ritual worship, and the function of natural religion to teach us the existence and powers of God: all of which leaves us, in fact, resting upon the not very solid foundation of design theology.

Here also, Brougham was partly conscious of the weaknesses in the design argument. In his *Discourse* he refers to Paley's watch and explains that we distinguish this as a man-made article from what grows wild because we learn this distinction by experience; which suggests that we do not make the distinction, as Paley asserted, because one thing has parts functioning together for a purpose while the other does not. He also points out that Paley 'assumes the very position which alone sceptics dispute. In combating him they would assert that he begged the whole question; for certainly they do not deny . . . the *fact* of adaptation.' However, far from abandoning the argument, Brougham reasserts it: when we contemplate the eye, constructed as it is to achieve vision, we rightly infer a maker, 'Because we nowhere and at no time have had any experience of any one thing fashioning itself, and indeed cannot form to ourselves any distinct idea of what such a process as self-creation means'. In that case, we wonder what Brougham meant by things growing wild and being found in the earth. The distinction between the artificial and the natural which he has just attributed to the spontaneous recognition of experience is now denied. 'Self-creation' and 'fashioning itself' have become identified with human modes of production and the whole argument thereby reduced to nonsense.

He also argues from the fact of adaptation to a divine maker in precisely the same way as Paley, but insists on the superiority of his own form of the argument because he believes he has demonstrated that mind always exists independently of matter. Therefore the purposeful mind evidenced in natural adaptation of means to ends must exist independently of nature, just as the human mind does.[32] To which sceptics would reply that the inference from the fact of adaptation to its origin in conscious design was just as much a *petitio principii* for Brougham as for Paley; and his assertion of mind's independence of matter simply contrary to observation. The facts concerning mental life appealed to by Brougham, although very significant, no more supported his conclusions than they did in the case of Paley. What is noteworthy is that he could be very much aware of Hume's scepticism and see the fatal objections to the orthodox natural theology, but still remain quite incapable of breaking away from it and embracing or producing a genuinely fresh philosophy.

The controversy over Robert Chambers' anonymously published *Vestiges of the Natural History of Creation* is well known, and it is possible to dismiss the book as an ill-informed anticipation of the much more securely grounded theory of evolution proposed by Darwin and Wallace; but this is to miss its real significance.

Chambers opens his book[33] with an acceptance of the nebular hypothesis, ruling out chance and emphasising the 'sublime simplicity' of the uniform laws which governs all, the necessary inference beyond the scope of science that 'there is a First Cause to which all others are secondary and ministrative, a primitive almighty will' beyond the grasp of finite faculties, and whom man can only contemplate with wonder and adoration. At the same time, Comte's calculations using mass, gravitation and distance in the *Cours de philosophie positif* are quoted with approval, along with reference to the work of the Herschels.[34] The next chapter concerns chemical elements, suggesting that there is a similar basic matter throughout space, appearing in different forms according to varying conditions. Geology figures largely in the book, and it teaches us 'that the same laws and conditions of nature now apparent to us have existed throughout the whole time'. Life originates naturally, the opposite assumption being 'directly opposed to the principles of philosophical investigation'. Endeavours to produce life experimentally are not impious, because this is merely an attempt to arrange the conditions under which divine creative energy could be 'pleased to work'.[35]

The argument for a natural development from simple to more complex forms of life over a very long period of time is supported by an appeal to the natural processes we can actually observe. Man takes his zoological place in the whole scheme, 'the true and unmistakable head of animated nature'; although 'without regard to the distinct character assigned to him by theology'.[36]

Chambers does not spend much time on biblical interpretation, but he concedes that if Scripture clearly supported the idea of direct creation, this would constitute 'a strong objection to the reception of any opposite hypothesis'. However, 'I do not think it right to adduce the Mosaic record, either in objection to, or support of any natural hypothesis', because 'there is not the least appearance of an intention in that book to give philosophically

exact views of nature'. The reader of *Vestiges* who had never
opened a Bible might conclude from these ambivalent remarks
that the subject of creation finds no mention in its pages, or only
the most cursory and imprecise reference; but Chambers himself
knew better, and he therefore had to say something about
Genesis chapter 1. According to Chambers, scientific discovery has
actually made clearer the real meaning of Genesis 1, which records
God's will and intent rather than his direct acts, references to
God's 'making' being few and stylistically subordinate to the main
idea.[37] Such comment on the text can only throw into relief
Chambers' primary interest in matters scientific.

His natural theology is no better. Adaptation, so well illustrated
by science, reveals design and therefore a designer, a creator. 'The
Natural Theology of Paley, and the *Bridgewater Treatises*, place the
subject in so clear a light, that the general postulate may be taken
for granted.' God creates by means of law and throughout the
whole universe. This is a far more impressive picture than one of
God creating every single creature or species which appears, an
idea 'too ridiculous to be for a moment entertained'. Nevertheless, 'the whole system is continually supported by his providence';
an idea Chambers does not elaborate.[38] A comparison of this pious
assertion with insistence upon the legitimacy of attempting to
recreate the conditions in which life appears must raise the question whether God would have the choice of displaying his creative
energy or not if those physical conditions should be successfully
reproduced. It is, of course, a question which defies an answer and
always will. If the great First Cause is beyond the grasp of finite
faculties, then we are going to have to rest content with the observation of secondary causes and dependence on the design argument. Chambers had no more a sound philosophical basis for his
assertion of religious belief than Paley and the Bridgewater
authors to whom he appeals.

Even worse is to come when Chambers enters upon the subject
of the mental and moral aspects of human experience. He refers
to insistence on the distinction between mind and matter, and the
distinction between the human mind and animals' instinct, and
argues that 'There is . . . nothing to prevent our regarding man as
specially endowed with an immortal spirit, at the same time that
his ordinary mental manifestations are looked upon as simple
phenomena resulting from organization, those of the lower

animals being phenomena absolutely the same in character, though developed within much narrower limits.'[39]

Mental action therefore belongs to the category of natural things; mental phenomena are physically caused and conditioned; the distinction between physical and moral is mere metaphysical confusion; and therefore mental and moral activities are subject to natural laws and statistical generalisation. The similarity of man and animals is illustrated, although man is much more highly developed. The whole is a reflection of 'Almighty Wisdom'.

Since man is a piece of mechanism and only part of a larger, extensive piece of social mechanism, some variety of morals is needed in society for its proper working. God has determined the working of the mechanism through his laws, but he cannot be blamed for evil, his purpose being the happiness of his creatures. The reality of human choice is clearly assumed by Chambers, although he quite fails to integrate this with the divine determinism.[40]

The 'Note Conclusory' shows that Chambers had no suspicion of what the actual reaction to his book was going to be. He was a journalistic layman anxious to put before the general public the overall picture of the universe which was emerging from scientific research. To this end he turned to experts for his scientific information and in subsequent editions showed himself very willing to correct errors and give a more accurate account of details: but criticism of details, while necessary and useful in the improvement of Chambers' volume, by no means explains the storm of controversy he let loose. This was caused by his insistence that the concept of development was essential for a proper understanding of how the whole organic world had come to be what it now is, just as the concept of gravitation was essential to a proper understanding of the workings of inorganic nature. In this assertion Chambers was simply being more honest and frank than many of his contemporaries and drawing the conclusion which they would have done if they had felt free to do so. Because religious thinkers had no philosophy with which to defend themselves against what they perceived to be the damning implications in his basic contention, they fastened on weakness of detail; while those who favoured an evolutionary hypothesis did not wish to be associated with a premature statement based on insufficient evidence. Nevertheless, the real problems raised by *Vestiges* are philosophical, and Chambers no more had an answer to them than did his critics.

In the various editions of the book Chambers refers favourably to Lyell, Murchison, Sedgwick, Darwin, Owen, Buckland, Agassiz, Paley and the Bridgewater authors, Babbage, the Herschels, Henslow, Hugh Miller and Pye Smith. Gentlemen like these, though, were not happy about having their names linked with others such as Laplace and Comte, as if they had all contributed to what must be a generally agreed picture of the universe in all its aspects. Adam Sedgwick, Professor of Geology at Cambridge and a conservative defender of the faith, reviewed *Vestiges* at some length, much of the review being taken up with criticism of details, designed to show that Chambers did not know what he was talking about; but the real cause of fear and displeasure is the 'material-ism' of *Vestiges*, referred to from time to time throughout the article and often with such epithets as 'dismal' and 'irrational' attached to it. Sedgwick insists that man's mind, however closely bound up with matter and its laws, can comprehend these laws and express them in general propositions, and that we have the capacity for moral and aesthetic feeling and thought which cannot be explained in purely naturalistic terms. Therefore 'there is an immeasurable difference between instinct and reason'.[41] Yet Sedgwick did not appreciate the problems raised by his own view.

Each organic structure is a miracle as incomprehensible as the creation of a planetary system . . . yet governed by laws and revolving cycles within itself, and implied in the very conditions of its existence. What know we of the God of nature (we speak only of natural means) except through the faculties he has given us, rightly employed on the materials around us?[42]

Confronted by passages like this, Chambers simply could not understand Sedgwick's opposition. It seemed to Chambers that the whole work of men like Sedgwick demonstrated the develop-ment of the world according to law, and that they displayed an unintelligible inconsistency in attacking his own explicit emphasis on it, while at the same time acknowledging it and illustrating it in their own writings.

Sedgwick produced a fifth edition of his *Discourse on the Studies of the University*, 'With Additions and a Preliminary Dissertation', the 'Preface' running from page ix to page ccccxlii, and the whole being a vastly enlarged and confessedly somewhat repetitious critique of *Vestiges*. The nub of Sedgwick's case, however, is given in a relatively brief introductory statement, from which the following is a quotation:

The kingdoms of nature are presented to our senses in a succession of material actions, so adapted to one another as to end in harmony and order. All these changes and movements among the things around us seem to be produced by powers of nature we call second causes: but the mind of man cannot and will not rest content with second causes, and is constrained to look above them to some First Cause. Among the things produced by the hands of man we are able to separate works of accident from works of design; we gain this knowledge by experience, and by reflecting on what passes within ourselves: it is by taking this knowledge with us in our judgments on the works of God, that we are naturally led to a conception of an intelligent First Cause, capable of producing all the phenomena of the visible world.[43]

Ironically, this could just as well have been written by Chambers. It is also the case that while Sedgwick correctly pointed out that Chambers' philosophy was utterly destructive of all moral and aesthetic value, he was himself as little able to find legitimate entry for such values into his own scheme.

That man, as a moral and social being is under law, we believe true; but when it is affirmed that this law, as comprehended by ourselves, is of the same order with the mechanical laws that govern the undeviating movements of the heavenly spheres, we believe the affirmation to be utterly untrue.

However, on the next page we learn that

In the sight of God every act of man, from childhood to old age, is, we believe, as certain as the ordained movements of the heavenly bodies; and we all allow that the Maker of the universe can work out the ends of his prescient will by the actions of responsible and moral beings.

Sedgwick's subsequent remark is only too well justified: 'Out of this conception of the God of nature spring some dark unsolved questions on fate and free will, by which the reason of man may well be staggered.' Nevertheless, he can confidently assert, 'I affirm then that the moral conduct of man (whatsoever it may be in the eye of God) is not, like the movements of the heavenly bodies, bound up in any conception of a constant, undeviating law.'[44]

Mere affirmation, unfortunately, in the whole context of

Sedgwick's argument was not good enough. Moral value had come to resemble the Queen of Spades: first you see her, then you don't. The length, repetitiousness and virulence of Sedgwick's comments on *Vestiges* suggest the struggles of a mind at war with itself, groping and grasping for that final demonstration which delivers us from a dead and Godless universe.

Chambers' *Explanations* was very largely a reply to Sedgwick's *Edinburgh Review* criticisms.[45] He clearly reasserts the universality of the rule of law, including human life, despite the mysterious unpredictability of the individual human being and the sense of moral responsibility. He emphasises that his chief aim in writing *Vestiges* was to show that God creates through law and not arbitrarily, and that this remains true even if a given scientific explanation such as the nebular hypothesis is false. Nor is Chambers prepared to find gaps in the working of nature's laws to use as props for religious belief.

It is not surprising that the idea of an organic creation by special exertion or fiat should be maintained by the advocates of these views, for it is one of the last obscure pieces of scientific ground on which they can show face. One after another, the phenomena of nature . . . have fallen under the dominion of order or law.

Indeed, with respect to the origin of the organic kingdoms he was prophetic:

So long as this remains obscure, the supernatural will have a certain hold upon enlightened persons. Should it ever be cleared up in a way that leaves no doubt of a natural origin of plants and animals, there must be a complete revolution in the view which is generally taken of our relation to the Father of our being.[46]

Chambers has no real reply to the charge of 'fatalism and materialism' implied by his hypothesis, but he was stung by it to castigate such critics for their fear of being themselves attacked by the 'narrow-minded'. Severe criticism is meted out to scientists for being too much concerned with narrow fields of research, the escape into congenial pursuits and profitable alliances with the realm of capitalist technology, to take a broader view and face profounder questions. Herschel's *Discourse* receives sharp comment for what Chambers considers its very limited view of the uses of science. 'Existing philosophy . . . leaves us only puzzled. We know not how to regard the phenomena of the world, and our own relation to them.'[47] The proper application of science, the recognition of the rule of law in all life, would save many from death, suffering and misery, and lead to a much more responsible attitude on the part of the educated, the wealthy and the influential; and also to a more enlightened attitude towards the creaturely world to which we are related.[48]

Chambers knew something of physical disability, as well as the struggles of youth against relative poverty. The moral passion which erupts in the *Explanations* is a signal that his development hypothesis was no mere academic exercise, but part of a vision of the unity and order of the world which, together with fierce democratic feeling and belief in a beneficent God, formed a deeply held gospel. In his Preface to the tenth edition of *Vestiges* (1853), he tells us that having rejected fiats, miracles and divine interferences as inconsistent with the unified rule of law, the idea came to him 'That the ordinary phenomenon of reproduction was the key to the genesis of species. In that process . . . we see a gradual evolution of high from low, of complicated from simple, of special from general, all, in unvarying order, and therefore all natural, although all of divine ordination.'[49] He also later shrewdly points out that if English naturalists set aside the development hypothesis because it cannot be demonstrated from present experience, they should set aside miraculous creative intervention for the same reason.

Nevertheless, Chambers can offer no real reason why we should believe in God, and although he teeters on the edge of adopting creatio continua in reply to Hitchcock, his rule of law certainly seems to annihilate moral value and leave us with a universe in which God has become the unnecessary hypothesis. For all his protestation Sedgwick was in no better position. His references to 'dead matter', 'dead elements' and 'laws of dead matter' assume the very point at issue; as does his determination to see God in the universe even though we know 'absolutely nothing' of actual divine power, must conceive God anthropomorphically, and see divine design in nature by reading our own experience into it.[50]

The one established academic and prominent thinker who appreciated the situation was Baden Powell, Savilian Professor of Geometry in the University of Oxford, and Fellow of the Royal Society. Powell recognised not only the great popularity of *Vestiges* and the flexibility of the author in dealing with scientific criticisms, but above all the essential similarity between the book and the commonly accepted works and arguments of natural theology. This led him to dismiss the vituperative criticism of *Vestiges* as no better than the expression of religious prejudice, and there can be no doubting the strength of his own feeling against what he regarded as a bigoted and ignorant refusal to face established scientific fact:

With a certain class of religionists every invention and discovery is considered impious and unscriptural – as long as it is new. Not only the discoveries of astronomy and geology, but steam, gas, electricity, political economy, have all in their turn been denounced; and not least, chloroform. Its use in parturition has been anathematised as an infraction of the penalty pronounced on Eve![51]

Powell was born at the end of the eighteenth century, and he carried with him into the nineteenth a vivid awareness of the way in which a certain class of conservative thinkers had denounced the application of reason to matters religious as carnal blindness and sinful presumption, preferring to rest their faith on the literal assertions of the Bible; and he was also aware of the impetus which had carried that view over into what must be a century of radical change quite inconsistent with it.[52] In consequence, he did not always fully appreciate the substance in conservative criticism of new ideas.

Furthermore, his professional work and the mathematical bent of his mind, along with the dominating influence of design theology, inclined him to favour a resolution of the conflict between science and religion which leaves the essential problem unanswered. Nevertheless, among those thinkers who had the opportunity to influence academic and public opinion in the debate over science and religion, perhaps Baden Powell came closest to finding a sound philosophical basis for religious belief. He knew that the whole method of argument which the author of *Vestiges* shared with his critics was wrong: 'a romance – a speculation more or less grounded on fancy', 'a fable', and that he must therefore try to offer a constructive alternative to this defective natural theology.[53]

This endeavour found expression in a relatively early work dedicated to Edward Stanley, Bishop of Norwich, who is commended by Powell for having 'asserted the revelation of God in the volume of nature as our best guide to the manifestation of Him in the pages of inspiration'.[54] Paley's work is referred to, and so is its 'reproduction' in the Bridgewater Treatises, but Powell expresses dissatisfaction with 'the mere accumulation of *particular instances* of design', and wishes to demonstrate instead an essential connection between natural science and natural theology such that the former, whatever the details of its discoveries, will always prove a sound basis for the assertions of the latter; while natural theology in its turn will provide the firm foundation upon which to rest both the concept and content of revelation. This leads him to consider the problem raised by the fear which religious believers often feel concerning the study of 'second causes', this fear being sufficiently widespread, even among the educated, to constitute a real obstacle to the proper development of scientific education.

Powell tries to remove the obstacle by giving an account of secondary causation which eliminates the element of necessity from it while at the same time recognising that it is something more than a mere generalisation from a number of instances. That is to say, the connection between causes and effects is something other than a mere regular sequence. When a loadstone attracts a piece of iron we not only correctly expect this to happen, but feel certain that it will. According to Powell, this is because we can relate the particular instance to a more general principle, and can relate this principle in turn to more general laws, all of which are based upon belief in the uniformity of nature as a fundamental assumption of our thinking. This in turn means that the greater the number of 'second causes' we discover, the greater the evidence for the general order of the universe, and it is this general order which shows that the universe is divinely created: a conclusion which remained of central importance for Powell to the end of his life.

He believed that in this way he had avoided the usual pitfalls of the design argument. He supported Brougham's criticism of Paley, that he was assuming precisely the point which sceptics dispute. He recognised the danger of circularity in the argument from final causes, and he referred to W. J. Irons' observation that it is 'altogether fallacious and illusory', the assertion that design implies a designer being a mere tautology. Powell warns against reading into nature our own felt sense of voluntary effort and being misled by words like 'chain', 'links', 'connexion' and 'production' in the description of causal sequences; and he commends Babbage's calculating machine analogy as correctly illustrating the fact that even exceptions to the overall order of the universe are only apparent.

Nevertheless, he could not agree with Irons that we must abandon natural theology for total dependence on revelation. Quite the reverse. 'The conclusions of natural theology are limited in extent, but demonstrative in proof: they are most important in themselves; and indispensable in the foundations of any evidence of revelation.'55 This also means that it is absurd to make revelation a guide to physical truth, and in any case 'scientific and revealed truth are of essentially *different natures*'. In religion we have moral proof and faith, not the demonstrations of science, and scientific truth cannot harm the moral and religious truth of revelation.56

At this point, though, the confusions in Powell's argument become apparent. If scientific and religious truth are so different, how can one be the essential foundation of the other? How do we get from the recorded facts concerning second causes to the fact of the great First Cause? Powell rightly insists that we are here using the term 'cause' in two different senses, and he rightly recognises that when we speak of the First Cause, we are using the word figuratively. In this way he thinks to overcome Irons' objection that finite reason cannot achieve the knowledge of Infinite Being. The knowledge is not direct acquaintance but based on analogy with works produced by voluntary agents and intelligent beings within our experience.57 But it must be confessed that this seems to be no better than the assertions of Paley and the Bridgewater authors, since analogy does not provide 'demonstrative proof' but requires its own justification. Nor is Powell's attempt to avoid recognition of the actual force and necessity at work in nature any more persuasive. When the loadstone draws the iron, we believe that it is because of its 'magnetic property/power', and the existence of necessitating force in nature cannot be explained away in terms of general principles subsumed under wider generalities. The hidden analogy with geometrical axioms, principles and conclusions is wholly misleading.

The mixture of insight and confusion in Powell's thought reflects the struggles of a mind trying to free itself from traditional approaches to the problems raised by new knowledge. In the *Essays* his main ideas are repeated and developed, and at the centre of them is Powell's recognition that the Paleyan design argument is invalid combined with his profound conviction that the overall rationality of the universe implies the existence of a transcendent intelligence. This has the interesting consequence that Powell regards the examples Paley uses as genuine illustrations of intelligence revealed through nature's works, while rejecting Paley's claim that he was presenting a valid inference from them to God; but it is difficult to see that Powell is in any better case. Powell extends consideration from specific items within nature, to nature or the universe as a whole; but with respect to the attempted inference from nature to a transcendent deity, does this make any difference?

Powell's central conviction was strengthened by the teaching of Hans Christian Oersted, Professor of Physics at Copenhagen and a disciple of Schelling. 'All effects obey natural laws; these laws stand in the same necessary connexion as one axiom in reason to another . . . Innumerable as are the effects determined by natural laws in every object in nature . . . I deeply feel an unfathomable reason within them . . . In short, nature is to me the revelation of an endless living and acting reason . . . All existence is a dominion of reason.' 'The laws of Nature are the thoughts of Nature; and these are the thoughts of God.'[58]

Such language is not to be dismissed as mere airy-fairy pseudo-philosophical speculation. Oersted was actively engaged in experimental research and Powell was a professional mathematician very much in touch with scientific work being pursued in various fields, and it was a source of wonder to such men that nature could present herself to the serious observer as dynamic, intricate and subtle to an unimaginable degree, and yet behave according to principles readily intelligible to the mind of man. Appreciation of nature's combined intricacy and simplicity, however, was one thing: the ability to conceive and create such a living system was another, and infinitely beyond anything attainable by humanity. Creation must therefore be attributed to a kindred but infinitely larger intelligence, to which human manufacture would provide some sort of remote analogy: a conclusion dangerously near to that of Hume in the *Dialogues*.

One is reminded of the profound conviction of a more recent physicist: 'Raffiniert ist der Herrgott aber boshaft ist er nicht'.[59] Powell was moved by the same conviction:

The actual laws and profound principles which regulate the mechanism of the universe are the originals, the conception and expression of them in the mind of man only the copies . . . All science is but the partial reflexion in the *reason of man*, of the great all-pervading *reason of the universe*. And thus the *unity* of science is the reflexion of the *unity* of nature, and of the *unity* of that supreme reason and intelligence which pervades and rules over nature, and from whence all reason and science is derived.[60]

Therefore to posit exceptions to the rule of law was to deny the most significant fact about the universe revealed to human knowledge. Even life itself must one day be explained in the terms and categories of the exact sciences:

But the truly inductive inquirer can never doubt that there really exists as complete and continuous a relation and connexion of *some kind* between the manifestations of life and the simplest mechanical or chemical laws evinced in the varied actions of the body in which it resides, as there is between the action of any machine and the laws of motion and equilibrium . . . and that this connexion and dependence is but one component portion of the vast chain of physical causation whose essential strength lies in its universal continuity, which extends, without interruption, through the entire world of order, and in which a real disruption of one link would be the destruction of the whole.[61]

It is not surprising that Powell could see the strength as well as the weaknesses in Robert Chambers' *Vestiges* and should give such a warm welcome to Darwin's *Origin* when it appeared. Yet the fears and objections of conservative religious thinkers had their foundation in something more than mere prejudice.

The idea that everything, including human life, was explicable in terms of second causes not unnaturally aroused alarm and opposition in many religious minds. With some justification conservatives felt that even if belief in God could legitimately be combined with this idea, such a God had become too remote to be identified with the God revealed in Scripture and worshipped by the Church. A reviewer dealing with Powell's contribution to *Essays and Reviews* referred to his 'scarcely-veiled Atheism'. 'These words, "the self-evolving powers of nature", convey no meaning to our mind if they do not intentionally resolve the notion of a Personal Creator into the misty hieroglyphic of the Atheist.' 'Mr Baden Powell, if there be meaning in words, gives up the very being of a God.'[62] It was in vain that Powell denied the existence of actual necessitating power in nature and endeavoured to replace the concept of mechanical, blind or fated necessity with that of rational necessity, logical sequence.[63] Nobody believed this, nor does anyone believe it now. Thousands of experiences every day confirm the inescapable fact of necessary, compelling causal connection. Human formulations, the laws, equations, principles, calculations, records and predictions which go to make up science, might well display necessary relationships and sequences best described as 'logical'; but the forces which make natural processes what they are display a different kind of compulsory connection.

This is not to deny Hume's suggestion that nature's processes might work according to an algebraic kind of necessity. The mathematical analogy emphasises the inevitability and regularity of causal sequences, but it does not identify human rationality and physical process, however closely connected we may believe them to be. Furthermore, Powell's critics not unjustifiably regarded his view as involving the destruction of human rationality. If all life, including human, was to be explained in terms of development out of lower forms, and ultimately out of chemical change, this must include the human mind and soul. If Powell was not prepared to allow real exceptions to the scope of scientific explanation, then there was no room for the creative activity of a transcendent deity, all must be deduced from principles of an immanentist kind, and if God was allowed to ring up the curtain, he was certainly not permitted to take any active part in the play.

Powell treated the concept of creation as having two meanings: the philosophical, in which it merely refers to our ignorance of the way in which the physical world came into being; and the scientific, which is the investigation of the physical antecedents of this world as far back as we can trace them. The evidence of geology and biology was appealed to, but above all, the principle that there cannot be real 'breaks' in nature, that the connections studied by science must be complete or otherwise science itself be rejected as impossible:

Physical philosophy . . . cannot investigate or conceive a condition antecedent to nature, or the case of its actual commencement. No science can carry us, even in imagination, into a state of arbitrary and disordered influences; a *chaos* has no existence in the ideas or the vocabulary of the inductive philosophy. A creation, in the same vocabulary, implies orderly evolution. If we entertain any ideas beyond these, it can only be from sources of quite another kind.[64]

Naturally, therefore, Sedgwick's idea of 'creative additions' had to be rejected; but this left men like Sedgwick and Owen wondering about the status of a divine power which had been relegated to an area of which human beings were necessarily for ever ignorant. Neither in time nor in space was science to be denied, and the rationality which was to be our bridge to transcendent Intelligence would itself be subsumed under categories of evolutionary process.

Powell himself refused to accept such conclusions from his own premises. The unbreakable links which form nature's processes produced man in so far as he is an animal, but not his spiritual nature, which belongs to 'A DIFFERENT ORDER OF THINGS';[65] a view which coincided with his assertion that science and religion are concerned with separate matters which are distinct in kind, and with his stress upon the moral and spiritual character of the truths expressed in the Bible. This aspect of Powell's philosophy might also have been very profitably linked with his belief that ideas of divine creation can only be justified by an appeal to considerations of a very different kind from those which occupy science, but this crucial link was not made. With reference to Christian theology and its relation to scientific discovery he stated,

Its peculiar aim is entirely different and independent: its objects *belong to another order of things*; and its representations of them are avowedly *not the realities*, but only their *images*; they can be seen by us only . . . 'by means of a mirror and in an enigma', in our present state; while it holds out a future when 'we shall see face to face, and know even as we are known'.[66]

On this point Powell had to confess disagreement with Oersted, who is quoted as saying,

If we are now thoroughly convinced that everything in material existence is produced from similar particles of matter, and by the same forces, and in obedience to the same laws . . . everywhere the creatures endowed with reason are the productions of nature in the same sense as ourselves, that is, their understanding is bound up with the organs of their body.

Powell, however, refuses to 'associate too closely the intellectual and spiritual nature of man with the physical, on the essential distinction between which I have before enlarged';[67] but he fails to justify the rather large break which he is now making in the continuity of nature's overall life and growth. Powell was rightly trying to do justice to all aspects of human experience, but dogmatic assertion could no more satisfy his critics in this respect than it could in the attempt to rid the world of efficient causation.

Failure to argue the matter through also left a very negative impression of commitment to a divine creator and acceptance of biblical authority. According to Powell, anthropomorphic pictures of the deity, whether arrived at by Paley's argument or derived from the Bible, create hopeless difficulties if taken literally, and so-called proofs of God's existence are only rationalisations of such already held ideas. We are led into misleading scholastic jargon about First and second causes and the problem of infinite regress; and we play into the hands of men like Comte and Feuerbach, the former pointing out the arbitrary character of nature's laws if they are dependent on the divine will, and the latter asserting that we make God in our own image. The Old Testament has been proved wrong in certain of its assertions about the physical world, it is a collection of documents adapted in style and content to the ideas and judgment of the ancient society which produced it, and can only be safely interpreted in the light of the distinctly superior New Testament, the truths of which rest on altogether different grounds from those dealt with by natural science. Yet the intrusion of the miraculous into religion is also a mistake, creating the unworthy idea of a God who has to interfere with his world to be effective, and demanding faith in that which we do not know or understand, a faith which cannot form the proper foundation for reasonable belief.

One is left wondering how such literature can lay any kind of claim to authority. When the bulk of the Bible, the Old Testament, is regarded as having lent support to bigotry and immorality as well as being a source of untruth about the main physical features of the universe, remarks about its literary characteristics, however true, are scarcely sufficient to restore flagging devotion to pretensions of revelation: 'our only alternative is to regard that which is *not history* as *poetry*, if we would avoid impugning the truth of these accounts altogether'. Yet Powell himself, in the same place, describes Genesis 1 as 'in the *form of a circumstantial narrative* of the origin of the world', which suggests that it is not poetry; and even if it were, it is difficult to see how one could avoid 'impugning' its truth, just as incitements to bigotry and immorality, however poetically expressed, would not normally be regarded as divinely inspired.[68] The New Testament, despite its supposed superiority, contains a highly significant element of the miraculous, and is not without some violence of expression and dogmatic emphasis which easily lend themselves to the service of intolerance and persecution. Powell's assertion that revelation must be based on a sound natural theology appears to be only too true.

If the concept of creation can only become meaningful by making it refer simply to the appearance of that which did not previously exist and applying it to the orderly evolution which is revealed to observation and careful inductive method, then biblical or any other religious assertions about divine creation must of necessity be figurative; and presumably descriptions of God must also be figurative and often anthropomorphic, because God himself is no more observable and measurable than his creative work. We must therefore depend on Powell's argument from the intelligibility of the universe to the transcendent divine intelligence as our justification for using language about God at all or attaching any value to biblical assertions about God and his demands on and promises to mankind: but Hume's scepticism dissolves Powell's argument as surely as Paley's. If the human mind has evolved and survived through the long eras of change in the life of the planet, it is not surprising that the world should be intelligible to it. Such intelligibility is an essential part of the mind's adaptation to its environment, without which it would not exist at all.

Nevertheless, much that Powell said about science, the Bible and the concept of creation was true even though at the time it seemed to be destructive of religious belief; and he also gave recognition to the element in human experience, and Kant's emphasis upon it, which could have provided him with the real basis for a fruitful natural theology. In 1854, as one of three judges appointed to award the Burnett Prizes for studies in natural theology, he read through 208 essays, noting the similarity of argument in most of them, and obviously looking for something fresh which showed a proper appreciation of the philosophical issues involved.[69] In his own reflections on these issues he shows some sympathy with Kant, who 'draws with a clear and masterly hand the important distinction between strict philosophical reasoning and that kind of moral persuasion which prevails among mankind at large, and suffices for all practical purposes'. Later Powell states that 'the language of theology expresses by the phrase creation . . . some act, the nature of which it is utterly beyond the power of human reason to conceive and which, so far from *explaining*, professedly shuts out all *explanation*, and can only be a conception of *faith*'.[70] It is here, in these two points, that Powell could have found the beginning of a fresh approach to natural theology, including the peculiar nature and position of mankind in the world, and a fruitful, unforced connection with what is of profound value in the biblical literature.

Unfortunately he failed to recognise the real value and the full implications of his own best insights, with the result that his thought taken as a whole is flawed and undeveloped. He was like a prisoner successful in his effort to escape the cell, but careful to take his ball and chain with him. His agnosticism, his emphasis upon faith and the moral and spiritual nature of man, his recognition of a kind of truth which persuades by an appeal to criteria unknown to scientific method, and his groping after an appreciation of the true character of the biblical literature could all have borne much fruit; but failure to break completely with design theology involved the inevitable frustration of any such promise. The ghost of ancient Jewish cosmogony was not the only one requiring exorcism. Although at the very outset of his argument Powell had reverently laid Paley to rest, watch and all, his mind, like many others, was still haunted by that genial, well-intentioned and persuasive shade.

CHAPTER 8

The later nineteenth century

The year 1860 may be taken as a convenient, if not perfectly precise, chronological marker with respect to thought about religion in Britain. The evidences in favour of a wholly naturalistic interpretation of life, including religion, had been growing stronger throughout the century, and by the year 1860 a kind of breaking point or turning of the tide had been reached. A profound and lasting trend was established, and it was the triumph of scientific method: not the consequence of some sudden revelation or discovery, but as the culmination of intellectual endeavour going back to the eighteenth century. Basil Willey links the publication of *The Origin of Species*, of *Essays and Reviews* and of Colenso's *The Pentateuch and the Book of Joshua Critically Examined* as 'Three great explosions . . . which rocked the fabric of Christendom and sent believers scuttling for shelter';[1] but while these events unquestionably made a sharp impact on thinking people, they did not of themselves establish some unheard of novelty which in turn set in motion or released forces hitherto dormant. They were symptomatic of a social and intellectual shift long since begun, and by expressing it they increased awareness of change already proceeding and encouraged it.

The idea of an evolutionary explanation for the appearance of life on the planet was by no means new; and the evidence in its favour was always gradually accumulating, a fact to which the Bridgewater Treatises themselves bore witness in contradiction to their main intention. Darwin and Wallace presented their hypothesis to the Linnean Society in 1858, having arrived at a similar conclusion wholly independently of each other. They welded evidence into an argument which now became too probably correct to be easily dismissed, and which demanded serious investigation by other biologists; but if these two had not produced the hypothesis, someone else would have done.

Taken along with progress in chemistry, physics, geology, astronomy and medicine, it was clear to any honest and unprejudiced person by 1860 that scientific methods could establish truths about the natural world with a probability often indistinguishable for all practical purposes from certainty. Of course, some conclusions were partial and subject to further refinement; disputes were commonplace, as, for example, over the age of the earth; sometimes scientists operated with hypotheses of greater or less probability; but even where there was argument and uncertainty it had to be accepted that it was scientific method which would sooner or later bring the truth to light, to the extent that truth was attainable at all.

Natural theology as understood by Paley was not suddenly rendered invalid by the advance of science. Invalid argument enjoys the privilege of transcendence over mere temporal change; but the developing view of nature enforced the point for all those who had eyes to see. A survey of the natural world with the intention of proving the basic tenets of religion gradually ceased to be a serious proposition.

At the same time genuine biblical criticism was beginning to appear as an intellectual force whose presence could not be removed and whose development could not be stopped. Such criticism had been practised in Germany for many years, and scholars in this country were well aware of the fact, although the general attitude towards it was one of hostility. Yet the textual, literary and historical problems which gave rise to such critical study were not the mere products of a perverse imagination. They were an integral part of the text, waiting to confront anyone who undertook the task of properly understanding it. At the same time, the picture of the universe and life on earth being developed by natural science was totally at variance with the biblical picture, and the adoption of the critical or scientific method of studying biblical literature avoided the embarrassment of trying to evade the discrepancy by means of forced reconciliations or futile attempts to deny the scientific evidence. Historical and literary criticism set the biblical documents firmly in their historical context and accepted that they were products of an ancient mentality which knew far less about the natural world than the educated population of nineteenth-century Britain.

The old idea that we should not seek information about the natural world in books which were intended to convey religious and moral truth was given a new and crucial significance. Scientific method applied to the Bible could claim the double advantage of removing any possibility of conflict between the Bible and the natural sciences, and of concentrating attention upon the spiritual messages intended by the ancient authors. By 1860 a sufficient number of British scholars appreciated these facts to ensure that historical and literary criticism became the dominating trend in biblical interpretation, and in this way the true nature of the ancient literature was brought to light and demonstrated beyond reasonable doubt, so that the Bible could be accepted for what it was, rather than for what it was not.

Scientific method triumphed therefore in the sense that it made claims to truth which no honest, unprejudiced and informed person could or would deny, and from about 1860 onwards increasing numbers of people in Britain accepted scientific method as the sole or chief means of establishing the truth, whether this was the truth in some specific area of inquiry or the truth about the universe as a whole. Natural scientists began to gain some real independence of ecclesiastical authority and its influence on social status and prospects for a career. T. H. Huxley became the best-known propagandist for this independence, and prophet of an agnosticism which regarded the positive propositions of religious belief as already destroyed by Hume's scepticism and Kant's critical philosophy.

Most people, of course, were no more able or willing to engage in serious experimental work than they were able or willing to engage in serious theological debate or biblical exegesis: conclusions and explanations had to be accepted on authority, and after 1860 that authority gradually but very definitely passed to the scientist and away from the priest and bishop. It became increasingly obvious to thinking people that the facts of science could not simply be denied; that the first eleven chapters of Genesis could no longer be regarded as unique or absolutely accurate as a portrayal of the origins of the world and mankind; that the biblical literature expressed religious and moral crudities as if they reflected truth about the nature of God; that many of the so-called events recorded challenged credulity beyond breaking point, while science and technology produced contemporary 'miracles' open to common inspection. Naturalistic explanation was convincing and displayed its triumphs daily. It could be readily appreciated at an unsophisticated level, like the errors of the Bible; and the general tendency to prefer it was established then and has increased its influence to the present day. It was also increasingly apparent that the Church had no generally agreed religious philosophy. The gospel was proclaimed and dogma recited, but no unified reply was offered to the inquirer or critic who wondered how any credence at all could be given to claims on behalf of a transcendent deity.

The dangers and limitations of historical generalisation must be admitted, and claims to truth may receive a response similar to Pilate's when confronted by the claims of Christ. It was the case then as it is now that issues in any individual mind or the collective mind of any given community were not necessarily either clear-cut or fixed. The sociological aspects of religious belief are complex and subtle; but when full weight has been given to qualifications and reservations, a general trend is discernible and has continued to the present day, and that is the production by natural science of increasing evidence that a wholly naturalistic explanation of life is the correct one. Unless we are to be utterly cynical about the capacity of the human mind to appreciate truth; unless we are prepared to see human thought as merely a species of instinct, dominated by prejudices which have their origin in the determining influence of heredity and environment, then we must recognise the possible willing correspondence of thought with fact, the possibility of real mental adjustment to what is demonstrably the case or made probable by the weight of evidence. That there was a distinctive approach to things which could be designated 'scientific', and that it developed a strong fascination for the Victorian imagination, is undeniable, and Sherlock Holmes is perhaps the most powerful symbolic expression of the fact. When we try to define 'scientific', as when we try to define 'religious', the complexities and subtleties of human life, both in its individual and in its social aspects, defy us, and what starts out as a definition must become encyclopaedic if it is to be comprehensive. Yet both terms refer to something readily recognisable and real in both individual and society: and after 1860 in Britain it was the scientific approach to nature and 'revelation' which seemed to increasing numbers of thinking people to offer the unprejudiced attempt to establish a proper correspondence between thought and fact.

It may seem natural to conclude from these remarks that those who rejected or ignored scientific claims, and even denounced them, were ignorant or prejudiced or just plain dishonest; but the situation was not and is not so simple. It was one thing to accept the positive gains afforded by commitment to scientific methods of inquiry, but a very different matter to accept the full implications of a wholly naturalistic explanation of life. Those who held to religious belief and who were not prepared to water it down to mere sentiment or some kind of subjective response to the greater world of which mankind is a part were confronted by the necessity of avoiding the wholly naturalistic conclusion. To some this seemed simple enough: the natural sciences revealed truth about nature, while religious experience down the ages, especially that recorded in the Bible, revealed truth about God, the supernatural. These were regarded as two essentially different kinds of truth which could never come into conflict with each other, and it was open to anyone to accept both. The answer to the science/religion conflict therefore was to be a sharp dualism.

It is not out of the question that the finite human mind should be compelled to rest content with a dualistic view of reality, however powerful the mind's own tendency is to seek satisfaction in a coherent and unified system; but if so, both aspects of the duality must display convincing evidence of their existence. Furthermore, religious belief in Britain not only asserted the existence of God, but that the world has been created, and is sustained and providentially governed by him. He is no absentee God. When therefore such a profound and significant relationship is asserted to exist between nature and God, it comes as something of a surprise to be told that assertions about God and assertions about nature not only do not, but cannot contradict each other because they are of a wholly different character; which also implies that they cannot confirm or illuminate each other either.

At first the explanation seems plausible enough, as can be seen by means of a simple analogy. We may say of a man that he is kind and generous and conscientious in his work, and we may say of the house in which he lives that it has three bedrooms, a dining room and kitchen and is semi-detached. Religious assertions about God are like those about the man, and scientific assertions about nature are like those concerning the house: the truth or falsity of one set of assertions has no connection with the truth or falsity of the other set. Yet it is at the point where the analogy breaks down that it becomes instructive. We find out what nature is like in basically the same way as we find out what the house is like: but how do we find out about God? In the analogy, the man and the house are both knowable in roughly the same sort of way, and if questions are raised about statements concerning the man, we know at least in principle how they can be checked, and this is not so very different from ways in which statements about the house can be checked; but if the man was never seen in the house, or leaving or entering it, if no one knew where he worked or actually met him; if the garden was overgrown and the house unfurnished, or occupied by people who said they knew the man but could not, even in answer to the most persistent inquiries, introduce us to him: we should accept verifiable statements about the house, and we should accept the distinction in meaning between propositions about the man and the house, but regard such a distinction as of no significance in the absence of any evidence that the man actually existed.

We can, of course, legitimately alter the analogy, and say that the man not only lives in the house, but made it and maintains it; and both the idea of 'living in' and that of 'making' can be more closely defined or explained so as to reflect more clearly just how we envisage God's relationship with his world. It is obvious in this case that at least some assertions about the man and his house might be connected, and even if we can never meet the man despite long Kafka-like searches for him, we may deduce ideas about him from the state of the house: and in the same way we may deduce ideas of God from nature.

In this case, however, the sharp dualism has been surrendered, with all the risks that that involves; risks vividly portrayed by Hume in his *Dialogues* and brought home to religious thought in the later nineteenth century by destructive criticism of Paley from varied quarters. If Paley's natural theology had been valid, there would have been a bridge from the natural to the supernatural; but even then, as Hume demonstrated, it would have been by no means certain that conclusions concerning the divine nature would have been at all in keeping with the teaching of the Church.

The reaction of conservative religious thinkers is therefore understandable and is not to be dismissed as the mere effusion of ignorance and prejudice. Religious philosophy was in a state of confusion. Some people still defended Paley's argument, even though they might believe that it required restatement in some supposedly modified form. Others rejected such argument altogether, but could only provide equally dubious alternatives; and there was no general agreement as to how philosophy should meet incipient atheism. He who eats with the devil must use a very long spoon: and those who were by temperament and upbringing suspicious of appeals to a corrupted human reason must have felt that attempts to meet unbelief by means of argument were futile endeavours to convert Satan on his home ground.

Liberal critical scholars believed that the Bible contained inspired religious truth, but they preferred to leave the justification of such belief to others. They willingly conceded the authority of the natural sciences in their own sphere, but also applied the principles of naturalistic explanation to the interpretation of the biblical literature. They did not regard themselves as engaged in or implying by their methods a wholly naturalistic interpretation of the Bible, and they looked upon it as containing profound religious and moral truth which God willed to reveal to mankind; but their method of study by its very nature involved, and does involve, the concentration of attention upon the human elements in its composition and transmission, and in all of its very varied contents. This is why such biblical study has at times been described as 'scientific'. Critical scholars assumed that the Bible was inspired revelation but set aside the assumption for the purposes of critical research, just as a natural scientist might assume that the world is God's creation, but rigorously set aside the assumption in the prosecution of his professional work. The liberal critical approach to biblical interpretation was essentially and inevitably a phenomenological exercise.

Liberal scholars freely acknowledged the problems of biblical interpretation and agreed that the biblical literature should be read and studied like any other. The Word of God comes to us as the words and deeds of men, and this means that the biblical literature must be amenable to explanation in naturalistic terms; indeed, it must demand such explanation. At the same time they assumed that sacred truth would shine by its own light in the eyes of the honest inquirer, and since sacred truth is not scientific, errors in matters scientific could be cheerfully conceded. The weakness of this position was that naturalistic explanations were self-explanatory, and the phenomenological approach could stand on its own feet; while the claim that religious truth had been revealed through nature and the affairs of men still remained to be justified.

This kind of criticism was utterly inconsistent with the simple understanding of inspiration and revelation which sees God as guaranteeing by his providential activity that the sense of every biblical text shall be open to every sincere believer, and unquestionably true. The proper critical study of the Bible involved the recognition of biblical error, error which could not have appeared if it were the product of direct and unambiguous divine revelation, even granted that God spoke in a language and by means of cultural concepts which his hearers could grasp.

Conservatives inevitably saw such scholarly criticism as a fatal concession to the spirit of the age. Liberal critical methods involved the surrender of the supernatural, and it was asking far too much of faith to put its trust in reason to reinstate God in his world. It was altogether simpler and more in keeping with the spirit of true piety to accept the biblical miracles as true and obvious signs of the divine presence and activity, setting the seal on a biblical message which, thus guaranteed, would make its own moral and spiritual impact on a lost humanity. Had not Our Lord himself appealed to the overwise in his own generation to believe at least for the very works' sake?

After all, the issue between belief and unbelief was not simply clear-cut. Only ignorance and desperate cynicism could dismiss the Bible as merely a collection of errors and moral crudities, and sceptics could no more produce an agreed philosophy than the Church. Immanent moral and aesthetic values were just as much a problem for unbelief as the transcendent was for belief; and, most fundamental of all, if sin and salvation mean anything, they denote something rather more than the exchange of an incorrect mental picture of the universe for a correct one. Conservatives made out their case under the powerful conviction that there were aspects of human life profoundly more important than the fallible conclusions of human reason and that such conclusions should not be allowed to undermine the supreme authority of the Word of God conveyed through the biblical revelation. The occupational hazard of conservative thought was the too cavalier

treatment of genuine intellectual difficulties and a tendency to
engage in unconvincing rationalisation.

Liberal thinkers were also moved by consideration for moral
and spiritual realities of central significance in human life and
which perpetually resist reduction to wholly naturalistic explanation; but they were also convinced that the results of rational
inquiry could not be so easily dismissed. Such results might be
refined and developed, but in many cases represented discovery of
fact which would remain substantially unaltered; and rational
inquiry could be put to good use in biblical study and by means of
honest exegesis bring to light religious truth which would otherwise lie unappreciated in the obscurity of its original cultural
setting. The occupational hazard of liberalism was too great a concentration on the human element in the Bible and failure to give
proper recognition to the significance of the supernatural in it.
Biblical theology on this basis was hamstrung from the start. The
biblical 'Theologies' which were to emerge in the liberal tradition
would be fine and illuminating descriptions of the religious ideas
to be found in the Bible, but to what extent these ideas might be
accepted as true for humanity regardless of the historical context
in which they appeared was a problem which could not be
addressed.

For both conservatives and liberals philosophy was a distinct
discipline regarded with more or less distrust by both parties. And
yet it was only by means of philosophy that the problems raised by
Hume and enforced by the natural sciences could be met, the
eternal distinguished from the ephemeral in the biblical revelation, and a true theology, or metaphysics, constructed.

Henry Longueville Mansel well illustrates both the need for a
correct philosophy and the profound change which had taken
place in British thought since the middle of the eighteenth century. His Bampton Lectures on the limits of religious thought,
given and first published in 1858, were a display of intellectual
power in argument distinctly more impressive than Darwin's
Origin or anything the contributors to *Essays and Reviews* could produce.[2] Dean Burgon has left us a vivid account of the excitement
created in St Mary's on the occasion of their delivery:

The interest which Mansel's delivery of his Bampton Lectures excited in
Oxford was extraordinary: the strangest feature of the case being, that
those compositions were so entirely 'over the heads' of most of those who

nevertheless every Sunday morning flocked to S. Mary's to hear them. The Undergraduates' gallery, which accommodates about half the congregation at S. Mary's, was always entirely filled with attentive and enthusiastic listeners; but it may be questioned if one in a hundred was able to follow the preacher. The young men knew, of course, in a general kind of way, what the champion of Orthodoxy was about. He was, single-handed, contunding a host of unbelievers, – some, with unpronounce-able names and unintelligible theories; and sending them flying before him like dust before the wind. And *that* was quite enough for *them.* It was a kind of gladiatorial exhibition which they were invited to witness: the unequal odds against 'the British lion' adding greatly to the zest of the entertainment; especially as the noble animal was always observed to remain master of the field in the end. But, for the space of an hour, there was sure to be some desperate hard fighting, during which they knew that Mansel would have to hit both straight and hard: and *that* they liked. If was only necessary to look at their Champion to be sure that *he* also sincerely relished his occupation; and this completed their satisfaction. So long as he was encountering his opponents' reasoning, his massive brow, expressive features, and earnest manner suggested the image of nothing so much as resolute intellectual conflict, combined with con-scious intellectual superiority. But the turning-point was reached at last. He would suddenly erect his forefinger. This was the signal for the final decisive charge. Resistance from that moment was hopeless. Already were the enemy's ranks broken. It only remained to pursue the routed foe into some remote corner of Germany, and to pronounce the Benediction.3

Burgon goes on to refer to the immense sensation which the publication of the lectures produced on the continent and in America as well as in England, but enthusiasm and thoroughly justified admiration for Mansel's intellectual athleticism were no substitute for a proper grasp of the issues which by then actually confronted religious believers in Britain. The future belonged not to Mansel but to Darwin, even in part to Colenso and *Essays and Reviews,* and the reason for this is instructive and not without irony. If the intellectual invaders who threatened the establish-ment were of German origin, so was the ally who provided the British champion with the weaponry necessary for their destruc-tion; and while the annihilating power displayed was exhilarating during the battle, more sober subsequent reflection shows it to have undermined the foundations upon which it was placed and which it was meant to defend. This was not the intention of the ally, but implied the need for more careful training in the employment of equipment which he had placed at Britain's disposal.

Mansel saw himself as a latter-day Butler, applying the approach of the *Analogy* to Idealist criticism of Christian theology in fundamentally the same manner as Butler had made out his reply to deism. Butler had strongly emphasised the limitations of human reason and couched his own argument in terms of the probability which guides common sense in the affairs of everyday life. The speculations of pure reason had been dismissed as worse than useless. Deists admitted that there was strong evidence in nature for the existence of an intelligent creator, but once this was granted there was no good reason to reject a biblically based Christianity and every reason to accept it. The analogy between belief in God based on a correct view of nature and belief in God based on a correct view of revelation was so close and mutually illuminating that they must stand or fall together: and a judgment based on the generally accepted principle of probability, the principle used for every other important decision in life, would bring in a verdict of acceptance for both.

Like Butler, and in accordance with the title of his lectures, Mansel stressed the limitations of human reason, and endeavoured to show that revelation offered Christianity's Idealist critics the belief in God which they wanted, and in terms which were within the capacity of reason to grasp. Futile speculation was to be replaced by the plain, readily accessible message of the Bible, and the revelation of God contained in a record of human experience and therefore intelligible to a mentality entirely adapted to this world's environment. Mansel wanted to inculcate a humility which would surrender the arrogant attempt to bring religious doctrine within the bounds of rational criticism, and to encourage a faith which would acknowledge revelation as the only possible source of knowledge about God.

Both Mansel and Butler, therefore, depended on a critique of reason, and a demonstration that if certain critics of Christianity re-examined their own argument, they would be obliged to accept revelation rather than rejecting it; but once this general similarity has been indicated, it must be admitted that there was a crucial difference between these two thinkers. This difference lay in the critique of reason, which Mansel borrowed from Kant both directly, and also indirectly through Sir William Hamilton. The

Kantian critique was far more extensive both in its negative and positive aspects than anything Butler dreamt of; and while Butler based confidence in revelation on the supposed truth of deistic natural theology and argued that acceptance of it should lead naturally to acceptance of Christian belief, Mansel demolished the foundations of German Idealism and hoped to rebuild confidence in Christianity on the ruins of the metaphysical systems he had now completely undermined.

It was one thing, however, to make a wreck of Idealism, but a very different matter to replace it with a convincing demonstration of biblically based truth. If concepts of the Absolute and Infinite are simply beyond the range of finite human reason, if in the very nature of the case they cannot be grasped by an earth-bound human understanding, then they were presumably beyond the grasp of the men and women whose experiences go to make up the biblical record; and if what is expressed in the Bible is something essentially other than the Absolute and Infinite, then the images of God presented to us could be the fruit of immanent forces at work rather than picturesque adaptations of the transcendent revealing itself to our limited intelligence. Feuerbach could be right, and God might be the glorified image of man, projected into the sky by culturally determined fancy, rather than the concretely evidenced ultimate reality. Mansel's demolition job was done so thoroughly that one is left wondering why we should not jettison Christian theology along with the works of Hegel, Fichte and Schelling.

Mansel might have claimed that the biblical revelation was based on unique knowledge, on modes of spiritual communication not open to the rest of mankind, but this line of approach was firmly rejected.[4] More to the point, he might have faced the problem squarely and considered more seriously and sympathetically Kant's own answer to it; and it is very significant for an understanding of nineteenth- and twentieth-century religious thought in Britain that he not only did not do so, but positively rejected the Kantian solution. For Mansel, the idea of religion within the limits of mere reason was a contradiction in terms: religion involved acknowledgement of the unconditioned transcendent, which was precisely what reason alone could not reach. He accused Kant of identifying religion with morality and maintaining that the supernatural and historical were not necessary to religious belief; and he also denounced Kant's attempt to find a firm basis for religious belief in our moral sense as inconsistent with his critical conclusions.

This firm rejection of Kant's positive aims left Mansel with no alternative but a straightforward appeal to the Bible as revelation, and this was no doubt his intention; but while such an appeal might be sufficient within the circle of the unquestioning faithful, it was wholly inadequate when dealing with the Church's critics, or even those among the faithful who could not suppress the rise of doubt. Some justification had to be offered for regarding a collection of ancient records as 'revelation', and Mansel was not unaware of the fact. Somehow he had to show that human cognition is capable of establishing contact through the Bible with that supernatural, unconditioned Absolute, the Infinite God, whom he has shown to be beyond the grasp of human reason, without at the same time rebuilding what he has pulled down.

Mansel emphasised that God is represented in the Bible by means of symbolic terms which are more or less adequate and which we rightly interpret personally. God is revealed through partial manifestations and indications of his nature which human beings can only appreciate in terms of personality, and without this consciousness of personality we could have no belief in God at all. Nevertheless Mansel recognises that concepts of the infinite and absolute have to be used in Christian theology, even though he has demonstrated that human reason cannot grasp them, since it is only by using them that we can express essential truth about God.

He easily gets round the apparent contradiction in his argument by insisting that such abstract ideas as they are used in Christian theology have a purely negative sense: we think of the love or wrath of God in human personal terms, but at the same time feel and acknowledge that no limit or condition can qualify the divine love or wrath as they do human love and anger, and in that sense the divine is infinite and absolute.

The natural response of critics and doubters would be to ask why we should believe that there is any being to whom such descriptions apply. If we can give positive content to concepts of infiniteness and absoluteness and produce evidence that such ideas represent real knowledge, then we can claim to have crossed the divide between nature and history on the one hand, and the supernatural, transcendent God on the other: but if we deny such positive content to these concepts, and insist that they can only be complementary to our consciousness of the relative and finite, then we are still trapped on the earthly side of the divide, left with only those ideas which Mother Nature has vouchsafed as fit for us to play with.

Mansel's answer to the question of critics and doubters was virtually no answer at all. According to Mansel, the biblical revelation was to be accepted in faith and humility. The testimony of Scripture should be accepted as a fact, intended for our practical guidance, in which case it would be plain and intelligible. It was only when treated as a subject for speculative analysis that it became incomprehensible.

Those who could accept this naive approach to the ancient literature would already have abdicated the use of reason, and placed themselves well beyond any risk of controversy; but Mansel's task was to offer a reasonable defence of Christianity, and while he was justified in deploying the Kantian critique against sophisticated flights of speculation, it was a very different matter to try to sidestep queries which went little beyond the demands of common sense. The faith of a rational being includes reasonable thought, and Mansel, of course, knew it:

Reason does not deceive us, if we will only read her witness aright; and Reason herself gives us warning, when we are in danger of reading it wrong. The light that is within us is not darkness; only it cannot illuminate that which is beyond the sphere of its rays . . . Within her own province, and among her own objects, let Reason go forth, conquering and to conquer. The finite objects, which she can clearly and distinctly conceive, are her lawful empire and her true glory. The countless phenomena of the visible world; the unseen things which lie in the depths of the human soul; – these are given into her hand; and over them she may reign in unquestioned dominion.[5]

Very well: but we must return yet again to the question how this earth-bound thought can claim union with the transcendent. To point us to the Bible is merely to reiterate the question.

It was hard for Mansel to kick against the pricks, and inconsistently with his criticisms of Kant he had to admit that it was the consciousness of moral obligation which compels us to assume the existence of a moral deity and to regard absolute standards of right and wrong as constituted by the nature of that deity.[6]

Combined with his correct emphasis on the central significance of the concept of personality in Christian religious thought, this could have formed the true basis upon which to construct a positive alternative to Idealism; but for Mansel it remained only an acknowledgement, prevented from further development by a misguided rejection of Kantian insights.

The attempt to make the Bible an all-sufficient testimony to truth independent of rational inquiry also placed Mansel in an awkward position in relation to the rise of scholarly biblical study. Once the problems uncovered by biblical criticism and related studies have been conceded, two consequences follow, neither of which was welcome to Mansel. First, the idea of a plain and readily intelligible biblical message, open to the grasp of any simple-minded inquirer, has to be surrendered. Second, it is precisely the very varied human element in the scriptural texts which is highlighted by criticism, thereby emphasising the central problem for Mansel of how to get from the human/historical/natural to the divine. If Moses and the prophets, the apostles and the evangelists could be treated as men like ourselves, then the Kantian critique was just as applicable to them as to Hegel, Fichte and Schelling.

Mansel showed himself very uneasy with Rowland Williams' ideas of biblical interpretation and expressed fears of the thoroughgoing rationalism 'determined at all hazards to expel the supernatural from Scripture': something which might be expected in Germany, but not in those 'who, like Dr Williams, hold fast the doctrine of the Incarnation of the Son of God'.[7] Williams for his part regretted the absence from Mansel's lectures of even the rudiments of biblical criticism: 'In all his volume not one text of Scripture is elucidated, nor a single difficulty in the evidences of Christianity removed', with the result that 'his blows fall heaviest on what it was his duty to defend'. Williams also realised the misleading nature of the supposed similarity between Mansel's argument and Butler's.[8] Nevertheless, although Williams' comments were justified, he did not go to the root of the problem. Once in the arena of honest doubt, free thought, reasonable questioning, controversy, the introduction of concepts like 'revelation' and 'incarnation', far from answering the problem, are merely a begging of the question:

We may seek as we will for a 'Religion within the limits of the bare Reason'; and we shall not find it; simply because no such thing exists; and if we dream for a moment that it does exist, it is only because we are unable or unwilling to pursue reason to its final consequences. But if we do not, others will; and the system which we have raised on the shifting basis of our arbitrary resting place, waits only till the wind of controversy blows against it, and the flood of unbelief descends upon it, to manifest itself as the work of the 'foolish man which built his house upon the sand'.9

There was something terribly prophetic in this statement which envisaged a future in which fierce Victorian religious controversies would appear at best as mere historical curiosities.

Not everyone was enthusiastically in favour of the lectures, and Mansel himself had to admit that his argument was in some respects controversial. Notable among his opponents was F. D. Maurice, who published several hundred pages of vigorous criticism based on a fundamental misunderstanding of Mansel's position.10 In the Preface to his volume Maurice makes a significant slip: Mansel is quoted to the effect that there cannot be a 'direct manifestation of the Infinite Nature of God', which becomes in Maurice's repetition, 'direct manifestation of the Nature of God', the omission of 'Infinite' being crucial. Maurice insisted that knowledge of God in this world can be genuine even if limited, and made much appeal to the Bible in support of his contention. Mansel could only reply that they were both saying the same thing, and there can be no doubt that he must have warmly supported much of the positive and still valuable exposition of the text which Maurice offered. When the difference between them is seen in relation to the future of religious thought in Britain, two comments are necessary.

First, Maurice like Mansel believed that any honest mind could and would find the biblical message plain and persuasive, and that the Church had nothing to fear from rational study of the text. He inveighed against the rationalistic approach to Paley's *Evidences* in the universities and warned of the evil consequences which followed upon the disillusionment of young men who felt cheated when they were promised objective, unprejudiced investigation, only to discover that they were being led along a well-worn path to predetermined conclusions. Yet no more than Mansel could

Maurice accept genuine biblical criticism, and his estrangement from Colenso illustrates the fact.[11]

Second, Maurice misunderstood Mansel's argument, but his rejection of it was probably the instinctive reaction of someone who sensed that Mansel had undermined belief rather than strengthening it. There was implicit in Maurice's response to Mansel the admission that if human knowledge is of necessity confined to experience of this world, this must apply to the human beings whose knowledge forms the foundation of the biblical record; in which case it must be illusion rather than revelation.

What might be called the human side of inspiration and revelation received full recognition in the Bampton Lectures for 1885 given by Frederic W. Farrar.[12] Farrar started out from the fact that the universal Church had never defined 'inspiration', and he firmly rejected the idea of 'mechanical' inspiration, by which he meant that the men and women who in various ways produced the Bible had not been somehow guided or addressed by God so as to override their natural human responses and prevent error. God reveals himself always in the same way to all men and women, and the degree of truth revealed depends on the capacity of the human receiver to respond to and grasp the revelation. The Bible has a particular claim on our attention because, simply as a matter of fact, some parts of the biblical record show a depth of understanding not generally to be found. As a record of divine revelation to certain people the Bible contains error and is overall of unequal value: but it also contains profound and essential truths which will be recognised by those who in the present are obedient to Christ and open their minds and hearts to the work of the same Holy Spirit who was at work in biblical times.

Farrar put his main point in another way by asserting that there was no essential difference between biblical history and history in general. The light of God destroys idolatry, and 'HISTORY is a ray of that light of God. A great part of the Bible is History, and all History, rightly understood, is also a Bible. Its lessons are God's divine method of slowly exposing error and of guiding into truth.' Quoting Fichte, 'God alone makes History, but He does this by the agency of man.' Again, 'secular History too is a revelation. It is, as Vico called it, "a civil Theology of Divine Providence".' And Farrar refers with approval to the view of Sebastian Franck: 'He regarded all history as a Bible.'[13]

It followed from this that Farrar would recognise the importance of biblical criticism, which endeavours to get at the original
meaning of the biblical writers by carefully studying the historical
context in which they worked and the historical circumstances in
which the men and women of the Bible lived; but he insisted that
the main spiritual truths conveyed by the Bible are few and clear
and open to any simple believer. Spiritual and moral truth were
not to be left to the mercy of technical skill, no matter how useful
the latter might be in illuminating the biblical text. He also
severely castigated much learned exposition as no better than a
perverted rationalisation of the text, produced by wrangling
clergy who had falsely set themselves above the rest of the Church.

Farrar regarded the concept of progressive revelation as essential to a proper understanding of the Bible and accepted as fruitful Lessing's view of God as the educator of the human race. It is
no doubt understandable that someone who wished to express
inspiration in dynamic terms and who believed that God was
continually revealing himself as knowledge increased should be
sufficiently impressed by the work of Darwin to see in ideas of
growth and development the chief clue to grasping the nature of
the biblical revelation; and Farrar was to speak with warm approval
of Darwin before the lectures were finished. Nevertheless, the idea
of progress in revelation raises more problems than it answers. In
so far as it draws attention to the adaptation of God's communication to the capacity of the receiver and emphasises the personal
character of the divine–human relationship it may be welcomed;
but in so far as it suggests an analogy with organic growth in man's
ever-changing knowledge of God it must be dismissed. Apart from
the insurmountable difficulty of making it fit the evidence, it
should, in the context of Farrar's argument, have meant that men
would know more of God centuries after the biblical period than
during it: a conclusion which he would not have accepted.

The problems of biblical interpretation, its wide variety and the
relationship between the readings of the simple-minded and those
of the sophisticated critic are acknowledged by Farrar, but not at
all adequately dealt with; but the basic problem for Farrar arises
from his assertion of the essential similarity between biblical
history and all other history. The question is not so much how we
can know when God is being revealed to us as against when he is
not, but how we can know there is any revelation of God at all. Why

should we believe that it is God who is making history and not just men? How would the history of the British Empire or the rise of modern Germany or the facts of life in Renaissance Italy tell us about God? And why should we not read the biblical account of Israel's birth and the rise of the monarchy in a purely secular sense, and regard the religious interpretation put upon these events as, from a later and more enlightened point of view, so much superstition? Farrar's assertion is not invalidated because it raises such questions, but they do demand an answer: and this means entering the realms of philosophical discussion. By 1885, however, serious biblical study and philosophy had become separated disciplines.

If Farrar unified the witnesses of biblical and more general history to the revelation of God, he wished to see natural science and religion as two distinct but equally legitimate areas of human activity. His eirenical aim in so doing should be fully appreciated. He spoke of the attitude of religious believers towards scientists as 'an attitude first of fierce persecution, then of timid compromise, lastly, of thankless and inevitable acceptance'. There was scarcely a nascent science 'which the accredited defenders of religion have not in their ignorance striven to overwhelm; scarcely a great discovery which, in the first instance, they did not denounce as heretical or blasphemous'. The Church record in this matter was 'Five hundred years of mistaken opposition, from the days of Roger Bacon down to those of Darwin'.[14]

Farrar accepted the solution of regarding science and religion as 'twin sisters, each studying her own sacred book of God . . . Let them study in mutual love and honour side by side, and each pronounce respecting those things which alone she knows.'[15] This was consistent with his view that the divine mind was being expressed in current events and movements; but the influence which he gladly acknowledged scientific discoveries and hypotheses had had, and could be expected to have, on religious belief give the lie to any hope of peaceful co-existence based on the utter dissimilarity of scientific and religious interests. Furthermore, according to Farrar the sacred book of religion included all history. If both history and nature reveal God, there must surely be some connection between them: a consideration made all the more likely by the obvious fact that human beings belong to both realms. We must also face the question with regard to nature which we have to face with regard to history: What is the evidence that facts or events reveal the transcendent God? How are we to counter the claim that what we really can know of facts and events suggests that complete knowledge would lead us to regard history/religion not as a separate book but as an appendix within the book of nature? This was precisely the tendency of Darwin's work, and this was why not all religious believers would share Farrar's enthusiasm for the man and his work.

Farrar's failure, however, was different from Mansel's. The latter looked backward to what was permanently outmoded; the former at least tried to look forward and appreciate the views which any credible future religious belief in Britain would have to satisfy. What they both needed was an adequate philosophy.

This need is also to be seen in *Essays and Reviews*, first published in 1860, and *Replies to 'Essays and Reviews'*, two volumes in which true and valid comment is by no means confined to one side.[16] The opening sentences of *Essays* are an acknowledgement of the fundamental threat posed by science to religious belief, which the remainder of the volume underlines rather than answering. 'In a world of mere phenomena, where all events are bound to one another by a rigid law of cause and effect', we may imagine endless cycles in a meaningless succession of events. 'This supposition transforms the universe into a dead machine.'[17] Temple might, at that stage in the nineteenth century, have substituted an organism for a machine, but this would only have strengthened the anti-religious case. Like Farrar, Temple wanted growing knowledge about nature to be regarded as a new book of revelation, without offering any reason why we should so regard it; and his view that intellectual studies in general would act upon the progress of mankind by using biblical study as a kind of centre and focal point was merely naive.

Rowland Williams' essay also resembled the later lectures of Farrar in that he wanted to reduce the difference between the experience recorded in the Bible and the general experience of mankind, and therefore depicted God acting through conscience and morality rather than through obviously supernatural inter-ventions in the normal course of events. Williams did not deny that unusual happenings could be consequent upon faith, but he did wish to deny any religious significance to what was merely strange and irrational. Geology had shown that changes in the earth's structure, even the most colossal, could be explained in terms of causes still in operation; and biblical criticism had likewise shown that God's work recorded in 'Revelation' was to be seen in just the same terms as his work among men in all times and places.

The reference to liberal criticism inevitably suggested German scholarship, and Williams explicitly based his essay on the work of the outstanding German scholar Baron Christian C. J. Bunsen, who spent much time in Britain. There could be as little doubt of Bunsen's piety as of his scholarship, and towards the end of his essay Williams mentions Bunsen's attempt to enrich the Lutheran liturgy through a collection of evangelical songs and prayers. He then goes on to make an interesting criticism:

> Yet if it be one great test of a theology, that it shall bear to be prayed, our author has hardly satisfied it. Either reverence, or deference, may have prevented him from bringing his prayers into entire harmony with his criticisms; or it may be that a discrepance, which we should constantly diminish, is likely to remain between our feelings and our logical necessities.[18]

H. J. Rose in *Replies* seized on this remark and gilded it with his own somewhat more sweeping comment:

> it often happens that a German will not cast off a certain phase of faith when he has demolished every ground which an Englishman would deem a rational and logical foundation for holding it. We ought not, therefore, to be surprised at finding that . . . Baron Bunsen . . . had a great love for devotional hymns, framed upon a very different hypothesis, and addressed to a very different frame of mind.[19]

Leaving aside Rose's absurd caricature of the typical muddled German over against the typical sensible Englishman, it must be conceded that he had touched on the fundamental weakness of Williams' essay, which lay behind Williams' own reaction to Bunsen's book of prayers and songs; and that is that prayer has no place in a world entirely explicable in naturalistic or humanistic terms. If the obviously supernatural, the miraculous, is denied as admissible evidence for religious belief, and if we are simply left with the common experience of humanity, some explicit justification is required for the claim that this experience points beyond its earthly limitations to the transcendent deity.

Nor did conservatives always agree among themselves, as can be illustrated from two *Quarterly Review* articles. In one, concerning

Essays and Reviews, Williams is criticised for asserting that it was the goodness of the works wherein lay the appeal of Christ. The reviewer comments, 'as if the appeal of Christ was mainly to the inherent goodness, and not to the manifest power of the works – a fallacy so utterly transparent that it is needless in exposing it to do more than enunciate its terms'. In the other, a review of *Aids to Faith*, we find a different emphasis: 'Even miracles themselves were not, properly speaking, instruments of conversion to those before whose eyes they were wrought; they did but call attention to the message which was the instrument of conversion.' This reviewer warmly commends the argument of Mansel's essay in *Aids*, according to which the exercise of the human will in the natural world can have effect, and therefore the divine will can also be exercised to influence events, and miracles are then seen as the consequences of action by a personal agent for moral purposes.[20]

The latter interpretation of the miraculous may seem obviously reasonable. We enjoy the best of both worlds, and there is apparently little to separate Mansel, Williams and the second conservative reviewer, while the attitude of the first reviewer can then be dismissed as an expression of mere hidebound prejudice; but because the fundamental issue has not been dealt with, the position was not, and is not, so simple. Williams insisted that narratives of the miraculous must be subject to the same kind of critical assessment as any other historical narratives, and he was bound to do so if he was persuaded by the work of Bunsen or any other liberal scholar. The uncompromising conservative would then rightly demand to know why any apparently miraculous event described in the biblical narrative should be regarded as really miraculous. It would seem to such a conservative that if events, however remarkable, are to be understood in terms of humanity's general experience and if the instruments of divine intervention are morality and conscience, the specifically biblical witness to God is dissolved away and there is no ground for equating the Bible with revelation.

C. A. Heurtley made precisely this comment on Baden Powell's essay. Powell welcomed Darwin's *Origin* as substantiating on undeniable grounds the origination of new species by natural causes, and as destined to revolutionise opinion in favour of the principle that nature's powers are self-evolving. Powell also made an emphatic distinction between the world of matter and the region of the spiritual, and asserted that human testimony was inevitably confined to the facts observable by normal perception and could not reach to the supernatural. It is not surprising that Heurtley saw in such argument the banishment of religion, and that the *Quarterly Review* should accuse Powell of 'scarcely veiled Atheism'.[21] It is also not surprising that Heurtley should make the basis of his reply to Powell an appeal to the incarnation and resurrection of Christ, since all the contributors to *Essays and Reviews* were notable members of the English Church; but it was precisely the case that the essayists had radically widened the terms of reference within which the argument had to take place. Real atheists and sceptics, and those who were to become known as agnostics, were no longer spectators at some colourful ecclesiastical tournament where little but personal honour was at stake; they were participants in the conflict, demanding satisfaction or rightfully claiming victory over liberals and conservatives alike.

The head-on nature of the disagreement between liberals and conservatives is also illustrated by Christopher Wordsworth's vehement and mindless attack on Jowett, and the fact that Samuel Wilberforce could write his Preface to *Replies* without having read the essays which comprised it. The whole issue seemed obvious to such men: once liberal critical principles had been admitted, the supernatural was ex hypothesi excluded and the Ark of the Lord had passed into the camp of the Philistines. Jowett, however, believed that explicit and willing acceptance of biblical criticism was the cure for two evils. The first was the large variety of interpretations which had arisen because men had sought in Scripture only the confirmation of views which they already held; and the second was the tendency to see critical observations which any intelligent person could make for himself as necessarily expressions of unbelief and atheism. Jowett wished to make scholarly biblical study a normal part of liberal education, like the study of Sophocles and Plato, and he was optimistic about the establishment of the original meanings of the biblical authors and the general effect this could have on the unity of Christendom; and although today we might make a more sober assessment of the achievements and potential of criticism, much in his essay is true and well said. The only serious problem which remains is the usual one concerning the inspiration of the Bible, its claim to authority as revelation.

Jowett remarked,

As the idea of nature enlarges, the idea of revelation also enlarges; it was a temporary misunderstanding which severed them. And as the knowledge of nature which is possessed by the few is communicated in its leading features at least to the many, they will receive with it a higher conception of the ways of God to man. It may hereafter appear as natural to the majority of mankind to see the providence of God in the order of the world as it once was to appeal to interruptions of it.[22]

For the conservative such words meant death to religion. The apparent equation of nature with revelation, Providence with history and the Bible with great literature, ruled out evidences of the supernatural. As Wilberforce stated, the claim that we can only give assent to that which is within the grasp of the unassisted human intellect must lead to an essentially atheistic pantheism, and there was something inherently absurd in asserting doctrines which were then held to be open to discussion.

Jowett and other liberals could only have replied to such criticism by entering the realms of metaphysical discussion, but they were satisfied with the self-evident rightness of many of their positions regarding detailed exposition of the biblical text or investigations into Church history. Therefore critical scholarship should be presented vigorously and clearly to the educated public, and it would persuade simply by means of its inherent correctness. This approach is very clearly illustrated by C. W. Goodwin's essay on the Mosaic Cosmology. Goodwin has no difficulty demolishing past attempts to reconcile Genesis and geology, and having conceded everything science can demand, has equally little difficulty stating the religious message of Genesis chapter 1. G. Rorison in *Replies* expresses a large measure of agreement with Goodwin; but there was a breaking point. Either one accepted the supernatural, or one did not; and if the supernatural were accepted, then along with the human element in the Bible there would be no difficulty recognising the divine; and the presence of the divine would guarantee the absence of positive error. This then leaves us with a dilemma: to accept Goodwin means, as Rorison correctly perceived, abandoning any clear evidence of divine revelation. The unity and design of the world, progressive revelation and a kind of divine pedagogy are wholly inadequate to the task of lifting us from nature to nature's God, and from history to providential rule and supervision. To accept Rorison means denying error in the biblical text, a counsel of despair which can only lead back to the kind of attempted reconciliation between science and the Bible already rejected by both writers. Rorison himself demonstrated as much by trying to maintain that the opening account of creation is to be understood in terms of poetic parallelism and symbolism. We must understand the influence of the Divine Spirit on the mind of the author to have been such that when new knowledge came 'the general dignity, congruity, and religious impressiveness of the lesson should suffer no harm from the advent of such knowledge': phraseology which can mean anything or nothing.[23] In fact, neither the public confession of biblical error nor the attempt to cloak and dissemble it before the face of the uncommitted will persuade any honest mind. However pious and however sophisticated, it will create the correct impression of being so much sales talk. Lists of errors will exhibit the fallibility of 'revelation'; lists of dodges will exhibit the fallibility of the expositor.

The publication of Darwin's *Origin of Species* in 1859 seriously aggravated what was already becoming a very difficult situation for defenders of the faith. If the concept of evolution was not new, in Darwin's hypothesis it provided significantly greater strength to the science side in the science/religion conflict, and to those who wished to use science as the justification for scepticism, and inflicted a correspondingly heavy blow on those who defended religion. Darwin and Wallace by their own research added greatly to the large number of facts already accumulated which suggested or demanded explanation in evolutionary terms, and Malthus was adapted to provide a plausible mechanism whereby mere change could be transformed into the inevitable development of varied species. The fearful spectacle of a world entirely explicable in naturalistic terms had taken another and massive step towards realisation.

Indeed, one could go further. A concept so broad in its reference and comprehensive in its scope could be taken as the expression of something more than the summation of findings in zoology and botany. 'Evolution', that is, causally determined change in directions fixed by purely immanent forces, could be taken to represent the whole naturalistic enterprise, describing the history of the earth, the solar system and the universe, as well as the long process whereby plants and creatures of very varied types had appeared on the planet. Robert Chambers, Darwin's notorious predecessor, had opened his book with reference to the nebular hypothesis, and if the concept of development was to be the key to understanding the antecedents and consequents of the appearance of life, the whole range of the sciences would provide contributions to its fuller understanding. Evolution therefore meant atheism, the all-sufficiency of scientific explanation, systematically excluding the supernatural, and making life itself the ultimate flowering of physical processes rather than a transcendent gift.

Much natural science was concerned with questions other than those directly related to biological evolution, and yet the evolutionary idea could be taken as bringing into focus the ultimate explanation of life implied by all scientific endeavour. If it were true, not only did this make it impossible to accept the details of Genesis chapters 1 and 2 at their face value; it also seemed to make the whole idea of divine creativity redundant. This devastating conclusion had long since been anticipated by religious believers, but Darwin and his supporters unified massive evidence into a justifiable and wholly naturalistic system which was too firmly based to be dismissed or rationalised away. Darwin's hypothesis was open to serious scientific question, and its publication was followed by many years of scientific argument and discussion; but the tendency of the argument was to prove its fruitfulness rather than its falsity.

Initially, therefore, it was possible for conservative religious believers to challenge Darwin with some show of reason. This is well illustrated by the notorious debate between Samuel Wilberforce and T. H. Huxley at the Oxford meeting of the British Association held in 1860: a contest which Huxley is supposed to have won by a knock-out blow, although it would be truer to say that it was won comfortably by Wilberforce on points.[24] Nevertheless, continued conservative attempts to solve a genuine problem simply by denying evolutionary theory have proved futile. At the same time, it must be confessed that liberal attempts to come to terms with Darwin were no better.

Exactly thirty years after the publication of Darwin's *Origin* a group of Anglican scholars published a collection of essays entitled *Lux Mundi*, generally remembered for the hostility it aroused among the conservatives on account of concessions to liberal ways of interpreting the Bible and what was taken to be an

undermining of Jesus' teaching authority.[25] Of far greater significance, however, was the attempt to come to terms with the theory
of evolution by seeing in it a revealed truth which recalled the
Church to a proper recognition of the immanence as well as the
transcendence of God, and which was a timely reminder of the
Johannine Logos doctrine linking the incarnate human life of the
second Person of the Trinity with his work in creation. If this
attempt to bring science within the framework of Christian
theology is open to severe criticism, it must nevertheless be recognised that the essays of Aubrey Moore and J. R. Illingworth on the
subject were bold and constructive and imply the need to make a
positive assertion concerning theology and science, or give up
Christian belief altogether.

Moore, on 'The Christian Doctrine of God', acknowledged that
religion saw man's relationship with deity in personal and moral
terms, while 'philosophy' insisted that the object of knowledge
must be a unity. That is, two mutually exclusive truths could not
simply be left side by side. This meant that Darwinism, from a
religious point of view, must be making clearer or re-emphasising
already revealed truth, and according to Moore this was precisely
the case:

Either God is everywhere present in nature, or He is nowhere. He cannot be here and not there. He cannot delegate His power to demigods
called 'second causes'. In nature everything must be His work or
nothing. We must frankly return to the Christian view of direct Divine
agency, the immanence of Divine power in nature from end to end, the
belief in a God in Whom not only we, but all things have their being, or
we must banish Him altogether. It seems as if, in the providence of God,
the mission of modern science was to bring home to our unmetaphysical
ways of thinking the great truth of the Divine immanence in creation,
which is not less essential to the Christian idea of God than to a philosophical view of nature.[26]

Moore chose to call his interpretation of the evidence a 'higher
pantheism', and this phrase was accepted, although with justifiable hesitation, by Illingworth, who saw in the opening of the
Fourth Gospel an assertion that the incarnation was not a unique
event, bearing no relation to the doctrine of creation, but the
supreme expression in human history of what is and always has
been true. The Logos is involved in the creation of life from the
beginning and continually.

mnetcentury

According to Illingworth this truth became neglected through concentration on the work of Christ in individual salvation, but its revival in the nineteenth century would mean the restoration of final causes to the realm of nature and give a sound intellectual grounding to that profound sense of the divine in nature felt by many scientists and expressed by poets and artists.

Of course, both Moore and Illingworth knew that they were putting a theological interpretation on to the scientific data. Christian theology was accepted as true, the theory of evolution was accepted as true, and this was the way in which both had to be understood in a unified scheme: but the question remained whether or not the interpretation could actually be made to fit the facts. The assertion that God is immediately at work in nature is not only not evident in nature itself, but appears to be contradicted by much that occurs. If God is so careful of the sparrow that falls, why is nature so organised that a great superfluity of them are created only in order to be inevitably annihilated? Venereal disease and AIDS, cancer and myxomatosis, death by starvation and violence, all these and much else of a painful and repulsive character are part of 'nature'.

The dismissal of secondary causation as in effect an illusion obscuring the immediate activity of God strikes not only at the heart of all scientific endeavour, but all common sense. Once we substitute immediately observable concrete facts for an abstract generalisation it becomes impossible to suppose, for example, that the wind blowing autumn leaves off the trees is really God at work, not least because God would have to be at one and the same time the force of the wind and the life of the tree, active in the leaves that fall and in the leaves that remain. Is God pushing up every blade of grass and guiding every worm, not to speak of the bird that eats the worm and the cat that stalks the bird? How is this omnipresent deity related to the processes of our own bodies? And how is divinity operating when the materials and forces of nature are bent to the purposes of men in the production of things?

The following passage from Moore's essay summarises his whole argument and illustrates its fundamental weakness:

The religious equivalent for 'immanence' is 'omnipresence', and the omnipresence of God is a corollary of a true monotheism. As long as any remains of dualism exist, there is a region, however small, impervious to

the Divine power. But the Old Testament doctrine of creation, by excluding dualism, implies from the first, if it does not teach, the omnipresence
of God. For the omnipotence of God underlies the doctrine of creation,
and omnipotence involves omnipresence. Hence we find the Psalmists
and Prophets ascribing natural processes immediately to God. They
know nothing of second causes. The main outlines of natural science, the
facts of generation and growth, are familiar enough to them, yet every
fact is ascribed immediately to the action of God. He makes the grass to
grow upon the mountains . . . [27]

Almost every assertion in this quotation is untrue or misleading:
the omnipresence of God, as well as being an ambiguous phrase,
is not a corollary of monotheism, and the insertion of 'true'
indicates that we are dealing with monotheism not simpliciter, but
as understood by Moore. The term 'dualism' is ambiguous. It is
evident from the Bible, all history and today's newspaper that
there are, and always have been, areas impervious to the divine
power, in the sense that in them there is no evidence of the actual
exercise of divine power and plenty of evidence to the contrary. If
Moore includes nature in such areas, then he is begging the question. If he means only realms of human affairs, he is wrong. The
facts therefore imply dualism in the sense that the world and God
are different, and that the world has a certain independence of
God; but it does not imply dualism in the sense that there are two
gods. The Old Testament account of creation denies dualism in
the second sense, but asserts it in the first; and it does not imply
the omnipresence of God in nature.

The term 'omnipotence' is vague, and does not necessarily
involve the concept of omnipresence. That it can be defined so as
to exclude it was well known to the older natural theologians.
Finally, psalmists and prophets do not ascribe natural processes
immediately to God, as Moore would have realised if he had
stopped to ask himself why he had felt it necessary to insert the
statement about the facts of generation and growth being well
known to them. All of the psalms, many of the prophecies and
almost the whole of Job are poetic expressions and contain, along
with much else in the Old Testament, abundant figures of speech.
The Old Testament can only be made to support the doctrine of
creatio continua by ignoring the fact.

Charles Gore in his essay on 'The Holy Spirit and Inspiration',
an essay which got him into such trouble with the conservatives,

wanted to depict all life as the gift of the Holy Spirit; yet he could also speak of the mere forces of nature which dominate human beings and prevent them realising their true freedom. A similar distinction was made in order to explain the imperfections of a divinely inspired Scripture: but we are left wondering how the concept of a merely natural life is related to the concept of life which in its entirety is the gift of the Holy Spirit.

The basic weakness from which *Lux Mundi* suffered is made clear in the Preface, also written by Gore. The aim of the volume was to present the ancient and unalterable truths of Christianity in terms which would be more readily intelligible to contemporary society: 'to put the Catholic faith into its right relation to modern intellectual and moral problems'; 'to present positively the central ideas and principles of religion, in the light of contemporary thought and current problems'.[28] Yet the challenge which faced the Church was not one of mere rephrasing or absorbing fresh material, but of getting to grips with an outlook wholly inimical to belief in the transcendent, the supernatural. Faith can scarcely be expressed in the language of scepticism or a naturalistic enterprise inherently atheistic.

Furthermore, Gore and his colleagues genuinely wanted fair and frank discussion, but they were continually aware of the strong conservative presence in the Church, and the desire to avoid offence meant that orthodox conclusions had to be guaranteed. This is not to say that the essayists were not themselves genuine orthodox believers, but there was never any chance that the radical rethinking necessary for a proper restatement could actually take place. Gore admitted that the three subjects sin, historical evidence and miracles could not be treated through lack of space; but he gave the assurance in so many words that the right conclusions would have been reached if more thorough treatment had been included. Both the omissions and the assurance were mistakes, since the attempt to handle these subjects in unprejudiced fashion would have taken any thinker to the heart of the conflict between belief and unbelief, and would have shown that the problems are by no means all on one side.

George J. Romanes was an eminent biologist and a man of deeply sensitive faith whose belief was seriously shaken by what he regarded as the double assault of Darwinism and negative biblical criticism. He realised the inadequacy of Paley's natural theology and at first regarded Christianity as 'played out' and destined to fall victim to a purely rational system;[29] but faith was restored partly by what might be called the conservative results of New Testament liberal criticism in Britain and partly by acceptance of the theology expressed by Aubrey Moore. Romanes recognised that there were some matters of a significance too far-reaching and profound to be settled by rational argument, but he also knew that some account must be given of Christian belief, and he could only cope with evolutionary theory by identifying causation with the divine will and, like Moore, seeing God active everywhere. His answer to the problem of evil and suffering raised in acute form by this view was that the waste and pain were justified by the results, the highest and best arising out of a struggle which eliminated the weaker and inferior; and this could be related to a hope which Illingworth expressed, that a new and greater humanity, fore-shadowed by Christ, might arise in later stages of the evolutionary process.

As pointed out earlier, the obvious objection to this essentially Utilitarian explanation for the existence of evil is that a genuinely omnipotent deity has no need to be a Utilitarian; and if we surrender the omnipotence, what happens to the corollary of omnipresence? John Stuart Mill gave forceful expression to the criticism:

If it be said that God does not take sufficient account of pleasure and pain to make them the reward or punishment of the good or the wicked, but that virtue is itself the greatest good and vice the greatest evil, then these at least ought to be dispensed to all according to what they have done to deserve them; instead of which, every kind of moral depravity is entailed upon multitudes by the fatality of their birth; through the fault of their parents, of society, or of uncontrollable circumstances, certainly through no fault of their own. Not even on the most distorted and contracted theory of good which ever was framed by religious or philo-sophical fanaticism, can the government of Nature be made to resemble the work of a being at once good and omnipotent.[30]

Mill could not accept that the God revealed in the teaching of Jesus was the same as the God of nature, and he pointed out that in practice believers sacrificed the omnipotence of God in the interest of preserving his goodness.

Mill's willingness to surrender prepossessions and evaluate the evidence for rational religious belief as objectively as possible only throws into relief the seriousness and difficulty of the problems which existed for any thinker on this subject in the late nineteenth century. He rejected the traditional natural theology, but still felt the tug of the argument from design, and was consequently somewhat at a loss to know how to estimate the evidence of evolution by natural selection in this respect. He was prepared to believe in a deity of limited power struggling with the evil or intractable forces of nature. He believed that good was accomplished by human beings, not in some kind of return to nature, but in controlling and restraining natural forces on a carefully selective basis; but he failed to follow up his own insight that it was possible to define 'nature' so as to include rather than exclude human nature. He regarded God as ruling nature through secondary causes and as not exercising any direct influence on the human will, leaving himself perilously dependent on the design argument if he was to retain natural theology at all; while at the same time he rejected the miraculous on similar grounds to those of Hume, and raised the perfectly reasonable question why, if God deviates occasionally from his ordinary mode of government in order to accomplish good, he does not do this more often. Yet, finally, he wanted to encourage hope, the outlook without which the quality of human life was liable to deteriorate greatly; and he was profoundly impressed by the ministry of Christ recorded in the gospels.

There was indeed a general concern among thinkers of all types to preserve the quality of life, which certainly included, whether or not it could be defined as, life's moral quality. This quality of life was to be recognised and justified, although some in effect destroyed it without in any way meaning to do so; while others veered towards making it the basis of their argument for religion, without actually doing so. Frederick Temple in his Bampton Lectures of 1884 asserted that the fundamental evidence for the existence of God 'is to be found in the voice of conscience',[31] but he envisaged the exercise of the will which is essential to morality as being a kind of occasional breaking into the uniformity of nature, this uniformity being general rather than absolute. Likewise, divine miracles were exceptional acts, and along with Paley and the argument from design, corroborations of the moral and spiritual message of the Bible. Needless to say, genuine insight, like the seed among thorns, stood not a chance in this environment.

St George Mivart believed that theism should have a rational basis, although the foundation upon which he built his justification of religious belief was not dialectical, but our awareness of free will, causation, morality and obligation. These are facts which can neither be explained nor explained away: they are 'primary and fundamental intuitions'.[32] The original creation of the world is no concern of physical science, which deals with the already created natural order ruled by secondary causes. The theist will see God acting on this order through natural laws, and he will detect intelligent guidance in the evolutionary process; but this will be because he already believes in God, the creator, on the basis of his fundamental intuitions, and he will bring this belief to the facts uncovered by science:

The theist, having arrived at his theistic convictions from quite other sources than a consideration of zoological or botanical phenomena, returns to the consideration of such phenomena and views them in a theistic light without of course asserting or implying that such light has been derived *from them*, or that there is an obligation of reason so to view them on the part of others.[33]

Nevertheless, if the basis of religious belief is a set of intuitions common to humanity, Mivart's argument implies that a sufficiently honest reflection upon experience will persuade anyone, and therefore that genuine religious belief will have a universal character, whatever cultural differences there may be in its expression.

It also implies that the laws of nature in themselves provide no foundation for faith, but there were others who tried to argue differently. The concept of law seemed to offer an appropriate means whereby the divine transcendence and immanence could be combined, and the demands of both theology and science satisfied. Perhaps the most famous attempt to argue along these lines was Henry Drummond's *Natural Law in the Spiritual World*, published in the summer of 1883. The vast number of copies sold and the correspondence which Drummond received bear witness to the profound anxiety created in many minds by the implications of a wholly naturalistic explanation of life. The book arose out of the fact that Drummond taught classes in both science and religion, and his awareness that science had a much more obvious power of persuasion than religion, especially if the latter meant dogma based on authority or appeals to the miraculous. Just as

Herbert Spencer and others had extended the principles of science into social theory, so Drummond wanted to extend them into religion. He rejected Bushnell's treatment of nature as providing mere symbols of religious truth, and tried to present concrete illustrations of a world ruled by law in both its spiritual and natural aspects, thus removing any reason for seeing the two as in some kind of opposition to each other.

Drummond wanted to see law operating in religious experience in just the same way as it is seen operating in nature, but the most he could hope to achieve was the establishment of analogies between scientific and religious experience, and the question whether or not the analogies were justified would still remain to be answered. As he himself put it, 'It is clear that we can only express the Spiritual Laws in language borrowed from the visible universe. Being dependent for our vocabulary on images, if an altogether new and foreign set of laws existed in the Spiritual World, they could never take shape as definite ideas from mere want of words.'[34]

Hume, and more recent thinkers such as Ayer and Russell, would not have been slow to draw the sceptical conclusion implied in the opening sentence.

Drummond himself came to regard the argument of the book as unsatisfactory, although to the end of his life he felt the need to make some kind of reconciliation between science and religion. The Duke of Argyll also appreciated the dismay which could result from the contemplation of a universe governed by iron necessity, and in his volume *The Reign of Law*, sought to replace this picture with one which took into account the amenability of natural processes to description in terms of intelligent purpose, and the fact that human beings could bend these forces to achieve their own ends on a large scale. The world was altogether more flexible and personal in character than the sceptic claimed. Argyll's account of the various meanings which could be attached to the term 'law' in science was lucid and accurate; and he accepted evolution as a fact, which should be interpreted as the history of creation. Huxley made a scathing attack on Argyll, but it is the latter who is persuasive on the subject of 'law' in science, and not Huxley, who seems to have been overwhelmed by resentment against any religious apologist who included in his apologia positive assertions about science.

Argyll's problem was to establish a possible view of the universe as the actual one, and while much of what he said was valuable and worth while, he could only appeal to the traditional design argument to reach the desired conclusion. He did this with full confidence in its validity, even though at the same time he made the fatal admission which concedes all to the sceptic: 'It is true, indeed, that in all human machinery we know by the evidence of sight the ultimate agency to which the machinery is due, whereas in the machinery of Nature the ultimate agency is concealed from sight.'35 What was supposed to be open to immediate inspection was the machine-like design of nature, a view which can only be regarded as a silent tribute to the influence of Paley.

John Henry Newman, like Drummond and Argyll, emphasised the unity of the world and the consequent unity which should mark our knowledge of it; and he argued for the recognition of theology as a science within what would be regarded as a normal university education. At the same time he rejected the idea that God was known through the processes and laws of nature, insisting that this would reduce religion to mere sentiment, a kind of pantheistic admiration which one person might feel and another might not, the one attitude being as much or as little justified as the other.

Newman's assertion that God is more than nature seems obvious enough to any Christian theist, but his conclusion that theology is therefore a science suggests that God is the object of theological or religious knowledge in the same way as nature is the object of the natural sciences. Newman's problem was to show how this is so bearing in mind the not insignificant number of people who disclaimed such knowledge or even asserted it to be impossible, or who claimed the knowledge but had doubts about it. It was one thing to display a 'scientific' theological knowledge when this comprised expertise in documentary evidence concerning doctrine, but confrontation with outright scepticism was another and very different matter. Within the walls of Christendom, Newman moved with a certain fundamental assurance, even if that movement involved a gradual, momentous and anguished change of belief; but when he peered out at the surrounding paganism he was at a loss. He could see traditional natural theology leading to the scepticism of Hume, but he could only dismiss that philosopher as 'This acute, though most low-minded of speculators', and along with Hobbes and Bentham brand him as 'simply a disgrace'.[36]

If Newman was at a loss, his work is nevertheless not without value. It has the character of 'clearing the decks'. He knew what line of argument not to follow, and he stated clearly the implications genuine religious knowledge would have for the authority of the natural sciences. In an address to medical students of the Catholic University of Ireland, November 1858, he pointed out that if belief in the God who is more than nature is true, then sometimes perfectly correct medical knowledge will have to give way to advice based upon very different, moral and spiritual, considerations. Absorption in scientific research could lead men to mistake the truth of their discoveries for their overriding lawfulness, but 'a thing may be ever so true in medicine, yet may be unlawful in fact, in consequence of the *higher* law of morals and religion having come to some different conclusion'.[37]

This raises the suspicion that the labelling of religious or theological knowledge as 'scientific' might be misleading, and there are indications in this collection of lectures and essays that later reflection led Newman towards a different view. In so far as Newman tried to justify religious knowledge in the terms he originally set out, he ran the grave danger of rehabilitating the kind of natural theology he had rightly rejected, but the following statements take us into a different realm of thought:

But the phenomena, which are the basis of morals and Religion, have nothing of this luminous evidence. Instead of being obtruded upon our notice, so that we cannot possibly overlook them, they are the dictates either of Conscience or of Faith. They are faint shadows and tracings, certain indeed, but delicate, fragile, and almost evanescent, which the mind recognizes at one time, not at another . . .

we depend upon a seat of government which is in another world; we are directed and governed by intimations from above.[38]

Newman was understandably horrified when he saw education developing in conscious distinction from the knowledge of God, but what he was doing in reply was not so much arguing for the inclusion of a subject in the curriculum, as feeling after a whole view of the world, a metaphysical system of quite different character from that which could be constructed from the purely empirical deductions permitted or encouraged by the natural sciences.

John Tyndall in his presidential address to the British Association gathered in Belfast reached a conclusion at the opposite
pole to Newman's although his argument was not without its paradoxical character. Part of it was an imaginary discussion between
Bishop Butler and a disciple of Lucretius. The conclusion of
Butler's reply to the Lucretian is that even a complete scientific
description of the world, including human beings, 'cannot satisfy
the human understanding in its demand for logical continuity
between molecular processes and the phenomena of consciousness. This is a rock on which materialism must inevitably split
whenever it pretends to be a complete philosophy of life.'39
Tyndall comments that such reasoning is unanswerable. Later we
read, 'Man the *object* is separated by an impassable gulf from man
the *subject.* There is no motor energy in intellect to carry it without
logical rupture from the one to the other.'40 Tyndall asserts the
inexplicable significance and mystery of life and morality, and
points to the deep-seated feelings of awe, reverence and wonder
which form the immovable basis of religion; and we begin to
wonder why he should have suffered such bitter attacks from the
faithful. We seem to have here genuine clues to the distinct but
essential contributions which both religion and science must
make to our proper understanding of the world and man's place
in it.

Hopes, however, are doomed to disappointment, and we realise
that fierce opposition to Tyndall was far from being the mere
fulmination of bigotry. His conclusion is that religion becomes
'grotesque' and 'mischievous, if permitted to intrude on the
region of *knowledge,* over which it holds no command', but is
'capable of being guided to noble issues in the region of *emotion,*
which is its proper and elevated sphere'.41 According to Tyndall,
though, all life is indissolubly joined with matter; mind is controlled by matter; and all events are to be explained in terms of
absolutely unbroken causal sequence. He refuses to regard this
explanation of things as materialistic because he wants to regard
the power at work behind all phenomena as a mystery; but taken
with his dismissal of ideas of a transcendent deity as merely anthropomorphic, the best we can hope for by way of religious belief is
pantheism. The believer is relieved of even that which he hath.

J. R. Seeley approached the controversy from a different angle
but tried to promote a similar point of view. According to Seeley,

the supernatural was not essential to Christianity but a mere 'accident', and he proferred as an alternative uniting science and religion a kind of Spinozism in which both scientific method and the sentiments and insights of great literature would join to give us a rounded and true appreciation of the world and our life in it. 'The present question relates not to any God who is beyond Nature, but to a God who is only Nature called by another name. And the question whether any worship worth calling worship can be offered to such a Deity'.[42] Seeley's answer was positive, and he was pained that in consequence he should have been thought to deny Christianity and the Bible.

William James, in his classic Gifford Lectures, given around the turn of the century, made explicit comment on Newman's attempt to justify theology as a science. James clearly understood what Newman was aiming at, but believed that the role of reason could only be to find evidences in favour of already established feeling, however complex the relation between feeling and rational reflection might be. This meant that philosophy could never satisfy the hope of producing a demonstration that this or that religion was true, that there was a God of this or that nature; and not without considerable justification, James claimed that the history of religious belief and practice proved as much. His conclusion was that philosophy must abandon metaphysics and deduction in favour of criticism and induction, and theology be transformed into 'science of religions'.[43] He referred favourably to Seeley's *Natural Religion*, regretting that it was too little read, and in his Postscript he even pleaded that polytheism should be taken more seriously, as being in any case the real religion of common people; thereby returning to an idea which Hume had cynically floated a century and a half before, and which was also not distantly related to Mill's belief in a God of finite power.

Finally, reference must be made to two thinkers who expressed and by their own work encouraged intellectual tendencies which passed into the twentieth century and, directly or indirectly, powerfully influenced the minds of those who gave serious thought to religion. The first is S. R. Driver, who became Regius Professor of Hebrew and Canon of Christ Church in the University of Oxford, and the second, Thomas Henry Huxley.

It is precisely their representative character which makes these two men significant for British thought, and certainly not any original, unique contribution to knowledge. Driver's influence was crucial because of his learning, his caution, the balanced and objective character of his judgment, his integrity and commitment to religious belief and his position both in academic circles and the Church.[44] First he became persuaded through the most careful study that German critical scholarship was the correct method of attaining a right understanding of the biblical text, and then during the last two decades of the century proceeded to establish this method as the dominant one in all serious biblical study. Driver summed up in himself all that was best and most constructive in liberal criticism, and because he had taken time to be convinced by it himself, and because he did not enter the field with some theoretical axe to grind, the sheer reasonableness of this approach shone through his work and was able to make its own impression by means of its own undeniable weight.

Furthermore, Driver once and for all relieved students of any obligation to render consistent the literal assertions of Scripture and the literal assertions of science when these are in obvious conflict, and he unambiguously drew attention to the essentially religious and moral character of the biblical message. Henceforth critical study should proceed quite undistracted by findings in the natural sciences, using the whole apparatus of scholarship to make clear the unchanging spiritual truths couched in the language and forms of ancient Near Eastern peoples.

Driver, however, felt the need to give some justification of this procedure by making clearer exactly what was going on when some biblical assertions were dismissed as wrong or of mere secondary importance, while others were taken to be expressions of eternal truth. He did this by distinguishing between the form of the biblical message, and its content. H. E. Ryle likewise referred to the 'form' of the Hebrew narrative, which 'is but the shell and husk of the Divine Message'.[45] Criticism, according to Driver, was concerned with the outer form, or human aspect, of the Bible, and signs of human error and weakness could be willingly conceded since this in no way affected the value of the treasure to be found in the earthen vessels:

It is impossible to doubt that the main conclusions of critics with reference to the authorship of the books of the Old Testament rest upon reasonings the cogency of which cannot be denied without denying the ordinary principles by which history is judged and the evidence estimated . . . the conclusions which satisfy the common unbiassed and unsophisticated reason of mankind prevail in the end . . . Those conclusions affect not the *fact* of revelation, but only its *form* . . . They do not touch either the authority or the inspiration of the scriptures of the Old Testament.[46]

The character of any particular passage was therefore not to be decided a priori but by applying the canons of judgment normally employed in historical and literary study:

There is a human factor in the Bible, which, though quickened and sustained by the informing Spirit, is never wholly absorbed or neutralized by it; and the limits of its operation cannot be ascertained by an arbitrary a priori determination of the methods of inspiration; the only means by which they can be ascertained is by an assiduous and comprehensive study of the facts presented by the Old Testament itself.[47]

When Driver employed the historical method in the interpretation of the Book of Genesis, using material from earlier lectures in the Oxford School of Theology, he readily admitted that this revealed uncertainties in certain parts of the book, but insisted that this did not detract from the spiritual value of its contents. For example, the truth about God's relationship with the world had been grafted on to the false science of antiquity. The first eleven chapters contained much that could not be regarded as a record of historical fact, but 'the seemingly historical narratives' conveyed an implicit spiritual message.[48] At this point, however, we must question the innocent-looking distinction between form and content, external form and inner substance, spiritual truths and the material fabric once necessary to give them substance and support. It conjures up pictures satisfying to the imagination, the worthless husk or shell being removed in order to release for our consumption the nourishing grain or kernel: but can the distinction, so plain to observation in the analogy, be so readily applied to the biblical text? An illustration may make the problem clearer.

Let us suppose that we are introduced to someone who, we are most earnestly informed, has messages to convey of the most profound significance for mankind, but whose mode of expression creates difficulties for the listener. He speaks in a strange tongue, but the mutual friend will translate. His diction is unclear and his grammar imperfect,but repetition and careful attention will solve these problems. The content of the messages will amply repay the effort, we are assured.

So far, the distinction between form, the manner of expression, and content, the matter to be expressed, is sensible and helpful. We do not wish to miss something of great importance merely because it comes to us in an odd, at times garbled and piecemeal form and in a foreign language; and we respect the mutual friend.

Let us suppose, however, that as we listen we are first of all regaled with statements of fact which we know to be untrue, and which our friend agrees are well wide of the mark; and that as we proceed we are further regaled with many narratives concerning the ancestors of the stranger, some of which are entertaining but incredible, and some of which are more or less repulsive. Therefore, after some time we ask for a pause in the proceedings, and not wishing to appear discourteous to the stranger, ask our friend when we are going to get to the important part. He then tells us, to our astonishment, that it was important from the beginning, and that he had warned us not to be put off by the foreign tongue, the indistinct speech, the repetition and inconsistency. We reply that we were quite prepared for a difficult mode of expression, and are still happy to put up with it, and even to learn the stranger's language and habits of expression ourselves; but we can see little of value in what has so far been said, the content of the so-called message.

Our friend sympathises with the difficulty, but then explains that much of what we call the content of the message is really only part of the mode of expression. Not only are the language and pronunciation and general 'style' of the stranger inescapable cultural characteristics, but so also what he says: the antiquated picture of the world he expounds, the wheelings and dealings of long-deceased ancestors, tales of envy, deceit, murder, genocide, revenge, the slaughter of countless animals, not to speak of natural events which strain credulity to breaking point; and all of these not merely presided over and connived at by some primitively conceived deity, but actually commanded by the same. These are all part of the form, the mode of expression.

Whatever the limitations of this caricature might be, two related truths are at this stage apparent: first, the distinction between form and content has ceased to be properly observed and the words are being used in a manner not generally understood, and confusing rather than helpful. Second, if profound and permanent truth is really contained in the stranger's utterances, some way of eliciting it must be discovered quite other than merely translating his language and learning to appreciate his cultural characteristics. Driver's approach was not wrong, but inadequate. His actual method of getting at the religious truth of the Bible was to select what he already believed to be the truth and ignore the rest as part of the dispensable form in which it appeared; but this is merely to leave unanswered the question why we should accept one part of the text rather than another.

An even more fundamental question left unanswered is why we should accept any part of the text at all in so far as it claims to reveal truth about God. Driver thought that he had disposed of science's challenge to biblical authority by relegating its relevance to parts or aspects of the text which have no doctrinal significance, but the scepticism based on scientific success not only calls into question the inspired character of given documents, but the very existence of the one who is supposed to have inspired them. Not only is doubt cast on the envoy's credentials, but also on the existence of the kingdom which he is supposed to represent.

Even conservatives could not avoid being influenced by the critical method which Driver did so much to establish in Britain, and yet conservative circles have only accepted such scholarship in part and with varying degrees of reluctance or even hostility. This has left conservative groups in the Church stranded between extremes of banality and near superstition on the one hand, and cautious willingness to receive acceptable conclusions supported by scholarship on the other.

Yet the conservative criticism has point: if we treat biblical books just like other literature, we are ignoring their essential character. The biblical documents belong to the world of nature and human affairs, but they proclaim a deity unique, transcendent and immanent. The severance of God and nature implied in the liberal critical approach is untrue to the fundamental character and purpose of the documents themselves, as well as leaving naturalistic explanations free to run rampant through every department of the natural order, including the human.

If liberal critics confine themselves entirely to treating biblical books by means of literary, historical and critical methods recognised in all fields of similar research, they are merely participating in the naturalistic enterprise. What is required, however, is not that this participation should be surrendered, but that it should be set within a wider context. Surrender would mean failure to acknowledge what is only too true, that the documents belong very much to this world. The addition of philosophical reflection, on the other hand, is not a mere appendix to the main enterprise, but an attempt to grapple with the problems raised by taking the proclaimed purpose of the documents seriously. To do this only for the sake of developing an historical understanding of the documents involves a self-defeating abstraction of one area of human history and literature from all the rest, and a denial of what the biblical authors themselves strenuously maintained.

In biblical study, Driver typified the general approach to religious matters suggested by James: whatever private belief might be held, the student or scholar as such should concentrate upon what reason could establish with certainty or probability. The enterprise was to be a purely phenomenological one, to which personal religious affirmation might or might not be attached. The self-proclaimed envoy was to be treated simply as a human being, like everyone else. If, however, he should turn out to be the genuine ambassador of a real kingdom with which one had to enter into some kind of relationship, what then? Being thoroughly informed about the nature of the representative is scarcely a substitute for decision making about that which he represents.

Ironically, T. H. Huxley fully appreciated the situation. Huxley was bitterly opposed to 'the clergy', 'ecclesiasticism', 'theology', that is to say, the religious establishment and its dogmatic systems; but he claimed to be a genuine believer in the Bible and its highest moral and religious teaching. He welcomed German biblical scholarship and had some acquaintance with critical methods, and he was obviously pleased to find support among churchmen for the rational undermining of conservative positions and consequent weakening of conservative influence in society. At the same time he believed in scientific method as the one sure path to discovery of the truth, rejected the distinction between the natural and the supernatural, and looked upon the universe as entirely governed by causal connections which were, at least in principle, describable and explicable in rational terms. Human nature and human artefacts were part of nature as a whole, the products of natural forces which must provide the ultimate explanation for all human thinking and willing.

When Huxley was taxed with being an atheist, or materialist, or disciple of Comte, and in effect destroying the religion and morality which he claimed to support, he hotly denied the charge. Criticism, however, forced him into making positive declarations about his overall outlook, what might be called his philosophy, and inventing a title which would correctly reflect this philosophy over against such unwanted labels as 'atheist' or 'materialist'. The title which he produced was 'agnostic': one who does not know.

Huxley's philosophy, on his own admission, owed much to Hume, and something to Kant. It could be described as a kind of garbled Kantianism. According to Huxley the ultimate nature of reality is and must be utterly unknown to us. This puts materialism and idealism, spiritualism, on an equal footing. We cannot know reality in itself; we can know only states of our own consciousness. Sometimes it is convenient to describe these states in material, physical terms; sometimes it is convenient to describe them in spiritual, idealist terms. We should never, however, read back into reality the materialist or idealist modes of expression which we happen to find convenient. About that we must be, and forever remain, agnostic.

At this point Huxley might appear to be an awful warning of what happens when philosophy is allowed to infiltrate discussions on serious topics, but it is truer to say that he is an awful warning of what happens when philosophy is dabbled in and merely plundered to provide impressive-looking rationalisations of an already adopted position.

Huxley did not actually believe that meeting people and agreeing or arguing with them was merely encountering states of his own consciousness, or that examining rocks or fossils was simply giving concentrated attention to his own states of mind. If he really had thought this he would have explicitly embraced some kind of idealism, but in fact he did the exact opposite. After brave attempts to pretend that the material and spiritual had equal claims to expressing a kind of pragmatic truth, Huxley made quite clear his real opinion, which was that descriptions and explanations in physical terms were vastly more helpful and fruitful than those in spiritual terms. That is to say, we are back with the view which characterised Huxley's whole working life: the natural sciences alone can tell us the truth about the world and our life in it.

The complicated prevarications and confusions into which Huxley occasionally lapsed reflected a war between his head and his heart. Something in him wanted to cling to morality and religion, while at the same time his reason, allied with anti-clerical prejudices, produced a view of the world destructive of moral value and religious hope. Agnosticism was Huxley's method of trying to dodge the consequences of a wholly naturalistic explanation of life, an attempt to keep what he wanted, and profoundly needed, of morality and spiritual hope, while keeping science free from any kind of interference from or subjection to external authority.

Huxley was the type of things to come, a nation and society ruled by agnosticism, science and technology free from all but financial restraint, and a highly selective appeal to morality and religion when convenient.

The liberal scholarly version of biblical religion could offer no challenge to such an outlook; it could only suffer the dubious compliment of being invited to join the club. Huxley well characterised its weakness:

Inspiration, deprived of its old intelligible sense, is watered down into a mystification. The Scriptures are, indeed, inspired; but they contain a wholly undefined and indefinable 'human element'; and this unfortunate intruder is converted into a sort of biblical whipping boy. Whatsoever scientific investigation, historical or physical, proves to be erroneous, the 'human element' bears the blame; while the divine inspiration of such statements, as by their nature are out of reach of proof or disproof, is still asserted with all the vigour inspired by conscious safety from attack. Though the proposal to treat the Bible 'like any other book' which caused so much scandal, forty years ago, may not yet be generally accepted, and though Bishop Colenso's criticisms may still lie, formally, under ecclesiastical ban, yet the church has not wholly turned a deaf ear to the voice of the scientific tempter.[49]

Biblical criticism could therefore be recognised as a scientific method of establishing truth, but only at the expense of surrendering theology.

It was pointed out to Huxley in his own lifetime that his so-called agnosticism must lead to the death of religion and the collapse of morality: a prophecy which can perhaps be better appreciated a century later than it could at the time.

CHAPTER 9

Immanuel Kant

It has been maintained that in the nineteenth century 'The main philosophical influence was that of Immanuel Kant'; that Kantianism was the guiding principle in the religious thought of the century, mediated by Schleiermacher and Ritschl; and that Kant's many-sidedness 'was to make of him . . . a power from which the mind of the ensuing century seemed to have little wish to free itself'.[1] As far as British religious thought was concerned it would appear that nothing could be further from the truth; and if it had really been the case, there would be some difficulty accounting for the dominating influence of Paley and the general confusion which marked the latter part of the century. There is no denying that the name of Kant was well known and that some acquaintance with his philosophy was not uncommon, and there is also no denying that thinkers were entitled to take from Kant's teaching what they regarded as valuable and reject what they regarded as false; but to speak of a dominating influence implies general understanding and acceptance of the critical philosophy, and there is little evidence of either.

In his substantial study of *Essays and Reviews*, Ieuan Ellis has referred to the influence of German thought on the essayists, an influence which went far beyond that of Baron Bunsen and which was to be seen at times more clearly in their other works. Kant is one of those singled out for particular mention; but the Germanic influence was also subject to significant qualification. Idealism would appear to have been at least as important as Kant. Even Idealism, however, had not taken sufficient root in English thought to provide or suggest a clear alternative to the old theologies which had been rejected. There was widespread hostility to or distaste for German philosophy, shared to some extent by Jowett; and Ellis' remark, 'From these references it should be obvious that the essayists used the German teachers for their own purposes',[2] indicates a fundamental weakness in the idea of a dominating Kantian or more general Germanic philosophical influence.

Frederick Temple was, apparently, faithful to Kant to the end of his life and often based sermons on him, and Temple was also no doubt not alone in being impressed by Kant's emphasis on morality and conscience; but Temple's assertion in his Bampton Lectures of the occasional interference which could be made by a morally guided will in what was otherwise the general uniformity of nature was far removed from Kant's answer to the problem of free will in a world ruled by causal necessity. Furthermore, if religious thinkers liked to make use of Kant now and again to support belief, Huxley appealed to the Kantian epistemology to support agnosticism. Henry Mansel was another who tried to employ Kant for his own purposes rather than allowing a proper grasp of the critical philosophy to guide his own thinking. To speak of influence in such a case is merely misleading. The analogy of a child playing with fire would be nearer the mark.

To say that Kant exercised significant influence over nineteenth-century British thinkers would mean that they understood his critical philosophy, at least in its main features, and that this knowledge changed their thinking, or determined its direction from the start. This would not necessarily be by way of agreement. The explicit and clearly worked out rejection of the critical philosophy, or parts of it, would equally indicate influence. Kant himself openly acknowledged the revolutionary impact of Humean scepticism on his own mind, while at the same time he rejected scepticism, and aimed to replace it and the dogmatic systems which it destroyed with a well-grounded metaphysics.

It was Paley who exercised an almost mesmeric influence over British religious thinkers, directly or indirectly reinforcing the appeal of a long-established natural theology, and this was the influence from which they found it almost impossible to free themselves.

The difference between Kant's response to Hume and Paley's is of crucial significance. As we have seen, Paley met the scepticism of the *Dialogues* with a flat denial and simply reasserted the argument which Hume had destroyed. Kant, on the other hand, accepted what was correct in Hume's contention, and welcomed Hume's scepticism as a force which could bring about much-needed change. Paley wished to reforge the broken link with tradition; Kant recognised that something altogether new must be forged to replace it. In the words of Gerald Cragg, 'An age which had ventured to challenge revelation had assumed that natural religion was impregnable; Hume reduced it to a tenuous shadow of its former self.' Cragg also correctly points out that Hume's position as a neutral observer was at the same time his greatest weakness and that the true sequel to Hume was provided by Kant's critical philosophy.[3]

OUR KNOWLEDGE OF THE WORLD

Kant's own reference to Hume's influence is well known: 'I freely admit that it was in fact the recollection of David Hume which first, many years ago, interrupted my dogmatic slumber and gave a completely different direction to my investigations in the field of speculative philosophy.'[4]

The opening words of his most famous work in its first edition also bear indirect testimony to the power of Humean scepticism: 'Human reason has this peculiar fate that in one species of its knowledge it is burdened by questions which, as prescribed by the very nature of reason itself, it is not able to ignore, but which, as transcending all its powers, it is also not able to answer.'[5]

Hume's insistence that human knowledge is confined to human experience in and of this world was accepted by Kant as a starting point. Time and again Kant asserts that human knowledge is only possible because objects are presented, given to us, and we know them through their effect upon our senses. Without this presentation of objects to our sight, hearing, touch, smell and taste, we should know nothing. Sense perception, therefore, forms an essential part of what Kant calls *Erfahrung*, translated 'experience'. Without the objects presented to us through the senses there could be no knowledge, no 'experience'.[6]

There is, however, another essential element in knowledge; and that is the active contribution of the knowing mind. What we might call the raw material provided through sensation would remain an undifferentiated, unintelligible mass if it were not set in order by the active, constructive mind; and it is this ongoing activity of the mind working on the objects given through the senses which constitutes knowledge, experience:

But though all our knowledge begins with experience, it does not follow that it all arises out of experience. For it may well be that even our empirical knowledge is made up of what we receive through impressions and of what our own faculty of knowledge . . . supplies from itself. If our faculty of knowledge makes any such addition, it may be that we are not in a position to distinguish it from the raw material, until with long practice of attention we have become skilled in separating it.7

The *Critique of Pure Reason* was Kant's attempt to separate out the mind's contribution to knowledge, and thereby establish just what reason could achieve and what was beyond it. He accepted Hume's claim that reason often overreaches itself in asserting so-called truths and demonstrations which carry human thought beyond what it can possibly know. This is essential to the main theme of the *Critique of Pure Reason* but is repeated time and again in the other Critiques. The acceptance of what is true in Hume's empiricism and scepticism was a great strength in Kant's critical philosophy. Kant, as it were, absorbed beforehand criticism of religious belief based on empirical discovery, and willingly conceded to the sceptic that which scepticism could rightfully claim. There was, nevertheless, a fundamental difference of aim between the two men. Hume's critique of reason was meant to weaken reliance upon it in the interests of a demand for tolerance in social life, especially in its religious and political aspects. Hume wanted to destroy dogma and zealous prejudice by undermining their supposedly rational foundations, and to replace them with a healthy and tolerant scepticism operating within the limits of common sense. This was scarcely an adequate basis for religious belief, and one is left with the impression, as far as Hume is concerned, that such belief is an optional extra.

Kant's aim was to recognise not only the limits but also the legitimate uses of reason in order to place metaphysics on a sound basis, and the very title of the *Prolegomena* clearly says as much. The severe limits imposed by Hume on the capacity of reason to discover truth were largely endorsed by Kant, who time and again insists that there can be no knowledge except that which is related to the objects given through sensation: but with one crucial exception, which makes Kant's critique the preparation for a well-founded metaphysics rather than the confirmation of mere scepticism. This exception is moral knowledge, hinted at in the *Critique of Pure Reason* and playing an essential role in the later development of the critical philosophy.

Surprisingly but consistently Kant includes space and time in the mental contribution to experience. It is easy for anyone to appreciate that what an object looks like, or sounds like, or tastes like depends very much on the state of our own seeing, hearing and tasting. This is very obvious in the case of sound, which we hardly regard as belonging to the object at all. A ringing bell or a vocal ensemble may be described as making or producing a sound rather than possessing it. If we stop to reflect on the taste of something, we realise that it is in us rather than in the object. The same is actually true of colour, although in this case it is by no means obvious that this is so. Light travels so fast and our perception works so swiftly and unconsciously that colour is naturally and spontaneously attributed to the object.

Variations in, for example, sight and taste lead different individuals to ascribe different colours or shades, or different degrees of sweetness or bitterness, to the same object: and yet it is qualities such as these which actually help to make up the object of our experience. If this 'object' is so dependent for its character and constitution upon our mental state and our senses, why not regard it as wholly the product of our own mind and sensation? In order to preserve the independent reality of the object we can attribute to it so-called primary qualities, over against the so-called secondary qualities dependent on our capacity for varied sensations. These primary qualities, such as extension, place and shape, were supposed to constitute the unchangeable substance and character of the object, over against the changeable qualities such as colour and touch which varied according to the observer's senses.

Kant rejected this explanation and argued that both spatial and temporal qualities, far from belonging to the objects which are given to the senses, belong instead to the perceiving human mind. According to Kant, they are certainly different from the qualities which exist through sensation, and must be thought of rather as a framework imposed on the raw materials of experience provided through the senses. The human capacity to perceive and know the world is so constituted that it spontaneously and unconsciously imposes dimensions of space and time on everything presented to it:

Space . . . as condition of outer objects, necessarily belongs to their appearance or intuition. Taste and colours are not necessary conditions under which alone objects can be for us objects of the senses. They are connected with the appearances only as effects accidentally added by the particular constitution of the sense organs. Accordingly, they are not a priori representations, but are grounded in sensation . . . Further, no one can have a priori a representation of a colour or of any taste; whereas, since space concerns only the pure form of intuition, and therefore involves no sensation whatsoever, and nothing empirical, all kinds and determinations of space can and must be represented a priori, if concepts of figures and of their relations are to arise. Through space alone is it possible that things should be outer objects to us.[8]

However strange Kant's view may seem, it does render his account of our knowledge of the world thoroughly consistent and coherent. Instead of supposing that we perceive things to some extent according to the dictates of our own faculties and to some extent as they really are, as if everything in our experience were partly our own creature and somehow also partly the thing as it really is in itself, Kant recognised that everything is wholly and inevitably viewed according to our total integrated mental and physical make-up. It is in the nature of the case impossible that something, some chunk of reality, should present itself simply as it is, should somehow break through to our self-conscious awareness without being affected by our senses and cast of mind. Although he was much impressed by the scientific work of Isaac Newton, Kant's account of space and time was very different from that of Newton. Newton looked upon them as vast receptacles within which objects were positioned or moved and events took place, and throughout which existed the omnipresent and eternal deity. It does not follow, therefore, that because Newton's ideas have been refined or superseded, and because Euclidean geometry is not the unique and absolute truth which Kant took it to be, that the main features in Kant's account of human knowledge have been destroyed. Kant's view of time and space remains, independent of the particular mathematics and physics he mistakenly believed to be the last word on the subject.

Karl Heim has given an excellent account of the way in which Kantian epistemology should be seen in relation to modern developments in mathematics and physics:

Modern physics . . . has been recognizing ever more clearly that physical facts cannot be completely described or exactly defined at all without including the cognitive subject in the definition from the very outset. In reaching this conclusion modern physics has provided a surprising confirmation of the Kantian critical principle that there is no objective experience which is not the experience of a subject whom reality objectively confronts. The ego and the object can indeed be distinguished from one another by means of an abstraction, but they cannot be concretely detached from one another. But if the subject and object cannot be isolated from one another at all as separable quantities, then the entire dispute between the physicists and the Kantians rests on an error in the posing of the problem. It is quite meaningless to ask whether the subject carries within himself the structural law of space or whether this is contained in the object.

Heim points out that the different 'spaces' with which mathematicians deal can be 'transformed' into one another, thereby reflecting the fact that the structure of the space in which reality becomes perceptible to us is always founded on the actual nature of that reality:

This indicates clearly that behind the various spaces there is something which is common to them all, something which cannot be exhibited in an intuitively perceptible form, but which can nevertheless be formulated mathematically in terms of equations of transformation. From the other point of view, in the latest phase of contemporary physics, quantum mechanics, even more than in Einstein's theory of relativity, the observing subject is more than ever involved as a factor in the physical process. This has resulted in the calling in question of the objectivity and the general validity of space.[9]

Kant attached very great importance to his emphasis on the dynamic and constructive part played by the mind in our knowledge of the world. He likened it to the Copernican revolution in astronomy. Copernicus had found the basic solution to intractable astronomical problems by focussing attention on the contribution which the rotating earth-bound observer makes to his own view of the universe. This had made possible the vast development of astronomical knowledge we now take for granted. Likewise, Kant focussed attention on the observing, knowing self, and was thereby able to offer a solution to otherwise insuperable problems, and, he hoped, open the way to the development of a well-founded metaphysics.

Nevertheless, Kant insisted time and again on the existence of the vast world of interrelated objects independent of the observer, and he seems to have regarded the existence of this world as so obvious as to require no argument, and perhaps to be so basic to experience as not to be capable of further demonstration at all. This feeling of the obviousness of the fact seems to lie behind Kant's remark that we must be able to *think* things in themselves, since 'otherwise we should be landed in the absurd conclusion that there can be appearance without anything that appears'.[10]

Throughout the *Critique of Pure Reason* and the *Prolegomena* there is a powerful sense of the sheer givenness of things, and the need to posit their objective existence in order to make experience intelligible, even though we cannot know them just as they are in themselves. Because things in themselves must be understood, in the sense of being assumed, Kant called them *noumena*, 'things-assumed-by-understanding'; while things as they appear to us he called *phenomena*, 'appearances'. The term 'noumenon' and 'phenomenon' in any given case, therefore, refer to the same thing, either denoting it as it is in itself, or else denoting it as it is known in human experience.

The distinction between noumena and phenomena is simple enough, but could be misleading. It is easy to slip into the assumption that we are thinking about two different sets of things, two different kinds of world, whereas both terms, as already pointed out, denote the one world of things, but regarded from two different points of view.

Kant himself was often anxious to stress the mental and sensuous contribution to our experience of the world, and this was, after all, his own 'Copernican revolution'; but it sometimes led to a correspondingly negative attitude towards the utterly unknowable noumena, encouraging the misleading impression already referred to of two worlds, and raising a serious doubt about the existence of noumena, although such doubt makes no sense at all in the context of Kant's whole critical philosophy.

Nor are phenomena 'appearances' in the sense of being mere illusions or simply subjective states of consciousness. On the contrary, phenomena are the actual things, whether natural or artificial, which make up the whole world of our experience. Despite the misleading character of some Kantian phrases taken out of their context, the overall Kantian picture of the universe is of a vast collection of things, among them human beings capable of self-conscious awareness and of reflection upon the other things which surround them and impinge on them. Genuine knowledge exists and is commonplace; and where there is such knowledge, it is a knowledge of things, not the mere apprehension of mental images cast upon some purely subjective screen.

The transcendental idealist is, therefore, an empirical realist, and allows to matter, as appearance, a reality which does not permit of being inferred, but is immediately perceived. Transcendental realism, on the other hand, inevitably falls into difficulties, and finds itself obliged to give way to empirical idealism, in that it regards the objects of outer sense as something distinct from the senses themselves, treating mere appearances as self-subsistent beings, existing outside us. On such a view as this, however clearly we may be conscious of our representation of these things, it is still far from certain that, if the representation exists, there exists also the object corresponding to it. In our system, on the other hand, these external things, namely matter, are in all their configurations and alterations nothing but mere appearances, that is, representations in us, of the reality of which we are immediately conscious.[11]

Kant himself set out from the problem of causation raised by Hume, combining acknowledgement of the correctness of Hume's argument with acknowledgement of the growing success of the sciences. No purely rational basis or justification for scientific research can be given. It is impossible to observe or demonstrate necessary connection in nature, and for all we know or can prove, such necessity may not really exist; and yet nature *as we know it* is ruled by such necessity, and we can neither think of nature nor live our lives as human beings nor carry out the experimental work of science without assuming and consciously accepting the apparent fact.[12]

Kant resolved the paradox by seeing necessary connection as part of the mind's contribution to knowledge and experience. The part or faculty of the mind concerned was called by Kant *Verstand,* translated 'understanding'; and he meant by this the capacity which the mind has to take the impressions made on the senses by things in themselves and turn these into consciously recognised objects, related to one another and unified into an harmonious whole in the experience of the individual. Furthermore, Kant firmly rejected the idea that this was a psychological description of human learning, experience and knowledge, and claimed that it was a process proceeding according to logical rules which must characterise the activity of any rational being. In this way Kant insisted that what he was describing and explaining was not what merely happens to be the case, but is what must be the case.

Therefore, the necessity linking cause and effect, as part of the work of *Verstand*, understanding, had the force of logic: it existed in the mind before ever sensation was stimulated and experience made possible.

Kant insisted on this because he was anxious to distinguish this kind of explanation from the one offered by Hume, which made the necessity lie only in a mental habit engendered by the customary association of certain objects. As Kant pointed out, this was not a truly necessary connection between things, but the substitution for it of a contingent connection between ideas.

There is both strength and weakness in the Kantian argument, but it is strength which preponderates. It is true that the distinctions which Kant makes are both useful in our attempt to understand human knowledge, and also very misleading when they are made too sharp to be properly reintegrated into what is, after all, a single personal experience: as if the ingredients of a recipe were somehow rendered incapable of properly combining into the finished cake. Kant also overstressed the part played by rules in knowledge and experience, and seemed to believe that they could bestow objectivity and order on what would otherwise remain merely subjective. For example:

The 'understanding' is therefore not simply a capacity for developing rules out of the comparison of 'appearances': it is itself nature's lawgiver. That is to say, without 'understanding' we should not be aware of any such thing as nature . . . since 'appearances' by their very character cannot occur independently of us, but exist only in our capacity for sense-perception.[13]

When Kant raises the question how our sensations, or sense-perceptions, can come to be regarded as independently existing objects, he refers this to the rule-making capacity of the mind which brings everything together into one ordered consciousness. For example:

If then we inquire what kind of new quality is produced by referring our sense-perceptions to an object, what new dignity is thereby conferred on them, we find that it consists in nothing more than binding together such sensations according to a certain kind of necessity and subjecting them to a rule. Or, conversely, that the only means whereby our sensations can be given objective significance is that there must be a certain regulated order in their temporal sequence.[14]

It is not altogether surprising that this aspect of the Kantian critique should have been seized on and developed so as to create systems in which mind becomes the fount and origin of all reality; but Kant himself repudiated such developments as quite out of keeping with his real intention. This intention is revealed in his repeated insistence on the independent reality of things as they are in themselves apart from the knowing mind, and his explicit rejection of any idealist philosophy inconsistent with this independent reality. The consequence in Kant's philosophy, however, is that there are two kinds of objectivity, each one sharply separated from the other: one belonging to things in themselves, and the other belonging to things as they appear to us. The serious difficulty in the way of accepting this view is not the existence of the two kinds of objectivity, but the sharpness of the distinction between them.

Kant believed that the certainties of mathematics and the sciences had to reflect the logical structure, the rationality of the human mind: only if nature is the creature of the mind can we gain unquestionable knowledge of its constitution and working. This meant that things in their noumenal aspect had to become totally, absolutely unknowable and without influence, so that in our quest for knowledge of nature this aspect of things could be and ought to be left entirely out of account. We could then rest assured that our present knowledge, as the product of the mind's own investigation of its own construction of nature, was both real and certain. The remaining problem was to explain how the constructions of mind and sense could appear as external objects.

The sheer objectivity of things, however, requires no explanation, and not only are Kant's attempts to explain objectivity unconvincing in themselves, but they are also inconsistent with his own fundamental insights. Objectivity is simply the givenness of things and their relationships in their unknown, noumenal aspect. Objectivity, the sheer confrontational quality of the world in relation to any given individual self, lies on the noumenal side of the divide but produces its own phenomenal consequence in our knowledge and experience. Furthermore, as Kant explicitly recognised, the individual self is also in itself a thing, a noumenon, which can be presented to its own observation and self-consciousness as a phenomenon, an 'appearance', a fact of nature. That is to say, on Kant's own showing the sharp division between noumena and phenomena does not exist. The individual

self is the sensitive and dynamic meeting place of things as they are
in themselves and the same things as they are known and felt.
There is no gainsaying Kant's fundamental point that absolutely
everything we know comes to us through the determining influence of our own perceptual apparatus and frame of mind; but it is
things and their relationships which we know, and not a set of
phenomena triggered off in the imagination by a quite different
set of noumena existing wholly independently of the thinker. Men
and women, after all, not only observe and reflect upon things, but
frequently manipulate them, and are continually subjected to
their own force and resistance. The true position has been well
expressed by F. R. Tennant:

> Kant teaches that we can know only the existence of the thing in itself:
> yet we must suppose that it determines and conditions our knowledge in
> some way – there must be some kind of *rapport* between us and noumena,
> or otherwise we could not even know that noumena exist.
>
> But while we thus have *acquaintance* only with the sensible or phenom-
> enal, we are having *rapport* with, and phenomenal knowledge of or about,
> the noumenal. We do not, in this latter sense of 'knowledge', know the
> phenomenal only: rather, we know the noumenal through the phenom-
> enal. The phenomenon is, so to say, the utterance of the ontal *to us*; if the
> noumenal shines forth or appears to us, as the phenomenal, it cannot be
> totally unknowable.

Tennant goes on to suggest that what is important for us is not
that our knowledge should be an exact replica of reality, but that
it should be a reliable guide to it; just as a map of the Lake District
is not a picture or model of it, but nevertheless fulfils its purpose
as an accurate guide.[15]
This implies that distinguishing the mind's contribution to
knowledge and experience from that of the things we know and
experience can never be fully accomplished. It is a distinction
which can only be approximated. We cannot stand outside the situation and measure each contribution, and there is an unbroken
continuity between the self-conscious experience of the individual
and things which he is experiencing. Sounds, tastes and smells are
only loosely connected with objects, although we still regard them
as somehow part of the object. Colour, and hardness or softness to
the touch seem to be much more part of the object; while shape
and size we regard as utterly independent characteristics of the
object, although it is perfectly obvious that size and shape vary

continually according to the viewpoint of the observer, just as do the implements which we use to measure them. The Kantian critique of empirical knowledge therefore encourages a healthy agnosticism concerning its ultimate objective validity, and suggests that we might do better to confine ourselves to pragmatic criteria when trying to appreciate and evaluate scientific discovery and progress.

Although Kant was himself greatly impressed by the knowledge gained through scientific investigation, he was also quite explicit about its provisional nature. Questions about the world which are answered in empirical terms can never satisfy reason because they always give rise to further questions, and this has its implications for mathematics and the sciences since they are, in the nature of the case, confined to answering questions about phenomena, 'appearances'. Their scope is unlimited within the vast field of things as they are grasped through human sense-perception, but beyond that field they cannot go.

Mathematics is concerned only with 'appearances'. That which cannot be an object of knowledge through sense perception, such as the concepts belonging to metaphysics and morality, lies completely outside its sphere and it can never lead us to, nor does it have the slightest need of such an object . . . Natural science will never reveal the inner nature of things, that nature which is not 'appearance' but which can in fact serve as the ultimate, fundamental explanation of 'appearances'; yet it is equally true that natural science has no need of this for its own physical explanations. Indeed, if such an ultimate explanation were offered to it from elsewhere, for example, the influence of immaterial beings, natural science should firmly reject it and give it no place whatever in its developing powers of explanation. Rather should natural science always base its explanations on what belongs to experience as the object of the senses and can be brought into connection with our actual perceptions according to the laws of empirical knowledge.[16]

Developments in mathematics and the sciences since Kant's time have fully borne out his belief concerning their colossal scope for increasing our knowledge of the natural world; and the capacity of the senses to receive information about that world has been extended to a very remarkable degree through the use of instruments and apparatus. The understanding has been fed with a vast amount of raw material well beyond the capacity of technically unassisted sense-perception to take in, with a corresponding stimulus to curiosity and determined inquiry. It would be

astonishing if all this knowledge turned out to be only a highly
sophisticated acquaintance with the mind's own productions, and
if the real world of things in themselves, things in their noumenal
aspect, should turn out to be completely different; but the fundamental Kantian position still holds true. We know what is
presented to the senses, however developed those senses may be
through the use of instruments and however ingenious the
apparatus of presentation may be; and we know according to the
faculties of our knowing mind. That which we know is the independent, external world; but we know it in our own way, and there
is an impassable barrier between our knowledge and things as they
truly are. We trust that such knowledge does not mislead us, and
we have good reason to do so as long as it produces practical
consequences which we can foresee and manipulate; nor do we
have any alternative; but when reason strays beyond the control of
fact and tries to reach the ultimate nature of things in themselves
or the origin of things in creation, physics has become metaphysics of the type forbidden by both Humean scepticism and the
Kantian critique.

The uncertainty and randomness which to some extent characterise the behaviour of atomic energy as at present understood do
not contradict the basic Kantian picture of the universe. Human
thought and action are still dominated by the experience of
necessary causal connection which comes to us as a fundamental
and absolutely inescapable feature of the world as we know it, and
without which the strange and paradoxical discoveries of modern
physics would themselves never have been made. If real indeter-
minacy and randomness do lie at the root of all change, we must
remember that Kant, following Hume, explicitly denied that
causal necessity was either discoverable or demonstrable. Kant was
concerned with the world as it is in our experience of it and not
with the world as it might be if what is genuinely random should
become its dominating feature; and human beings, simply as a
matter of fact, experience very varied kinds of force, and not
statistical probabilities.

MORALITY

Human experience is reflected in human language. Some
assertions are based on experience, resulting from the obser-

vations made through sense-perception and directly or indirectly recording it. Other assertions are based on language itself and the meanings attached to it. Kant called the first kind of statement *synthetic a posteriori* because it asserts a connection, a 'putting together' of things which we can know only 'following' actual perceptions.

The second kind of statement he called *analytic a priori* because it asserts something about the words and phrases we use which can be discovered by analysing their meaning, and which must be true or false by definition.

It was, of course, fundamental to Kant's whole philosophy that no knowledge at all is possible until we have had 'experience', that is, had objects presented to us through the five senses, *Sinnlichkeit*, and grasped them by means of 'understanding', *Verstand*;[17] but once granted this basic condition of human consciousness, Kant's distinction between the two kinds of statement is quite clear. The assertion that the cat is on the mat must be based on observation, and we can only know whether or not it is true *after, a posteriori*, looking in order to find out. On the other hand, what we mean by 'cat' and 'mat' is already determined *before, a priori*, we look, and no amount of looking would be of any use if such meanings were not already established and generally accepted. Whatever particular verbal expressions might be used, the concepts of 'cat' and 'mat' must already exist in our minds, along with ideas of a great many other things and their relationships, in order that we should make sense of things and communicate with one another.

Kant, however, recognised that human experience and thought include far more than what is provided simply through sense-perception or required by clarity of expression, and that this extra is also reflected in language. We do not assert only what is in fact or in principle observable through sense-perception, or what is tautologous or a matter of definition. Kant therefore posited a third kind of assertion, the *synthetic a priori*. This gives actual information, really connecting things and not expressing mere definition or clarification, while at the same time being absolutely certain and not merely justified by the data supplied through physical sensation. We often wish to say that something is true, not simply as a matter of fact, but that it must be true and that the necessity or compulsion is a logical one, and not merely a psychological one such as instinct or habit.

Kant believed that all mathematical reasoning and all the most important assertions of natural science are of the *synthetic a priori* type. Scientists spend much time simply trying to find out what, simply as a matter of fact, is the case; but their ultimate aim is to establish what must be the case, and this necessity is reflected in the mathematical expression of the laws and principles which, as we say, govern the universe. Certain chemical combinations and reactions take place because they must; other combinations and reactions do not take place because they cannot. Light behaves in certain ways because it must, and in consequence we can make reliable inferences about such things as the movements of planets, the constitution of the stars and the appearance of rainbows. When machinery fails or the milk goes sour we put it down to cause and effect, not gremlins or disgruntled fairies.

Whether or not the whole of mathematics is describable in terms of the *synthetic a priori* is a question for mathematicians to settle; but Kant's insistence that mathematics is the expression of real information and not merely an analysis or definition of terms is often true. Equations are tightly related to the discovery of fact and are also often exploratory in character. On the basis of prediction, experiments can be set up and observations made, and particular mathematical arguments vindicated, modified or rejected in consequence. The discovery of the elliptical shape of planetary orbits round the sun, of the existence of the planet Neptune, of the wobble in the orbit of Mercury and the bending of light in a strong gravitational field are famous examples of this interaction between mathematical 'necessity' and the contingency of facts which have to be sought out and confirmed or denied. The vast universe of objects is presented to us as a colossal contingency: for all we know it might have been quite different and it might become quite different; but within that great contingency necessity rules, and human knowledge and expression inevitably reflect these two intimately related aspects of the world of which we are a part, which is to some extent the creature of our own minds, and with which we must come to terms.

For Kant, the link between metaphysics on the one hand, and the natural sciences on the other, is that the essential subject-matter of both is expressed in statements of the *synthetic a priori* type. The ground of certainty in both may be different, but if the propositions of physics have a rational basis, so do the propositions of metaphysics.

There are elements in our overall, general experience of life which mere empiricism cannot adequately describe, let alone account for. Among these, moral values were of fundamental significance for Kant. According to Kant, we are all aware of moral good and bad, moral right and wrong, as facts of life which cannot be described or explained in any other terms, and which make a unique and unqualified demand upon our attention and obedience. Our duty is that which we are called upon to obey regardless of any other consideration, no matter what the cost may be in terms of health and welfare or even life. If what is required of us is a moral demand, then it is absolutely right, and if what is forbidden is a moral prohibition, then it is absolutely wrong.

Kant was perfectly well aware, of course, that morality is woven into the fabric of life itself and is worked out in terms of what people do and think and feel, but he was all the more anxious on that account to distinguish the specifically moral from all the other elements in any given situation. He repeatedly warns us that the moral cannot under any circumstances be justified in any other terms: moral obligation, duty, possesses a sovereign authority which owes nothing to any empirical circumstance and which cannot be derived from any external being, not even God. He even carries his argument to the length of asserting that an action can be considered moral only if it is done out of conscious and deliberate obedience to duty, the moral law. Obedience to the moral command must be the sole motive in such a case, and it is by no means sufficient for what claims to be a moral action that it has been done merely in conformity with the moral law.

Kant's point may seem to be far-fetched, but we must remember that he was trying to isolate and identify something specific and that this does lend his analysis a certain artificial character, but only of the type which is bound to characterise any such enterprise. Kant himself compared his argument with the endeavours of a chemist to sort out the elements in a given compound. An imaginary situation might help to make clearer and more plausible what he was aiming to achieve.

Let us suppose that we are walking along a beach with heavy seas pounding the shore. We suddenly see a man tearing off his shoes and clothes, plunging into the waves and striking out to sea. We then see a child in obvious difficulties, thrashing about in the waves but scarcely able to keep afloat and being carried further out to certain death. The man, however, is a strong swimmer and within a few minutes the child is rescued.

We instantly feel that this was a moral action, an act of bravery and compassion. That the child should be rescued is an obvious moral good and that the man should risk his life to accomplish this end is obviously a morally right action. When we meet Kant later in the evening and are discussing the incident with him over a drink we are inclined to be impatient with him when he asks us about the man's motives, and insists that the actual consequence of the deed cannot in itself justify our praise on moral grounds. We offer, with an ironic smile, to stand him a glass of hemlock. We then discover, however, that Kant has been leading us on: he knows more about the incident than we do. He puts it to us that if we had not been so anxious to rush back to town and be the first to spread the news we might have noticed some discreetly camouflaged equipment, and realised that the whole incident was no more than a stunt, the enactment of a dramatic scene from some epic film. The child was never in any danger and the swimmer was a well-paid stuntman who regarded the performance as easy money. That is to say, the events which we observed could in themselves tell us nothing about the moral quality of the deed, and once we have learnt more about the facts of the case we naturally conclude that it was not a morally commendable act at all: and we do so precisely because we now know that the man's motive was not at all what we supposed it to be.

Or let us suppose that we had been sufficiently observant to see the equipment and that we had actually been asked to remain still for a few moments while a brief scene could be shot on a deserted shore. We admire the skill of the actors and comment on this in our later evening conversation with Kant. The philosopher then tells us that the convincing display was actually the consequence of things going wrong: the child really had got into difficulties and a nearby technician who was a good but not exceptional swimmer really had risked his life getting the child back to safety. What we had witnessed was, as they say, a real-life drama: and we now agree with Kant in commending the man on moral grounds, and we do so precisely because we now know that the man's motive was a purely moral one.

Or let us suppose that the incident had nothing whatever to do with film-making and that the man really did rescue a child in real difficulties: but Kant then points out to us that, far from being the end of the matter, it was only the beginning. The child has very wealthy parents and the man is a notoriously unscrupulous criminal who has merely seized the opportunity to take the child hostage and drive a hard bargain with people whom he regards as well able to afford a very large ransom. Once more our judgment on the man's action changes, not merely because we have learnt more about the circumstances, but because these reflect his state of mind, his motivation, and it is this which is crucial in influencing our opinion.

Kant himself suggested an illustration to bring out the same point. A man has a strong desire for a particular woman. A gallows is erected outside his house and he is told that he can satisfy his desire for the woman on condition that he is hanged immediately afterwards. This sets up a conflict within the man between fear and desire. However, let us suppose, says Kant, that the man is invited to cooperate with the ruler of his country in an act of serious injustice against an honourable fellow citizen, with death as the penalty for refusal. This also sets up a conflict within him, but as Kant indicates, it is a conflict of a quite different type from the first.[18] The moral element makes all the difference.

There can be no doubt that the whole of Kant's lengthy argument concerning morality involves an implicit appeal to us to reflect upon our own experience, and there can be equally no doubt that when we do so, we are compelled to acknowledge the existence of something deeply rooted in our consciousness which we must recognise as having precisely the peculiar, unique and overruling character denoted by Kant. It is what gives meaning to terms such as 'conscience' and 'duty' and to the categories we so frequently use in decisions, arguments and discussions as to what is right or wrong, what people ought or ought not to do. Also, as Kant insisted, moral values cannot be explained in any other terms; and even those who believe that in theory they can be so explained, and therefore explained away, cannot in practice escape them. They are an integral part of what it means to be human.

Nevertheless, we feel that some kind of justification is needed for granting the legitimacy of demands which often involve, or would involve if we obeyed them, the denial of natural desires, the acceptance of pain and the sacrifice of much that is valuable to us, even including life itself. Kant himself acknowledged this and in a remarkable passage raised the question what possible origin there could be for so sublime a concept and force in human life as that of duty. His answer was that its origin lies in human personality, and in that aspect of it which belongs to the noumenal world, and which gives each person true freedom and independence of the phenomenal world of things. Every person belongs to both worlds, and even persons are, in their phenomenal aspect, subject to the laws of cause and effect, empirical necessity; but with respect to their reason and conscience they rise superior to the mechanism of nature, and enjoy the consciousness of pure practical laws given by reason. Not surprisingly, we accord all honour and respect to such rational laws because they express our real freedom and superiority to the merely natural world.[19]

Kant's moral philosophy well illustrates the importance of the distinction between noumena and phenomena already established in his theory of knowledge; but it also means that the weakness which characterises his handling of that distinction remains and threatens proper appreciation and development of his insights. The insights nevertheless remain, and are highly significant.

The foundation of Kant's moral and religious philosophy is the sheer fact of morality and the peculiarly authoritative character of duty, moral obligation. Starting out from this fact, Kant then argued that human beings must be free, since freedom is implicit in moral obligation. Someone cannot be obliged to do what is impossible for him: and Kant was very clear on the point that while genuine freedom is necessary for the existence of moral obligation, we can only know that we are free through our knowledge of the moral law:

The concept of freedom, in so far as its reality is demonstrated through the presence of an absolute law of practical reason, now becomes the keystone in the whole structure of pure, even speculative reason.

While freedom is the *ratio essendi* of the moral law, the moral law is the *ratio cognoscendi* of freedom. This is because we should never be justified in accepting that there is any such thing as freedom . . . unless we were already clearly aware of the moral law in our reason. On the other hand, if there were no freedom we should never be confronted by the moral law within ourselves.[20]

Kant readily agreed and even emphasised that a human being has no freedom from an empirical point of view. As an item in the phenomenal world every human being is subject to the same laws of cause and effect as everything else, and we can therefore know neither freedom nor morality simply by observing events, not even by observing them within our own experience. On the other hand we do know morality, and are even intimately aware of it. It is not, however, presented to us through the senses like all other knowledge, but is presented a priori to the reason; and freedom, which we cannot know directly, is implicit in it. We therefore frequently make, and feel compelled to make, moral judgments which are *synthetic* because we are convinced that they are assertions of fact; but are a priori because what is essential to them as *moral* judgments is contributed by reason and not to be found by empirical investigation, any more than necessary causal connection is to be found by that method.

However awkward and artificial Kant's description of the individual's overall experience may be, there can be no doubt that it is true to life. There is a striking honesty about his attempt to do justice to every aspect of the human situation and his refusal to simplify matters by ignoring something or by reducing one element or aspect to another. The sharpness of his distinction between the noumenal and the phenomenal is once more a weakness in his exposition, leaving us with the superficial impression that each person suffers a kind of Jekyll and Hyde existence, enjoying freedom and morality in the noumenal world but existing simply as a predetermined beast in the phenomenal or natural world. Kant continued to wrestle with the problem of giving proper expression to his thought in the *Critique of Judgment*, first published in 1790, and in the following passages Kant faces and tries to overcome the danger of being taken to assert a hopeless dualism:

If, then, a vast gulf has in fact been fixed between the realm ruled by the concept of nature as known through sense perception, and the realm, beyond the senses, ruled by the concept of freedom, so that no crossing over is possible from the first to the second, not even through the theoretical use of reason, just as if they were completely different worlds of which the first could have no influence on the second . . . The understanding [*Verstand*] gives laws a priori for nature as the object of sense-perception to produce a theoretical knowledge of nature in a possible

experience. Reason [*Vernunft*] gives laws a priori for freedom and its particular kind of causality, as that which lies within the subject beyond the
senses, to produce an unconditional practical knowledge. The realm
ruled by the concept of nature under the one legislation and that ruled
by the concept of freedom under the other are completely cut off from
all reciprocal influence which they could have on one another, each
according to its own basic rules. This is because of the great gulf which
divides appearances (phenomena) from that which lies beyond what can
be grasped through the senses. The concept of freedom determines
nothing with respect to the theoretical knowledge of nature; and likewise, the concept of nature determines nothing with respect to the practical laws of freedom: and it is to that extent impossible to throw a bridge
from one realm over to the other.[21]

Nevertheless, the first passage is followed by the statement that
there must be some means whereby freedom can fulfil its moral
purposes in nature, and nature must somehow be understood so
as to be amenable to such influence; and the second is followed by
the assertion that free choices must have their effect in the
phenomenal world. That is, moral ends must be actually attainable in the natural world of which man is a part.

It is not surprising that Kant was accused of self-contradiction in
this matter, although it was an accusation which he firmly repudiated. The problem arises out of his oversharp distinction between
noumena and phenomena, of which talk about two realms or
worlds is an illustration. There is only one world, a fact which Kant
had no wish to deny, but which he simply assumed while at the
same time insisting upon distinctions which he rightly regarded as
necessary and useful. Reiterated emphasis upon distinctions, however, created a false impression, perhaps sometimes even in his
own mind. In the present instance the need to recognise the ultimate unity of the world, including mankind, was wrung out of
Kant, but in no way does it actually contradict his basic theory of
knowledge, and it was to this that he appealed as a solution to an
unnecessary dilemma.

In so far as we are considering things as observers, even
happenings and facts within ourselves, they are phenomena and
we inevitably see them in terms of determined relationships. They
are events in which one thing or set of circumstances arises of
necessity out of another, or in which various elements help to
determine one another's character and place in the overall
scheme. In such an incident as that already imagined, in which a

child is rescued from drowning, we can at least in principle give a complete description of events as they are observed along with the constitution of the participants and elements in the situation, and such a description, *in so far as it concerns itself with that which can be perceived*, will involve only one type of causality, that of the necessary connection of cause and effect. At the same time, we shall make moral judgments about such a situation, and many others, and we shall feel certain that such judgments concern real elements in these situations even though these elements are not open to observation. These elements of moral value and freedom of will cannot be presented to us as objects through what we might call the filter of the senses; but it is necessary to remember that even the objects which can be so presented – the child, the sea, the man, etc. – cannot be presented to us as they are in themselves. The phenomenal is an aspect of things, and we are not at all entitled to regard it as the whole or as conveying to our understanding and knowledge the true and ultimate nature of things.

Kant was so profoundly concerned to assert the reality of duty and human freedom that he was equally anxious that people should not expect to find them, or evidence of them, by looking in the wrong place. For Kant this was Hume's fundamental mistake, and it was a mistake which could only result in barren scepticism. If we would understand the world in its ultimate nature, to the extent that is granted to us, we should stop expecting to find it in empiricism, in that which is presented to us through sense-perception. Hence Kant's much repeated insistence on the distinction between noumena and phenomena, and an almost fierce determination that this distinction should be observed by all those who take the trouble to think about such things. Yet 'noumena' is just another name for things in their true nature, and moral values are noumena which we can know direct through reason, and freedom is that which we can know by implication through reason. This is genuine a priori knowledge, and is the only genuine knowledge of an object a priori through reason that there is; at the same time, carrying the certain knowledge of freedom with it, even though freedom cannot actually be known directly.

The moral law is as it were presented as a fact of pure reason of which we are ourselves conscious *a priori* and which is absolutely certain. What follows from this is that no example of the moral law can be found in merely empirical knowledge, and this is exactly what might be concluded. Therefore the objective reality of the moral law cannot be demonstrated through any deduction or any effort of theoretical reason, whether speculative or empirically supported. Nor can it be demonstrated a posteriori through being willing to surrender its absolute certainty and thereby get it confirmed through empirical knowledge. Nevertheless, it stands firm in its own right.[22]

What is very remarkable, however, is that an idea of reason is actually to be found among real objects, although it cannot be perceived, and therefore its possibility cannot be demonstrated. That is the idea of freedom. As a special kind of causality its reality is revealed in experience through the practical laws of pure reason and actual deeds in accordance with them, although considered as a theoretical concept it would go beyond what can have meaning for us. It is the only one of all the ideas of pure reason whose object is a fact and which must be reckoned among those things whose existence can be known.[23]

According to Kant, therefore, the moral is reason's a priori contribution to experience, giving us concrete information and therefore making possible synthetic judgments; but not of the sort which can be verified empirically, however bound up with empirical elements they may be. The moral is as much an expression of the noumenal in our experience as the physical objects we encounter, and with the same objectivity, but presented to us through reason and not the senses.

It must be repeated that Kant's argument is ultimately an appeal to experience. If what he says is true, then we are indeed aware of moral obligation, duty, which is quite different from desire or inclination, even it if happens to chime in with both. We believe and even assume that there is a very significant difference between things which happen because they must, and things which happen because of human choice and decision; and while we feel that people can be praised or blamed for that over which they have the power of choice and decision, we feel that such praise or blame is pointless, senseless, when mere force compels consequences. At the same time we know that we cannot hold up moral values for inspection, and that in searching for free will we are chasing a will o' the wisp. The deep and inalienable sense that the power of responsible choice and decision is an essential part of our very selves nevertheless remains, no matter how much of a mystery it may be for the investigator; and as Kant himself pointed out, it is the great stumbling-block for all empiricists, and therefore, we may add, for all sceptics who take empiricism as the foundation of their unbelief.

Kant himself gives the simple illustration of rising from a chair as an example of a freely accomplished action, while at the same time recognising that from the point of view of an observer who wants to give a full explanation of nature, including human behaviour, the sense of freedom must be an illusion, or otherwise nature becomes chaos.[24] We could develop this criticism of free will by claiming that a detailed biochemical description of the action would reveal an unbroken chain of causes and effects; and if the person concerned were the subject of psychological examination, his own description of his inner consciousness would be made up of explanations strongly suggesting the working of compelling forces, masking their compulsive force by a swift and subconscious spontaneity. Do people rise out of chairs for no reason at all? If we reply that the reason is choice, we are merely entering a vicious circle from the observer's point of view, including that of the subject in so far as he has been put into the position of an observer of his own actions, feelings and motives. It turns out that he wanted light or warmth, to communicate with someone, to find a book, to attend a meeting; and the action then becomes part of a web of events which extends in ever-widening horizons from tastes and inclinations related to the chemistry of the body, to the influences of home and upbringing, sub-cultural and wider cultural influences, genetics, education, etc., etc.

And yet, when the observer's case has been made out as fully as it can be, I myself still insist upon and cannot avoid the distinction between the compelled and the chosen and the concept of freedom which goes with them: a concept which Kant rightly asserted, which cannot by itself be given any positive content, but which is nevertheless a rational idea from which we cannot escape.

Kant's noumena and phenomena are two sides of the same coin. The coin observed is made up of phenomena linked for the observing mind in chains of cause and effect. Yet reflection upon observation compels us to admit that phenomena are noumena as we perceive them, things in themselves presented to us and become things-for-us; and the causal connection is part of the way we perceive things. No amount of observation can uncover the actual necessity in the connections of things, and we can therefore neither assert nor deny it of things in themselves; but this is the way we must perceive the world, while in a quite different fashion we are compelled to acknowledge and assume genuine freedom. We are left with the paradox that seen in one way all events are determined, but seen in another way there are very significant breaks in the causal connections, inexplicable fresh beginnings to interrupted causal sequences.

It follows from this that no amount of scientific research will ever discover or demonstrate the existence of morality and free will, both of which are essential elements in the Christian, and much other, religion. Commitment to scientific procedures as the sole methods of determining truth entails the denial of morality and free will before ever investigation begins. Whether intentionally or not, those who are dedicated to objective observation and rational argument strictly based upon it as the means to establishing truth have already decided that morality and freedom no more belong to the real world than fairies and demons. Nor is the analogy merely flippant: fairies and demons represent active personal wills, and intentions which are either good or bad, and systematic scientific research cannot tolerate the possibility of such forces in its explanations, as Kant himself pointed out.

There is no small irony in this situation. The decision to commit oneself wholly to the scientific outlook is itself an ongoing act of will, and the person so committed does not cease to be human, and continues to make genuine moral judgments; but this does not alter the fact that there is a contradiction between the two frames of mind, and an unhealthy tension between the two outlooks. T. H. Huxley, the father of modern agnosticism, well illustrates the fact. Time and again he denied freedom and destroyed the basis of morality, and time and again he sincerely repudiated any such implications of his scientific outlook. The consequence was his muddled agnosticism, bequeathed by the nineteenth century to the twentieth in lieu of a proper assessment of the relationship between science on the one hand, and morality and religion on the other. Huxley typified in his own person the future character of a whole society which he himself helped to create.

The alternative was and still is to recognise the highly significant limitations of science, and the fact of duty, the inescapable moral responsibility of men and women which demands that the whole of life, including science, shall be brought under its sway.

RELIGION

When we return to Kant's question about the origin of duty, it must be confessed that his answer to the question is open to the same kind of objection as his attempt to justify the objective character of phenomena: there is too much emphasis on the significance of law and a certain forgetfulness, very strange in Kant, that morality, duty, carries with it a striking appearance of self-authentication.

Kant started from the fact that all deeds imply some principle or maxim according to which they have been done. In the case of moral actions this might be some principle such as 'A promise must be kept', or 'Do not steal'. According to Kant, if such a maxim could be turned into a universal rule which all men could obey, then it was morally right; whereas if it was a morally wrong maxim, the attempt to universalise it would reveal a self-contradiction. For example, to say that lying is justified when it brings advantage to the liar could not be universalised, since it would lead to a breakdown of all trust and would destroy itself as a practical principle by which people could live. The principle of keeping promises, on the other hand, strengthens mutual trust and could be the more easily observed for being universally acknowledged.

It takes little reflection, though, to realise that there are quite selfish maxims which can be cheerfully universalised by the sinner without any fear of self-contradiction, and Kant came perilously close to admitting as much. A man might wish for a life of moderate pleasure and ease, and there would be no contradiction in supposing that everyone should make it their aim in life. Talents would be neglected, of course, but talents can be used for ill as well as good; and even if the man felt some moral unease about such neglect, this would in no way demonstrate a contradiction in the rule by which he lived and which he was happy to see other men live by. Kant tries to escape from this conclusion by saying that the man as a rational being could not actually *will* such a state of affairs, but this is merely importing into the situation the moral principle which he was supposed to be explaining.

Similar remarks apply to the case of a man who does not wish to put himself out in order to help other people. It is not to the point that the man might find himself in the position of needing help and then think differently: the point is that there is no *self-contradiction* in willing that all people should act according to the original principle, and we must therefore surrender this idea as a test of any given maxim's moral value.[25]

It is in fact impossible to find moral rules which can be regarded as absolutely and universally binding. Principles that we should never lie or steal or that we should always be kind and generous either become mere tautologies, or suffer from the contradiction of easily imaginable circumstances in which they cannot be applied. Let us suppose that a woman and her baby are starving, while nearby a wealthy farmer enjoys plenty – a not altogether far-fetched scenario. The farmer knows the woman's plight, but ignores it. The woman takes milk from the farmer's dairy and survives with her child. We may say that in this case she was stealing, but that stealing is not always wrong: it may be defined as taking something belonging to someone else without their knowledge or permission, but in the circumstances, such taking was justified. The woman had an obligation to her helpless child, and so, in fact, did the farmer, who is the one to be blamed for not responding properly to the demands of the situation. Or we may put the same argument in another way, insisting that stealing is always wrong by definition, but refusing to apply the concept to this kind of action. The woman was simply taking a step towards the more equitable distribution of wealth, and doing so in obedience to the demands of duty regarding her child.

Kant was not, of course, wrong to connect universality with morality, and in a sense we readily sympathise with the connection. If something is right, we feel that it must be right for everyone; and not just sometimes right, but always so. If something is morally right or wrong for X in a given situation, then it is true for everyone in the world that placed in the same position as X, they are under the same obligation. The rules cannot as it were be bent in order to satisfy privilege or grant special favours.

Nevertheless, even when this has been granted, it remains the case that ostensibly similar circumstances can be crucially different, and rules remain a crude instrument for dealing with the complexities of human existence. Furthermore, and of greater significance, the universality must depend on the morality, and not vice versa. If someone enjoys eating apple pie, it matters not how many other people share his taste; but if we think it right that someone has surrendered his apple pie in the interests of sending a donation to Oxfam, then we believe that it is right for everyone in a similar position to take similar action, however reluctant we might be to admit it and follow his example.

If, then, we reject Kant's explanation of duty, moral obligation, in terms of rational law, we must either rest content with the acceptance of it simply as a fact, a revelation to reason and conscience with self-evident authority; or we must look elsewhere for its authentication. In deciding between these two alternatives, it is worth while considering other things which Kant had to say about morality and the overall situation in which human beings find themselves, although we shall be led to a conclusion which was explicitly rejected by Kant himself.

While he repeatedly and rightly insisted upon the absolute and unique nature of duty's demand upon us, Kant also recognised the obvious fact that human beings often do not do what is right, and often find it extremely difficult or apparently even impossible to avoid preferring what is wrong and sometimes appallingly wicked. He also recognised that every person naturally desires his own happiness. For Kant, of course, this meant the kind of happiness which is morally good, but it is equally clear that he meant real happiness and true welfare. To deny such happiness and welfare to human beings is itself immoral; and therefore the truly good and upright person legitimately expects happiness in proportion to his moral deserts. Yet in this world it is frequently the case that moral good can only be achieved at personal cost and sacrifice; and it is certainly very far from being the case that virtue is consistently rewarded and wrongdoing punished.

With regard to the last point, Kant even rejected it as a desirable state of affairs, pointing out that any such system of rewards and punishments is destructive of freedom, and therefore, of course, morality. 'Yet especially to regard all punishment and reward only as the instrument wielded by a higher power, which should have the sole purpose of setting rational beings in motion towards their final end, happiness, is all too plainly a mechanical manipulation of the will totally destructive of freedom.'[26]

According to Kant, then, human beings are confronted by a moral demand which no excuse can evade, but which human weakness prevents from being fulfilled in this world. Nevertheless, the freedom to accomplish moral perfection does exist in every person, and it is integral to morality that that perfection should be achieved. Duty cannot, as it were, compromise and rest content with something less than perfection in human nature, either in its individual or its corporate aspect. As long as duty remains to be performed and right accomplished then, by definition, they must be performed and accomplished. It is in the nature of morality that this should be so.

Since, however, this is never achieved in this world and seems to be impossible of achievement, there must be some future state beyond death in which progress towards this end can be made until it is accomplished: morality by its very nature only makes sense if the universe extends far beyond the phenomenal existence we know at present, and a so-called morality which is confined to this world is no morality at all. Therefore, every time we make a sincere moral judgment we are not only asserting something of the immediate situation with which we are concerned, but by implication saying something very significant about the whole nature of the universe.

Kant reached a similar conclusion by a different approach. Virtue deserves to be united with happiness, but this is far from being the case in this world. The uniting of virtue with happiness is, however, itself a moral demand, and there must therefore be some future life in which this state of affairs is brought about; and there must also be some power in the universe capable of bringing it about. This power must also will that this be accomplished, and, indeed, have a will which is in perfect harmony with the moral law. This power or being we call God: and therefore every sincere moral judgment we make entails acknowledgement of the existence of God.

Thus, in Kant's own words,

Moral also führt unumgänglich zur Religion, wodurch sie sich zur Idee eines machthabenden moralischen Gesetzgebers außer dem Menschen erweitert, in dessen Willen dasjenige Endzweck (der Weltschöpfung) ist, was zugleich der Endzweck des Menschen sein kann und soll.

Morality therefore leads inevitably to religion. It is enlarged to include the idea of an all-powerful lawgiver existing apart from mankind, in whose will lies that final end of creation which at the same time both can and should be the ultimate aim of humanity.[27]

The acceptance of morality, therefore, entails the acceptance of human freedom, immortality, and the existence of God. It is important at this point, however, to recognise the distinction upon which Kant insisted between pure reason and practical reason. It is not that we are aware of two quite distinct mental faculties, but it is the case that we employ our reason in two quite different ways. We may use our reason in argumentative fashion, relating ideas to one another and drawing conclusions. Or we may use our reason for practical purposes, deciding what is right both in the moral and non-moral senses, working out how things should be achieved, thinking about ends and the means to accomplishing them.

Kant denied that it was possible to prove the existence of freedom, immortality and God by using pure reason, reason in the first sense. The attempt to demonstrate the truth of religion by some purely theoretical argument must fail. Kant also believed that it was impossible to provide a firm foundation for the natural sciences by this means. Hume had done his work well in this respect. Whatever theoretical model of the universe was proposed to justify religion or science, scepticism could always legitimately suggest some other model. In the case of religion, it is always possible to deny the real existence of its foundation, morality. It is always possible to argue, without self-contradiction, that moral values are purely subjective feelings and ideas generated in the course of evolution, just as instincts, nervous systems, personalities and societies have been generated. Those who are committed to empiricism must argue in this way, but any agnostic can leave the matter as an open question.

When we employ practical reason, on the other hand, we find ourselves compelled to accept the legitimacy of scientific argument within its own sphere, and we are equally compelled to accept morality and what goes with it. Whatever may or may not be true in theory, the attempt to live as if morality were false does not work, at least not as long as we remain normal human beings. Acceptance of moral obligation and commitment to what is right and morally good is very inadequate, while commitment to what is wrong and morally evil is all too evident; but even acknowledgement of this basic fact of human life is an acknowledgement of morality. The total surrender of belief in morals is no more open to a human being in practice than the total surrender of belief in necessary causation: and once this is accepted, what is entailed is accepted, too, even if there is no conscious recognition of the fact.

It is, of course, possible to play fast and loose with moral ideas in a way which is impossible within the sphere of natural science, but this is also a reflection of the greater profundity and significance of moral considerations in our lives than anything even the most sophisticated empiricism can provide. The perfect argument for the truth of religion would destroy human freedom, that is to say, human personality. The cast-iron conclusion of an irresistible argument would not only overwhelm the mind, but would reflect a kind of reality in which atheism was no longer an option: God would have become as evident as the noonday sun and rejection would be possible only at the expense of sanity. Rejection of the knowledge of God would mean that the machine had broken down, its mental apparatus lost in confusion, the total illusion which bears no relation to the facts. As Kant clearly recognised, this is neither true for the world in which we actually live, nor could it be true for any world in which genuine human personalities are possible and real.

Kant's main insights, therefore, must be accepted, although that 'must' is of the peculiar nature which pure reason may reject. Nevertheless, a serious problem is raised by Kant's argument, and it must now be considered.

No matter how important freedom may be for a proper understanding of morality and human life, it frequently seems to be the case that men and women are influenced by forces of evil and powers of temptation which they are powerless to resist. To relegate such force to the world of phenomena while retaining a superior noumenal freedom is not as it stands a sufficient reply to the problem. We have already seen that there is a problem of relating the noumenally free individual to the determined sequence of phenomena of which he is a part, and we have seen that this could only be overcome by abandoning Kant's oversharp distinction between noumena and phenomena and recognising that noumenal freedom does have its phenomenal aspect. Human beings do make choices and decisions which really do influence the course of phenomenal events, even though such freedom may not be observable; and this is, in fact, something which we accept and take for granted in everyday life.

The weakness of the moral will, however, cannot be explained in terms of the limitations of observation and purely empirical explanation. When we ask the question, Are people really free to choose the good and the right? we are compelled to face the fact that very often they seem not to have such freedom at all but to be overwhelmed by powerful inner drives and unalterable outward circumstances.

In a lengthy discussion concerning the difficulty of relating noumenal freedom to phenomenal necessity, Kant firmly rejects the idea that immorality can be excused by relegating it to the stream of caused, and therefore unavoidable, events, and insists that personal character is under the control of freedom and the moral law; but the discussion is more complex than convincing.[28] In fairness to Kant it must be said that he acknowledged both the difficulty of the subject and his own attempt to deal with it; but the power of evil to paralyse the will and pervert both reason and conscience cannot be explained away by insistence on the distinction between the noumenal and the phenomenal self, no matter how illuminating in many ways the distinction may be.

This situation in which we find ourselves creates a not unfamiliar kind of dilemma: in a given case we believe that a man is morally obliged to act in a certain way, and that this implies that he is actually free so to act if only he chooses to do so; and we praise or blame him according to whether he acts rightly or not. On the other hand, the man is under considerable, perhaps irresistible, pressure to act in one way rather than the other; his real freedom to choose is in doubt; and if he claims that the pressure was irresistible and we believe him, then we feel that we cannot praise him for doing right, or blame him if he does wrong. Yet we go on believing that one course of action was morally right, and the other morally wrong. Kant himself, as we have seen, distinguished action which follows inclination from action done solely out of obedience to the moral law, and believed that only the latter was praiseworthy as a moral deed.

When we think of concrete examples of situations in which a moral judgment is called for, we remain grateful to Kant for the essential distinctions and implications which he has made clear, but realise that some modification of his argument is necessary. The modification will lead to a conclusion which he rejected, but which is nevertheless closely related to his own ideas.

If someone reacts violently against attempts at blackmail or some persistent form of grossly unfair and hurtful persecution, we may well be compelled to recognise that the action was the inevitable consequence of natural feeling and deep-rooted instinct, and yet still believe that it ought not to have been done. We hesitate or refuse to blame the person concerned, and yet we condemn the act as immoral. Or it may be that someone risks injury in order to rescue a trapped animal. We learn that this individual has had a natural and lifelong love of animals and simply could not bear to see a helpless creature suffering, and derived profound satisfaction from the success of his attempt; but we still praise the deed as morally worthy, even though the person acted spontaneously, gave no thought whatever to duty, and would have undergone mental suffering if the creature had been neglected.

There are many situations in which men and women act wrongly and gain popularity and approval or make substantial sums of money out of so doing. These people were under pressure, perhaps considerable pressure, to act wrongly; and yet we often feel in these cases that some power of choice and decision remained. The morally right could have been willed. Or we feel that the situation has developed out of a series of previous choices and need never have arisen if moral obligation had been properly considered from the start. People may do what is right out of natural affection, as when parents make sacrifices for their children, and they may derive great satisfaction from such action and its consequences, but we do not on that account withhold praise on moral grounds. The happiest state of affairs is that in which obedience to duty no longer appears as such, but when the moral will has become blended with natural feeling to produce a wholly integrated personality.

Kant was therefore right to insist on the peculiar and highly significant nature of morality in our lives, and the implication of human freedom which this carries with it. He was also right to recognise the elusive character of this freedom, which is combined in our consciousness with a profound sense of its reality. He was above all right to argue that morality only makes sense in a universe of a certain character: we cannot justify the absolute demands of duty and the frequent self-denial and even sacrifice which this entails merely within the confines of experience in the present world. If explanations in terms of phenomena are the only valid ones, then morality is an illusion. If, however, the claims of duty and moral obligation are justified, they must be enlarged to include religious assertions of the most profound and far-reaching significance.

On the other hand, we cannot do justice to the true nature of moral good and bad, moral right and wrong, in terms of law; and while freedom is essential to morality, this is true only in a general sense and does not mean that in every situation every individual is actually in a position to exercise genuine choice. Freedom exists to different degrees in different individuals and in the same individual at different times, and it implies the capacity for development, change in a given direction, rather than the ability to accomplish a given act at a given moment. Each human being is a single whole, swayed by dispositions, feelings, motives, ideas, subject to the influence of feeling and will. The individual human being is also more or less bound up in a corporate life of family, friends and acquaintances, and the larger life of society; and this individual and corporate life appears at a moment in history, inheriting the complex influences of the past and being taken up into the stream of continual dynamic change.

The will operates as an element within and integral to the whole personality as thus seen, itself influencing and influenced like the rudder of a small sailing ship in a vast, and at times stormy, ocean.

Kant's claim to offer compass and chart was well justified, as was his claim to have shown that the existence of neither ocean nor vessel is explicable merely in terms of what is open to immediate sense-perception. It is unfortunate, however, that he read back into the whole unified situation distinctions necessary for thought, but much too sharp for reality. Although not intended by Kant, the illusion is created that man is the master of his own fate, and this means that his appreciation of the need for religion, although genuine and significant as far as it goes, is also inadequate.

It is the case, then, that the morally right and wrong, the good and the evil remain, quite regardless of whether or not the individual is capable of achieving the one and avoiding the other in any particular situation. The moral comes to us as the expression of a reality beyond our immediate circumstances and which lays upon us an absolute demand to respond, regardless of whether or not we are actually able at that moment to respond fully or not.

Kant himself repeatedly referred to the demands of duty as the commands of God, meaning by this that duty and the will of God coincide, as we might expect in the case of the supreme and perfect being. He firmly rejected the conclusion that duty and the will of God are identical; that is, that the moral is simply another name for the will of God, the expression of the divine nature as apprehended by human beings. According to this latter view, what we recognise as morally good and bad, morally right and wrong, is simply the expression of God's nature and will and derives its peculiar and absolute authority from that fact: it reflects the unique relationship which we have with the author and source of all life, and the kind of demand which the creator alone can make upon the creature.

Kant refused to let morality depend upon the will of God because he wished above all to assert and defend the inherent authority of the moral law, its absolutely binding quality independent of any other consideration. What is morally right, morally good, morally binding, is in itself quite simply that, and it must not be allowed to suffer contamination with any other circumstance. According to Kant, to make morality dependent upon the will of God would be to destroy its absolutely binding character by founding it on something essentially arbitrary. Kant needed the existence of God as an assurance that virtue would ultimately be united with the blessedness which it deserves, but nevertheless,

It must not be understood from this that it is necessary to accept the existence of God as a reason for all obligation whatever; since this is founded, as has been sufficiently shown, simply upon the autonomy of reason itself.

In this way the moral law leads through the concept of the highest good as the object and final purpose of pure practical reason to religion, that is, the knowledge of all duties as the commands of God: but not as sanctions, that is, the arbitrary decrees accidentally suited to a foreign will, but rather as the laws which are essential to every free will in itself . . . [29]

Kant's insistence upon the unique, irreducible character of the moral law was correct, and must not be lost sight of; but his attempt to present that character as derived from the logic of human rationality failed. The idea that we are aware of rational universal moral rules which we must obey regardless of the consequences, rather as we have to accept self-evident axioms and principles in Euclidean geometry, certainly seems to remove the idea of arbitrariness from moral obligation; whereas making it depend on some other being's will is indeed reminiscent of that last refuge of adult authority when confronted by precocious infantile defiance, 'Because I say so'. Yet morality cannot be convincingly presented as a set of rules: the facts of life are too varied and complex, morality is itself too intimately bound up with them, and the will is too often too weak to provide the moral imperative with the reality which it rightfully demands.

There is something far more arbitrary about Kant's argument as it stands. We are asked to assume the existence of an all-powerful being who is not actually the source of morality, but whose will happens to coincide with duty as conceived by the clear human conscience, and who also guarantees that blessedness will ultimately be bestowed according to virtue; even though the concepts of duty and happiness are quite distinct, and the obligations laid upon us by the former have an absolutely binding quality regardless of whether the latter follows from obedience to them or not.

The second passage quoted above continues:

but which nevertheless must be seen as commands of the highest being. This is because the moral law is set before us as our duty by the highest good, the object of our striving; but we can only hope to achieve the highest good through agreement with a will which is morally perfect, holy and good, and at the same time all-powerful.[30]

Kant goes on to emphasise that behaviour which results from selfish hope or fear utterly destroys its moral worth: but the highest good, which must be the ultimate aim of all behaviour, includes the combination of blessedness and moral perfection, and only a holy and good creator can bring this about, and therefore my will must unite with his.

Apart, however, from the problem of seeing how fear and hope can be excluded from a person's attitude in such circumstances, the impossibility of separating moral intention in practice from knowledge or belief about the consequences of action, and the acknowledged reasonableness of wanting to be happy, it is above all impossible to see why morality should not be included in the work of a being whom we regard as the creator. This being is perfectly holy and good, and he has made creatures who can appreciate holiness and goodness, but we are then asked to believe that the holiness and goodness somehow owe their origin to the rational faculty of the creatures. Even if pure reason is regarded as an adequate source of morality, that reason must exist to perfection within the creator; and we must then believe that he has made creatures who can to some degree share in that rationality and therefore enjoy what we might call moral potential. The creature shares in the nature of the creator, including the rational–moral aspect of that nature. If there be a creator, he is the origin and source of the whole universe; and if it is a universe in which morality makes sense, that is because the creator has willed it to be so.

Kant knew very well that hope of the final union between virtue and happiness must play an important part in the moral endeavour of any person. He condemned supposedly moral action done out of selfish motives of hope or fear, but at the same time recognised the need for reasonable hope that a life of moral endeavour would issue in a personal life of real well-being; and he also recognised the fundamentally immoral or amoral nature of a universe in which virtue and true happiness remain for ever separated. Human beings are often deceived and led astray by delusive ideas of happiness. If there be such a thing as virtue, it is in fact the sign of where true happiness lies: Kant's sharp distinction is a warning not to see happiness as some kind of reward for virtue bearing no relation to that for which it is the return. Virtue and happiness, if the first really is what it claims to be, are two sides of the same coin, and it is therefore not surprising that moral evil is that which tends to keep them apart.

Kant, in his role of ethical chemist, carried out an uncompromising isolation of the elements in experience; but if we take his analysis seriously and accept its truth as a piece of analysis, we can nevertheless only properly understand it and appreciate its implications by remembering that the elements do not actually exist in isolation from one another but in intimate, subtle and complex interrelationship. If the moral is what it claims to be, it sheds light on the whole and reveals not just some aspect of existence, but the fundamental character of the universe. The moral imperative does indeed have its universal character, but one which has to be expressed in terms of creation rather than law.

Kant opened the Conclusion to his *Critique of Practical Reason* in words which have become famous. The two things which inspired increasing awe and wonder in his soul were the starry heavens above, and the moral law within. We are reminded of Psalm 19. We are also reminded of Kant's claim to have brought about a 'Copernican revolution', and the analogy with the revelations concerning the size of the physical universe, with its countless stars upon stars and galaxies upon galaxies, which were made possible and initiated by the Copernican hypothesis, is very much to the point. As Kant claimed, reflection upon our inner experience leads us to conclude the existence of an endless unseen universe, just as reflection upon the evidence of the senses leads us to realise the existence of an apparently endless physical universe: and in both cases we are ourselves part of this universe, however great may be its extent. In relation to the physical aspect I am reduced to nothing, an animal whose material remains will return to the speck in the universe from which they once emerged; but in relation to the moral law, a personality with possibilities of development far beyond the limitations imposed by an earthly existence.

If we accept this picture of the universe we must include God in the picture, the author of the whole, and above all its most significant part. We might adapt Kant's remark concerning the relationship of morality and freedom to the relationship of morality and God: morality is the *ratio cognoscendi* of God, but God is the *ratio essendi* of morality. The answer to the old conundrum, Does God will it because it is good? or is it good because God wills it? is that both statements are true. The first expresses our belief in our own capacity truly to perceive the good, to be aware of moral values in their actuality, and that if this is so they must be in accordance with the will of God. The second expresses our belief in the necessary origin of the good if it is truly to be the most significant characteristic of the created order: without a good God, our perceptions of the good are merely illusions.

CONCLUDING REMARKS

Nineteenth-century British religious thinkers were alarmed by the growth of natural science. It depicted the realm of nature as one controlled by the predetermined operation of secondary causes, with a growing tendency to include mankind in that realm, culminating in Darwin and Wallace's theory of evolution. God was systematically excluded from scientific hypotheses, which was equivalent to the total exclusion of God from nature, unless one conceded the exceptional occurrences referred to as miracles. As science advanced, however, miracles became correspondingly more and more miraculous and therefore unbelievable; while scientific method applied to ancient documents and records, including the Bible, made naturalistic explanation more and more persuasive even in that sphere of religion known as revelation.

Those who looked to natural theology for an answer to these problems relied upon the teleological, or design, argument for the existence of God. If the Kantian critical philosophy had been widely known and accepted in Britain, this approach to the defence of religious belief could never have been employed, and if considered at all, would have been firmly rejected. Kant had shown that knowledge of nature was just that and nothing more. Reason could work with the facts presented to it through sense-perception, and might make profitable guesswork about facts which in principle could be presented to it; but the ultimate nature of reality was not open to observation. There is an absolute bar on the knowledge of things in their noumenal aspect. 'To resort to God as the creator of all things in the attempt to explain the arrangements of nature or their alteration is, to say the least, no physical explanation, and is in every case a confession that one has come to the end of philosophy.'[31]

Kant therefore rejected all three of the classical arguments for the existence of God. The ontological failed because existence could not possibly be derived from a mere concept; and the cosmological failed because any concept of cause which we could know and understand must belong to phenomena and therefore itself require further explanation, while a noumenal 'cause' would be beyond both knowledge and understanding.

Kant's comments on the teleological argument and teleological judgment in general require more extended consideration, partly because of the dominating significance of this argument in nineteenth-century Britain and partly because of the deep-seated appeal which it makes to the imagination. Kant himself acknowledged its strong appeal and spoke of the way in which it could deceive rather than properly convince the intellect:

An illusory proof of this kind is the one brought forward in natural theology, perhaps with the best of intentions, but nevertheless with a wilful concealment of its weakness: if one drags in a great pile of evidence concerning the origin of natural things according to the principle of purpose, and makes capital out of what is a purely subjective ground of human reason . . .

then we shall inevitably come to the conclusion that there is a single all-powerful and all-sufficient intelligent cause of these things rather than a lot of different causes.[32]

Kant very willingly granted that we see purpose at work in nature and that this is of the utmost use to scientists in understanding plants and organisms. This may lead us to imagine a purposeful author of nature; but what is useful and imaginable is by no means therefore proved to be true, or even given any degree of probability. Kant would have sympathised with both the title and the intention of Richard Dawkins' book, *The Blind Watchmaker*. To a human mind the workings, the evolution of nature do appear to express purpose and are to that extent just like Paley's watch; but in fact there is no such conscious purpose in nature, and nature is in that sense 'blind'.

Furthermore, Kant pointed out that the machine analogy fails precisely where it must hold if it is to succeed as an argument. Nature is simply not like a machine. Let us think of any natural object, fruit, vegetable or animal:

In such a product of nature every part is thought of as being there only through the agency of all the rest, and also as existing for the sake of the others, and for the sake of the whole; that is, as a tool, instrument. But this view is inadequate, since it could just as well be an artificial tool and therefore be represented merely as a possible end. It should rather be thought of as a tool actually producing the other parts, and consequently every part should be thought of as being in the same reciprocal relationship with the others. No artificial tool can be like that . . . And only then and for that reason could such a natural product, as an organised and self-organising entity, be called a natural end. In a watch one part is the instrument whereby another part is set in motion, but a wheel is not the effective cause whereby another is brought into existence. One part is indeed for the sake of another, but it does not appear through the agency of the other.[33]

The teleological principle, then, governs our thinking, but this cannot justify us in using it to determine our judgment about the ultimate nature of the world. When we allow this illegitimate judgment to occur in trying to demonstrate the existence of God, we merely create a vicious circle on the one hand, and falsify our view of nature on the other. In commenting on the principle that an organised product of nature is one in which every part is reciprocally both end and means; that nothing is purposeless or to be ascribed to a blind mechanism, Kant points out that this is a very useful, even necessary, maxim guiding botanists and zoologists and enabling them to understand why things are as they are. Kant was prepared to go so far as to say that such scientists could no more dispense with the idea of purpose in nature than they could dispense with the idea of necessary causation. Yet this purpose must be seen as a principle guiding human understanding and not as the assertion of something actually to be found in the natural world.

If it were to be treated as an actually inherent characteristic of nature and then used as the basis for theological assertion, nothing but confusion could result:

So if the concept of God is introduced into the context of scientific research and for the sake of science, in order to explain the purposeful-ness to be found in nature, and then afterwards this purposefulness is needed in order to prove that there is a God: then in neither of these sciences [natural science and theology] is there any inner constancy. A misleading interchange creates uncertainty in each because it allows their boundaries to overrun each other.[34]

In no way, then, can we infer the existence of God from the scientific or any other picture of nature, and if nineteenth-century British religious thinkers had taken on board Kant's message a great deal of fruitless argument would have been avoided and there would have been no temptation to enter a plainly signposted blind alley. There would have been no fear of science confined within its own boundaries, because those boundaries would have been sufficiently clearly drawn. Kant himself saw the possibility of evolutionary theory and looked forward hopefully to its establish-ment. British thinkers sometimes spoke of the legitimacy of sci-ence within its own bounds and claimed that the religious believer need have no fear of it; but it was an assurance with a hollow sound because, unlike Kant, they had not clearly seen just what the limitations of science are. A theory of evolution was a useful touch-stone for what claimed to be soundly based religious confidence, and in this respect the general religious reaction to Darwin in Britain, even down to the present day, needs no further comment.

While, therefore, Kant destroyed traditional attempts to defend fundamental religious belief, he also put a severe restraint on scientific claims to truth. Within those realms ruled by empiricism scientific methods serve their master well, and we can set no limit to discovery and explanation; but the overall scientific method has

an essential, inherent and inescapable limitation which lies within
the scientist himself as a human being. In a sense no subject can
be exempted from rational inquiry, and Kant was explicit about
the dangers to religious belief of trying to protect itself by claiming such exemption; but once the scientific attitude is adopted
towards any field of human experience, there are certain matters
which are systematically removed from its capacity to affirm or
deny.

These matters are those of the most profound concern to any
human being, but they carry us beyond what can be discovered by
empirical investigation or demonstrated by rational calculation.
The clear recognition of this fact, primarily a truth about human
nature, would have revealed the real nature of the conflict
between religion and science. Confronted by scepticism, religious
belief would willingly concede the justification for such scepticism
based upon purely empirical attempts to explain the nature of
reality, and would go even further and insist that scepticism was
the inevitable and unavoidable consequence of empiricism. Nor
would religious belief pretend to offer any demonstration that
empiricism's claim to be the sole method of attaining the truth
was false. Religious belief, however, would insist on indicating the
further and very far-reaching consequences of adopting this
position, and raise the question whether or not normal or
properly recognisable human life was really possible on such
terms. It is, in a sense, easy to dismiss the ideas of God, freedom
and immortality as ostensibly remote and unintelligible; but the
dismissal of morality is not, on even a moment's reflection, a
simple matter at all.

Once the significance of morality in human existence is
accepted, an altogether different approach to questions concerning life and reality has been adopted from that of the empiricist,
and therefore that of the natural scientist as such. Kant was substantially correct in his argument that a whole view of the universe
is being asserted in any seriously meant moral judgment and that
we cannot have the one without the other. Science can neither
confirm nor deny such a view, and religious belief will be able to
provide convincing proof that this is so. Those who wish to believe
that the natural sciences are the sole means of discovering truth
will be at liberty to do so, but they will not be at liberty to deny the
consequences of their stance; and while they will continue, as

human beings, to make sincere use of moral concepts, they will have to confess themselves living examples of a contradiction between the denial of practical reason on the one hand and its employment on the other.

Furthermore, the recognition of morality's significance not only entails a religious view of the universe but also the subordination of scientific activity to the authority of the moral and religious. How such subordination should work out in practice is another question, but problems of medical ethics and those concerning the use of nuclear energy, along with many others, show that the idea is neither novel nor unreasonable even though there may be widespread resistance to it.

The nineteenth-century conflict between science and religion in Britain was a real one. It would be absurd to suppose that Kant's insights were not shared to some extent by British thinkers, and Kant himself believed that one reason for the success of the design argument was the hidden importation into it of moral considerations. British thinkers, however, did not see the significance of the truths they grasped with the clarity and conviction found in Kant, nor did they work out the proper relationship between such truths, or even begin to approach the construction of a system such as the Kantian critical philosophy. Had they done so, they must have grasped the true nature of the conflict between science and religion far better than they did, and seen it as the rival claims of two world-views rather than a matter of mutual contradiction, and fundamentally a challenge to choice, will and commitment.

It is a great strength in the Kantian foundation of metaphysics, including theology, that we may choose to accept or reject it, and yet that the full implications of rejection are almost impossible to accept in practice. 'Ich mußte also das Wissen aufheben, um zum Glauben Platz zu bekommen': 'I must destroy knowledge in order to make way for faith.'[35] Coming from Kant this statement must be taken with the utmost seriousness. Like Elijah on Carmel, Kant challenges us to make a decision, while at the same time sober contemplation of the real nature of that decision clearly shows us what we ought to choose.

It is not simply that the power of choice is one which is integral to the Kantian moral philosophy and only to be denied at the price of self-contradiction. Far more to the point is the fact that Kant's thought here reflects paradoxes woven inextricably into the fabric of human experience: that we are free to reject both morality and freedom; that obedience to the moral law must be freely accepted if it is to be meaningful at all, but that the demand upon obedience is an absolute one; that our choice is a practical one and that we make it consciously or unconsciously every day; and that it produces consequences in terms of our own character and personality and the welfare of others. These truths are part of what the intellect must face as it tries to give expression to facts of experience which take us to the borders of the intelligible.

When we have completed the fullest possible description of the world and experience, and analysed away both freedom and morality, we are still left with a deep-seated sense of responsibility, justice and duty. Moral good and evil are our daily companions; and yet it is part of the very nature of the moral law that we may disobey, ignore or endeavour to escape from it. The daily practical demand upon every rational being, however ignorant or little given to reflection, is for commitment one way or another, with no ultimate proof one way or the other to destroy that freedom which belongs to a truly rational being.

CHAPTER 10

Critical philosophy and the Bible

INTRODUCTION

There is no greater field of human experience than that referred to as religion, and the believer rightly feels that there is a great deal more to religious thought than finding answers to scepticism. Worship and prayer and the attempt to put into daily practice what are conceived to be the commands of God, loyalty to centuries or millennia of tradition, participation in human fellowship and the giving and receiving of mutual comfort, all the many and greatly varied activities, feelings and ideas which we call religious seem to be quite incompatible with persistent doubt and the spending of time and trouble on questions which imply that the whole enterprise is nothing better than an elaborate charade. How can anyone worship and obey the God whose existence is a source of perennial doubt?

The beginning of an answer to this question is that belief and doubt are not so sharply or clearly divided as the question assumes. The idea that any human being can attain to a state of religious knowledge, which really is knowledge and which excludes even the possibility of doubt, is open to serious question. The spectacle provided by those who lay claim to such knowledge, often in rival and violently hostile groups, does not encourage acceptance of the idea by any reasonable and honest person.

When different religious parties lay claim to *knowledge* of mutually contradictory *truths*, the door to scepticism is not closed but thrown wide open. It was precisely the intolerance attendant upon dogmatism which evoked what was perhaps the most devastating expression of religious scepticism ever known in the English-speaking world, Hume's *Dialogues Concerning Natural Religion*.

Religious believers who command our profoundest respect, and they are by no means necessarily famous people, and may from a social and political point of view be utterly obscure, do display a kind of assurance which might be called knowledge. At any rate, there are some things they would claim to know and concerning which they would firmly refuse to admit doubt; and a sense of the presence and reality of God would be the foundation of all the rest. Yet even here it may be better to speak of assurance rather than knowledge. F. D. Maurice was right when he complained that the word 'knowledge' is a slippery customer, too often used in undefined and misleading ways. It may also convey a certain brashness which has already settled possible objections before they are uttered and which displays a consequent impatience with awkward facts and considerations which pose a threat to its unique authority.

The most deeply religious are those whose sensitivity would prevent any such claim. The joy, peace and serenity which we associate with a genuine assurance concerning the existence or presence of God must be surrounded by a profound awareness of the tragedies and mysteries of human life. Confronted by literally unspeakable, verbally inexpressible suffering and evil, who can claim in any recognisable sense of the term to *know* that God exists, to *know* that that which we call God really answers to some reality worthy of the name? Doubt and the willing confession of ignorance would seem to be essential ingredients of that religious belief which is worthy of respect, and very necessary restraints upon the uninhibited excesses of religious enthusiasm.

Genuine assurance must not, however, be watered down to a kind of reverent agnosticism. It is in part the grasping of truths which are held to outweigh in significance the ignorance and uncertainty inevitably attached to much with which we are acquainted; and in part a commitment to certain ideas, feelings and motives, to certain experiences, because we want to be so committed, because we feel that this is right. Certain claims on our attention and will are conceded through conviction that for us there is no alternative. In that sense, Martin Luther's famous words express something universal in religious commitment: 'Here I stand! I can no other.'

The relevance of these considerations to the present argument is this: unless religious belief is of the most superficial nature it involves conscious commitment, and conscious commitment involves confrontation with doubt. Even a very imperfect appreciation of the promises and demands of the Christian religion must raise the question whether or not such promises can be true and such demands justified, and it is difficult to believe that the same is not the case for other world religions. The state of assurance in which doubt no longer exists or has been weakened to the extent that it is no longer a motivating force is one which has to be attained, it is the fruit of growth. If there are exceptions to this rule, they only go to prove it as a generalisation; and the believers who have not faced and overcome doubt, or are not facing and overcoming it, have in all probability built their house upon sand.

In Great Britain doubt has been for many years sufficiently widespread and sufficiently strong to prevent serious commitment to religion on the part of the great majority of the population. The development of natural science strengthened scepticism and encouraged the belief or assumption that there is an alternative empirical explanation of life which can dispense with belief in God; and, indeed, ought to do so since such belief can do nothing but place stumbling-blocks in the way of real progress. Such scepticism seemed to be confirmed by a glance at the Bible, with its antiquated views of the universe and superstitious fears of demonic possession and divine wrath and its vain hopes of divine intervention and angelic sustenance. Admittedly, there are passages of great beauty and moral worth in its pages, but it was no part of the empiricist case that we should surrender aesthetic and moral values. Scepticism was reserved for the specifically religious.

This does not mean that religion has been surrendered in favour of a positively embraced atheism; far from it. Many would still confess to some kind of vague belief in God, and no doubt some kind of vague hope of a future life for themselves and their loved ones; but empty churches, general ignorance of the Bible and the degraded state of religious education in schools tell the true story, along with a positive faith in science and technology revealed time and again in the practicalities of life. These are the gods, it is believed, which will deliver us from evil. The proper word to describe the general outlook in Britain is 'agnostic', in a sense strikingly similar to that proclaimed by Thomas Henry Huxley, and often expressed explicitly or implicitly in a variety of ways by the more articulate.

Those acquainted with this challenge to religion, and those brought up in a society whose ethos has been increasingly dominated by it, need and deserve a proper reply from the religious side. Replies have been made, and it would be grossly unjust to those concerned not to acknowledge the real value of many of them; but the only person to construct a systematic and thoroughgoing critique of both scepticism and dogmatism, and provide the basis for reasonable religious belief, was Immanuel Kant. It may be readily admitted that religion is not simply a matter of reason, any more than domestic happiness is summed up in the possession of an efficient watchdog; but the members of the household can rest all the more easily for knowing that the dog is on their side rather than the leader of a dangerous pack seven times worse than itself. Religion must include reason, and once this faculty has come under the control of persuasion, it can perform its rightful functions not only in the defence but in the development of the faith.

If we approach Kant from the point of view of already held Christian belief we shall be struck by the inadequacies of his attempt to give a positive account of morality and religion; but if we start where Kant started, with the question whether or not there is any reasonable basis for religious belief at all, we shall become aware of the insights of his philosophy which are of permanent value. We shall find these insights leading us to revelation and fulfilling the hopes so frequently expressed by the advocates of natural theology. Even more, we shall find his insights casting light on revelation itself, since human nature does not and did not cease to be such when receiving and conveying the Word of God. There is no essential difference between reason and moral sense in modern and in biblical man.

BIBLICAL RELIGION: GENERAL REMARKS

The Bible is a literary collection, made from a wide variety of sources over a long period of time. Whatever may have been the original intentions of the sources, the collection is presented to us with the claim, implicit throughout and sometimes explicit, that we are being given information of the most profound importance concerning our life and the world in which we live. It is by no means always obvious that this is so, and no one can take the claim seriously without being selective with respect to it. At the most elementary level this is because there are inconsistencies in the text, such that if one text is accepted as true the other cannot be. There are also assertions of fact which cannot be taken at their face value, even though it is obvious that this is the way we are supposed to take them; and this is so even if we exclude all stories of the miraculous as a special case. These basic facts are common-place in liberal scholarship, and the mind which is open to honest persuasion cannot possibly deny them.

There is much else of a wide-ranging variety, in which we should probably include all the miracle stories, which makes a demand upon the judgment of the reader. Two perfectly serious readers may come to very different conclusions concerning much of this literature, and the history of the Jewish and Christian Churches amply demonstrates the fact. It is also true that there is and has often been widespread and substantial agreement on the value of many texts; but even in agreement we are aware of the personal judgment of the reader or hearer. As in other literature, as in other means of communication such as film, music or painting, the personal involvement of those receiving the communication is essential and inescapable if the communication is to be meaning-ful; and the more significant the communication, the more truly is this the case. Judgment, choice, selection: these are not only unavoidable but accepted as normal in any genuine desire to understand and either accept or reject a given communication.

The judgment and selection we exercise in reading the Bible is based upon already accepted ideas about right and wrong, what is likely and what is unlikely, and so on. Our own conscious belief, and even more powerfully, our assumptions influence our response to the biblical text. It is not surprising that much in an ancient and foreign literature should be unacceptable to us, and in some or even many cases it may be obvious that the modern reader is more advanced than the ancient author; but in other cases it may be that our own assumptions and beliefs are being fairly challenged and that we are being offered insights into the truth which only a fool will refuse to consider.

This brings us back to critical philosophy: the examination of assumptions, beliefs and claims to knowledge; and the construc-tion of a sound metaphysics. The two functions are not discon-nected, and in any attempt to work out a proper overall view of the world we need to start with what we think we cannot reasonably deny. Common sense by itself is quite unable to deal with serious intellectual problems, but it can play an essential role as a controlling factor in serious intellectual debate. No matter how sophisticated a rational system may be, it will neither persuade nor deserve to persuade if it cannot stand the test of daily belief and practice. If we are presented with what might be called a Heath Robinson metaphysics we might, if we are that way inclined, admire its ingenuity, but we shall not take it seriously as a practical guide to running the household.

This was precisely why Kant published his own extensive reflections on the possibility of producing a genuinely plausible, believable theology. Those reflections are to be found primarily in the three great Critiques of Pure Reason, Practical Reason, and Judgment; but they were also employed in an examination of religious belief itself, which included some comment on biblical passages. This was in *Die Religion innerhalb der Grenzen der bloßen Vernunft, Religion within the Limits of Pure Reason,*[1] and it was necessary that this should be so. The critical philosophy concerns human beings as such, and if justified is quite as applicable to the men and women of biblical times, quite as applicable to the biblical authors and the personalities who appear in their narratives, as to men and women now. Bearing in mind the powers and limitations of human reason, what can we make of the claims of the biblical authors and those whom we meet in their pages to be vehicles of 'revelation'?

The word *bloßen* in the title of Kant's book means 'bare', as in barefoot, or bare skin. We might be put off an examination of religion's claims which sounds so emphatically intellectual, but this work is not to be dismissed, nor should the general relevance of the critical philosophy to an understanding of biblical religion be ignored. If Kant's work displays weakness as well as strength, it is the better part which provides a firm link between the men and women of the Bible and the rest of humanity. If Kant's attempt to evaluate biblical religion falls distinctly short of a full appreciation of its subject, it is nevertheless sufficient to prepare the ground for rich development.

Kant's own comments on the Christian religion and biblical passages will be considered later. First, some indication must be given, however brief and selective, of the general relevance of the critical philosophy to biblical interpretation.

Biblical passages vary considerably in length, from the brief proverb or parable to whole books like Jeremiah or Job or St John's Gospel. What we regard as a 'passage' already depends upon that process of selection already referred to. In any given case such a passage or collection of them may or may not assert or assume a particular metaphysical, theological view; but since the general purpose of the Bible is to make metaphysical, theological assertions, any passage which seems not to convey such a message will have to be taken up into a larger context which does do so, if we are to remain true to this fundamental aim of the biblical writers. When we are told that a battle took place or that Jesus travelled from Jericho up to Jerusalem, these assertions in themselves are of merely historical interest; but if we are told in the larger context that the outcome of the battle was determined by the judgment of God and that Jesus went to Jerusalem in order to die for the sins of men, we are being presented by claims which, if true, are of significance for human belief and behaviour always and everywhere.

The critical philosophy will help to make us aware of our own ideas and assumptions and their influence upon our approach to the Bible in the first place, and it will help us to assess the metaphysical claims presented to us in the text. This will constitute a fair challenge to scepticism, whether expressed by an individual or group or in our own doubts and indifference, and also a fair challenge to the biblical religious message. What can we reasonably believe? and what ought we to believe?

The Bible asserts the existence of God and that the world was created by God, and that there is evil in the world even though the original purpose of the creator was wholly good.[2] The first three chapters of Genesis deal specifically with these matters, although there is much else in the Bible of direct relevance to them. When we read these three chapters we come across difficulties in understanding them, not least their incompatibility with the picture of the universe built up by modern science. Some of these difficulties have been dealt with by liberal scholarship, and excellent commentaries have been produced by liberal scholars which enable us to appreciate the way in which the writers have chosen to convey their message and the way in which editors have been at work putting together originally disparate sources. These chapters are related as literature to other Near Eastern documents and we are made fully aware of the fact that we are reading the work of a very different culture from our own, and that we must enter sympathetically into the minds of the ancient writers and editors if we are to do them justice. When inconsistencies, scientifically untenable statements and what might strike us as rather strange tales are set in their cultural context and viewed in terms of the history of traditions handed down over centuries, or even millennia, we begin to distinguish the wood from the trees and lay aside our own natural assumptions in the interests of grasping the significant content of the narratives. Nevertheless, we are left with the all-important question: Is that which is asserted true?

The opening account of creation in Genesis 1:1–2:3 makes very clear the unique character of that which is being described. The repeated assertions of God's purpose and that that purpose has been fulfilled and approved convey a sense of finality, and this culminates in the statement of 1:31 that God surveyed everything and found it very good. Even more important in this connection is the divine sabbath referred to in 2:1–3. Sheer repetition of the assertion that God's work is finished and the very nature of the sabbath itself emphasise beyond doubt and without the slightest ambiguity that creation does not continue. The original divine creation 'In the beginning' stands in splendid isolation from everything which follows. The divine sabbath represents an unbridgeable gulf between the world of nature which we experience and of which we are a part, and the essential condition for the appearance of that nature and our experience of it.

Nature is marked by continual change and growth and the whole universe is in constant movement, all the result of life and force which belong to the natural world as such. There is a fertility and power of reproduction which are divine in origin, but which now belong to nature itself. This is quite clear from chapter 1, but seems to be confirmed in 2:4a by the word often translated 'generations', but which more accurately should be 'generatings', 'begettings', explicitly referring to the active production of life, as in 5:1ff.; 6:9ff.; 10:1ff.; and 11:10ff., 27ff. In these other chapters the word refers to what follows, but in 2:4a this is scarcely appropriate, and it is much more likely that the whole sentence refers back to the account in chapter 1, and the life-giving properties bestowed

upon the whole natural order in the act of creation. 'The usual
placing of the phrase at the head of the narrative was, in this one
unique case, impossible, since this narrative's prime assertion is of
God's creative activity from which the power to produce life is
itself derived. All other uses of the phrase concern significant
moments within the continuing life of the already established
natural order.'[3]

It follows from this that the observation and knowledge of
nature will not in itself carry us back to the creator. As Kant maintained, the concept of creation takes us beyond the bounds of
what human beings can know. In biblical terms, the perfect fulfilment of God's will in creation, and even more the intervening
sabbath rest of God, place creation in what can only be thought of
as a period or moment utterly beyond the reach of human investigation. Creation belongs to the noumenal world, whereas our
whole knowledge of nature belongs to the phenomenal. God has
given to the earth and heavens their own life, movement and
force, and however much we learn of the created order of which
we are ourselves a part, we cannot get beyond that life, movement
and force.

It has already been argued that talk of noumenal and phenomenal worlds can be misleading, and this is true if it makes us forget
the intimate union and continuity between noumena and
phenomena: that they are two aspects of the same single world of
things. On the other hand, once this fact of central importance for
Kant's theory of knowledge has been firmly grasped, we must
admit that the extent of the world beyond the range of our
perceptions is one upon which we can place no limit, and this
admission is implicit in the biblical account of creation. And it is
an admission forced upon us by an examination of empiricism
alone, regardless of any other consideration.

This can, of course, be dangerous. We can fill this limitless
emptiness with objects corresponding to our own ideas without
any fear of contradiction, and with no better confirmation than
that they correspond to our own desire and fancy. It matters not
whether our ideas are the product of sophisticated rational reflection, as in the classical arguments for the existence of God, or a
lively imagination, as in the case of those fairy-tale and pantomime
characters which still appeal to the child in us: as far as proof,
demonstration and observation are concerned, we must confess

total and unqualified agnosticism. Neither atheist nor religious dogmatist have a scrap of evidence whereon to stand.

Nevertheless, we want to know what lies beyond the bounds of empirical knowledge, and it is because of deep-seated questions which belong to humanity as such and which stir men, women and children totally regardless of capacity or inclination for intellectual reflection that the Bible and the critical philosophy of Kant, along with much other literature, have been produced. In the light of a genuine agnosticism, how are we to regard the dogmatic utterances of Genesis 1? or the claims of cosmologists to be approaching ever nearer to an unfolding of the secret of the universe's origins? Asking the question how the universe began conceals the question why it began, and seems to demand an answer which only the expert or the deeply initiated can try to give; but thinly disguises the much more personal question why 'I' began and all the other 'I's who help to make the self what it is. And the question put in terms of origins is just as much a question which might be put in terms of future destiny: What is left when the wholly empirical has been stripped away? The point that this is no mere academic exercise scarcely needs labouring.

A recent attempt has been made by Professor Stephen Hawking to sum up in language intelligible to a layman the views of cosmologists concerning the nature and origin of the universe in so far as these are open to highly sophisticated empirical investigation.[4] The layman is genuinely grateful to Professor Hawking and other experts for taking time off from fascinating specialist inquiry to share their results and speculations with the general public; but the attempt by experts to express in relatively plain terms what are their aims, achievements and methods has another use than the very worthy one of keeping the rest of us informed. It lays bare the more general questions and assumptions which lie behind the details of daily research. Furthermore, the attempt by the expert to make plain what he is about is itself a discipline of no small value to the expert as well as the layman. Properly carried out, it becomes an essay in critical philosophy. If the general picture of the universe which emerges from advanced research cannot be put into meaningful plain language, is it meaningful at all?

Much of Hawking's book, of course, is concerned with purely scientific matters and as such makes fascinating reading; but he does not hesitate to consider what might be the implications of scientific research for religious belief. Carl Sagan concludes his Introduction with the explicit assertion that the book is about God, 'or perhaps about the absence of God'. According to Sagan, Hawking is trying to answer Einstein's famous question as to whether or not God had any choice in creating the universe, but comes to the unexpected conclusion that in a universe with neither spatial nor temporal boundaries, there is nothing for a creator to do.

The existence of God is not denied by Hawking, but doubt is repeatedly cast upon the idea of divine creation, and by the time we come to the end of the book we feel that yet another nail has been driven by the scientific establishment into the coffin of religious belief. The scientific expert seems to have demonstrated for the umpteenth time that religious affirmations such as Genesis 1 are merely objects of curiosity in some kind of intellectual *Antiques Roadshow,* and regrettably of no actual value.

Hawking describes the big bang theory of the universe's origin, and tells us on page 50 that 'nowadays nearly everyone assumes that the universe started with a big bang singularity'. He goes on, however, to question this theory and to offer an alternative suggestion. His main objection to the big bang theory is that it posits a point at which the existence of the universe began, but leaves us with this beginning as an absolutely arbitrary event, in itself totally beyond the power of science to explain. We can trace back the life of the universe to the big bang by using what we know of the laws of nature, but once we have reached it, these laws cease to apply and the big bang itself remains an event for ever inexplicable.

Hawking proposes another view based on the quantum theory of gravity.

Because one is using Euclidean space-times, in which the time direction is on the same footing as directions in space, it is possible for space-time to be finite in extent and yet to have no singularities that formed a boundary or edge. Space-time would be like the surface of the earth, only with two more dimensions. The surface of the earth is finite in extent but it doesn't have a boundary or edge.[5]

Hawking makes it quite clear that these different views of the universe's origin must stand or fall according to the scientifically gathered and assessed evidence, but his own preference is also influenced by the desire to produce a completely unified scientific theory, and ultimately 'a complete *understanding* of the events around us, and of our own existence'.[6] In Hawking's opinion, the big bang theory involves the denial of this hope, and provides instead the ultimate inescapable gap in our knowledge which religious believers are only too happy to fill with 'God'. Hawking supports this view by referring to the official pronouncement of the Catholic Church in 1951 that the big bang model is in accordance with biblical teaching; but he also has to admit that some scientists have deliberately tried to avoid the assertion that time had a beginning at the big bang precisely because it seems to suggest the idea of divine intervention.[7]

Hawking twice refers to a conference he attended in the Vatican, organised by Jesuits to receive the advice of experts on cosmology. At this conference, held in 1981, the Pope himself laid it down that the evolution of the universe after the big bang could be legitimately studied by the scientists, but not the big bang itself, because this was the moment of divine creation. Hawking believed his own alternative theory to be quite at variance with this religious affirmation, since according to his own theory there was no moment of creation. For Hawking the universe should be regarded as completely self-contained, with nothing outside it, and therefore nothing apart from itself which could affect it; and with no beginning or end, and therefore no moment at which a creator could operate. For Hawking this is the consequence of the idea that 'space and time may form a closed surface without boundary'.

The idea that space and time may form a closed surface without boundary also has profound implications for the role of God in the affairs of the universe . . . So long as the universe had a beginning, we could suppose it had a creator. But if the universe is really completely self-contained, having no boundary or edge, it would have neither beginning nor end: it would simply be. What place, then, for a creator?[8]

In commenting on Hawking's theory it is necessary to distinguish between the scientific evidence which he presents, and which forms the main content of his book, and the religious and philosophical views which he mentions. The scientific debate is a matter for experts, and it is out of the question for a layman to pronounce in favour of one scientific theory rather than another. We are, however, in a different case with regard to the religious and philosophical questions raised by Hawking.

Early in his volume reference is made to Kant and St Augustine.9 Hawking refers to the antinomies found in the *Critique of Pure Reason* and correctly points out that one of them is meant to demonstrate that there are equally compelling arguments for believing that the universe had a beginning and for believing that it has existed for ever. As Hawking recognises, this is one of the illustrations Kant gives of the self-contradictions into which pure reason can get itself; but he then seems to forget that Kant's whole aim in the antinomies is to show the limits of reason and that the antinomies are simply illustrations used by Kant, merely repeating long-familiar arguments which never get anywhere. Hawking accuses Kant of making the unspoken assumption that time goes back for ever, but this was the assumption made by the thinkers whom Kant criticised, and which he rightly believed he had reduced to absurdity by demonstrating its consequences. Kant's own view of time was very different.

Hawking dismisses the *Critique of Pure Reason* as monumental but very obscure, thereby fostering a popular illusion but probably giving expression to widespread feeling among scientists about philosophy in general. Yet closer attention to Kant would have saved Hawking, and no doubt other scientists engaged in speculation about the nature of the universe, from real obscurity.

Hawking seems to believe that he has dodged the dilemma expressed by the first antinomy. His model of the universe is unlimited in space and time in the sense that it has no spatial or temporal boundaries; but at the same time it is spatially and temporally finite. No matter how far our explorations reach, or how long we carry them on, we shall always find the same laws of science at work, and we shall never come to a mysterious point where such laws break down and we have to call in God to supply the deficiency.

As far as scientific evidence about the physical structure and working of the universe is concerned, this view may be true: but it tells us nothing about creation. If Kant were alive today he would regard both Hawking's remarks about God and those of the Vatican as reported by Hawking as a modern antinomy; that is, an illusory conflict of opinions, neither of which is justified, and which are the consequence of ignoring a soundly based critique of reason.

If, on the one hand, the big bang theory is correct, scientists can only confess total and unqualified ignorance concerning what lies beyond it. A confession of absolute and inevitable ignorance, however, is no basis for either the assertion or the denial of God's existence, either the acceptance or the rejection of divine creation. If, on the other hand, Hawking's theory is correct, we are presented with the model of a self-contained physical universe with all its working parts, as it were, open to inspection from within. This still leaves us with the question, however, why and how such a universe should exist. If we imagine a great series of cycles, with universes succeeding one another over vast aeons of time, yet always according to the laws of science, this may be very consoling to the natural scientist, but the human mind will simply rephrase its questions about the origin of the universe into questions about the origin of the series.

Interestingly enough, this is precisely what Hawking does. He confesses that even if there is only one possible unified theory, the rules and equations which comprise it could not explain why the universe which they describe actually exists. If we could construct a perfect model of the universe, we should still be left with the question why there was a universe for the model to depict.[10]

According to Hawking, scientists have been too preoccupied with theories describing what the universe is, to spend time on the question why it is; but he virtually admits that the latter question is not one which scientific method is competent to deal with. The question why is one for philosophers, and Hawking castigates them for not keeping up with the advance of science and allowing philosophy to degenerate into mere linguistic analysis. There may well be truth in the criticism, but it is ironic that he should be so dismissive of the one great philosopher who anticipated and solved before the end of the eighteenth century the problems which were to be raised by the sciences for religious belief.

It is also ironic that Hawking's understandable desire that the laws of science shall always be found to operate in the universe, no matter how far our explorations take us into time and space, should be fully in keeping with the Kantian critique. The consistency, however, arises from the fact that the laws of science, like the phenomena with which science and common sense alike deal,

are in part, and crucially, determined by the observing and understanding self or subject; just as space and time are the framework
which the observer continually carries around as part of his own
perceptual and mental apparatus and spontaneously imposes on
what is given. At the same time, this sets the limit on what empirical investigation can achieve, no matter how sophisticated, and it
matters not at all to metaphysics whether this limit be described as
a big bang, or as a spherical surface which is in itself an impassable
boundary between the empirically knowable and the unknowable.

Hawking's view also raises another fundamental question concerning knowledge, and it is one which he recognises and tries to
answer. If the entire universe is governed by laws which can be
combined into a complete unified theory, this implies that all
human action, including the theory itself, is already determined
by it. 'And why should it determine that we come to the right conclusions from the evidence? Might it not equally well determine
that we draw the wrong conclusion? Or no conclusion at all?'

Hawking goes on to find the answer in Darwin's principle of
natural selection. Truth is the correct correspondence of our
thoughts with the facts, and this is what has survival value. Intelligence and scientific discovery have already demonstrated this, and
we may therefore reasonably expect the evolving world to throw
up the right answers to our questions about the universe, including the complete unified theory.[11]

If we include moral ideas and judgments in human intelligence
and thought, as we should, it is not difficult to see that this hypothesis is totally destructive of all real morality and implies consequences of an horrific nature. It also repeats, as so much in this
century has done, the ideas of T. H. Huxley, barren of hope for
anything beyond a lucky draw in this life. We might also query the
claim that intellectual achievement has been of such marked
survival value. Short-term, and unquestionably very valuable, gain
by some has to be set against destruction of life on a colossal scale
and vast ecological problems which would never have been possible without scientific and technological discovery; and not least
among these is the incalculable danger posed by precisely those
discoveries most closely associated with talk of a complete unified
theory, that is, work on the atom and nuclear energy. It is also
perhaps a little premature for men to speak of survival in evolutionary terms: compared with the dinosaur and the cockroach

mankind has hardly begun. Most serious of all, however, this survival-value explanation of 'truth' does not at all correspond to what we mean by 'truth', the direct evidences of our own consciousness.

Sir Arthur Eddington faced the same problem as Hawking in his Swarthmore Lecture for 1929. Eddington contemplated the situation in which we knew that the whole truth about the physical universe would be revealed within a few years, and he tried by means of a simple illustration to show what this could be taken to imply. Let us suppose that every thought in the mind is represented in the brain by a characteristic configuration of atoms and that such configurations succeed one another according to determined causal connections; and that therefore our thoughts are simply determined according to the laws of nature. In that case, what do we make of one person's thought, $7 \times 9 = 65$, and another person's thought, $7 \times 9 = 63$? According to the theory we cannot say one is correct and the other false: we can only regard both thoughts as the latest state in a predetermined causal chain; but this is manifestly not the way we do regard them, and such a theory has no plausibility.[12]

As a final comment on Hawking's book, we must return to the fact that the opening account of creation in the Book of Genesis has anticipated Professor Hawking and his colleagues by quite a few centuries in maintaining that the physical universe is 'completely self-contained'; and it may well be that we should see in the chaos which precedes the appearance of a knowable universe a symbol of that impenetrable veil which lies between human curiosity and the original creation. How the author of Genesis could then leap the unbridgeable gap to God will be a matter for separate consideration.

Hawking's book is an illustration of what so often happens when major scientific work is placed before the general public. What we might call the intellectual spin-off is the implication that an ever-developing empiricism has rendered religious belief obsolete, especially that expressed in the Bible. Yet empiricism itself, however impressive, cannot get us any closer to answering those questions that really matter. Nor does it in itself invalidate religious belief. It is an alternative to religion which must stand or fall by the test of our whole experience.

This is also the test which must be applied to, say, Genesis chapters 1 and 2, both of which deal with the creation of the world, although from different angles. The test, therefore, is not empirical or scientific. Empiricism is the alternative to what is offered in Genesis, and as a rival for our affections cannot act as judge, even though it may boast of those respects in which it is superior to the biblical text. The biblical authors, however, might claim some superiority of their own.

Both accounts of creation, 1:1–2:4a, and 2:4b–25, depend upon analogical modes of expression. There is no pretence in these narratives as they are presented to us in the Bible that a straight account is being given of that which was observed, or which can be extrapolated from what is observed now. In certain details the two accounts are plainly inconsistent, and if such details had been in themselves of significance there must have been some omissions, or attempts at reconciliation of the type favoured by misguided modern conservatives. It is obvious to any unprejudiced reader that we are here in the world of metaphor, analogy: but instead of regarding this as a weakness to be excused, as some commentators have done, it should be welcomed as the only mode of expression possible when dealing with such matters as creation and the relationship between man and God. Kant himself insisted that analogy was the only possible way in which man could conceive of the attributes of God,[13] although, of course, he was careful to rule out any attempt to *argue from* analogy. This characteristic of the biblical text, which meets us in the first two chapters, is to be found throughout; and it is interesting to reflect that the faith which so powerfully emphasised and enforced the ineffability of God by the refusal to tolerate any kind of manufactured image should nevertheless unselfconsciously adopt verbal imagery, sometimes of a very striking nature, as the proper mode of describing God and his dealings with men. God unquestionably belongs to the noumenal world, but is revealed in unquestionably phenomenal language.

This does not, however, prove that there is anything, or anyone, corresponding to our analogies, nor does the Bible offer demonstration or explicit argument to justify them: once more in keeping with the Kantian critical philosophy. In order to find the justification for the assertions of Genesis 1–2, we have to set these chapters in a much larger context, and understand that they are based upon the profound moral sense which also characterises the literature throughout. Sometimes moral issues are being dealt with explicitly or by very obvious implication; at other times we temporarily lose sight of the moral, or we may even be repelled by the moral judgments clearly approved in the text. Nevertheless, it is a major and obvious characteristic of the literature as a whole that there exists that which is morally good and bad, morally right and wrong, and that this moral awareness is identified or intimately associated with the will of God. The values and the claims upon humanity are absolute, and they emanate from a source not only independent of humanity and the world, but possessing the unique authority and power which alone can justify the recognition of such values, such rights and wrongs as real and legitimate.

This point is crucial for biblical religion and any metaphysics, any theology which we wish to construct out of it, just as it is in Kant's critical preparation for metaphysics. This is not a question of morality in any narrow sense, nor does it imply that we shall agree with every moral judgment favoured in the Bible; nor is such agreement possible, since there is significant variety in the moral judgments of the Bible. It is a question of acknowledging or refusing to acknowledge that there is that which is truly good and really evil, truly right and really wrong; that what we call our moral sense, with the widest and deepest meaning we can give to the concept of the moral, actually does put us in touch with what exists independently of ourselves but which can become part of ourselves, even more truly than the five physical senses put us in touch with the world of things and make them part of our experience. Just as our sight or hearing or taste may mislead us, so may our moral sense. Just as our sense of smell or our sense of touch may become damaged and dulled, so may our moral sense: but we either believe or we do not believe that this capacity really can establish contact between ourselves and something with an objective reality of its own, however faulty the connection may be.

The Bible and Kant both regard the claims of the good and the prohibitions of the bad as the commands of God, and for both morality can only make sense in a world created and ruled by God. For the Bible, however, God not only wills and commands what is good, but in so doing simply expresses his own nature, which is the source of the good. As for Kant, so for the men and women of the Bible, human beings are free, but their freedom is not the essential condition for the existence of moral good and evil: it is rather the essential condition for the participation of human beings in what is good. In a sense, human freedom is the essential condition of morality. That is, human beings can themselves only truly participate in good, do right, if they are free, and the same freedom implies the capacity to refuse the good and choose the evil; but the good exists regardless of whether or not human beings participate in it.

In the Bible, good and evil, right and wrong, are conceived very much in personal terms. The good is a right relationship with God and the bad is its denial. Human freedom is the essential condition for being human, and according to the Bible we become most truly ourselves when we have a right relationship with God. In this respect we must regard the Bible as providing us with a much more powerful and persuasive analogy than Kant could offer. The philosopher provided secular thought with a profound insight by his insistence that all persons must be regarded as ends and never as means, but his justification of this view by an appeal to the rational faculty in mankind is by no means sufficient to bear the weight put upon it. It is an attitude which needs to be more intimately related to an overall view of the nature of the world of which we are a part, and the Bible provides that integration. In language which is startling, even extravagant, man and woman are declared to be created in the image and likeness of God: an assertion rich in its implications, with a meaning not to be confined within the narrow bounds of definition. One feels, for example, that the stern law forbidding the construction of images is related to the truth about human beings as well as the ineffability of God, and conveys the warning that when men make idols out of the created order they contradict their own nature and become alienated from their environment.

There is good reason to believe that the opening account of creation in Genesis was composed around 500 B.C. However ancient some of the material used in it may be, it seems to have been moulded in the light of prophetic teaching, most notably that associated with the exile in Babylon. The moral element in this teaching is extensive and profound, and it is this which provides the answer to the question how a biblical author can leap the gap between the noumenal and the phenomenal. It may seem purely artificial to associate the arguments of an eighteenth-century

Prussian philosopher with the 'revelation' contained in the Bible, but what is more striking is that two such divergent sources should be in such profound agreement. It is an agreement which could only result from comparable honest reflection upon common human experience, and the determination to insist upon recognition of the claims of that which alone can give value and hope to human existence; and a corresponding determination to resist the claims of a superficially plausible empiricism.

To put the matter crudely, the biblical writers, like the great philosopher, offer us a package deal, morality with strings attached. If we want to recognise good and evil as realities in our lives, then we have to take God with them, along with a spiritual universe more vast and incalculable than the physical which defies our imagination and intelligence. The strings attached to morality form a ladder across to the noumenal world, rapidly lost to our sight, but firm and real enough at the phenomenal end.

The empiricist remains free enough in a purely intellectual sense to reject this view, but empiricism has already decided the issue before it is put into operation. Empiricism will inevitably produce a Godless universe, and it will also produce an amoral one. It, too, is a package deal: but the strings which are attached do not lead anywhere. They only serve to make the self-contained parcel in itself more secure.

BIBLICAL RELIGION: THEODICY

The overall picture of the universe given in Genesis 1:1–2:4a is of a self-contained natural world, a great organism with its own life, ruled by its own inherent forces. God no longer intervenes in this world, and in that sense miracles do not happen. What is natural remains uninfluenced by any direct contact with the supernatural. God is 'resting' from that particular kind of work, and rumours of the miraculous which suggest that kind of divine activity must be put down to superstition, or the desire to convey a spiritual message by means of an impressive tale.

This picture of the universe is saved from deism by the intimate relationship between man and God. Even after the Fall described in Genesis chapter 3, God does not cease to communicate with men and women, and the significance of that communication is of central importance throughout the whole biblical literature.

Humanity provides the link between the divine and the natural, and where there is genuine influence of the supernatural upon the human it would be unwise to set limits to the possible effects of this influence in the physical world.

Questions concerning the miraculous will scarcely be settled by these few bald statements, but they do seem to sum up the picture given in Genesis 1, and they are in keeping with Kant's critical foundation for theology. It may be argued that it is precisely the character of the miraculous to be exceptional, and this is true; but the plain and emphatic assertions of the Genesis account seem deliberately designed to rule out exceptions of this sort, and along with the rest of the biblical literature present true religion as only properly conceivable in terms of a personal relationship. And once we move into the area of personal, moral value, we have eschewed the idea of development through compulsion, including the kind of mental and emotional submission induced by overwhelming demonstrations of sheer power.

The attempt to understand the miraculous element in the biblical literature, therefore, raises questions of fundamental importance concerning the nature of God, the nature of man and the relationship between the two. Dividing the Red Sea and making an axe-head float may influence people, but they are not means to creating true friendship; nor do they seem to have been very effective as genuine instruments of conversion in their Old Testament setting. Furthermore, we wonder why God does not intervene more often to remove, or, better still, prevent the atrocious evil and suffering which so often mar human and animal existence. Once a single exception is conceded to the generalisation that God does not intervene directly in the life of the natural world, including human beings in so far as they are creatures of nature, the question becomes very pressing indeed; so pressing that only atheism or a concept of God radically different from that which is usually entertained seem to be reasonable answers to it.

Therefore, faced by the problem of evil we may seek to defend God (theodicy); deny God; or surrender the idea of achieving an intellectual resolution of the problem in terms of pure reason alone, and see it instead in terms of pure practical reason. Kant, consistently with his whole critical philosophy, adopted the third solution; but he was not alone, and was himself happy to acknowledge the anticipation of his view by an ancient writer many centuries before his own time.[14]

There is ample recognition throughout the Bible of the existence of evil in the world, including the suffering of the innocent, but there is nowhere any considered defence of the deity's justice and mercy despite the existence of that which is apparently so contrary to his will. This is all the more remarkable because for most of the very long period covered by the biblical literature there was no belief in an after-life, and therefore no opportunity for wrongs to be righted on the other side of the grave. The simplest defence of God in these circumstances is, of course, to suppose that there is really no innocent suffering, and that God, who has a perfect knowledge of human deserts, apportions bane and blessing according to the real, if unperceived, guilt or merit of the receiver. Publicly observable prosperity and suffering then become sure signs of a person's real spiritual worth, and we do well to govern our own attitude towards him in the light of the fact, since otherwise we run the risk of inviting the visitation of divine wrath upon ourselves. The well-known 'Servant Songs' included in the prophecies of Isaiah 40–55 bear witness to this belief: the Servant is despised and rejected because of his physical pain, disease and weakness; although it is made clear in the Songs that this was a bad misjudgment.

The most devastating refutation of the belief comes, however, in the Book of Job. According to the story, Job is a very wealthy man surrounded by a large and loving family. He is also a good man, sincerely determined to obey God and avoid wrongdoing. Even God bears witness to his innocence, his upright and God-fearing nature. Suddenly, his fortunes change radically for the worse. He loses both possessions and family, and a little later is himself afflicted with a loathsome and painful disease. His horrified friends visit him, and at some length beg him to examine his conscience: he must have sinned in some way for God to inflict such suffering on him. Yet Job vigorously protests his innocence, and not surprisingly makes some bitter complaints about the treatment he has received at God's hand; but he maintains his faith in God, and unable to reconcile his suffering with God's justice, can only give vent to devastated bewilderment.

One thing upon which both Job and his friends are agreed is that it is God who gives, and God who takes away. This does not imply that God is directly at work in the world, and the story says otherwise; but if God is the creator of the world, then he is ultimately responsible for what goes on in it, and there is no attempt whatever to avoid that conclusion in the Book of Job.

The story ends with the restoration of Job's health and fortunes and handsome compensation for all he has gone through. His friends, on the other hand, are condemned and only saved from the wrath of God by Job's intercession.

The opening and close of the story are told in prose, while the bulk of it, Job's encounter with his friends, is expressed in poetry. The opening prose passage sets the scene, but interestingly, this includes goings-on in heaven as well as Job's life on earth. With this insight we know from the very start that Job's friends are badly wrong in their interpretation of his suffering. God has boasted of Job's goodness, but Satan has challenged this commendation on the ground that anyone would be good if rewarded by God in the way that Job has been. When Job remains steadfast despite his losses, the challenge is repeated, and consequently Job's own health is destroyed. The principle expressed in Satan's challenge is not denied. It is Satan who does the dirty work, but only with God's permission. God could be wrong about Job, and there is only one way to find out.

In a famous essay on the inevitable failure of theodicy published in 1791, Kant made direct reference to the story of Job.[15] It well illustrated his argument that theodicies must fail simply because those who undertake to defend God cannot possibly know enough. Before the bar of pure speculative reason it is not good enough to offer a defence which *would* succeed if only we knew it to be true. Hard evidence must be produced, and that is what no human being is in a position to provide. Job himself taxes his critical friends with their hypocrisy in pretending to know the mind of God. They are condemned and Job praised because they rashly attributed to God what was not only wrong, but what they could not possibly know to be right; while Job simply trusted in the divine justice, even in the midst of his bitter protests. Job's trust in the moral law is vindicated, while speculations about the noumenal go badly awry.

The prose account of the scenes in heaven is therefore a figurative description of noumenal reality. It could not be proved true, but it does depend for its effectiveness on a principle which can easily be appreciated on the phenomenal side of the divide. Rewards and punishments handed out as only God could dispense them would destroy morality, that is to say, the possibility of a right relationship with God, altogether. The noumenal has its phenomenal counterpart; Satan moves freely between the two worlds; God knows and influences what is going on in the world, although the influence is of a somewhat indirect and subtle nature. The poetic substance of the book represents the thoughts and feelings of those on the phenomenal side of the divide and reflects no knowledge of proceedings in heaven; and yet every phenomenal occurrence has its noumenal counterpart, including the wrath of God against the wilful misapprehension of Job's friends. Wilful, because they had the same light to guide them as Job: a sense of the moral law, and a potential awareness of the limits of reason.

The lesson is enforced by God's answer out of the whirlwind in chapters 38–41, the revelation of God as creator. It is an extended and eloquent reflection on the wonders of the created order, not in order to demonstrate the existence of God, which is already assumed and fundamental to the argument of the whole book, but to emphasise the ineffable nature of God and the mystery of creation itself. When reason presses its anxious questions beyond a certain point, it loses itself and can only be redeemed through a sense of the sublime.

Finally, Job more than regains what he has lost. The prose conclusion has in fact also removed us from the world of phenomena and it presents us, like the opening descriptions of heaven, with a figurative account of the noumenal, that kingdom of God in which virtue and blessedness are united in a single experience. It is to be attained, however, not by demonstrations at the bar of speculative reason, but by recognising and obeying the dictates of a reason as pure as the speculative, but of a moral, 'practical' nature.

The atheistic alternative remains. Just as human personality cannot participate in the good by accepting a bribe, neither can it do so by drawing an infallible conclusion or submitting beneath the weight of irresistible evidence. The powerful poetic expression of human agony and the futility of attempts to justify it will find a ready response in any sensitive reader, but there is nothing to prevent the conclusion being drawn from the poetic dialogue that scenes in heaven and a parabolic happy ending are merely relics of ancient superstition, comforting illusions which offer refuge from the realities so eloquently portrayed in the greater part of the book.

Nevertheless, if this is our conclusion, we must face a paradox. The empiricist alternative destroys not only the comforting illusion but also the evil. The lightning and the tempest are no more than chemical reactions, with further chemical reactions as their consequences. The destruction of human and animal life is just another complex effect in the ever-continuing chain of pre-determined connections; and so is Job's disease, and so are his agonised protests, and so are the ideas, feelings and arguments of his friends. The evil which we feel to be a denial of God ceases to exist, but by the same token the empiricism which confirms the denial loses the ground on which it stands. Health and disease remain, the one desirable and the other very undesirable, but no more susceptible of moral evaluation than coffee white or coffee black. Empiricism itself becomes a refuge in which we can lose all sense of responsibility and instead live for the moment: but an awkward and profound sense of having made a choice remains, as does the awareness of the awful reality of evil and the hope of the good.

Before moving on, it is worth noting that Jesus, like the author of Job, refuses to tolerate the idea that suffering is inflicted as the punishment for individual guilt, and equally refuses to offer any alternative explanation. Speculation and special revelation of what goes on behind the phenomenal scenes are replaced by emphasis upon the demands of practical reason: 'Unless you repent . . . '; 'we must work the work of him who sent me'.[16]

BIBLICAL RELIGION: 'DIE RELIGION'

A detailed examination of Kant's *Die Religion* would lead directly into the construction of a biblical theology, at least in outline, and is therefore well beyond the scope of this book. Nevertheless, Kant's own comments on the Bible, mainly the New Testament, cannot be ignored. We naturally wish to know what the philosopher himself made of 'revelation' in the light of his critical philosophy, and some consideration must now be given to various points, even if in rather summary fashion.

It must be admitted that his characterisation of Judaism as

revealed in the Old Testament is far worse than inadequate. According to Kant, Judaism in its essence was not a true religion at all but a political organisation, in which law was used solely to regulate external behaviour, and therefore had no moral significance; and in which there was no belief in any future life, and consequently no heaven or hell, and therefore no basis for the adoption of a moral outlook on life. If individual Jews had a religious faith and observed the moral law, this was no thanks to official teaching.[17]

It is fortunate that this breathtaking dismissal of Judaism does not follow from the critical philosophy, but is rather a reflection of Kant's personal ignorance and prejudice. Nor, happily, was he consistent in this approach to the Old Testament. He was able to make very apposite use of the Book of Job in his critical analysis of theodicy, and the following remark about the Jewish Law is truer both to the spirit and intention of that Law and also to Kant's own philosophy:

Perhaps there is no more sublime passage in the Law Book of the Jews than the command: You shall not make for yourself any image, nor any likeness, either of what is in heaven or on the earth or under the earth. This law is in itself sufficient to explain the enthusiasm which the Jewish people felt for their religion in their moral epoch whenever they compared themselves with other peoples, and that pride which Mohammedanism inspired. The very same holds true for the idea of the moral law and the capacity for morality within ourselves.[18]

The last two paragraphs in §28 of the same *Critique of Judgment* read almost like a reflection on Elijah's experience at Horeb, and if Kant had paid closer attention to the prophetic writings he must surely have been profoundly impressed, not only by their repeated emphasis on morality, but their insistence that the phenomenal world can be understood only in terms of the noumenal, the reality beyond the profane gaze of a humanity clothed in flesh and subject to an outlook framed by the dimensions of space and time.

He must also have been challenged, not by contradiction of his own best insights but by fruitful suggestions for their development. First, his uncompromising assertion that the morally good and right, regarded simply as highly significant features of human experience, bear the stamp of their own unqualified authority without need of external justification would have been fully endorsed. This would have been partly because of the direct appeal which the prophets often made to human conscience; but it would also have been seen as the inevitable outcome of disbelief in a future life. It is paradoxical that Kant should have so severely criticised precisely that aspect of Old Testament religion which focusses attention upon the here and now, and thereby strengthens that which is the tendency of his own philosophy, not least in its 'practical' aspect. To do what is good and right because we hope thereby to win a reward vastly outweighing present pain and inconvenience is, as Kant saw, utterly destructive of moral worth. If the moral imperative is really categorical, we are not allowed to introduce surreptitious qualifications, either in this world or some other.

Second, Kant would have been challenged by the prophets' natural identification of the good and right with the will of God, but he might have been led to see that the contradictions and implausibilities of his own system were thereby overcome. If the moral law stands absolutely secure in its own rationality, it matters not whether virtue is rewarded or ignored. That which carries with it the cast-iron validity of logical justification cannot, by definition, be denied. Yet Kant knew better. He knew that included in the absolute authority of the moral imperative there is the *moral* demand that virtue shall not be ignored, and in effect punished, and that any such idea makes nonsense of morality. It would be somewhat as if a car were sold with an unqualified warranty from the manufacturer that it was perfectly constructed from the best materials, when in fact it was poorly constructed from the cheapest materials, but the manufacturer felt that this was the kind of warranty he *ought* to give to his customers, and the customers for their part felt that such a warranty was due to them. If the warranty which comes with the moral sense and our attempt to respond to it are only part of some universal charade, there is no morality, any more than there is a cooling drink corresponding to a mirage.

On the other hand, if morality is the will of God, then the nature of God expressed in that demand upon us will also be reflected in the whole of creation, in both its noumenal and phenomenal aspects. The uniting of the categorical imperative and the concept of creation means that in the kind of world we inhabit, virtue is even more firmly grounded than the laws of physics, chemistry and biology; and that just as obedience to the latter brings its own rewards and disobedience spells disaster, so obedience to the moral law is just another name for true happiness, and disobedience the way of destruction. The world is made in a certain way, and we either go along with it, or we try to go against it. It is quite true that if we commit ourselves to this belief, we shall have to enlarge our view of life to include hopes which take us beyond the horizons provided by phenomena, but what Kant deduced in the course of argument came to Israel as the fruit of experience; and what is reasonable is to accept both. The practical consequence, however, is not that we do right now in the hope that an all-powerful deity will add happiness to our virtue in the future, but that by doing right we are becoming more truly ourselves, better adapted to that ever-developing life which the all-powerful deity has created.

Kant's attempt to interpret the biblical story of the Fall as support for his own moral philosophy runs into serious difficulty. He rightly sees the narrative as expressing in temporal terms what is meant to be a truth concerning human nature, and the root cause of evil in that nature. The primacy is not temporal, referring to some supposed historical event, but is rather concerned with the prime cause, or ground of evil in everyone, always. The problem arises, however, from Kant's location of morality in a law which human beings are free to accept or reject. Although there is essential truth in Kant's view, it is unsatisfactory as an ultimate explanation: if a person is in a state of innocence, then there cannot be any inclination to do evil; but if there is such an inclination, there is no state of innocence. The moral law should be welcomed as a friend into the mind of the innocent, and yet it appears as an irksome duty which is disobeyed. Furthermore, Kant lays great stress throughout *Die Religion* on the need for men and women to improve and save themselves by their own moral effort, which implies their capacity to do this, and he is therefore reluctant to admit a force of evil which incapacitates them in this respect. He has to confess the inexplicable nature of the fundamental cause of evil in human beings.

The ancient story also tacitly admits the mystery, not least by being a piece of ancient folklore rather than by being a piece of history, but in Kantian terms it is the kind of mystery which inevitably shrouds the noumenal while at the same time we are not left without highly significant phenomenal clues sufficient to satisfy our understanding here and now. According to the story, the moral law is in no way narrow or irksome: the man and the woman are placed in a delightful garden and may partake of the rich variety of fruit growing on a rich variety of trees, while they are surrounded by animals with which they enjoy close kinship and over which they exercise benevolent control. They have a kind of natural, instinctive knowledge which enables them to tend the garden and understand the animals, and the whole scene is one of physical, mental and emotional bliss reflecting the perfect harmony between the deity and his human creatures.

Nevertheless, there is a divine prohibition, and evil consists in deliberate disobedience, the motive for such disobedience and the consequences of it. It is not simply that God lays down a law and that this law is broken. This is an essential element in the situation, but there are others, too. The prohibition is not arbitrary, but is a warning, such as a caring mother impresses on her child. The motive to ignore the warning is depicted as the sly suggestiveness of the serpent, which finds a ready response in the woman and a weak, culpable surrender in the man. The temptation is not altogether a lie. Their eyes really are opened and they really do gain a knowledge which they did not previously possess: but it is a knowledge which belongs properly only to the gods and it wreaks havoc with human nature, bringing degradation and guilt and destroying the life originally intended by God. The fruit of the tree of life which might have been consumed in the state of innocence is out of the question for a creature with pretensions to divine status.

Kant himself raised the question how the evil spirit could appear in a world originally perfectly good; but this is only another form of the question how complete innocence can become a prey to evil. We might also ask why God places a tree in the garden which he knows poses a danger to mankind and then draws attention to it by forbidding the fruit thereof. The answer to all such questions is that, taken as a parable, every element in the story corresponds to an essential element in human experience. It is precisely because men and women are human and not mere beasts, precisely because they have a potential for development which can belong only to free beings created in the image and likeness of God, that they can also feel a temptation which no beast can feel. It is precisely because freedom is what it claims to be that it can choose a personal relationship with the deity of trust and obedience, or reject this in favour of a futile attempt to exchange likeness for substantial identity with the divine. And it is precisely because the desire for equality with the gods is possible for men and women that such desire is depicted as temptation: it is a real feeling and motive within the human creature, but it is also that which is alien and hostile to real human health and welfare.

The whole story can be understood within the context of the Kantian critique of reason, at the same time modifying that critique in legitimate ways and taking us beyond it. If it be asked why we have to understand the ancient story within the context of modern philosophy, the answer is that we do not have to if we are no longer a prey to the doubt and scepticism fostered by dependence upon modern knowledge; but where doubt and scepticism rule or threaten, the Kantian critique is a more than useful means of redressing the intellectual balance and strengthening the claim that the message of the Bible is not to be lightly dismissed and rewards serious attention.[19]

When commenting on the New Testament, Kant inevitably stresses the moral appeal of Jesus, both in his person and his teaching. Jesus is the model whom we should imitate, and if he is truly imitable then he must have been truly human. We could not be required to reproduce in our own lives what could only belong to the superhuman divine. There is therefore no doubt about the true humanity of Christ since without it there could be no Christian gospel of salvation. God's forgiveness or grace is the reward of genuine moral endeavour, it is God's encouragement and strengthening of our own efforts, and moral progress is the fruit of cooperation between man and God. The death of Christ seen as a sacrifice assures us of God's love and makes moral achievement worth while. Without that sacrifice humanity would be confronted by what might be called a spiritual debt beyond any hope of repayment, but the atoning death puts settlement within reach, and covers that which men and women cannot out of their own meagre resources afford. For Kant it is a dangerous anthropomorphism to take the language concerning Christ's sacrifice literally, since it suggests that someone else can pay my debt and achieve holiness for me; whereas it is meant, on the contrary, to encourage every endeavour on our part to become better than we are.

Since all men know the moral law and all are under the same rule of duty, the supreme example of Christ makes Christianity the true universal religion and the supreme natural religion. Kant was not prepared to deny outright that miracles had happened and could happen again, nor did he deny that the appearance of the Bible itself might be a miracle; but he refused to allow the miraculous any essential part in true religion. The only test of faith is the moral one, and Kant gives the impression of simply not wishing to be drawn into argument about miracles, since whether they happened or not is irrelevant to the practical decisions and choices which form the substance of religion and everyday life. He gives the illustration of a judge who is told that the accused was tempted by the devil, whose power he could not resist. The judge proceeds precisely as if nothing had been said, even though he might believe in both the devil and the miraculous, for the simple reason that the claim is untestable and of no practical consequence; although, as Kant points out, it would be if it were known to be true.

Kant draws the further conclusion that historical knowledge forms no essential part of religion, including knowledge of the ministry of Jesus. For Kant it would be dangerous nonsense to suggest that a man cannot know and obey the moral law because he lacks historical knowledge concerning Jesus of Nazareth, however inspiring and helpful such knowledge might be. Even with respect to the latter consideration, much would depend for Kant on the frame of mind in which the person concerned approached the information given in the gospels, or the content of any other biblical text. For Kant, the biblical documents cannot in themselves provide us with true morality; it is we who bring to the text our own moral sense and find in it confirmation or correction of our judgment, or, it may be, sentiments which we must ourselves reject. Kant was happy to quote from II Timothy 3:16–17 and find in these words confirmation of his own view. This means that revelation is not and cannot be something merely objective presented to us from without, and which we either imbibe or refuse to imbibe. Revelation is the Word of God to every man, woman and child, and the moral sense found in every man, woman and child is the means whereby that Word is made known and the instrument through which the moral Word becomes effective in our lives, or is rejected. The Bible is a vast record of the way in which many others have responded to the Word revealed in their lives, and we shall find genuine inspiration in the Bible to the extent that the response recorded there was true, and to the extent that we are ourselves capable of recognising it.

Kant recognised that religion finds outward expression in organisation, ritual, the ministrations of priesthood, scriptural scholarship and theological learning. Human beings are social creatures, and the Church is the means to mutual help. Nevertheless, he seems to have been more impressed by the failures of the outward organisation than its helpfulness, more anxious to warn of the distractions and illusions it could foster than to commend the support it could offer in the daily struggle to obey the moral law. He regarded the Bible as a means of binding people together in one Church, and he granted the biblical scholar the important, but definitely subordinate, task of establishing the authenticity of the biblical documents and making sure that they were properly understood. This would strengthen the authority of the Church, but would do nothing of itself to strengthen the authority of religion, an authority to be found only within the reason of the individual believer, a moral law immune to the vagaries of scholarship and the actual facts of history alike.

No doubt the views Kant expressed in *Die Religion* reflect the influence of his pietistic upbringing, but they are not on that account to be merely pigeon-holed and dismissed. It is not difficult to distinguish between expressions of personal inclination and prejudice on the one hand, and the outworking of the critical philosophy on the other, and it must be admitted that Kant's understanding of religion has much to commend it. His emphasis upon the central and essential significance of the moral demand in Christianity is massively supported in the New Testament, and is needful precisely because it is in this respect that human beings fail time and again. The continual reminder of moral weakness is not pleasant, and confrontation with the moral ideal is often a humiliating experience, but there is no escaping the firm insistence on it by Christ and the early Church, and Kant was right to assert it as essential to a proper understanding of the Atonement. He was also right to associate closely with it the concept of the imitation of Christ, and two texts readily spring to mind which confirm his teaching in this respect, but which also indicate the way in which we must go beyond Kant without, however, losing what is true in his exposition.

St John tells us that at the Last Supper Jesus washed the disciples' feet, and then told them that if he, their Master and Lord, was prepared to carry out such a humble task, they should likewise be prepared to serve one another. He had set them an example, and true satisfaction would consist in following it. Similarly, St Paul, in trying to encourage mutual help and understanding among the believers in Philippi, appeals to the example of Christ: let this mind be in you which was also in Christ Jesus our Lord.

At the same time, both passages bring out the early Christian belief in the unique, ineffable character of the work of Christ. Although the washing of disciples' feet is an example to them, it is also the symbol of a cleansing which only Jesus can accomplish; and if the apostle can exhort the recipients of his letter to think and behave like Christ, he is rapidly led into a eulogy of the sacrifice and exaltation of Jesus which celebrates what belongs to Jesus alone.[20]

This reflects a view of evil which attributes to it a force and extent far beyond anything contemplated by Kant and which cannot be summed up as the refusal to obey the moral law as revealed to the individual conscience. Kant's illustration of the judge and the tempted criminal is true as far as it goes: we cannot make the miraculous, whether good or bad, the excuse for dodging moral responsibility. On the other hand, even a system of justice, which is of necessity designed to deal with matters of behaviour and the most obvious expressions of motive and feeling, and which cannot delay to survey its own verdicts before the bar of pure reason, has to take some account of the forces unleashed within the human constitution, and which lie beyond the control of the individual. A realistic survey of phenomenal evil powerfully suggests a noumenal origin infinitely incomprehensible to the human mind, and this is precisely the picture presented to us in both Old and New Testaments.

It is the picture given in much other literature, too, and the universalism which belongs to the truth and which was rightly insisted upon by Kant means that we may expect to find 'revelations' of both good and evil in other authors besides the biblical. We shall also find such revelations in all forms of art, although whether or not an actual 'revelation' takes place will depend as much on the one who reads, hears, looks or handles, as upon the creative artists themselves. Nor does this constitute a denial of the uniqueness of the Bible, or of Christ, since in this instance it is precisely the uniqueness which gives to both the literature and the historical figure their universal significance. If it is the 'Word' which is expressed in both, and supremely in the latter, it would be very strange if such expression were confined to that with which we happen to be familiar.

Kant's failure to appreciate the real force of evil is, therefore, actually out of keeping with his own fundamental insights; and this is also true of his appreciation of the good. The moral ideal of Jesus, radical and almost ruthless, cannot be summed up as obedience to the moral law, and the truly good in the world of phenomena has its intimately related counterpart in the world of noumena. Jesus did not proclaim a moral ideal, he proclaimed the kingdom of God; and while he unquestionably strove for a willed response from his hearers and companions, and regarded such a willed response as of crucial significance for the ultimate fate of the individual and nation, he saw the conflict of good and evil as something infinitely more than the acceptance or rejection of moral law. There is a dynamic and depth to be found in both the prophetic teaching and that of Christ which cannot be found in the Kantian critique, even though the latter may be developed to include it.

Such development would include Kant's recognition of God's grace and his acknowledgement of Christ's sacrifice, but both elements would require considerable enlargement in any attempt at a proper understanding of religion. Nevertheless, the enlargement would be thoroughly coherent with Kant's best insights.

Finally, at the heart of biblical religion lies belief in the knowledge of God, in both senses of that ambiguous phrase: our knowledge of God, and God's knowledge of us. Once more, Kant surely prepared the way for acceptance of such an idea in modern thought by his assertion of our knowledge of the moral law, the noumenal character of that law, and its coincidence with the commands of God. It is obvious that we do not know God and are not known by him in just the same way as is the case with other human beings, but the analogy of personal communication is of profound significance in the Bible and the experience of the Church down the ages. The rigour of the Kantian critique is a safeguard against the illusions of an unfettered enthusiasm, but the safeguard should not be allowed to become a straitjacket. The commands of an earthly sovereign are mediated through elements in a system external to both sovereign and subject alike; but the commands of God come direct and unmediated into the mind of the creature moulded in his image, and it is surely no great leap to suppose that communion between the two may be expressed in other than merely legal terms.

Among modern thinkers, Rudolf Otto has gladly emphasised the limits of reason as demonstrated by Kant, but he has also argued for a genuine awareness of God, an *Ahn(d)ung* of the divine.[21] Otto's use of Kant was subjected to severe but fair-minded criticism by H. J. Paton, but it is a discussion which needs to be continued. It is no mere academic exercise, but a bringing into the open of the questions everyone has to answer in one way or another: What can I know? What may I reasonably believe? What ought I to do?

Conclusion

If Kant instead of Paley had been the dominating influence on nineteenth-century British thinkers, the strength of the case for religion and the weakness of an empirically based scepticism would have been made clear. The conflict between science and religion would still have taken place, but the nature of the conflict, and therefore the nature of the respective claims to allegiance involved in it, would have been much better understood.

This nineteenth-century war, with its truth, half-truths, confusions and misunderstandings, has been continued throughout the twentieth century, to the detriment of religion and the increase of a materialist and often escapist outlook on life. The spiritual and moral ideas, feelings and motives natural to human beings have continued, too, but without the encouragement and development they might have had. The churches have continued to do much good; but with respect to the churches, the vast majority of the population have voted with their feet. There have been several reasons for this, but the failure to offer a convinced and convincing reply to the doubts engendered by empiricism has been a major contributory factor.

The historical survey clearly indicates a profound need to accept the discipline of the Kantian critique and to appreciate the rich development which it makes possible in the life of both individual and community. The neglect belonging to the past is not only no excuse for present failure, but once recognised should stimulate a radical reappraisal of those attempts to expound religion's claims known as metaphysics or theology, and at the same time provide criteria for an assessment of the metaphysics implied in the biblical literature.

That literature need no longer remain in not very splendid isolation from the rest of the world's cultural heritage, obscured by dogmatic presuppositions concerning inspiration and revelation, but may be allowed to shine with its own peculiar brilliance along with the genuine light shed on human life by other great writings and works of creative art; and the Church, with its immense potential, may aspire to a genuine catholicity which welcomes the truth wherever it is to be found, and whatever the form of its cultural expression.

The alternative can scarcely be the continuation of the present state of affairs into and throughout the twenty-first century. The immense power which the success of scientific methods has put into the hands of a select few can only be properly controlled by a community which has learnt to judge with right judgment, and which has a firm grasp of values which are not to be bargained away in return for short-term or illusory benefits. It is a matter of choice: but the consequences of the choice are very far-reaching, and unavoidable once it has been made.

Notes

1 THE GENERAL PICTURE

1 John Rogerson, *Old Testament Criticism in the Nineteenth Century: England and Germany* (London, 1984).
2 T. H. Huxley, *Collected Essays*, Vol. v (London, 1894), pp. 25–6. From the Prologue, 'Controverted Questions', 1892.
3 Owen Chadwick, *The Secularization of the European Mind in the Nineteenth Century* (Cambridge, 1975), p. 161.
4 Ibid., p. 167.
5 Ibid., p. 175.
6 Ibid., p. 165.
7 B. M. G. Reardon, *Religious Thought in the Nineteenth Century* (Cambridge, 1966), p. 26.
8 B. M. G. Reardon, *From Coleridge to Gore: A Century of Religious Thought in Britain* (London, 1971), p. 288.
9 James R. Moore, *The Post-Darwinian Controversies: A Study of the Protestant Struggle to Come to Terms with Darwin in Great Britain and America, 1870–1900* (Cambridge, 1979).
10 Ibid., p. ix.
11 Ibid., pp. ix–x; 15–16. See also quotations from Arthur Hugh Clough's 'The Bothie of Tober-na-Tuolich' on p. viii; and Huxley, *Collected Essays*, Vol. v, p. 1.
12 Quoting J. W. Gruber, *A Conscience in Conflict: The Life of St George Jackson Mivart* (New York, 1960).
13 Moore, *Post-Darwinian Controversies*, p. 121. See also pp. 64–5.
14 Ibid., p. 349. See *Fortnightly Review* (1 November 1892), 557–71.
15 Ibid., 567.
16 Ibid., 568.
17 Ibid., 568.
18 See, for example, Moore, *Post-Darwinian Controversies*, pp. 280–98 on the American George Frederick Wright; and pp. 307–45, largely on Charles Darwin himself.
19 Ibid., pp. 250–1.
20 Tess Cosslett, *Science and Religion in the Nineteenth Century* (Cambridge, 1984).

299

21 Ibid., p. 25.
22 Ibid., p. 26.
23 Ibid., p. 172.
24 Ibid., p. 187.
25 Ibid., p. 242nn.
26 Ibid., pp. 1, 2.
27 Ibid., p. 2.
28 Ibid., p. 10.
29 John Tyndall, *Address Delivered before the British Association Assembled at Belfast, with Additions* (London, 1874), p. vii.
30 J. H. Newman, *The Idea of a University: Defined and Illustrated* (London, n.d.; Preface, November 1852; Dedication and Advertisement, November 1858), p. 503. See pp. 487–504.
31 John Locke, *An Essay Concerning Human Understanding* (London, 1947; 1st edn, 1690), Book IV, chapter XVIII, and the famous statement in chapter XIX, 4, pp. 333–9; 340.
32 *Collected Essays*, Vol. IX, *Evolution and Ethics* (London, 1903), p. 140. Part of Huxley's essay 'Science and Morals', 1886.
33 John Henry Cardinal Newman, *Apologia Pro Vita Sua* (London, 1902 (2nd edn of 1865)), p. 28.
34 Ibid., for example pp. 14, 48–9; Note A, 'Liberalism', pp. 285–7. S. L. Ollard, *A Short History of the Oxford Movement* (London, 1915), pp. 9–11.
35 David McLellan, *Karl Marx: His Life and Thought* (St Albans, 1976), p. 424. Charles Darwin, *The Origin of Species*, ed. J. W. Burrow (Harmondsworth, 1968), Editor's Introduction. p. 45. Cf. Isaiah Berlin, *Karl Marx* (Oxford, 1978, reprint 1983), p. 182n.

2 DAVID HUME

1 See, for example, *A Treatise of Human Nature*, Vol. 1 (London & New York, 1911), Book I, Part III, section III; section XIV, pp. 153–7; section XVI; Part IV, section I, pp. 178–9. See also *Hume: Theory of Knowledge*, ed. D. C. Yalden-Thomson (Edinburgh, 1951); and *An Essay Concerning Human Understanding*, section IV, pp. 34–8; section VII, pp. 63–5, 76–8; section IX, 'Of the Reason of Animals'. See also Norman Kemp Smith, *The Philosophy of David Hume* (London, 1949), pp. 407–9.
2 *Dialogues Concerning Natural Religion*, ed. with Introduction by Henry D. Aiken (London & New York, 1948), close of Part X, p. 70; near the end of Part XII, p. 90.
3 Ibid., pp. 86, 94–5.
4 *Treatise*, Vol. 1, p. 159n.
5 Hume, *Essays Literary, Moral and Political* (London & New York, 1894), pp. 514–52.
6 *Dialogues*, Part XII, p. 88.

7 Ibid., p. 94. *Essays*, p. 568. The essay 'Of Miracles' may also be found as section x of *An Essay Concerning Human Understanding*.
8 *Dialogues*, p. 9.
9 Ibid., pp. 15–17.
10 Ibid., Part vii, p. 50.
11 Ibid., Part iv, p. 34.
12 Ibid., Part v, p. 39.
13 Ibid., p. 50.
14 Richard Dawkins, *The Blind Watchmaker* (Harlow, 1986), p. 6.
15 Ibid., pp. 59, 60.
16 *Treatise*, Vol. i, Part iv, section v, pp. 228–38.
17 *Dialogues*, Part xi, pp. 78–9.
18 Ibid., p. 79.
19 See Sir Leslie Stephen, *History of English Thought in the Eighteenth Century*, 2nd edn (London, 1881), Vol. i, pp. 1–2.
20 *Hume's Dialogues Concerning Natural Religion*, ed. with Introduction by Norman Kemp Smith (Oxford, 1935), p. 96.
21 G. R. Cragg, *Reason and Authority in the Eighteenth Century* (Cambridge, 1964), pp. 125, 141.

3 WILLIAM PALEY

1 *The Complete Works of Percy Bysshe Shelley*, ed. Roger Ingpen and Walter E. Peck (London & New York, 1965). From the Preface to *Prometheus Unbound*, Vol. ii, p. 174. (First published 1820.)
2 Ibid., p. 270. In 'Note on "Prometheus Unbound"'.
3 *The Complete Works of William Hazlitt in Twenty One Volumes*, ed. P. P. Howe, centenary edition (London & Toronto, 1930). From 'The Late Dr Priestley', published 14 June 1829. Vol. xx, p. 237.
4 From 'My First Acquaintance with Poets', in *The Complete Works of William Hazlitt*, Vol. xvii, p. 114. For other remarks on Paley see Vol. i, p. 296n; Vol. vii, pp. 252–53, 'On the Clerical Character'.
5 Quoted by D. L. LeMahieu, *The Mind of William Paley* (Lincoln & London, 1976), p. 157.
6 *Aids to Reflection* (London, 1913), pp. 272, 273. (First published 1825.)
7 Letter, 11 August 1863. *The Life of Frederick Denison Maurice*, ed. Frederick Maurice (London, 1884), Vol. ii, p. 450.
8 I am indebted to Dr C. D. Watkinson, Secretary to the University Library, Durham, for this information.
9 Frida Knight, *University Rebel: The Life of William Frend* (London, 1971), p. 25.
10 *Autobiography of Charles Darwin*, The Thinker's Library (London, 1929), p. 22. Reprinted from *Life of Charles Darwin*, ed. Francis Darwin.
11 *Paley's Natural Theology Revised to Harmonize with Modern Science*, ed. F. le Gros Clarke (London, 1875), p. v.

12 W. H. Turton, *The Truth of Christianity*, 7th edn (London, 1908), pp. 12–29.

13 Colin A. Russell, Open University Arts: A Third Level Course. *Science and Belief: From Darwin to Einstein*, Milton Keynes (1981), p. 32.

14 See Dawkins, *The Blind Watchmaker*, pp. 4–5; 37.

15 *Theological Essays of the Late Benjamin Jowett*, ed. Lewis Campbell (London, 1906).

16 LeMahieu, *The Mind*, p. 207. M. L. Clarke, *Paley: Evidences for the Man* (London, 1975), p. 97. See also Leslie Stephen's article 'William Paley', *Dictionary of National Biography*, ed. Sidney Lee, Vol. XLIII (London, 1895).

17 *The Existence of God*, ed. John Hick (London & New York, 1964), pp. 103–4. See also A. N. Whitehead, *Science and the Modern World* (Cambridge, 1938), p. 95.

18 *The Encyclopaedia of Philosophy*, ed. Paul Edwards (New York & London, 1966), Vol. I, p. 386; Vol. VI, p. 20.

19 *From Coleridge to Gore*, p. 4.

20 *History of English Thought in the Eighteenth Century*, pp. 408, 409.

21 *The Works of William Paley D.D.* (5 vols., London, 1819), Vol. IV, p. 400. Hume, *Dialogues*, ed. Aiken, p. 76. See also Ann L. Loades, 'Theodicy and Evolution: Aspects of Theology from Pierre Bayle to J. S. Mill', unpublished doctoral thesis, University of Durham, 1975, pp. 239, 242.

22 *Essays Literary, Moral and Political*, p. 568.

23 LeMahieu, *The Mind*, pp. 31–2.

24 Ibid., p. 171. Cf. pp. 53–4.

25 Ibid., pp. 55–8.

26 Ibid., p. 89.

27 Ibid., p. 90.

28 Ibid., p. 53.

29 Ibid., pp. 30, 67, 71.

30 *The Works of William Paley D.D., A New Edition, with Illustrative Notes and a Life of the Author*. Editor's name not given (London, William Smith, 1838).

31 Ibid., p. 26.

32 *The Works of William Paley D.D.* (1819), Vol. IV, p. 11.

33 *Science and Religion*, p. 27. See also p. 219 n. 3.

34 *Natural Theology*, section VIII of chapter I.

35 *Natural Theology*, in *The Works of William Paley D.D.* (1819), Vol. IV, p. 31. See pp. 30–3.

36 Ibid., pp. 44–7. Cf. pp. 57–9.

37 Ibid., p. 88.

38 Ibid., pp. 143–4.

39 Ibid., pp. 162–5; 167–9; 191.

40 Ibid., p. 228.

41 Ibid., pp. 229–30; 305.

42 Ibid., pp. 351–5.
43 Ibid., p. 345. Conclusion of chapter xxiii, 'Of the Personality of the Deity'.
44 *Thoughts on Religion*, ed. Charles Gore, 5th edn (London, 1895), p. 58. Cf. J. S. Mill, *Nature, The Utility of Religion, and Theism* (London, 1874; republished Farnborough, 1969), p. 168. P. B. Shelley, 'A Refutation of Deism in a Dialogue', in Ingpen and Peck (eds.), *The Complete Works*, Vol. vi, p. 46.
45 *Dialogues*, ed. Aiken, opening of Part iii, p. 26.
46 T. S. Kuhn, *The Copernican Revolution: Planetary Astronomy in the Development of Western Thought* (Cambridge, Mass. & London, 1957), p. 184. Cf. Kuhn's remarks on Darwin, *The Structure of Scientific Revolutions*, 2nd edn (Chicago, 1970), pp. 171–2.
47 *Natural Theology*, opening of chapter xxvi.
48 See *Natural Theology*, the whole of the first part of chapter xxvi.
49 *The Origin of Species*, ed. Burrow, chapter vi, p. 229.
50 *Natural Theology*, chapter v, sections 3, 4 and last part of chapter xxvi, sections 1–2.
51 Cf. A. R. Peacocke, *Creation and the World of Science* (Oxford, 1979), pp. 90–2.
52 *Natural Theology* in *The Works of William Paley D.D.* (1819), Vol. iv, pp. 411–13.

4 BIBLICAL CONSERVATISM

1 Ingpen & Peck (eds.), *The Complete Works*, Vol. v, pp. 299–300; Vol. vi, pp. 205–7; 360.
2 Samuel Horsley, *Biblical Criticism* (London, 1820).
3 Ibid., Vol. i, pp. 4–7.
4 C. M. Burnett, *The Power, Wisdom, and Goodness of God, as Displayed in the Animal Creation; Shewing the Remarkable Agreement between this Department of Nature and Revelation* (London, 1838). Reference to Paley, p. 298.
5 Ibid., pp. 1–107. See also Preface, pp. v–vii. On the origin of the world, pp. 15–18; fossils, pp. 23–31; the Flood, pp. 31–40; light, pp. 41–2; the Genesis day, pp. 105–6.
6 Ibid., pp. 16, 43–4.
7 The full title of Sumner's treatise: *A Treatise on the Records of the Creation and on the Moral Attributes of the Creator: The Consistency of the Principle of Population with the Wisdom and Goodness of the Deity* (London, 1816). The bequest was made by a Mr Burnett, a Scotsman.
8 Ibid., Vol. i, pp. x–xvii.
9 Ibid., pp. 16–17.
10 Appendix i, pp. 268–9; and Vol. ii, pp. 18–19.
11 Sumner, *A Treatise*, Vol. i, p. ix.

12 Ibid., p. 89.

13 Ibid., p. 40n.

14 See whole of Appendix I, ibid., pp. 267–85.

15 J. H. Pratt, *Scripture and Science not at Variance*, 2nd edn (London, 1856).

16 Ibid., pp. 25; 27; pp. 29–30n.

17 Ibid., pp. 2; 5; 79; 95.

18 Donald MacDonald, *Creation and the Fall: A Defence and Exposition of the First Three Chapters of Genesis* (Edinburgh, 1856), p. 15.

19 Ibid., pp. 2; 9–10; 223.

20 Ibid., quotation on p. 27.

21 Ibid., pp. 82; 86–108.

22 George Holden, *A Dissertation on the Fall of Man in which the Literal Sense of the Mosaic Account of that Event is Asserted and Vindicated*, 2nd edn (London, 1823), p. 3; pp. 7–8nn.

23 Ibid., pp. 35; 28.

24 Ibid., p. 222. On literary critical analysis, see chapter II, pp. 32–68.

25 *A Comparative Estimate of the Mineral and Mosaical Geologies*, 2nd edn, revised and enlarged (London, 1825), Vol. I, p. xiv.

26 Ibid., pp. lv–lvi. Also xvi; xix–xx.

27 Ibid., pp. xvii; xix; xxvi; xl–xli.

28 Ibid., pp. 117; 120–1.

29 *Essays and Reviews*, 12th edn (London, 1865), p. 253. Also Rogerson, *Old Testament Criticism*, pp. 182; 197–8.

30 T. H. Horne, *Deism Refuted: OR, Plain Reasons for being a Christian*, 2nd edn (London, 1819).

31 Ibid., pp. 1-31.

32 Ibid., pp. 32–3.

33 Ibid., pp. 33–40.

34 Ibid., pp. 41–2; 50. See pp. 41–64.

35 T. H. Horne, *An Introduction to the Critical Study and Knowledge of the Holy Scriptures*, 3rd edn corrected (London, 1822), Vol. I, pp. viii; 1–2.

36 *An Introduction to the Criticism of the Old Testament and to Biblical Interpretation*, revised and edited by Revd John Ayre (London, 1860), p. 514. See pp. 514–18.

37 Cf. Rogerson, *Old Testament Criticism*, pp. 182–3.

38 Horne, *An Introduction to the Criticism*, pp. 264–5.

39 Ibid., pp. 514; 516–17.

40 Ibid., p. 516.

41 Ibid., Preface, p. vi.

42 Rogerson, *Old Testament Criticism*, pp. 197–202.

43 Horne, *An Introduction to the Critical Study*, Vol. I, pp. 4; 9–18.

44 Horne, *Deism Refuted*, pp. 3–4.

45 Horne, *An Introduction to the Critical Study*, Vol. I, pp. 4; 10.

46 Ibid., p. 634.

47 Horne, *Deism Refuted*, p. 36.
48 Adam Clarke, *The Holy Bible: Containing the Old and New Testaments according to the Authorized Version* (Liverpool, 1813), p. i. See also p. vi. Cf. *Commentary on the Old Testament*, Vol. 1 (London, 1825), pp. xv–xvi, part of General Preface dated London, 2 July 1810.
49 Clarke, *The Holy Bible*, p. ii. *Commentary*, Vol. 1, p. xv.
50 Clarke, *The Holy Bible*, p. 5. Cf. *Commentary*, Vol. 1, Preface to Genesis.
51 Clarke, *Commentary*, Vol. 1, pp. xvii; xxiii; xxv–xxvi.
52 Ibid., Vol. 1.
53 Ibid., Vol. 1, on Genesis 3:1; 1:2. *The Holy Bible*, pp. 10–11.
54 Clarke, *The Holy Bible*, p. 5. *Commentary*, concluding remarks on Genesis 1.
55 Clarke, *The Holy Bible*, p. 6.
56 Clarke, *Commentary*, on Genesis 1:14.
57 For further information on Horne and Clarke, see Rogerson, *Old Testament Criticism*, pp. 180–4.
58 *On the Whole Doctrine of Final Causes* (London, 1836).
59 Ibid., p. 9.
60 Ibid., pp. 110; 206.
61 Ibid., p. 100n.
62 Ibid., pp. 117–18.
63 Ibid., pp. 122–7.
64 Ibid., pp. 137–42.
65 Ibid., p. 83.
66 Ibid., p. 143.
67 Ibid., p. 87.
68 Ibid., pp. 172–80.
69 Ibid., note B, p. 209.
70 Ibid., p. 215.
71 Ibid., pp. 194–6. See also pp. 129–37.

5 CONSERVATIVE NATURAL THEOLOGY: PALEY'S DESIGN ARGUMENT

1 Stephen, *History of English Thought in the Eighteenth Century*, Vol. 1, p. 411.
2 William Prout, *Chemistry Meteorology and the Function of Digestion considered with reference to Natural Theology* (London, 1834). Cf. Paley, *Natural Theology*, chapter XII, section 1.
3 Prout, *Chemistry*, Introduction; and Preliminary Observations, pp. 1–14. See also pp. 233–4.
4 William Whewell, *Astronomy and General Physics: Considered with reference to Natural Theology* (London, 1833), p. 344.
5 Ibid., p. vi.
6 Peter Mark Roget, *Animal and Vegetable Physiology considered with reference to Natural Theology* (London, 1834), Vol. 1, pp. 13–14n.

7 John Kidd, *On the Adaptation of External Nature to the Physical Condition of Man* (London, 1833), pp. 46; 55; 63–70; 72.
8 Ibid., pp. 210–11; 309–11; cf. 307; 329–34.
9 Ibid., pp. vii–x.
10 Roget, *Animal and Vegetable Physiology*, Vol. I, pp. 24; 124–5.
11 Ibid., Vol. II, pp. 1–15; 582.
12 Ibid., Vol. II, pp. 362–3.
13 Ibid., Vol. I, pp. 48–55.
14 Whewell, *Astronomy*, pp. 22; 31.
15 Ibid., pp. 173–7.
16 Ibid., pp. 349; 48.
17 Kidd, *On the Adaptation*, pp. 207–9.
18 William Buckland, *Geology and Mineralogy considered with reference to Natural Theology* (London, 1836), Vol. I, pp. 1–4; 7; 11.
19 Ibid., pp. 97–9; cf. pp. 535–8. Also pp. viii; 8.
20 Whewell, *Astronomy*, p. 29; on the solar system, pp. 150–72.
21 Charles Bell, *The Hand: Its Mechanism and Vital Endowments as Evincing Design* (London, 1833), p. 221. Roget, *Animal and Vegetable Physiology*, Vol. I, p. 28.
22 William Kirby, *On the History Habits and Instincts of Animals* (London, 1835), Vol. I, p. 58. Prout, *Chemistry*, pp. 86–91.
23 Roget, *Animal and Vegetable Physiology*, Vol. II, p. 21.
24 Bell, *The Hand*, p. 38.
25 Stephen, *History of English Thought in the Nineteenth Century*, pp. 413; 414.
26 Thomas Chalmers, *The Adaptation of External Nature to the Moral and Intellectual Constitution of Man* (London, 1833), Vol. I, pp. 49–53.
27 Whewell, *Astronomy*, pp. 211–12; 365.
28 Kirby, *On the History*, Vol. I, pp. lxxxi; ci–cii. Cf. Vol. II, chapter XVIII, 'On Instinct', pp. 220–80.
29 Prout, *Chemistry*. See, for example, chapter I of Book I, p. 551.
30 Ibid., pp. 85; 164; cf. pp. 166–7n; and p. 150.
31 Ibid., pp. 223–5.
32 See Job 12:6; 14–25.
33 Kirby, *On the History*, Vol. I, pp. i; ciii; lxxxi; xci.
34 Buckland, *Geology*, Vol. I, pp. 22–5, esp. 24. The whole argument is on pp. 16–26.
35 Dr Nigel M. de S. Cameron, 'Criticism in Controversy: Conservative Biblical Interpretation and Higher Criticism in Nineteenth Century Britain: A Study in a Conflict of Method', unpublished doctoral thesis, University of Edinburgh, 1982, Appendix D, p. 317.
36 Buckland, *Geology*, pp. 14–15; 26–8. The whole discussion in chapter ii, 'Consistency of Geological Discoveries with Sacred History', pp. 8–34.

37 Bell, *The Hand.* Whole passage from bottom of p. 220 to end of Concluding remarks, p. 233.
38 Whewell, *Astronomy*, p. 374.
39 Roget, *Animal and Vegetable Physiology*, Vol. II, pp. 68–9. Cf. Vol. I, chapter II, pp. 34–58.
40 *Goethe: Selected Verse*, ed. D. Luke (Harmondsworth, 1964), 'Das Göttliche', pp. 67–9.

6 CONSERVATIVE NATURAL THEOLOGY: THOMAS CHALMERS

1 Chalmers, *The Adaptation*, pp. 35–7.
2 Gilbert Ryle, *The Concept of Mind* (London, 1949), pp. 8; 15–16.
3 James Ward, *Naturalism and Agnosticism*, 4th edn (London, 1915), pp. 43–4; 287–8. Fred Hoyle, *The Intelligent Universe: A New View of Creation and Evolution* (London, 1983). See, for example, pp. 11–12; 25–49; 243. Cf. Dawkins, *The Blind Watchmaker*, p. 234.
4 A. N. Whitehead, *Adventures of Ideas* (Harmondsworth, 1942; first published 1933), pp. 150. Cf. pp. 146–8.
5 *The Blind Watchmaker*, concluding pages, 316–18.
6 Thomas Chalmers, *On Natural Theology*, in *The Works of Thomas Chalmers*, Vols. I and II (Glasgow, n.d.; Preface dated 15 December 1835).
7 *Natural Theology*, p. 169.
8 Ibid., p. 277.
9 Ibid., in order of quotations, pp. 113; 112; 105. Cf. Whitehead, *Adventures*, pp. 147–8.
10 *Natural Theology*, p. xii.
11 Ibid., pp. 17–18.
12 *The Adaptation*, Vol. II, pp. 236–7; 88–100.
13 *Natural Theology*, pp. 30; 34; 51.
14 Ibid., pp. 30; 34; 51.
15 *The Adaptation*, Vol. II, p. 100.
16 Ibid., p. 106.
17 Ibid., pp. 112–16. Cf. Vol. I, pp. 98–132. *Natural Theology*, Vol. II, pp. 278–86.
18 *Natural Theology*, Vol. II, p. 388.
19 *The Works of Thomas Chalmers*, Vol. VII, pp. x; 238; 260.
20 E. W. Grinfield, *The Connection of Natural and Revealed Theology* (London, 1818), pp. 30–1.
21 Ibid., pp. 178; 189; cf. pp. 269–70.
22 William Buckland, *Vindiciae Geologicae; or the Connexion of Geology with Religion Explained* (Oxford, 1820).
23 Ibid., pp. 11; 18; 19; 21; 27.

24 Buckland, *Geology*, Vol. 1, p. 49. Cf. p. 13.
25 James Kennedy, *Lectures on the Philosophy of the Mosaic Record of Creation*, Vol. 1 (London, 1826), pp. xii–xiii. Cf. pp. xviii; 51–6.
26 Ibid., pp. v–vi.
27 Ibid., pp. xi–xii; xiv; xvii.
28 John Anderson, *The Course of Creation* (London, 1850), p. iii.
29 Ibid., pp. 347–9. On developmental ideas, see chapter ii of Part 4, pp. 325–45.
30 Thomas Pearson, *Evangelical Alliance Prize Essay on Infidelity; its Aspects, Causes, and Agencies* (London, 1854), pp. 80–3.
31 Ibid., p. 192.
32 Ibid., pp. 129; 173–6.
33 Horace Bushnell, *Nature and the Supernatural as together constituting the One System of God*, 4th edn (New York, 1859). According to the Preface, written some years earlier, p. 19.
34 Ibid., pp. 36, 37.
35 Ibid., pp. 37–63.
36 T. A. G. Balfour, *The Typical Character of Nature: or, All Nature a Divine Symbol* (London, 1860).
37 T. A. G. Balfour, *God's Two Books: or, Nature and the Bible have One Author* (London, 1861).
38 Ibid., pp. 80–1.
39 Review of Cuvier's *Essay on the Theory of the Earth*, with notes by Professor Jameson, in *The Edinburgh Christian Instructor* (April 1914).
40 Ibid., 271.
41 Ibid., 272.
42 William Buckland, *Reliquiae Diluvianae: or, Observations on the Organic Remains contained in Caves, Fissures, and Diluvial Gravel, and on other Geological Phenomena, attesting the Action of an Universal Deluge* (London, 1823).
43 Buckland, *Geology*, Vol. 1, pp. 94–5n.
44 Kennedy, *Lectures*, Vol. 1, p. ix.
45 Ibid., pp. 38–40; 45; 47–8. Vol. 1, pp. 105–6; Vol. 11, pp. 26–8; 70–103.
46 John Pye Smith, *On the Relation between the Holy Scriptures and some parts of Geological Science* (London, 1839), pp. 105–64; 262–77; 285–90; 299–315. John Medway, *Memoirs of the Life and Writings of John Pye Smith* (London, 1853), pp. 522–3.
47 Hugh Miller, *The Testimony of the Rocks or, Geology in its bearings on the Two Theologies, Natural and Revealed* (Edinburgh, 1857), pp. 265; 290–1; 375; 377.
48 'The Mosaic Account of the Creation', *The Edinburgh New Philosophical Journal*, N.S., 10, 214–25.
49 *The Old Red Sandstone* (London, 1906; 1st edn, 1841), p. 281.
50 Miller, *The Testimony*, pp. 200, 201.
51 Smith, *On the Relation*, pp. 27; 40; 69; 79; 280–82.

52 Renn D. Hampden, *An Essay on the Philosophical Evidence of Christianity* (London, 1827), pp. 5–7; 20–1; 23–4.
53 Balfour, *The Typical Character*, pp. xi–xii; 130–3.
54 Gillispie, *Genesis and Geology* (Harvard, 1951), pp. ix; 105.

7 LIBERAL NATURAL THEOLOGY

1 *Edinburgh New Philosophical Journal*, N.S., 15, 79–113, esp. 80–1, and 86.
2 *Edinburgh Review*, 2 (1803), 492; 494.
3 Bushnell, *Nature and the Supernatural*, pp. 19; 31–5; 84.
4 John Herschel, *A Preliminary Discourse on the Study of Natural Philosophy. A Facsimile of the 1830 Edition*, London, With a new Introduction by Michael Partridge (New York & London, 1966).
5 Ibid., pp. 73; 360.
6 Charles Babbage, *The Ninth Bridgewater Treatise: A Fragment*, 2nd edn (London, 1838).
7 Ibid., pp. 92; 120–31.
8 Letter dated 31 October 1829. See *Life Letters and Journals of Sir Charles Lyell*, edited by his sister-in-law, Mrs Lyell (London, 1881), Vol. 1, p. 256.
9 Medway, *Memoirs*, p. 431.
10 Letter dated 7 April 1831. *Life*, Vol. 1, p. 318.
11 *Life*, Vol. 1, p. 356.
12 *Principles of Geology*, 7th edn (1847), p. 27.
13 Letters to Gideon Mantell, 7 June 1829, and G. Poulett Scrope, 9 November 1830. *Life*, pp. 253; 310.
14 *Life*, Vol. 11, p. 168.
15 Quoted by J. Y. Simpson, *Landmarks in the Struggle between Science and Religion* (London, 1925), p. 165.
16 *Autobiography of Charles Darwin*, p. 36.
17 *Life*, Vol. 1, pp. 467–9.
18 Letters to Hooker, 9 March 1863; to Haeckel, 23 November 1868, *Life*, Vol. 11, pp. 361; 436–7. Cf. letters to Whewell, 7 March 1837, and to Sedgwick, 20 January 1838; pp. 5; 36–7.
19 *Principles*, p. 59.
20 *Life*, Vol. 1, p. 382.
21 Letter to Gideon Mantell, March 1831, *Life*, Vol. 1, p. 316.
22 *Life*, Vol. 1, pp. 263; 276; 397. Vol. 11, pp. 82; 169; 172. On Milman, see Rogerson, *Old Testament Criticism*, pp. 184–5.
23 Thomas Dick, *The Christian Philosopher; or, the Connection of Science and Philosophy with Religion*, 21st edn (Glasgow & London, 1856). The Preface to the 2nd edn is dated December 1824. The later edition is used here.
24 Gillispie, *Genesis and Geology*, pp. 202–3. Cf. D. S. L. Cardwell, *The*

Organisation of Science in England (London, 1972), pp. 40–4; 71–5; 127. Pye Smith, *On the Relation*, pp. 237–9.

25 Dick, *Christian Philosopher*, p. 574.
26 Ibid., pp. 573, 574.
27 Ibid., p. 576.
28 See Henry Brougham (ed.), *Paley's Natural Theology*, the reissue (London, 1845), Vol. i, p. 8.
29 Ibid., pp. 152–3.
30 Ibid., p. 149.
31 Ibid., p. 154. On Hume's Essay, Note v, pp. 183–6.
32 Brougham (ed.), *Paley's Natural Theology*, reissue, p. 65n. See also pp. 38–9.
33 *Vestiges of the Natural History of Creation* (London, 1844).
34 Ibid., pp. 9–10; 17–18; 25–6.
35 Ibid., pp. 146; 177; 188–9.
36 Ibid., pp. 272–3.
37 Ibid., pp. 154–6.
38 Ibid., pp. 324; 154; 157.
39 Ibid., pp. 325–6.
40 Ibid., pp. 331–2. Comparison of man and animals, pp. 332–47. Morals and society, pp. 348–86.
41 *Edinburgh Review*, Vol. 82, No. 165 (July 1845), 16.
42 Ibid., 62.
43 *A Discourse on the Studies of the University*, 5th edn (London, 1850), pp. x–xi.
44 Ibid., pp. cxlviii–cl.
45 *Explanations: A Sequel to 'Vestiges . . . '* (London, 1845).
46 Ibid., pp. 142; 149.
47 Ibid., pp. 175–82.
48 Ibid., pp. 183–5.
49 *Vestiges*, 10th edn (London, 1853), pp. vii–viii.
50 *Discourse*, 5th edn, pp. xv–xvi. See also p. cxlix; and review article, pp. 63–4; 67.
51 Baden Powell, *Essays on the Spirit of the Inductive Philosophy, the Unity of Worlds, and the Philosophy of Creation* (London, 1855), p. 455n.
52 *Oxford Essays* (London, 1857), pp. 178–80.
53 Ibid., pp. 189–90.
54 Baden Powell, *The Connexion of Natural and Divine Truth; or, the Study of the Inductive Philosophy considered as Subservient to Theology* (London, 1838), p. iv.
55 Ibid., p. 273.
56 Ibid., pp. 229–36.
57 Ibid., pp. 179–85.
58 *Essays on the Spirit*, pp. 38–9; 113. Quoting Oersted's *The Soul in Nature* (1852).

59 Abraham Pais, *'Subtle is the Lord . . . ': The Science and the Life of Albert Einstein* (Oxford, 1982).
60 *Essays on the Spirit*, pp. 80–1.
61 Ibid., p. 67.
62 Ibid., pp. 114–32.
63 *Quarterly Review*, 109 (January 1861), 251; 262; 287.
64 See *The Philosophy of Creation*, part of *Essays on the Spirit*, p. 439. See also pp. 348–62; 374–91.
65 *Essays on the Spirit*, p. 76.
66 Ibid., p. 311.
67 Ibid., pp. 233–4. See also pp. 242–8.
68 *The Journal of Sacred Literature*, Vol. 2, No. 4 (October 1848), 'On the Application and Misapplication of Scripture', 261; 264; 265.
69 *Oxford Essays*, pp. 168–203.
70 Ibid., pp. 177; 189.

8 THE LATER NINETEENTH CENTURY

1 Basil Willey, *Darwin and Butler: Two Versions of Evolution* (London, 1960), p. 9.
2 H. L. Mansel, *The Limits of Religious Thought Examined in Eight Lectures*, 3rd edn (London, 1859).
3 John William Burgon, *Lives of Twelve Good Men*, 2nd edn (London, 1888), Vol. ii, pp. 185–6.
4 Mansel, *The Limits*, Preface to 1st edn, pp. xxix–xxx.
5 Ibid., pp. 198–9.
6 Ibid., p. 112. Cf. n. 11, p. 360.
7 Ibid., n. 11, pp. 419–21. Cf. n. 18, pp. 430–3.
8 *Essays and Reviews*, 12th edn (London, 1865), p. 79n.
9 Mansel, *The Limits*, p. 183.
10 F. D. Maurice, *What is Revelation? A Series of Sermons on the Epiphany to which are added Letters to a Student of Theology on the Bampton Lectures of Mr Mansel* (London, 1859).
11 Rogerson, *Old Testament Criticism*, pp. 234–5.
12 F. W. Farrar, *History of Interpretation* (London, 1886).
13 Ibid., pp. xii; xiii; 10; 341, n. 3.
14 Ibid., p. 427.
15 Ibid., p. 428.
16 The 12th edn of *Essays and Reviews* is used here (London, 1865). *Replies to 'Essays and Reviews'* (Oxford & London, 1862).
17 *Essays*, p. 1. The opening of Frederick Temple's essay on 'The Education of the World'.
18 *Essays*, p. 108.
19 *Replies*, pp. 65–6.
20 *Quarterly Review* (January 1861), 284; (October 1862), 457.

21 *Quarterly Review* (January 1861), 251.

22 *Essays*, p. 422.

23 *Replies*, p. 328.

24 P. Addinall, 'Huxley and Wilberforce: The 19th-Century Legacy in Religion and Science', *Epworth Review* (May 1989), pp. 66–73. Cf. J. R. Lucas, 'Wilberforce and Huxley: A Legendary Encounter', *Historical Journal*, Vol. 22, No. 2 (1979).

25 *Lux Mundi: A Series of Studies in the Religion of the Incarnation*, 2nd edn, ed. Charles Gore (London, 1890).

26 Ibid., pp. 99–100.

27 Ibid., p. 94.

28 Ibid., pp. vii and ix.

29 Romanes, *Thoughts on Religion*, ed. Gore, 5th and 6th edns, pp. 154–5, where Romanes' book of about twenty years earlier, *A Candid Examination of Theism*, is referred to.

30 Mill, *Nature, The Utility of Religion, and Theism*, p. 38. The first two essays were written between 1850 and 1858; the third between 1868 and 1870.

31 Frederick Temple, *The Relations between Religion and Science* (London, 1884).

32 St George Mivart, *On the Genesis of Species* (London, 1871), pp. 251–2. Cf. p. 274, n. 1.

33 Ibid., pp. 257–8.

34 Henry Drummond, *Natural Law in the Spiritual World*, 19th edn (London, 1887), p. 51.

35 The Duke of Argyll, *The Reign of Law* (London, 1867), pp. 108–9.

36 Newman, *The Idea of a University*, pp. 40; 319.

37 Ibid., p. 510. See pp. 509–13.

38 Ibid., pp. 514, 515.

39 Tyndall, *Address*, pp. 33–4. Cf. p. 54.

40 Ibid., p. 59.

41 Ibid., pp. 60–1.

42 J. R. Seeley, *Natural Religion*, 2nd edn (London, 1882), p. 82.

43 William James, *The Varieties of Religious Experience* (Harmondsworth, 1982), p. 455.

44 See Rogerson, *Old Testament Criticism*, chapter 20, esp. pp. 273–5, and 282–5. T. K. Cheyne, *Founders of Old Testament Criticism* (London, 1893), pp. 248–372.

45 H. E. Ryle, *The Early Narratives of Genesis* (London, 1892), pp. 30–1. See also pp. 12–13; 136–7.

46 S. R. Driver, *An Introduction to the Literature of the Old Testament*, 9th edn (Edinburgh, 1913). Quoted from Preface to the Eighth Edition, pp. vii–ix. The 1st edn, of which the Preface was substantially a repetition, is dated September 1891.

47 Ibid., p. xi.

48 *The Book of Genesis*, 11th edn (London, 1920), pp. 1; 33. This edn is a reprint of the 9th (April 1913), the last to be revised by Driver. Commentary first published 1904.

49 Huxley, *Collected Essays*, Vol. V (1909 reprint), pp. 25–6.

9 IMMANUEL KANT

1 B. M. G. Reardon, *Religious Thought in the Nineteenth Century* (Cambridge, 1966), pp. 5–6; 9.

2 Ieuan Ellis, *Seven Against Christ: A Study of 'Essays and Reviews'*, Studies in the History of Christian Thought, ed. Heiko A. Oberman, Vol. XXIII (Leiden, 1980), p. 308, and *passim*.

3 Cragg, *Reason and Authority*, pp. 125; 141; 143.

4 *Prolegomena zu einer jeden Künftigen Metaphysik, die als Wissenschaft auftreten können*, ed. Karl Vorländer (Hamburg, 1976), pp. 6–7. (First published 1783.)

5 *Immanuel Kant's Critique of Pure Reason*, trans. Norman Kemp Smith (London, 1964), p. 7, Avii.

6 See, for example, the opening words of the Introduction to the 2nd edition of the *Critique of Pure Reason*, trans. Kemp Smith, p. 41, B1.

7 Ibid., p. 42, B1–2.

8 Ibid., pp. 73–4, from 1st edition of the *Critique*. See whole of the Transcendental Aesthetic, pp. 65–91.

9 Karl Heim, *Christian Faith and Natural Science* (London, 1953). Quotations taken from pp. 127–38, the whole of which should be consulted. Translation by N. Horton Smith of *Der Christliche Gottesglaube und die Naturwissenschaft*, Vol. I (Tübingen, 1949). See also *The Transformation of the Scientific World View* (London, 1953), pp. 103–5. Translation by W. A. Whitehouse of *Der Christliche Gottesglaube und die Naturwissenschaft*, Vol. II, *Die Wandlung in naturwissenschaftlichen Weltbild* (Hamburg, 1951).

10 *Critique*, trans. Kemp Smith, p. 27. Last sentence of Bxxvi.

11 Ibid., p. 347, A371–2.

12 On Hume and the problem of causality see *Prolegomena*, ed. Vorländer, pp. 3–4; *Kritik der praktischen Vernunft*, ed. Joachim Kopper (Stuttgart, 1961), pp. 85–94. Cf. *Critique*, trans. Kemp Smith, pp. 606–7.

13 *Kritik der reinen Vernunft*, ed. Ingeborg Heidemann (Stuttgart, 1966), p. 904, A126–7.

14 Ibid., p. 276, A197–8, B242–3.

15 F. R. Tennant, *Philosophical Theology*, Vol. I (Cambridge, 1928); Vol. II (Cambridge, 1930). See Vol. I, pp. 246–7; 252.

16 *Prolegomena*, ed. Vorländer, pp. 117–19.

17 *Kritik d.r.V.*, ed. Heidemann, p. 80. Opening of the Transcendental

Doctrine of the Elements, B33/A19. Cf. *Critique*, trans. Kemp Smith, p. 65.

18 *Kritik d.pr.V.*, ed. Kopper, p. 53.

19 Ibid., pp. 139–40.

20 Ibid., p. 10, including footnote.

21 *Kritik der Urteilskraft*, ed. Gerhard Lehmann (Stuttgart, 1976), pp. 28, 58. Taken from the Introduction, sections II and IX.

22 *Kritik d.pr.V.*, ed. Kopper, p. 79.

23 *Kritik d.U.*, ed. Lehmann, p. 488. Part of §91 (2).

24 *Critique*, trans. Kemp Smith, p. 414. See whole of 3rd antinomy of reason, pp. 409–15. Cf. *Kritik d.r.V.*, ed. Heidemann, pp. 488–96, A444–50/B472–8.

25 *The Moral Law: Kant's Groundwork of the Metaphysic of Morals*. Translated and analysed by H. J. Paton (London, 1948; reissued in paperback), pp. 85–6.

26 *Kritik d.pr.V.*, ed. Kopper, p. 66.

27 *Die Religion innerhalb der Grenzen der bloßen Vernunft*, ed. Rudolf Malter (Stuttgart, 1974), pp. 7–8.

28 *Kritik d.pr.V.*, ed. Kopper, pp. 156–60.

29 Ibid., pp. 200; 205. See the whole of section V, 'Das Dasein Gottes, als ein Postulat der reinen praktischen Vernunft', in chapter II of Book II, Part I.

30 Ibid., p. 205.

31 Ibid., p. 219.

32 *Kritik d.U.*, ed. Lehmann, p. 477. Near the opening of §90.

33 Ibid., pp. 339–40. Part of §65.

34 Ibid., p. 352.

35 *Kritik d.r.V.*, ed. Heidemann, p. 38, BXXX.

10 CRITICAL PHILOSOPHY AND THE BIBLE

1 Cf. *Die Religion*, ed. Malter, p. 67n. In this reference to the subject-matter of his book, Kant uses the word *reinen* instead of *bloßen*, which strongly suggests that in this context he regarded them as interchangeable.

2 See my article 'What is Meant by a Theology of the Old Testament?', *Expository Times* (August 1986). See 'Hume's Challenge and Paley's Response', *ET* (May 1986), for an outline of the relationship between Hume, Kant and Paley.

3 Addinall, 'What is Meant by a Theology of the Old Testament?', 333.

4 Stephen W. Hawking, *A Brief History of Time* (London, 1988).

5 Ibid., pp. 135–6.

6 Ibid., p. 169.

7 Ibid., pp. 46–7.

8 Ibid., p. 136; pp. 140–1. Cf. p. 116.

9 Ibid., pp. 7–8.
10 Ibid., p. 174.
11 Ibid., pp. 12–13.
12 A. S. Eddington, *Science and the Unseen World* (London, 1929), pp. 35–6.
13 See, for example, *Kritik d.U.*, ed. Lehmann, p. 468; *Die Religion*, ed. Malter, pp. 80–2n.
14 See also 'What is Meant by a Theology of the Old Testament?'.
15 '*Über das Mißlingen aller philosophischen Versuche in der Theodizee*', in *Was ist Aufklärung? Aufsätze zur Geschichte und Philosophie*, ed. Jürgen Zehbe, 2nd edn (Göttingen, 1975), pp. 77–93. See esp. pp. 86–9.
16 Luke 13:1–5; John 9:1–5.
17 *Die Religion*, ed. Malter, pp. 165–7.
18 *Kritik d.U.*, ed. Lehmann, p. 182.
19 *Die Religion*, ed. Malter, pp. 51–4; see also p. 100. Genesis 2:4b–3:24.
20 See John 13:1–15; Philippians 2:1–11.
21 Rudolf Otto, *The Philosophy of Religion: Based on Kant and Fries*, trans. E. B. Dicker (London, 1931). Cf. Jacob Friedrich Fries, *Dialogues on Morality and Religion*, ed. D. Z. Phillips, trans. David Walford (Oxford, 1982): selections from *Julius und Evagoras*, 2nd edn (Heidelberg, 1822).

Bibliography

The Bridgewater Treatises are listed under the authors' names.

Addinall, P. 'Hume's Challenge and Paley's Response', *Expository Times* (May 1986).
   'What is Meant by a Theology of the Old Testament?', *Expository Times* (August 1986).
   'Huxley and Wilberforce: The 19th-Century Legacy in Religion and Science', *Epworth Review* (May 1989).
Alexander, Cecil Francis. *Poems*, ed. William Alexander, London, 1896.
Anderson, B. W. (ed.). *Creation in the Old Testament*, Philadelphia & London, 1984.
Anderson, John. *The Course of Creation*, London, 1850.
Anselm, St. *Basic Writings*, trans. S. N. Deane, 2nd edn, Illinois, 1974.
Argyll, Duke of. *The Reign of Law*, London, 1867.
Attenborough, David. *Life on Earth*, London, 1979.
Ayer, A. J. *Language, Truth and Logic*, 2nd edn, London, 1960.
Babbage, Charles. *The Ninth Bridgewater Treatise: A Fragment*, 2nd edn, London, 1838.
Baillie, John. *The Idea of Revelation in Recent Thought*, London, 1956.
Balfour, Thomas A. G. *The Typical Character of Nature: or, All Nature a Divine Symbol*, London, 1860.
   God's Two Books: or, Nature and the Bible have One Author, London, 1861.
Barbour, Ian G. *Issues in Science and Religion*, London, 1966.
Beauchamp, Philip (Bentham, Jeremy). *Analysis of the Influence of Natural Religion on the Temporal Happiness of Mankind*, new edn, London, 1875 (first published 1822).
Bell, Charles. *The Hand: Its Mechanism and Vital Endowments as Evincing Design*, London, 1833.
Berlin, Isaiah. *Karl Marx*, Oxford, 1978, reprinted 1983.
Blomfield, Charles James. *Sermons*, London, 1829.
Bonney, T. G. *Sermons on Some Questions of the Day*, Cambridge, 1878.
Bonnor, W. B. 'Fifty Years of Relativity', in *Science News*, Harmondsworth, 1955.

Born, Max. 'Physics and Metaphysics', in *Science News*, Harmondsworth, 1950.

'Fifty Years of Physics', in *Science News*, Harmondsworth, 1951.

British Review, Vol. 13, No. 25 (London, 1819): review of Thomas Gisborne, *The Testimony of Natural Theology to Christianity*.

Brougham, Henry, Lord. *Paley's Natural Theology; with Illustrative Notes and an Introductory Discourse of Natural Theology*, 2 vols., London, 1835; revised 1845.

Dissertations on Subjects of Science connected with Natural Theology: Being the Concluding Volumes of the New Edition of Paley's Work, 2 vols., London, 1839.

Brown, Stewart J. *Thomas Chalmers and the Godly Commonwealth in Scotland*, Oxford, 1982.

Buckland, William. *Vindiciae Geologicae; or the Connexion of Geology with Religion Explained*, Oxford, 1820.

Reliquiae Diluvianae; or, Observations on the Organic Remains contained in Caves, Fissures, and Diluvial Gravel, and on other Geological Phenomena, attesting the Action of an Universal Deluge, London, 1823.

Geology and Mineralogy considered with reference to Natural Theology, London, 1836.

Burgon, J. W. *Lives of Twelve Good Men*, 2nd edn, London, 1888.

Burnett, C. M. *The Power, Wisdom, and Goodness of God, as Displayed in the Animal Creation; Shewing the Remarkable Agreement between this Department of Nature and Revelation*, London, 1838.

Burtt, R. A. *The Metaphysical Foundations of Modern Physical Science*, 2nd edn, London, 1932.

Bushnell, Horace. *Nature and the Supernatural as together constituting the One System of God*, 4th edn, New York, 1859.

Butler, Joseph. *The Analogy of Religion to the Constitution and Course of Nature: also, Fifteen Sermons, on Subjects Chiefly Ethical*, ed. Joseph Angus, London, n.d.

Calderwood, Henry. *The Relations of Science and Religion*, Morse Lecture, 1880, London, 1881.

Cameron, Nigel M. de S. 'Criticism in Controversy: Conservative Biblical Interpretation and Higher Criticism in Nineteenth Century Britain: A Study in a Conflict of Method', unpublished doctoral thesis, University of Edinburgh, 1982.

'Inspiration and Criticism: The Nineteenth Century Crisis', *Tyndale Bulletin*, 35 (1984).

Campbell, Lewis (ed.). *Theological Essays of the Late Benjamin Jowett*, London, 1906.

Capra, Fritjof. *The Turning Point: Science, Society, and the Rising Culture*, London, 1983.

Cardwell, D. S. L. *The Organisation of Science in England*, London, 1972.

Chadwick, Owen. *The Victorian Church*, Parts I and II, London, 1970.

The Secularization of the European Mind in the Nineteenth Century, Cambridge, 1975.

Chalmers, Thomas. *The Adaptation of External Nature to the Moral and Intellectual Constitution of Man,* London, 1833.

On Natural Theology, in *The Works of Thomas Chalmers,* Vols. I and II, Glasgow, n.d. (Preface dated 15 December 1835).

Discourses on the Christian Revelation viewed in connection with the Modern Astronomy. To which are added Discourses illustrative of the connection between Theology and General Science, in *The Works,* Vol. VII.

Lectures on the Epistle of Paul the Apostle to the Romans, in *The Works,* Vol. XXII.

Chambers, Robert. *Vestiges of the Natural History of Creation,* London, 1844; 10th edn, London, 1853.

Explanations: A Sequel to 'Vestiges . . . ', London, 1845.

Vestiges of the Natural History of Creation. With an Introduction by Gavin de Beer, Leicester & New York, 1969.

Cheyne, T. K. *Founders of Old Testament Criticism,* London, 1893.

Church, R. W. *The Oxford Movement,* London, 1891.

Clarke, Adam. *Commentary on the Old Testament,* Vol. I, London, 1825.

The Holy Bible: Containing the Old and New Testaments according to the Authorized Version, Vol. I, London, 1913.

Clarke, F. le Gros (ed.). *Paley's Natural Theology Revised to Harmonize with Modern Science,* London, 1875.

Clarke, M. L. *Paley: Evidences for the Man,* London, 1974.

Clements, R. E. *A Century of Old Testament Study,* Guildford & London, 1976.

Cockshut, A. O. J. (ed.). *Religious Controversies of the Nineteenth Century: Selected Documents,* London, 1966.

Coleridge, S. T. *Aids to Reflection,* London, 1913.

Copleston, Frederick. *A History of Philosophy,* Vol. VII, London, 1963.

Corsi, Pietro. *The Age of Lamarck: Evolutionary Theories in France 1790–1830,* trans. Jonathan Mandelbaum, Berkeley & Los Angeles, 1988.

Cosslett, Tess. *Science and Religion in the Nineteenth Century,* Cambridge, 1984.

Cragg, Gerald R. *Reason and Authority in the Eighteenth Century,* Cambridge, 1964.

Crenshaw, J. L. (ed.). *Theodicy in the Old Testament,* Philadelphia & London, 1983.

Darwin, Charles. *Journal of Researches into the Geology & Natural History of the Various Countries Visited during the Voyage of H.M.S. Beagle Round the World,* London & New York, 1906.

Autobiography of Charles Darwin, The Thinker's Library, London, 1929. Reprinted from *Life of Charles Darwin,* ed. Francis Darwin.

The Origin of Species, ed. J. W. Burrow, Harmondsworth, 1968.

Davies, Paul. *The Cosmic Blueprint,* London, 1989.

Dawkins, Richard. *The Extended Phenotype*, Oxford, 1982.
The Blind Watchmaker, Harlow, 1986.
Dawson, J. W. *Archaia; or Studies of the Cosmogony and Natural History of the Hebrew Scriptures*, Montreal, 1860.
Descartes, René. *A Discourse on Method, Etc.*, London & New York, 1912.
Despland, Michel. *Kant on History and Religion*, Montreal & London, 1973.
Dick, Thomas. *The Christian Philosopher; or, the Connection of Science and Philosophy with Religion*, 21st edn, Glasgow & London, 1856.
Douglas, James. *Errors Regarding Religion*, Edinburgh, 1830.
Douglas, Mrs Stair. *The Life and Selections from the Correspondence of William Whewell*, London, 1881.
Draper, J. W. *History of the Conflict between Religion and Science*, 20th edn, London, 1887. Preface, New York University, December, 1873.
Driver, S. R. *An Introduction to the Literature of the Old Testament*, 9th edn, Edinburgh, 1913.
The Book of Genesis, 11th edn, London, 1920.
Drummond, Henry. *Natural Law in the Spiritual World*, 19th edn, London, 1887.
Eddington, A. S. *Science and the Unseen World*, London, 1929.
The Nature of the Physical World, Cambridge, 1930.
New Pathways in Science, Cambridge, 1935.
Edinburgh Christian Instructor (April 1814); (December 1814).
Edwards, Paul (ed.). *The Encyclopaedia of Philosophy*, New York & London, 1966.
Eichrodt, Walther. *Theology of the Old Testament*, trans. J. A. Baker, Vol. I, London, 1961; Vol. II, London, 1967.
Einstein, Albert. 'My Attitude to Quantum Theory', in *Science News*, Harmondsworth, 1950.
Einstein, A., & L. Infeld. *The Evolution of Physics*, Cambridge, 1938.
Elliott-Binns, L. E. *Religion in the Victorian Era*, 2nd edn, London, 1946.
English Thought 1860–1900: The Theological Aspect, London, 1956.
Ellis, Ieuan. *Seven Against Christ: A Study of 'Essays and Reviews'*, Studies in the History of Christian Thought, ed. Heiko A. Oberman, Vol. XXIII, Leiden, 1980.
Essays and Reviews. 12th edn, London, 1865.
Fairweather, Eugene R. (ed.). *The Oxford Movement*, Oxford, 1964.
Farrar, F. W. *History of Interpretation*, London, 1886.
Feuer, Lewis S. (ed.). *Marx and Engels: Basic Writings on Politics and Philosophy*, New York, 1959.
Fisher, James C. 'The Mosaic Account of the Creation', *The Edinburgh New Philosophical Journal*, N.S., 10, 214–25.
Fries, Jacob Friedrich. *Dialogues on Morality and Religion*, ed. D. Z. Phillips, trans. David Walford, Oxford, 1982. Selections from *Julius und Evagoras*, 2nd edn, Heidelberg, 1982.
Gardiner, Patrick. 'The German Idealists and their Successors', in

Germany: A Companion to German Studies, ed. Malcolm Pasley, London, 1972.

Gillispie, C. C. *Genesis and Geology: A Study in the Relations of Scientific Thought, Natural Theology, and Social Opinion in Great Britain, 1790–1850*, Harvard, 1951.

Gisborne, Thomas. *The Testimony of Natural Theology to Christianity*, London, 1818.

Gore, Charles. *Belief in God*, Harmondsworth, 1939.

Gore Charles (ed.). *Lux Mundi: A Series of Studies in the Religion of the Incarnation*, 2nd edn, London, 1890.

Grinfield, Edward W. *The Connection of Natural and Revealed Theology*, London, 1818.

Gruber, J. W. *A Conscience in Conflict: The Life of St George Jackson Mivart*, New York, 1960.

Gundry, D. W. 'The Bridgewater Treatises and their Authors', *History*, N.S., No. 31 (September 1946).

Habgood, John. *Religion and Science*, London, 1972.
'By Wayward Values to New Vulnerabilities', *The Times* (13 February 1987).

Haeckel, Ernst. *The Riddle of the Universe*, Thinker's Library, London, 1929.

Hampden, Renn D. *An Essay on the Philosophical Evidence of Christianity; or, the Credibility obtained to a Scriptural Revelation from its Coincidence with the Facts of Nature*, London, 1827.

Hampshire, Stuart. *Spinoza*, Harmondsworth, 1951.

Hardy, Alister. *The Divine Flame: An Essay towards a Natural History of Religion*, London & Glasgow, 1966.

Hawking, Stephen W. *A Brief History of Time*, London, 1988.

Heim, Karl. *Christian Faith and Natural Science*, London, 1953. Translation by N. Horton Smith of *Der Christliche Gottesglaube und die Naturwissenschaft*, Vol. I (Tübingen, 1949).
The Transformation of the Scientific World View, London, 1953. Translation by W. A. Whitehouse of *Der Christliche Gottesglaube und die Naturwissenschaft*, Vol. II, *Die Wandlung in naturwissenschaftliche Weltbild*, Hamburg, 1951.

Herschel, J. F. W. *A Preliminary Discourse on the Study of Natural Philosophy*, A Facsimile of the 1830 Edition, London, With a new Introduction by Michael Partridge, New York & London, 1966.

Hey, Tony, & Patrick Walters. *The Quantum Universe*, Cambridge, 1987.

Hick, John (ed.). *The Existence of God*, London & New York, 1964.

Higgins, W. M. *The Book of Geology*, London, 1842.

Hoeres, Professor Walter (Freiburg). 'Die Achtung vor dem moralischen Gesetz'. MS of broadcast on Südwestfunk, W. Germany, 21 April 1985.

Holden, George A. *A Dissertation on the Fall of Man in which the Literal Sense of the Mosaic Account of that Event is Asserted and Vindicated*, 2nd edn, London, 1823.

Horne, Thomas Hartwell. *Deism Refuted: OR, Plain Reasons for being a Christian*, 2nd edn, London, 1819.

An Introduction to the Critical Study and Knowledge of the Holy Scriptures, 3rd edn, corrected, London, 1822.

An Introduction to the Criticism of the Old Testament and to Biblical Interpretation, revised and edited by Revd John Ayre, London, 1860.

Horsley, Samuel. *Biblical Criticism*, London, 1820.

Howe, P. P. (ed.). *The Complete Works of William Hazlitt in Twenty One Volumes*, Centenary edition, London & Toronto, 1930.

Hoyle, Fred. *Astronomy*, London, 1962.

The Nature of the Universe, Harmondsworth, 1963.

The Intelligent Universe: A New View of Creation and Evolution, London, 1983.

Hume, David. *Essays Literary, Moral and Political*, London & New York, 1894.

A Treatise of Human Nature, Intro. A. D. Lindsay, London & New York, 1911.

Dialogues Concerning Natural Religion, ed. with Introduction by Henry D. Aiken, London & New York, 1948.

Huxley, T. H. 'An Apologetic Irenicon', *The Fortnightly Review* (1 November 1892).

Collected Essays, Vol. iv, *Science and Hebrew Tradition*, London, 1893; Vol. v, *Science and Christian Tradition*, London, 1894, reprinted 1909; Vol. vi, *Hume: with Helps to the Study of Berkeley*, London, 1894; Vol. ix, *Evolution & Ethics*, London, 1903.

Ingpen, Roger, & W. E. Peck (eds.). *The Complete Works of Percy Bysshe Shelley*, London & New York, 1965.

Irons, W. J. *On the Whole Doctrine of Final Causes*, London, 1836.

Irvine, Alexander. *My Lady of the Chimney Corner*, London & Glasgow, n.d.

James, William. *The Varieties of Religious Experience*, Harmondsworth, 1982.

Jeans, James. *Physics and Philosophy*, Cambridge, 1942.

Kant, Immanuel. *The Critique of Judgement*, trans. J. C. Meredith, Oxford, 1928.

The Moral Law: Kant's Groundwork of the Metaphysic of Morals. Translated and analysed by H. J. Paton, London, 1948; reissued in paperback.

Immanuel Kant: Critique of Practical Reason, trans. Lewis White Beck, Chicago, 1949.

Prolegomena to any future Metaphysics that will be able to present itself as a Science, trans. Peter G. Lucas, Manchester, 1853.

Kritik der praktischen Vernunft, ed. Joachim Kopper, Stuttgart, 1961. (Reclam).

Immanuel Kant's Critique of Pure Reason, trans. N. K. Smith, London, 1964.

Kritik der reinen Vernunft, ed. Ingeborg Heidemann, Stuttgart, 1966. (Reclam).

Die Religion innerhalb der Grenzen der bloßen Vernunft, ed. Rudolf Malter, Stuttgart, 1974. (Reclam).

Was ist Aufklärung? Aufsätze zur Geschichte und Philosophie, ed. Jürgen Zehbe, 2nd edn, Göttingen, 1975.

Kritik der Urteilskraft, ed. Gerhard Lehmann, Stuttgart, 1976. (Reclam).

Prolegomena zu einer jeden künftigen Metaphysik, die als Wissenschaft wird auftreten können, ed. Karl Vorländer, Hamburg, 1976 (first published 1783).

Kennedy, James. *Lectures on the Philosophy of the Mosaic Record of Creation*, Vol. I, London, 1826; Vol. II, London, Dublin & Edinburgh, 1827.

Kennedy, John. *A Popular Handbook of Christian Evidences*, London, 1880.

Kidd, John. *On the Adaptation of External Nature to the Physical Condition of Man*, London, 1833.

Kirby, William. *On the History Habits and Instincts of Animals*, London, 1835.

Kirkpatrick, A. F. *The Divine Library of the Old Testament*, London, 1911.

Kitto, John (ed.). *A Cyclopaedia of Biblical Literature*, Edinburgh, 1845/76.

Knight, Frida. *University Rebel: The Life of William Frend*, London, 1971.

Körner, Stephan. *Kant*, Harmondsworth, 1955.

Kuhn, T. S. *The Copernican Revolution: Planetary Astronomy in the Development of Western Thought*, Cambridge, Mass. & London, 1957.

The Structure of Scientific Revolutions, 2nd edn, Chicago, 1970.

Kurtz, J. H. *The Bible and Astronomy: An Exposition of the Biblical Cosmology and its relations to Natural Science*, trans. T. D. Simonton from 3rd German edn (1852), London, 1857.

LeMahieu, D. L. *The Mind of William Paley*, Lincoln & London, 1976.

Loades, Ann L. 'Kant's Concern with Theodicy', *Journal of Theological Studies* (October 1975).

'Theodicy and Evolution: Aspects of Theology from Pierre Bayle to J. S. Mill', doctoral thesis, University of Durham, 1975.

'Coleridge as Theologian: Some Comments on his Reading of Kant', *JTS* (October 1978).

'Moral Sentiment and Belief in God', *Studia Theologica*, 35 (1981).

'Immanuel Kant's Humanism', *Studies in Church History*, 17 (1982).

'No Consoling Vision: Coleridge's Discovery of Kant's "Authentic" Theodicy', in *An Infinite Complexity: Essays in Romanticism*, ed. J. R. Watson, Edinburgh, 1983.

Kant and Job's Comforters, Newcastle-upon-Tyne, 1985.

Locke, John. *An Essay Concerning Human Understanding*, London, 1947 (first published 1690).

The Reasonableness of Christianity, with a Discourse of Miracles, and part of a Third Letter Concerning Toleration, ed. I. T. Ramsey, London, 1958.

Losee, John. *A Historical Introduction to the Philosophy of Science*, 2nd edn, Oxford, 1980.

Lucas, J. R. 'Wilberforce and Huxley: A Legendary Encounter', *Historical Journal*, Vol. 22, No. 2 (1979).

Luke, D. (ed.). *Goethe: Selected Verse*, Harmondsworth, 1964.

Lyell, Charles. *Principles of Geology*, London, several edns from 1830 to 1875.

 The Geological Evidences of the Antiquity of Man, 4th edn, London, 1873.

 Life Letters and Journals of Sir Charles Lyell, edited by his sister-in-law, Mrs Lyell, 2 vols., London, 1881.

MacDonald, Donald. *Creation and the Fall: A Defence and Exposition of the First Three Chapters of Genesis*, Edinburgh, 1856.

Mackay, D. M. (ed.). *Christianity in a Mechanistic Universe*, London, 1965.

McLellan, David. *Karl Marx: His Life and Thought*, London, Macmillan, 1973; St Albans, Paladin, 1976.

Malthus, T. R. *Essay on the Principle of Population as it Affects the Future Improvement of Society*, London, 1914 (first published 1798).

Mansel, H. L. *The Limits of Religious Thought Examined in Eight Lectures*, 3rd edn, London, 1859.

Martineau, Harriet. *Biographical Sketches*, 2nd edn, London, 1869.

Mascall, E. L. *Christian Theology and Natural Science*, London, 1956.

Mason, S. F. *A History of the Sciences*, New York, 1962.

Maurice, F. D. *What is Revelation? A Series of Sermons on the Epiphany to which are added Letters to a Student of Theology on the Bampton Lectures of Mr Mansel*, London, 1859.

Maurice, Frederick (ed.). *The Life of Frederick Denison Maurice*, London, 1884.

Meadley, G. W. *Memoirs of William Paley*, Edinburgh, 1810.

Medway, John. *Memoirs of the Life and Writings of John Pye Smith*, London, 1853.

Mill, J. S. *Nature, The Utility of Religion, and Theism*, with an Introductory Notice by Helen Taylor, London, 1874; republished Farnborough, 1969.

Miller, Hugh. *The Testimony of the Rocks or, Geology in its bearings on the Two Theologies, Natural and Revealed*, Edinburgh, 1857.

 The Old Red Sandstone, London, 1906 (1st edn 1841).

 My Schools and Schoolmasters, London & Edinburgh, 1874.

Mivart, St George. *On the Genesis of Species*, London, 1871.

Moore, James R. *The Post-Darwinian Controversies: A Study of the Protestant Struggle to Come to Terms with Darwin in Great Britain and America, 1870–1900*, Cambridge, 1979.

Moore, James R. (ed.). *History, Humanity and Evolution*, Cambridge, 1989.

Morley, Henry. *Illustrations of English Religion*, London & Paris, n.d. (selections up to 1877).

Newman, J. H., Cardinal. *The Idea of a University: Defined and Illustrated*, London, n.d. (Preface, November 1852; Dedication and Advertisement, November 1858).

Ollard, S. L. *A Short History of the Oxford Movement*, London, 1915.

Olson, Richard. *Scottish Philosophy and British Physics 1750–1880*, New Jersey, 1975.

Otto, Rudolf. *Naturalism and Religion*, trans. J. A. & M. R. Thomson, London, 1907.

    The Philosophy of Religion: Based on Kant and Fries, trans. E. B. Dicker, London, 1931.

    Religious Essays: A Supplement to the Idea of the Holy, trans. Brian Lunn, London, 1931.

    The Kingdom of God and the Son of Man, trans. Floyd V. Filson and B. L. Woolf, London, 1938.

    The Idea of the Holy, trans. John W. Harvey, Harmondsworth, 1959.

Pais, Abraham. *'Subtle is the Lord . . . ': The Science and the Life of Albert Einstein*, Oxford, 1982.

Paley, William. *The Works of William Paley D.D.*, 5 vols., London, 1819, Vol. III, *Evidences of Christianity*; Vol. IV, *Natural Theology*.

    Natural Theology, Illustrated by James Paxton, plus 'Botanical Theology', by John Shute Duncan, Oxford, 1826.

    The Works of William Paley D.D., A New Edition, with Illustrative Notes and a Life of the Author. Editor's name not given. London, William Smith, 1838.

    A View of the Evidences of Christianity, a new edition, ed. Revd T. R. Birks, London, n.d. (but after 1852).

Paton, H. J. *The Modern Predicament: A Study in the Philosophy of Religion*, London & New York, 1955.

Peacocke, A. R. *Creation and the World of Science*, Oxford, 1979.

Pearson, Thomas. *Evangelical Alliance Prize Essay on Infidelity; its Aspects, Causes, and Agencies*, London, 1854.

Peat, C. J. Review of: *Earth's Earliest Biosphere: Its origin and evolution*, ed. J. William Schopf. *Times Higher Educational Supplement* (August 1984).

Penn, Granville. *A Comparative Estimate of the Mineral and Mosaical Geologies*, 2nd edn, revised and enlarged, London, 1825.

Powell, Baden. *The Connexion of Natural and Divine Truth; or, the Study of the Inductive Philosophy considered as Subservient to Theology*, London, 1838.

    Essays on the Spirit of the Inductive Philosophy, the Unity of Worlds, and the Philosophy of Creation, London, 1855.

    'The Burnett Prizes: The Study of the Evidences of Natural Theology', in *Oxford Essays*, London, 1857.

Powys, L. *The Pathetic Fallacy*, Thinker's Library, London, 1931.

Pratt, John H. *Scripture and Science not at Variance*, 2nd edn, London, 1958.

Prout, William. *Chemistry Meteorology and the Function of Digestion considered with reference to Natural Theology*, London, 1834.

Quarterly Review, 106 (October 1859); 108 (July 1860); 109 (January 1861); 112 (October 1862); 113 (January 1863).

Raven, C. E. *Natural Theology and Christian Theology. First Series: Science and Religion. Second Series: Experience and Interpretation*, Cambridge, 1953.

Reardon, B. M. G. *Religious Thought in the Nineteenth Century*, Cambridge, 1966.
From Coleridge to Gore: A Century of Religious Thought in Britain, London, 1971.
Kant as Philosophical Theologian, Basingstoke & London, 1988.

Redford, R. A. *The Christian's Plea against Modern Unbelief: A Handbook of Christian Evidence*, London, 1887.

Replies to 'Essays and Reviews', Oxford & London, 1862.

Robertson, J. M. *A History of Freethought in the Nineteenth Century*, London, 1929.

Robinson, J. H. *The Mind in the Making*, Thinker's Library, London, 1934 (first published London & New York, 1921; new and revised edn with Introduction by H. G. Wells, London, 1923).

Rogerson, John. *Myth in Old Testament Interpretation*, BZAW 134, Berlin, 1974.
Old Testament Criticism in the Nineteenth Century: England and Germany, London, 1984.

Roget, Peter Mark. *Animal and Vegetable Physiology considered with reference to Natural Theology*, London, 1834.

Romanes, E. *Life and Letters of George John Romanes*, London, 1896.

Romanes, G. J. *Thoughts on Religion*, ed. Charles Gore, 5th edn, London, 1895; 6th edn, London, 1896.
Symposium contributor, *Proceedings of the Aristotelian Society*, Vol. 1, No. 3 (1887–8), Johnson Reprint Corporation, New York & London, 1963.

Russell, Colin A. Open University Arts: A Third Level Course. *Science and Belief: From Darwin to Einstein*, Milton Keynes, 1981.

Ryle, G. *The Concept of Mind*, London, 1949.

Ryle, H. R. *The Early Narratives of Genesis*, London, 1892.

Schuster, J. A. and R. R. Yeo (eds.). *The Politics and Rhetoric of Scientific Method*, Dordrecht.

Sedgwick, Adam, *A Discourse on the Studies of the University*, 3rd edn, Cambridge, 1834; 5th edn, London, 1850.
Review of *Vestiges, Edinburgh Review*, Vol. 82, No. 165 (July 1845).

Seeley, J. R. *Natural Religion*, 2nd edn, London, 1882.

Shelley, Mary. *Frankenstein or, the Modern Prometheus*, London, 1818.

Simpson, J. Y. *Landmarks in the Struggle between Science and Religion*, London, 1925.

Smart, W. M. *The Origin of the Earth*, Harmondsworth, 1955.

Smith, John Pye. *On the Relations between the Holy Scriptures and some parts of Geological Science*, London, 1839.

Smith, N. K. *The Philosophy of David Hume*, London, 1949.

Smith, N. K. (ed.). *Hume's Dialogues Concerning Natural Religion*, Oxford, 1935.

Sorley, W. R. *Moral Values and the idea of God*, Cambridge, 1918.

A History of British Philosophy to 1900, Connecticut, 1973; reprint of Cambridge, 1965 (first published 1920).

Spence, H. D. M., & J. S. Exell. *Pulpit Commentary: Genesis*, new edition, London, 1897.

Spinoza, B. *Ethics*, London & New York, 1910.

Stace, W. T. 'Metaphysics and Meaning', *Mind* (1935).

Stanley, A. P. *Sermons on Special Occasions*, London, 1882.

Stephen, Leslie. *History of English Thought in the Eighteenth Century*, 2nd edn, London, 1881.

'William Paley', in *Dictionary of National Biography*, ed. Sidney Lee, Vol. XLIII, London, 1895.

Student's Cabinet Library of Useful Tracts, Vols. II, III, Edinburgh, 1836; Vol. V, Edinburgh, 1839; Vol. VIII, Edinburgh, 1840.

Sumner, John Bird. *A Treatise on the Records of the Creation and on the Moral Attributes of the Creator: The Consistency of the Principle of Population with the Wisdom and Goodness of the Deity*, London, 1816.

Taylor, Charles. *Hegel*, Cambridge, 1975.

Temple, Frederick. *The Relations between Religion and Science*, London, 1884.

Temple, William. *Nature, Man and God*, London, 1934.

Tennant, F. R. *Miracle and its Philosophical Presuppositions*, Cambridge, 1925.

Philosophical Theology, Vol. I, Cambridge, 1928; Vol. II, Cambridge, 1930.

Trench, R. C. *Notes on the Miracles of our Lord*, 8th edn, London, 1866.

Turton, W. H. *The Truth of Christianity*, 7th edn, London, 1908 (first published 1895).

Tyndall, John. *Address Delivered before the British Association Assembled at Belfast, with Additions*, London, 1874.

Tyrrell, D. A. J. Review of *Evolution from Space*, by F. Hoyle and C. Wickramsinghe, London, 1981, *Nature*, 294 (3 December 1981).

Urmson, J. O. (ed.). *Concise Encyclopaedia of Western Philosophy and Philosophers*, London, 1960.

Ward, James. *Naturalism and Agnosticism*, 4th edn, London, 1915 (1st edn, 1899).

Whewell, William. *Astronomy and General Physics: Considered with reference to Natural Theology*, London, 1833.

White, A. D. *A History of the Warfare of Science with Theology in Christendom*, New York, 1960.

Whitehead, A. N. *Adventures of Ideas*, Harmondsworth, 1942 (first published 1933).

Science and the Modern World, Cambridge, 1938.

Willey, Basil. *Nineteenth Century Studies: Coleridge to Matthew Arnold,*
London, 1949.
More Nineteenth Century Studies, London, 1956.
Darwin and Butler: Two Versions of Evolution, London, 1960.
Wood, A. W., & G. M. Clark. *Immanuel Kant: Lectures on Philosophical
Theology,* Ithaca & London, 1978.
Yalden-Thomson, D. C. (ed.). *Hume: Theory of Knowledge,* Edinburgh,
1951.
Zweig, A. *Kant: Philosophical Correspondence,* Chicago, 1967.

Index